The Anthro
Buddhism and

The Anthropology of Buddhism and Hinduism

Weberian Themes

David N. Gellner

OXFORD
UNIVERSITY PRESS

OXFORD
UNIVERSITY PRESS

YMCA Library Building, Jai Singh Road, New Delhi 110 001

Oxford University Press is a department of the University of Oxford. It furthers the
University's objective of excellence in research, scholarship, and education
by publishing worldwide in

Oxford   New York

Auckland   Bangkok   Buenos Aires   Cape Town   Chennai
Dar es Salaam   Delhi   Hong Kong   Istanbul   Karachi   Kolkata
Kuala Lumpur   Madrid   Melbourne   Mexico City   Mumbai   Nairobi
São Paulo   Shanghai   Taipei   Tokyo   Toronto

Oxford is a registered trademark of Oxford University Press
in the UK and in certain other countries

Published in India
By Oxford University Press, New Delhi

First published 2001
Second impression 2002
Oxford India Paperbacks 2003

ISBN 019 566611 9

Typeset in Goudy
by Eleven Arts, Keshav Puram, Delhi 110 035
Printed in India at Saurabh Print-o-Pack, Noida, U. P.
Published by Manzar Khan, Oxford University Press
YMCA Library Building, Jai Singh Road, New Delhi 110 001

For Nick, Martin, and Sofia

Contents

Tables and Figures

Plates

Preface

Republishing essays which have already appeared elsewhere requires some justification. It is for readers to judge whether I am right in thinking that the articles collected here have sufficient unity of theme to appear together and whether the whole is greater than the sum of the parts. But even if that judgement is negative, I can still make an argument from convenience, since several of the papers were published in relatively obscure places and will not have been readily available, especially to readers in Nepal and South Asia.

Acknowledgements are given for each of the essays separately, but it is a pleasure to be able to acknowledge more general debts in a more general way here. My basic education in the classics of sociology came from Steven Lukes. My doctoral supervisor, Richard Gombrich, first introduced me to the notion of soteriology in the South Asian context. It was with Nick (N.J.) Allen that I first attempted a close reading of Dumont. My wife, Lola Martinez, has read every one of the essays in this book: they have all benefited from her keen eye and her warnings not to quote Sylvain Lévi every time.

My initial two years' fieldwork in Nepal was funded by a Leverhulme Study Abroad Studentship. Subsequently I held a Junior Research Fellowship at St John's College, Oxford, and a British Academy Postdoctoral Fellowship at the Institute of Social and Cultural Anthropology, Oxford, with a Research Fellowship at Wolfson College, Oxford. Since then I have been a lecturer at Oxford Brookes and (since 1994) lecturer (and, from

October 2000, reader) in social anthropology at Brunel University, West London. The British Academy has supported several field trips to Nepal; others have been funded by Brunel University and by the International Centre for Ethnic Studies, Colombo. To all these institutions I am extremely grateful.

I would like to put on record two other institutional debts. The rise of the 'audit society' has had some beneficial and some pernicious effects. Perhaps this book will be judged to be both. Were it not for the approaching 2001 RAE (Research Assessment Exercise), a form of bureaucratic discipline introduced under Margaret Thatcher and continued by both Conservative and Labour governments subsequently, I would not have couched my request for study leave in terms of producing a book to order; this collection would have remained a distant aspiration. For non-British readers I should explain that—as in some long-winded party game— each member of every British university department has to submit their 'four best publications' of the last five years to a panel of subject experts. On this basis the panel then ranks each department in the country on a scale of 1 (the worst) to 5 (the best); higher rankings, weighted for the number of staff submitted, then score higher government research funding. Persistent rumours, as I write, that the 2001 RAE may be the last give this debt added poignancy.

The second, and more fundamental, debt is to Sue Lomas, Cheryl Cox, Maureen Hetherington, Joyce Spooner, Tracey Brett, Bette Yates, and the rest of the team at Wolfson College Day Nursery without whose devoted care for this book's dedicatees at least half of the chapters would never have been written in the first place.

The various chapters appeared previously in the following places and are republished by kind permission:

Chapter 1:   first published in *Sociology* (British Sociological Association, now published by Cambridge University Press) 16(4), 1982; this version first published in R. Roberts (ed.), *Religion and the Transformations of Capitalism: Comparative Approaches*, Routledge, 1995.

Chapter 2:   in *JASO: Journal of the Anthropological Society of Oxford* 21(2), 1990.

Chapter 3:   in *Social Anthropology* (Cambridge University Press) 7(2), 1999.

Chapter 4:   in *Pacific Viewpoint* (now published by Blackwell, Oxford, as *Asia Pacific Viewpoint*) 29(2), 1988.

Chapter 5:   in *Purusartha* 12, 1989.

Chapter 6: in N. Gutschow and A. Michaels (eds), *Heritage of the Kath-mandu Valley*. Sankt Augustin: VGH Wissenschaftsverlag, 1987 [papers from Lübeck conference of 1985].

Chapter 7: in S. Lienhard (ed.), *Change and Continuity: Studies in the Nepalese Culture of the Kathmandu Valley*, Alessandrio: Edizioni dell'Orso/CESMEO, 1996 [papers from Stockholm conference of 1987].

Chapter 8: in *Man: The Journal of the Royal Anthropological Institute* 29(1), 1994.

Chapter 9: in G. Toffin (ed.), *Nepal, Past and Present*, Paris: CNRS, 1993 [papers from Arc-et-Senans conference of 1990].

Chapter 10: not previously published.

Chapter 11: in *Man* (Royal Anthropological Institute) 26(1), 1991.

Chapter 12: in Z. Uherek (ed.), *Urban Anthropology and the Supranational and Regional Networks of the Town* (Prague Occasional Papers in Ethnology), Prague: Institute of Ethnology, 1993.

Chapter 13: in the *International Journal of Hindu Studies* 1(3), 1997.

Chapter 14: in *Social Anthropology* (Cambridge University Press) 5(3), 1997.

Chapter 15: in *JASO: Journal of the Anthropological Society of Oxford* 27(3), 1996.

Introduction

'... Weber tends to frighten anthropologists ...'
Clifford Geertz, *The Interpretation of Cultures*, p. 330

'... the concept of the self-regulating and self-justifying society and culture has trapped anthropology inside the bounds of its own definitions.'
Eric Wolf, *Europe and the People without History*, p. 18

The conjunction 'Weber and anthropology' is sufficiently unusual to warrant justification.[1] There is no such place as 'Weberian anthropology' on the maps that anthropologists draw themselves of their own discipline, or if there is, its inhabitants call it something else. By contrast Weberian sociology is a well-known, much fought-over, and highly desirable piece of real estate within the larger sociological empire. Given the considerable overlap in the intellectual histories of the two subjects, this difference is rather strange.

The history of social and cultural anthropology since the 1960s could be written in terms of a long march away from Durkheim (or at least from the views attributed to him): that is, the history of anthropology could be interpreted as a long struggle to overturn the assumptions that there are distinct and bounded societies, that the human sciences should seek general laws in imitation of the natural sciences, and that the significant fact is the presence of the social within individuals.[2] One might have expected that when anthropologists grew dissatisfied with one of the great founding fathers of social scientific theory, they would turn for inspiration to another.[3] Weber stands for everything that Durkheim did not—history, conflict, domination, ideology, change—so why not Weber? Of course, the salience of these very themes in Marx is responsible for his popularity in some quarters of anthropology. But why not Weber? I believe that a broad Weberian approach has much to recommend it, and can encompass many of the concerns of social and cultural anthropologists working today.

The present collection shares a general approach and ambition with Randall Collins' book, *Weberian Sociological Theory* (1986). Collins wished to contextualize and to establish just what Weber was arguing in his famous 'Protestant ethic thesis', rescuing him from all-too-common misunderstandings, much as I seek to do in Chapter 1.[4] At the same time, as I have in the other chapters, he sought to use a Weberian framework to explore a number of geo-political, social, and comparative questions empirically—questions that Weber himself did not necessarily consider. There is, however, one obvious difference between Collins' collection of essays and mine. As an anthropologist, whose particular area of expertise is the Kathmandu Valley, Nepal, I have mainly derived my questions from the ethnography of that region, and so I have been correspondingly less ambitious in pursuing historical or regional comparisons. Both Collins and I think that Weber's legacy is important, but unlike many Weber enthusiasts we do not think it necessary to stick to the questions and examples that he used. What Weber himself would have said on any particular question is less important than whether or not a broadly Weberian approach to tackling it is fruitful.

Only a few of the essays collected here are directly concerned with Weber's ideas; but the first—the kernel of which I can trace back to an undergraduate essay written for Steven Lukes in 1979, subsequently elaborated during discussions with Mark Elvin in 1980—does attempt to look at the place of the famous 'Protestant ethic thesis' in Weber's work as a whole, and to suggest how scholars of South Asia should approach it. The other essays, even those which directly mention Weber (and with the partial exception of Chapter 4), are empirical explorations in a broadly Weberian framework. These demonstrate, I hope, that such a framework is useful, comparative, and stimulating, without in any way being a straitjacket. But they were not written with that aim in mind. They exemplify the conviction—more frequently held by anthropologists than sociologists, but common among both—that general arguments are best made by means of contextualized particular cases.

This is a collection of previously published essays (excepting only Chapter 10). So it is only fair to qualify my ambitious title with the subtitle. I do not provide a systematic treatment of the anthropology of Buddhism, and even less of Hinduism. What I hope I have provided is some indication of what such a systematic treatment might include, and a stimulus to further research.

The Weberian heritage in anthropology

Unlike many sociologists, most anthropologists have only a limited acquaintance with Weber's writings. Most have vague memories of *The Protestant Ethic and the Spirit of Capitalism* (henceforth PESC) from introductory social science courses. Most know that he is identified with a method called 'verstehen' (the use of the German verb makes it sound particularly profound) and they may also be aware that Talcott Parsons' interpretation of Weber is nowadays thought to have been overly positivist. In so far as they associate Weber with a contemporary theoretical position, they have two rather contradictory images of him: on the one hand they see him as a founding father of Geertz's interpretivism, but, on the other, he is viewed as a naïve modernization theorist.

Interpretivism is the doctrine (or at any rate general attitude) that cultures consist of meanings. The *locus classicus* of this position is the introduction to Geertz's collection, *The Interpretation of Cultures* (1973). If cultures are collections of meanings, then the anthropologist's job is to interpret those meanings for others. No interpretation can ever be final; each interpretation is partial. The anthropologist's job is not to search for causal hypotheses, still less to test them. Geertz implicates Weber at the outset of his discussion of culture: 'Believing, with Max Weber, that man is an animal suspended in webs of significance he himself has spun, I take culture to be those webs, and the analysis of it to be therefore not an experimental science in search of law but an interpretive one in search of meaning' (Geertz 1973: 5).

Yet Geertz himself knows that there is far more to Weber than this, as a glance at the references to Weber in *The Interpretation of Cultures* shows. (Parsons' enthusiasm for Weber clearly rubbed off.) Weber is cited on the rationalization process of world religions, on patrimonialism, and on the necessity for ideas to have institutional grounding ('to be carried by powerful social groups', ibid.: 314) if they are to have social effects. Discussing developments in the understandings of pre-industrial peasant states, Geertz remarked that 'The comparative-institutions approach has been less frequently pursued, partly because Weber tends to frighten anthropologists ...' (ibid.: 330).

It is not, of course, the interpretivist Weber who frightens anthropologists, but Weber the writer of world history and Weber the builder of world-historical comparisons. But, funnily enough, and partly through Geertz's influence, this Weber is virtually unknown to anthropologists. By the time Geertz wrote the introduction to *The Interpretation of Cultures* he had already moved beyond the concern to construct explanations that animated many of the essays he was introducing (especially those on politics in Part IV). Geertz's subsequent writings emphasized Weber the semiotician; the other Webers were forgotten. Thus *The Interpretation of Cultures* has had an enormous impact, but, like the curate's egg, only in parts. The introduction and two of the essays, 'Person, Time, and Conduct in Bali' and 'The Balinese Cockfight', have been cited extensively and widely imitated. Geertz's attempts to construct a dialogue with political scientists and historians in Part IV of his book have been largely ignored, not least by his own later self.[5]

The other, very different Weber known to anthropologists is Weber the theorist of modernization. Anthropologists seem to assume that he was some kind of Pollyanna figure, predicting and celebrating the monolithic advance of rationality and bureaucracy. Contemptuous references are therefore made to 'Weberian rationality' or 'Weberian bureaucracy': the utter naïvety of these notions in the face of anthropologists' gritty experience of real people in faraway places is apparently self-evident.[6]

Whichever view of Weber is held, it follows that Weber is of no help to anthropologists. Who needs Weber the interpretivist when you have Evans-Pritchard or Geertz? In any case the notion of interpretation is sufficiently obvious to anthropologists, and sufficiently grounded in their practice, barely to need elaborate justification from outside the discipline. The modernization-theorist Weber, on the other hand, is not a model but a warning: a symbol of the egregious errors of sundry developmentalists and economists. All this means that, as Peel (1993: 97 n. 3) has remarked, 'Weber tends to be relevant for [anthropologists] not for the overall character of his sociology, but for what he had to say about particular topics, ...', charisma, stratification, or particular world religions, for example.[7]

Anthropologists in search of a paradigm

Anthropologists have a method—ethnographic fieldwork based on participant observation and open-ended interviews—but they cannot agree on what to make of the results so produced. The method has been much copied and is now practised far beyond the narrow confines of anthropology, but only anthropology can say that, as a discipline, it is defined by this method. As is well known, the method was first worked out and then institutionalized for the study of small-scale, non-literate cultures by Malinowski in the Trobriand islands and by Boas with native American Indians. Both Boas and Malinowski came from central Europe and both, in different ways, adapted the tradition of nationalist ethnography which flourished there. The key Herderian idea was that different nations or ethnic groups have their own culture, a distinct and distinctive interlocking set of practices and associated beliefs, which it is the folklorist-ethnographer's task to record before it disappears. The idea that each identifiable people—whether thought of as a nation, a race, or a tribe—had its own distinctive culture (conceived of as internally more or less homogeneous) was, and remains, very widespread. Neither Malinowski nor Boas shared the 'one tribe, one culture' model: on the contrary, they opposed it, as any reflective student of human societies must. None the less, the model was virtually built into their fieldwork *method*. Long-term, face-to-face ethnography with a single linguistic group, whether carried on in the name of science or not, tends, naturally enough, to lead to a series of monographs on 'The Nuer', 'The Navaho', etc. This is especially so when it is assumed that there are discrete societies operating as some kind of organic whole, as in Radcliffe-Brown's theory. Of course Radcliffe-Brown himself thought culture a flimsy thing, suitable for folklorists to study perhaps, but not worthy of attention from social scientific anthropologists or sociologists. Thus with him the 'one tribe, one culture' model became the 'one tribe, one society' model. Despite Radcliffe-Brown's relatively sophisticated handling of this assumption in his own work, the effect on his followers was much the same.

The history of anthropological theory since the founding figures, or at least since the 1960s, can be read as a series of attempts to grapple with and overturn this once-dominant 'one tribe, one culture' view. Of course, there have been, and still are, anthropologists who remain experts on one culture and one language and some of these are happy to cooperate enthusiastically with 'their' people's ethnonationalist spokespersons. But the dominant trend has been to attack, fairly fundamentally, the assumptions of the 'one tribe, one culture' model and, more recently, the methodology which makes it so plausible.[8]

In the first place, as soon as anthropologists began to study peasants or tribes who were part of a wider literate civilization, it became obvious that the village they happened to have chosen as a fieldsite could not be treated as an isolated cultural universe. This led Redfield to coin the terms Great Tradition and Little Tradition as labels for the ways of doing things that prevailed at sophisticated and literate centres, on the one hand, and in the socially (and often geographically) peripheral villages, on the other. The terms were unfortunate for several reasons (there may be more than one Great Tradition; it is misleading to think of what villagers do as part of a single Little Tradition over a large area: it is not even organized as a tradition in the same way as the Great Tradition; and so on). But despite these disadvantages (see further Chapter 4 below), the terms continue to be used (and I have used them) because they pick out a key analytic dimension in all complex societies.

Not only did it become clear that the culture of villages was complex and highly layered, with different actors evaluating it differently and sharing it to very different degrees; it also became evident that people could live together without necessarily sharing the same culture. Once different sub-cultures are recognized, which may interlock differently with overarching or neighbouring cultures, the notion of 'one tribe, one culture' becomes increasingly untenable.

By a series of ever more extreme formulations this insight has led to the complete rejection of the notions of culture and society in some quarters of the anthropological profession.[9] What has replaced it is a deliberately unsystematic view of individuals involved in shifting networks, constructing their culture as they go along in a process of never-ending negotiation with others. As many have noted, there is more than a touch of irony in anthropologists' rejecting the culture concept at the very moment when it has attained unparalleled popularity in other disciplines and outside the academy.

This spread of actor-centred, post-modern theorizing in anthropology is motivated by several key criticisms of the 'one tribe, one culture' view which is supposed to underlie conventional anthropology, whether derived from the structural-functionalism of Radcliffe-Brown or the cultural particularism of Boas:

1. it had a far too systematic, determining, and homogeneous view of culture;
2. it was very poor at handling questions of power and control, frequently ignoring the colonial context as well as 'internal' structures of inequality;
3. it had a very static view of the cultures it posited: change was explained either in terms of outside influences or in terms of a biologically inspired model of an organism interacting with its environment.

Many other faults were identified in the old paradigms, for example, the fit of structural-functionalism with the requirements of the British Empire.

Anthropologists have turned in a number of different directions in response to the awareness of these drawbacks. In many cases, a simple empiricist eclecticism has served, for which some justification can be drawn from the method of anthropology, which, after all, requires the voices of informants to be given pride of place, if not privileged explanatory power. But often either Marxist or Foucauldian approaches have been adopted: these have the advantage of trying to place cultures in some kind of explanatory framework, not taking them as given; of putting questions of power at the heart of the analysis; and of putting culture, in so far as it is the object of study, in a historical and global politico-economic framework.[10] A study that I admire—for its clear-headed response to precisely these theoretical considerations, for its combination of ethnography and history, and for its insistence on the necessity of simultaneously holding on both to an objectivist world-systems approach *and* to an actor-centred viewpoint—is Sherry Ortner's *High Religion* (1989).

I would suggest that, properly read, Weber offers much inspiration in this theoretical context. He was about as far from the 'one tribe, one culture' view as it is possible to be. His work, while centrally concerned with how people themselves define the situation, is simultaneously shot through with a materialist awareness that ideas do not and cannot act on their own, that they are weapons in the inherent struggles and inequalities of social life. He was as clear in his opposition to positivist and objectivist ways of describing social phenomena as Durkheim was entranced by them; yet he never abandoned the aims of generalization and comparison. He was not afraid to attempt typologies or causal explanations—but never confused the analyst's constructs with 'social reality', seeking rather to test them against it. He was, above all else, a historian with an acute sense of change and development; yet all the while he perceived—as perhaps no other significant theorist of his time did— that the teleological, evolutionist assumptions dominating nineteenth-century thought (which were to become the common sense of the twentieth century) were false. Power, status, and wealth (economic power) are at the heart of all his empirical analyses—except, unfortunately, PESC, which has consequently misled generations of his readers. Weber was, much of the time, as materialist as Marx, without any of the latter's utopianism or metaphysical realism. His work possesses a wonderful, almost philosophic unity, but at the same time has a very modern flavour in its rejection of totalizing system-building. As his friend Karl Jaspers remarked, 'No vision of the whole of human history, no construction of world history is permissible to him ... If [Weber] had a system, it could only be a system of temporary methods and basic ts' (Jaspers 1989: 94). What Jaspers meant, I presume, is that had no vision of human history of the common nineteenth-century ort. Weber's understanding of historical development and social types would certainly count as a 'vision of history' by today's standards.

There have been many misconceptions about Weber's ideal types. Sometimes the elementary error is made of assuming that 'ideal' meant that Weber was recommending them, rather than pointing to their abstraction. They are in fact models, which are developed by means of some basic structural distinctions. Weber himself lacked the positivist streak which might have led him to represent them in terms of diagrams or mechanical models; or perhaps it was simply that German professors of his day were not expected to make use of visual aids. However that may be, Schluchter's reconstructions of Weber's thought (Schluchter 1981, 1989) present it, accurately in my opinion, as, among other things, the working out of the implications of a massive series of empirically grounded complex structural categories. I have attempted to do something similar in these essays, both in relation to Weber (see, e.g., Chart 4.1 below) and when analysing material from Nepal or Japan.

Was Weber an Orientalist?

Edward Said's classic polemic, *Orientalism* (1985), struck a very deep chord. Although he himself was concerned with the Middle East, he intended the ideas to be applied elsewhere, and they have been.[11] The basic ideas are that:

1. the Western 'experts' who wrote about 'the Orient' in the nineteenth century did so in a demeaning way, denying agency to the people described by ascribing to them the vices of childishness, barbarity, irrationality, femininity, and corruption—the obverse, in fact, of the virtues supposedly displayed by the European and North American nations who were conquering the globe;
2. Orientalist writings were created in order to legitimate the imperial ambitions of the European powers, and to establish the writers' own positions as authorities over the Orient;
3. they constructed an authoritative discourse—a powerful form of knowledge—about the Orient that undermined traditional forms of knowledge, prevented the emergence of dissident voices, and led eventually to Orientals themselves adopting similar research strategies and questions as the 'authorities' in the metropolis;
4. this form of discourse continues even after decolonization to distort the way in which westerners are presented with 'the Orient'.

There have been many critiques of Said's ideas. Crude and/or politically motivated stereotypes are no monopoly of westerners viewing the East, as the case studies assembled by Carrier (1995) fully demonstrate. Nor is it the case that all writers of the imperial age fit Said's thesis equally well: there are very significant differences between them. The connection between Orientalism and imperial interests is not always as tight as the theory predicts: ironically, Britain, the imperial power, produced far fewer Sanskritists than Germany, which had no strategic interests in South Asia, and Britain regularly had to import them.[12] Many writers who displayed most clearly the Orientalist syndrome in relation to Buddhism likewise came from countries without imperial ambitions in Asia, e.g. Italy (Lopez 1995). Turner has criticized Said for adopting in *Orientalism* a pessimistic and Foucauldian view of ideas as irrevocably implicated in structures of power, whereas he appears in the guise of a straightforward positivist and humanist in other works, notably *Covering Islam* (Turner 1994: 6). In fact even in *Orientalism* he states quite explicitly: 'I would not have undertaken a book of this sort if I did not believe that there is scholarship that is not as corrupt, or at least as blind to human reality, as the kind that I have been mainly depicting' (Said 1985: 326). Said goes on to exonerate Geertz, Berque, and Rodinson from the charge of Orientalism.[13] However, simply picking out a few modern scholars by name is not enough. It is necessary to go beyond mere *ad hominem* exculpation and distinguish, as Trautmann does, between 'Orientalism[1] (knowledge produced by Orientalists, scholars who know Asian languages) and Orientalism[2] (European representations of the Orient, whether by Orientalists or others) (1997: 23)'. Much of the substance of Orientalism[2], Trautmann points out, was produced in direct opposition to the Orientalists[1]. Trautmann quite rightly concludes: 'We cannot do without a critical and expert winnowing of their [the Orientalists'[1]] work' (ibid.: 25).

Said's ideas have had an undeniable and justifiable impact. Many have castigated Weber for propagating Orientalist notions about South Asia. Are Weber's ideas on South Asia entirely vitiated by his reliance on outdated and biased sources? Did he simply propagate stereotypes of the passive and fatalistic Indian? I argue in Chapters 1 and 4 below that— even if there are many specific remarks which have to be discarded— the overall framework does not suffer from these drawbacks. Weber was not arguing that Hindus are fatalistic; he was making a much subtler argument about potential connections between the wholehearted practice of Hindu ideals in a pre-modern environment and a specific kind of economic ethic. Clearly Weber was arguing that there was a key contrast between the West and 'the Rest' and if all arguments of this sort are to be considered 'Orientalist' then Weber is guilty as charged. However, if the term is reserved for intellectually lazy pseudo-explanations which posit essences such as 'the Arab mind', 'the Russian soul', 'Indian spirituality', or 'Japanese uniqueness', then Weber was about as far from being 'Orientalist' as it is possible to be. For Weber the uniqueness of the West was a problem to be investigated and a painful predicament to be explored, the surprising outcome of an unlikely set of circumstances. It was certainly not inevitable, nor was it any reason for triumphalism or self-congratulation.

Dumont and Weber

Another great sociologist, whose connections with Weber are briefly mentioned in Chapters 1 and 4, was Louis Dumont (1911–98).[14] He spent much of his life as an ethnographer and theorist of Indian anthropology, and so of course his knowledge of South Asia was incomparably deeper and more extensive than Weber's. But although he sought to be as complete and thorough as possible in his knowledge of the relevant sources on India up to the appearance of his classic *Homo Hierarchicus*, thereafter he turned his back on South Asia and devoted himself to the history of what he took to be the dominant ideology of the West, namely economics and the individualist and rationalist model of human beings that it implies. His project was therefore a variation on Weber's, an attempt to pin down the origins of the uniqueness of the West (though he engaged surprisingly little with Weber).

No other recent theorist of South Asian society approaches the stature and comparative range of Dumont (though I suggest in Chapter 13 that Levy's impressive volume, *Mesocosm*, approaches Dumont's in the ambitious scope of the historical and sociological questions it poses and attempts to answer).[15] This iconic status has made Dumont's work, particularly *Homo Hierarchicus*, the frequent target of specialists, eager to make their name by pulling it down a notch or two. Their hopes of demolishing the structure altogether by means of one or two well-placed blows utterly fail, in my opinion, because they have nothing to put in its place and because they often fail to understand what they attack. There is a striking parallel with the enormous, but frequently misguided, critical literature on Weber's *Protestant Ethic and the Spirit of Capitalism*.

There are, however, certain points at which Dumont's vision of South Asia does seem to have been lacking. Important lacunae or problematic points include: his rather too static and structuralist picture of history;

his overdrawn picture of the 'secularized' Hindu king (Gupta and Gombrich 1986); his essentialist picture of the Hindu–Muslim confrontation in South Asia (Gaborieau 1993: 408); his rejection of the 'sociological reality' of the Indian village (Srinivas 1987); his insistence that the 'religion of the gods' is secondary to the 'religion of caste' (Dumont 1957: 20); his overwhelming emphasis on the hierarchy of purity and impurity, to the exclusion of other forms of hierarchy that might work against the pre-eminence of brahmans (Raheja 1988, Quigley 1993, Burghart 1996: Chapter 1).[16] On all these points a rather more open, less totalizing, and, dare I say it, more Weberian, historical and empirical approach would have been in order.

None the less, Dumont's achievement is still important and impressive and one that should be built on rather than destroyed. He showed that it is still possible for detailed empirical work to be combined with a global vision of Weberian proportions. The notion of hierarchy that he discerned as underlying the caste system may have been more contested and more protean than he portrayed it, but he provided both a sophisticated synthetic account of its empirical, institutional, and historical bases and a systematic theoretical analysis. Furthermore, Dumont stood for an aspiration that is still worth working towards, namely the integration of solid anthropological and ethnographic work with literate and Sanskritic studies. In my own case, reading his work inspired me to study Sanskrit and the Indological literature, in an Oxford MPhil under Richard Gombrich and Alexis Sanderson, as preparation for fieldwork in South Asia. I eventually chose to carry out my research among the urban representatives of one of the Great Traditions of South Asia, albeit one that has been marginalized by the vagaries of history: the Tantric Buddhism of the Newars of the Kathmandu Valley (see Chapters 5–7 below).

The approach applied

Most of the essays contained in this collection were not written with Weber explicitly in mind. But in retrospect it seems to me that they are centrally concerned with the Weberian themes of legitimation, the developmental history of religions, the contrast between soteriology and mundane interests, and modernization.

One key Weberian theme is the empirical study of ideologies. Ideas in action are always 'carried' by particular social groups. Elite groups in particular only manage to maintain their position in so far as they persuade others of their own fitness to rule or lead. Six of the essays collected here are concerned with the different ways in which priests legitimate their authority in Nepal. In particular I have been concerned with the ways in which the traditional Tantric Buddhist priests of the Kathmandu Valley legitimate their authority. Since they are Buddhist priests who are married and form a hereditary caste, this is not a question which previous observers had spent much time considering—preferring instead to denounce them as corrupt. In successive chapters I look at rituals and doctrines (Chapter 5),[17] sacred sites (monastic temple complexes) (Chapter 6), text recitation and worship (Chapter 7), and the provision of this-worldly assistance for misfortune (Chapters 7, 8, and 9). In this form of religion, various hierarchies are taken for granted: hierarchies of social status, hierarchies of entitlement, and the hierarchy of gender.

Traditional Newar Buddhism is nowadays on the defensive. Rituals, texts, and teachings are today provided equally by the Theravada movement, introduced into Nepal only in the 1930s. In comparison to the Theravada movement—with its numerous international links, its yellow-robed monastics, its stress on literacy and openness, and (since the 1980s) a strong association with meditation—many Newars now believe that their traditional form of Buddhism is inauthentic and overly Hinduized. The way they view their world has changed radically (as described briefly in Chapter 12).

Chapters 8, 9, and 10 move beyond the sphere of organized religion and explore some of the ways in which freelance practitioners make use of authoritative means of religious legitimation to carve out a career for themselves and to provide assistance to lay people with everyday problems. Very occasionally such practitioners move on from this to challenge established forms of religion in the soteriological sphere as well. In fact, as other students of Buddhism have found (Gombrich and Obeyesekere 1988, Tambiah 1984a), there is at this level a conflation of soteriology and worldly benefits: in effect, a rejection of the Weberian distinction which is fundamental to the organization of more formal religion. This is where the anthropology of religion and medical anthropology intersect. The benchmark of excellence in medical anthropology, at least where South Asia is concerned, is provided in my opinion by the works of Mark Nichter. These are not nearly as well known as they should be, perhaps because his major collection of essays (with Mimi Nichter) is published in a specialist medical anthropology list with the unexciting title, *Anthropology and International Health: Asian Case Studies* (1996, first edition 1989). Nichter combines sophisticated emic explorations of local terms for medical conditions with detailed statistical analysis. His discussion (1996: Chapter 7) of the way in which biomedicine is understood within a religious framework that opposes low, but powerful and bloodthirsty divinities to peaceable, high, vegetarian, and Sanskritic divinities has, I suspect, wide applicability, probably throughout South Asia.

Hinduism is, however, a very protean phenomenon. Whether it even constitutes 'a religion' has been questioned (Fitzgerald 1990; Frykenberg 1991; von Stietencron 1991). Dumont's *Homo Hierarchicus* is often taken to be 'about' Hinduism, though it contains nothing on pilgrimage or worship or ritual. Other works, on the other hand, deal with Hinduism while barely touching on social organization at all. In this book I have been primarily concerned with the Weberian questions of the legitimation of priests and other specialists, the nature of brahmanical Hinduism as a social movement, and the nature of Hinduism as an organizing principle of urban space.

Thus Chapters 11, 12, and 13 deal with the general Hindu social framework of the Kathmandu Valley. An analysis of the ways in which the Newars are perceived by their neighbours, and by foreign observers, leads to a consideration of long-term historical change, and the emergence of what I call the north Indian brahmanical system (NIBS for short). I argue in Chapters 2 and 5 that it is essential to understand the hierarchical nature of traditional forms of Buddhism. Where Hinduism is concerned this is less controversial. But an important corollary is often forgotten: what are thought of as 'standard Hindu values' or 'typical Hindu practices' were traditionally put into practice only by an elite. The majority of the population respected them, but did not practise them, or did so only in part. The spread of Hinduism was and is the very gradual spread and adoption of these elite values, or of practices that reflect them. This process has been much accelerated by modernization.

Chapter 13 considers the contribution of Robert Levy's *Mesocosm*, a major study of the city of Bhaktapur, which likewise seeks to understand it historically as representative of the pre-modern Hindu social system. Levy provides a detailed and sophisticated picture of Bhaktapur, even if he does not engage with historians of India, or with Weber or Dumont. He could perhaps be criticized for not adopting a sufficiently dynamic model of Indian history. Be that as it may, I have sought to defend him against attack from another quarter, a more fashionable pluralist and individualist approach which would undermine all Durkheimian attempts to account for consensus and the compulsions of tradition.

The final section of the book contains two short studies inspired by three months in Japan in 1991. The Buddhism of Japan is distantly related historically to that of Nepal. Some of the same rituals (notably the Tantric fire sacrifice) and some of the same Sanskrit mantras are found in both. Interestingly, Buddhism in Nepal, so close to its origin point, has evolved to provide a religion of life in the world as well as a soteriology. By contrast, Buddhism in Japan, at the furthest geographical and temporal point from India, has remained true to the original focus on death and salvation, though also coming to provide, through its provision of ancestor worship, a symbolic expression of the household.

Throughout this book a fundamental Weberian analytical distinction—explored in detail in Chapters 3 and 4—is made between salvation religion (soteriology) and worldly religion, and within the latter between group-oriented communal or social religion on the one hand and individualistic, instrumental religion on the other. These distinctions are essential, I believe, to the understanding of religious phenomena everywhere; but they are particularly apposite in Asia, where there are often indigenous terms that correspond to them and where the last type—instrumental religion—is often belittled or overlooked as 'not really religion'.[18] These categories provide a clear analytical framework, an essential first step in overcoming common misconceptions about both Buddhism and Hinduism.

A note on transliteration and abbreviations

Since I hope that this collection will appeal to those who are not specialists on Nepal, I have anglicized the names of castes, gods, and places.[19] Indigenous terms have been transliterated following standard conventions (for Newari, see Gellner and Quigley 1995). I have not felt it necessary to provide the diacritics on frequently cited terms (e.g., in Chapter 6, for *bahah* and *bahi*), except at the first occurrence.

The following abbreviations are used:

Skt	Sanskrit
Np.	Nepali
Nw.	Newari/Nepal Bhasha
VS	Vikram Samvat, the official era in Nepal (subtract 57 to obtain the common era)
NS	Nepal Samvat, the era preferred by Newār activists (add 880 to obtain the common era)
PESC	*The Protestant Ethic and the Spirit of Capitalism* (Weber 1976)
ES	*Economy and Society* (Weber 1968)
ROI	*Religion of India* (Weber 1958)

Most of the essays are published as they were, saving only the correction of minor errors, the addition of one or two references, and the removal of repetitions. However, Chapter 2 (originally the introduction to a special issue on Buddhism of *JASO*, the *Journal of the Anthropological Society of Oxford*) is substantially rewritten, Chapter 5 is slightly shortened, and Chapter 6 substantially so, losing a whole section of the original and numerous footnotes dealing with obscure etymologies.

Notes

1. I thank N.J. Allen, R. Goodman, A. Kuper, J.D.Y. Peel, and C. Stewart for helpful comments on this introduction.
2. Ortner 1984 and Marcus 1998 could be cited as emblematic statements in such an interpretation.
3. Nadel acknowledged his debt to Weber and Talcott Parsons in his *The Foundations of Social Anthropology*, first published in 1951, but although the book seems to have been much read in the 1950s, hardly anyone remembers it today.
4. Collins' book appeared too late, unfortunately, to influence the initial formulation of my argument. See Turner (1993: Chapter 2) for a discussion of Collins and of some other attempts to extend Weber's historical sociology.
5. On Geertz, see Chapter 3 below.
6. For a serious anthropological survey of Weber on rationality, which cautions against the more simplistic neo-Weberian characterizations of 'traditional religion', see Hefner 1993. Brubaker 1984 is an excellent guide to what Weber actually thought about rationality; see also Schroeder 1992 for a reconstruction of Weber's sociology of religion which puts his comparative project at the heart of his understanding of cultural change.
7. See Tambiah 1984a on charisma, and Fallers 1965 and 1973 on bureaucracy and stratification, respectively. Smith 1964 also made some use of Weber's political sociology.
8. See Southall 1970 for a classic attack on it in the African context.
9. For the rejection of 'society', see Ingold 1996: 77ff; for 'culture', see Abu-Lughod 1991; for scepticism about 'ethnicity' on similar grounds, see Banks 1996.
10. See Wallerstein 1974, 1980, 1989 for the classic world-systems approach and Wolf 1982 for its application within anthropology.
11. On India, see Inden 1990; on Buddhism, Lopez ed. 1995.
12. Trautmann 1997 is particularly good on this.
13. Others have not been so sure that Geertz has not imposed his own conceptual agenda on Muslims (Munson 1986) or the Balinese (Crapanzano 1986, Kuper 1999: Chapter 5).
14. See S. Collins 1989 for some of the background to Dumont's study of India

and Fitzgerald 1996 for an interesting defence of Dumont against the charge of Orientalism.

15. Another scholar of Nepal of whom the same might be said is Richard Burghart. His premature death in 1994 robbed us of the mature synthesis he was working towards (see Burghart 1996).

16. However I think it rather unfair to blame Dumont for the fact that a generation of anthropologists has neglected the study of the Indian working class (Parry 1999: viii). Dumont was, after all, interested in what happens to caste under the conditions of modernization.

17. The ideas of Chapter 5 are to be found also in my monograph on Newar Buddhism (Gellner 1992a), but I have included this paper (despite some overlap with Chapter 4): (a) because it sums up the sociological theme in a far more streamlined form than the book, and (b) because it explicitly relates the question of priestly legitimation to Weber's ideas.

18. Reader and Tanabe's recent work on Japan (1998), by its scholarly and historical focus on precisely this kind of religion, provides the best kind of challenge—dispassionate historical and ethnographic documentation—to this prejudice.

19. Except that in Chapter 6, I refer to Cikā Bahi, not Chikan Bahi. While a capital 'Brahman' refers to the small Newar caste of Brahmans, the Rajopadhyaya; 'brahman' refers either to the *varṇa* category or to Nepalese brahmans in general.

PART I

General Approaches

1

Max Weber, Capitalism, and the Religion of India

Introduction

Max Weber's book *The Religion of India* (henceforth *ROI*) has suffered a strange and undeserved fate.[1] Unlike *The Protestant Ethic and the Spirit of Capitalism* (henceforth *PESC*) it has given rise to rather little discussion of the numerous stimulating theories it puts forward among the specialists most competent to judge them. Part of the reason for this must lie in the fact that South Asian studies,[2] to their detriment, tend to divide up three ways between (i) Sanskritists, (ii) historians of the Muslim and modern periods, and (iii) social scientists, either anthropologists or sociologists. Between these three groups there is only imperfect communication.[3]

Sanskritists frequently dismiss Weber's book out of hand on the ground that nobody who had to rely on secondary sources can have anything to contribute to the study of South Asian religion or society. Occasionally historians have in fact discussed or made use of Weber's work (Bayly 1983, O'Hanlon 1985), but they have tended to damn him with faint praise, or worse. Anthropologists and sociologists, on the other hand, are not in a position, in the nature of their study, to address the more specific historical theses which Weber advances; and they have frequently been ill at ease with Weber's comparative framework (e.g. Appadurai 1986). Thus Weber's book has remained little read and largely unused by those South Asianists most competent to tackle it. As for sociologists in the West, it is probably the only book on South Asia they ever read. That this is certainly the case with Weber's translators, Gerth and Martindale, is shown by the frequent obscurity and inaccuracies of the translation, the incredible number of misprints in the transliteration of Sanskrit and Pali words (for which they carry over unthinkingly the German transliteration), and by the fact that they translate *yajñopavīta* from the German as 'holy girdle' instead of the normal 'sacred thread'.

Three fallacies in the interpretation of the Weber thesis

In so far as Weber's work has been taken up at all by social scientists dealing with South Asia, the discussion has centred on the connection between Hinduism and capitalism, a debate sparked off by post-independence economic development or the lack of it. This debate, inasmuch as it deals with Weber, has been almost wholly vitiated by misunderstandings of his central concerns. As Marshall (1982: 168) concludes of the 'Protestant ethic' debate in general, 'Working often with a crude and bastardized version of [Weber's] thesis, most critics have pursued inadmissible data in the wrong times and places.' Weber's writings on South Asia and China, and the projected work on Islamic civilization, were of course the counterpositives to *PESC*: that is, the latter explained, or began to explain, why capitalism originated only in the West, the other works why it failed to originate elsewhere. Thus in order to understand *ROI*, and why the above-mentioned interpretations of it are invalid, it is necessary to deal with *PESC* at the same time.

The debate over Weber's 'Protestantism' thesis, both in the western and in the South Asian context, has been dominated by three fallacies. These fallacies, though they can be held separately, are related and when held together reinforce each other, as I hope will become clear in the ensuing discussion. In decreasing order of vulgarity, they are:
  (i) Weber was an idealist in the sense that he believed economic behaviour to be straightforwardly determined by religious beliefs, either of individuals or collectively or both.
 (ii) There is only one problem of development, or the origin of capitalism, which is the same in essentials in Medieval China, nineteenth-century Europe, and twentieth-century Peru.
(iii) Weber held a whenever-A-then-B Humean view of social causality; in other words, he thought that if A was the cause of B, it was necessary and sufficient, or at least a necessary, condition of B.

The truth is that Weber was certainly not an idealist in this sense. Though vulgar Marxists and vulgar Weberians may be diametrically opposed, it is quite wrong to suppose that Weber represents historical materialism stood on its head. Protestantism for Weber was an exception to the general rule that ideas do not have an independent power to produce social change.

As far as fallacy (ii) goes, there are three separate problems of development requiring different answers:

(A) Why did one pre-industrial society develop faster than another (say, China than Christian Europe)?

(B) Why did one civilization only (Europe) develop industrial capitalism 'from within itself'?

(C) Why are some societies better at (deliberate, imitative) development in the modern industrial and industrializing world than others (say, Japan and Singapore than China and Indonesia)?

Weber himself was above all concerned with (B) and very little with (C), which was not then the burning issue it was to become.

The truth corresponding to fallacy (iii) is harder to state briefly. But it should at least be clear from his methodological writings, if not from the consideration of 'social reality' itself, that for Weber society is causally complex. X may be a necessary precondition for Y only under certain circumstances. In another situation Y may be possible without X. Thus talk of causes, rather than conditions, is misleading, as we may be led to expect a single cause to be 'constantly conjoined', in Hume's phrase, with a given effect. Much misguided criticism of Weber has been based on the assumption that he claimed Protestantism and capitalism to be 'constantly conjoined'.

Examples of the fallacies

Fallacy (i) has not normally been committed by those who have read *PESC* closely. Weber's statement that 'it is not, of course, my aim to substitute for a one-sided materialistic an equally one-sided spiritualistic causal interpretation of culture and of history' (*PESC*: 183) is too prominently placed for that. This has not prevented it from entering the South Asianists' discussion. Mandelbaum, for example, aligns Weber with William Kapp and Gunnar Myrdal as explaining South Asia's backwardness by citing the attitudes inculcated by Hinduism (Mandelbaum 1970: 638).

Fallacy (ii) is more interesting and it is more important to be clear about it. A concise formulation of it (a confusion of (B) and (C) above) is to be found in the preface by Gerth and Martindale to *ROI*: 'The central concern of this and other of Weber's studies of countries we today describe as "developing" was with the obstacles to industrialization and modernization. Weber anticipated by several decades a problem that has come to occupy the post-World War II world' (*ROI*: v). Similarly, Surajit Sinha takes the Weber thesis with reference to South Asia to be that Hinduism is a 'major stumbling block for modernization' (Sinha 1974: 519). In fact, Weber's principal theme was an answer to problem (B): 'no community dominated by powers of this sort [viz. religious anthropolatry on the part of the laity and a strong traditionalistic charismatic clergy] could out of its own substance arrive at the "spirit of capitalism"' (*ROI*: 325). The sentences which follow this in *ROI* state two corollaries which are indeed relevant to problem (C): that South Asia could not take over capitalism developed elsewhere as easily as the Japanese; and that, though capitalism had already been introduced to South Asia, only Pax Britannica, according to some, prevented an outbreak of the old 'feudal robber romanticism of the Middle Ages'. But these are only asides, and not the theme of the book as a whole.

Fallacy (iii) has not directly and openly been espoused, as far as I know, but it lurks in the claim that Weber's project with regard to *PESC* and the studies of the world religions was an application of Mill's method of agreement and difference. Of course the cases in which Protestantism did not produce capitalism are too well known for such a position to be tenable by present-day Weberians.[4] Consequently, Weberians claim, not that Protestantism invariably produces capitalism, but that it has a potential to do so. However this does not seem to get us very far in the task of explaining why capitalism appeared in one place rather than another, unless it is analysed in turn in a way similar to that attempted below.

Most commonly, fallacy (iii) is committed tacitly along with (ii). It is assumed that Weber asserted the existence of a necessary and sufficient link between Protestantism and rational capitalistic activity, or at least that the former is a necessary condition of the latter so that even if all Protestants are not capitalists, no Catholic can be one. Put like this it may sound absurd, but much of the debate has been carried on at this sort of level. As H. Luethy (1970: 128) remarked, 'it was as though the essential thread had suddenly been discovered which would lead dialectically from the nailing of Luther's ninety-five theses on the Wittenberg church door to the assembly lines of Detroit and the ramifications of Standard Oil.'

In the Asian context Weber's claim that non-European civilizations could not have developed capitalism endogenously because they lacked the ideological resources to produce a capitalist spirit, i.e. an active rational this-worldly asceticism, is misinterpreted as the 'theory' that Chinese, Hindus, or whoever make bad capitalists. In other words, Weber's answer to problem (B) above is taken as an answer to problem (C), and the causal connection asserted is presumed to be an invariable one. In this way it is possible to attempt to refute his characterization of the Hindu 'spirit' by citing 'the evidence today before us of politically independent Asian states actively planning their social, economic and scientific and technical development' (Singer 1961: 150). This is of course to miss the crucial point that Weber was concerned with the *first* unplanned, endogenous appearance of industrial capitalism, and with South Asia's potential or lack of it for the production of a capitalist *spirit* which was its necessary condition.[5] Capitalist economic *organization* according to Weber is not at all the same thing; the latter may exist in pre-modern societies, carried on in a traditionalistic spirit, without having any potential to transform its environment.

In an approach similar to Singer's, Tambiah seems to assume that because Buddhism and Hinduism can be adapted to modernization, because they can, *ex post*, provide analogues of the Protestant ethic, Weber's theory is disproved (Tambiah 1973: 13–16). But since Weber is addressing problem (B), in order to refute him in this way, one must show that Buddhism and Hinduism had this potential before the impact of modernization. It is quite wrong to attribute to him the thesis that there is an innate hostility between Hinduism or other eastern religions and capitalism. In his book on China he explicitly repudiates such a claim:

It is obviously not a question of deeming the Chinese 'naturally ungifted' for the demands of capitalism. But compared to the Occident, the varied conditions which externally favored the origin of capitalism in China did not suffice to create it. Likewise capitalism did not originate in occidental or oriental Antiquity, or in India, or where Islamism held sway. Yet in each of these areas different and favorable circumstances seemed to facilitate its rise. (Weber 1951: 248)

What then was Weber's position? It was that the spirit of capitalism was a necessary precondition of the first appearance, or origination of capitalism. It was not of course a sufficient condition, as the case of Jainism, discussed below, shows. Nor was it a necessary condition of capitalism as such: once capitalism stands on 'mechanical foundations' it is capitalism which tends to produce a capitalist spirit, or aspects of it, rather than the other way round. The importance of Protestantism lay in the fact that it produced and legitimated a capitalist spirit; but there was no necessary and/or sufficient link between Protestantism and the capitalist spirit (see *PESC*: 91). It is therefore quite beside the point to cite against Weber examples of non-Protestant capitalists or of Protestant non-capitalists. Protestantism was one element of a situation which, taken as a whole, was sufficient to produce a capitalist spirit, which in turn was, as stated, necessary for the first unplanned appearance of industrial society.[6]

Weber's studies of South Asia, China, and Islam were designed to show that, although other elements necessary for the production of capitalism sometimes existed (such as the availability of capital and formally free labour, and other factors discussed in his *General Economic History*), a capitalist spirit did not and indeed could not develop. Without a Protestant ethic or some equivalent no traditional (i.e agrarian) civilization could develop industrial capitalism 'from within itself'. Only religious sanctions, Weber assumed, could induce men permanently to defer satisfaction in the way required to produce the capitalist spirit. No this-worldly religious ethic could produce an active rational this-worldly asceticism: only a particular type of soteriology could do so. In fact the studies revealed, in at least one case, an analogous ethic (Jainism) and the burden of explanation in the South Asian case shifted, as we shall see, to the absence of other conditions.[7]

Probable reasons for the prevalence of the fallacies

The three fallacies listed above are by no means always made, but even when they are rejected, the way in which they go together does not seem to have been grasped. Thus Giddens rejects fallacy (ii): 'Weber's concerns were with the first origins of modern capitalism in Europe, not with its subsequent adoption elsewhere' (Giddens 1976: 6). He also seems to reject fallacy (iii) when he says that it is quite valueless to take Weber to task for suggesting that 'Calvinism was "the" cause of the development of modern capitalism' (ibid.: 10). But then he goes on to cite 'the supposed lack of "affinity" between Catholicism and regularized entrepreneurial activity' as one of the 'elements of Weber's analysis that are most definitely called into question' (ibid.: 12).

Why then is it so easy to make the three mistakes listed above? Two reasons leap to the eye: (i) Weber's order of exposition in *PESC*, which makes it possible to mistake his *initial problem*, that other things being equal Protestants in nineteenth-century Germany were more likely to be entrepreneurs than Catholics, for his *theory*; and (ii) the different meanings which attach to Weber's use of the word 'capitalism'.[8]

It is indeed misleading that Weber begins *PESC* with a consideration of the fact that in nineteenth-century Germany Protestants showed
a greater proclivity for entrepreneurial activity than Catholics, even
where one would expect the opposite (i.e. in areas where Catholics are
a minority among Protestants). But proper attention to the text makes
it quite clear that this is merely the problem, namely the evidence that
at an earlier period there was a special connection between Protestantism and the origin of capitalism. That is to say, Weber was not making
the quasi-tautological claim that more Protestants are entrepreneurs
because they have an innate disposition to be so; rather he claimed
that the preponderance of Protestant entrepreneurs in late-nineteenth-
century Germany was a consequence of the fact that two or three hundred years previously it was the Protestant ethic which had produced
the spirit of capitalism and therefore it was above all among Protestants
that modern bourgeois capitalists emerged.

In Weber and in the debate over *PESC* 'capitalism' seems to have at
least three shades of meaning. In the first place it refers to a type of
economic activity to be found in all civilizations: 'The important fact is
always that a calculation of capital in terms of money is made ... at the
beginning of the enterprise an initial balance, before every individual
decision a calculation to ascertain its probable profitableness, and at the
end a final balance to ascertain how much profit has been made' (*PESC*:
18). The 'capitalistic adventurer' is of this type. Then there is what Weber
called modern, rational, or bourgeois capitalism: in addition to the above
criterion this is based on formally free labour and double-entry book-
keeping; it is separate from the household and 'attuned to a regular market'. Finally there is 'capitalism' as a name for industrial society, or one
kind of industrial society, a usage which perhaps owes more to Marx
than to Weber, but which Weber certainly encouraged because in looking for the origin of modern capitalism in the second sense, he clearly
believed he was also explaining the origin of capitalism in the third sense.
Thus in the first two senses 'capitalism' denotes a kind of economic organization, the latter a distinct type of the former; the third sense denotes a type or sub-type of society. The capitalist *spirit* on the other hand
comprises an historically unusual set of attitudes based on the pursuit of
profit for its own sake, which Weber illustrated with the maxims of
Benjamin Franklin (*PESC*: Chapter 2).

The connection between the three senses of 'capitalism' for Weber
is this: capitalist society (sense 3) results, not from the gradual development of capitalist economic organizations (sense 1), but from the latter's
infusion with the spirit of capitalism, which turns it into rational or

bourgeois capitalism (sense 2). Weber's central insight was that there was nothing inevitable or 'natural' about this (the appearance of industrial society) as evolutionist perspectives suggest: it was the result of a certain set of unique and unusual conditions.[9] Thus he states in the final sentence of *ROI*: 'The appearance of [a rationally formed missionary prophecy] in the Occident ... with the extensive consequences borne with it, was conditioned by highly particular historical circumstances without which, despite differences of natural conditions, development there could easily have taken the course typical of Asia, particularly of India' (*ROI*: 343).

Confusion has no doubt been increased by failing to notice that the capitalist spirit as defined by Weber is only invariably associated with capitalism in the second of these senses, and then only before it stands on 'mechanical foundations'. Of course, all institutions require certain attitudes on the part of the individuals within them, but what Weber has called the capitalist spirit was not necessarily required by capitalist economic organization. Thus 'the management, for instance, of a bank, a wholesale export business, a large retail establishment, or of a large putting-out enterprise dealing with goods produced in homes, is certainly only possible in the form of a capitalistic enterprise. Nevertheless, they may all be carried on in a traditionalistic spirit' (*PESC*: 65). This is indeed the way they always, or nearly always, have been carried on, and Weber made it clear that this type of economic behaviour has no power to transform society. Protestantism, by contrast, produced individuals imbued with the capitalist spirit, and as an unforseen consequence produced a new type of society based on its own attitude to work. In reply to the initial publication of *PESC*, Sombart had cited the case of Alberti, a Renaissance man, in both senses, who wrote a treatise on household management which displayed a thoroughgoing money-mindedness. Weber replied:

The essential point of the difference [between Alberti and Franklin] is ... that an ethic based on religion places certain psychological sanctions (not of an economic character) on the maintenance of the attitude prescribed by it, sanctions which, so long as the religious belief remains alive, are highly effective, and which mere worldly wisdom like that of Alberti does not have at its disposal. Only in so far as these sanctions work, and, above all, in the direction in which they work, which is often very different from the doctrine of the theologians, does such an ethic gain an independent influence on the conduct of life and thus on the economic order. This is, to speak frankly, the point of this whole essay, which I had not expected to find so completely overlooked. (*PESC*: 197)

The challenge to the Weber thesis

The real question which Weber's approach has to face has been missed by most of the literature. It is: Why was the development that occurred within pre-industrial societies (see problem (A) above) not sufficient to produce modern capitalism? From an evolutionist perspective such as that of Luethy, development within agrarian civilizations ought to be sufficient to produce industrial capitalism. The emphasis that Weber placed on Protestantism 'creating' capitalism is therefore misplaced: 'In the period of the Reformation all the bases of the modern world—capital, wealth, the highest technological and artistic level of development, global power, world trade—all these were almost exclusively present in countries that were and remained Catholic ... One century later all this was petrifaction and decay.' The real problem, which according to Luethy is missed by Weber and the Weberians, is to explain 'the sudden breaking of an ascendant curve of development' in the Catholic countries, not its continuance in the Protestant ones (Luethy 1970: 133).

A viewpoint very similar to Luethy's has been advanced by Hugh Trevor-Roper in his stimulating article, 'Religion, the Reformation and Social Change':

It was not that Calvinism created a new type of man, who in turn created capitalism; it was rather that the old economic elite of Europe were driven into heresy because the attitude of mind which had been theirs for generations, and had been tolerated for generations, was suddenly, and in some places, declared heretical and intolerable. (Trevor-Roper 1967: 27)

Consequently Europe was divided into Catholic states with a '"bureaucratic" system of the princes which may encourage state capitalism, but squeezes out free enterprise' and Protestant ones which were the inheritors of 'the mercantile system of the free cities' (ibid.: 38). Thus 'it was the Counter-Reformation which extruded [economic enterprise] from society, not Calvinist doctrine which created it, or Catholic doctrine which stifled it, in individuals' (ibid.: 42).

Two separate issues are raised by Trevor-Roper's criticism of Weber. First, he takes Weber's thesis to be that there is a necessary and sufficient causal connection between Calvinism and the capitalist spirit, i.e. that all Calvinists must be ascetic capitalists. I need not repeat the reasons for rejecting this. Trevor-Roper's proof that the capitalist spirit predates Protestantism, and his examples of the unascetic behaviour of the most successful Calvinist entrepreneurs (unlikely to be typical for that very reason), do not therefore attack the Weber thesis. The importance of

Protestantism lay in the fact that it brought active rational asceticism into the everyday world and provided it with religious sanctions; asceticism was no longer confined, as in Medieval Catholicism or in Asia, to virtuosos. Trevor-Roper ably documents the hostility of Catholic Europe to the capitalist spirit when it threatened the former's political dominance. It was only much later, when the political advantages of Protestant economic attitudes became overwhelmingly clear (and it is important to remember that they were anything but clear beforehand), that Catholic writers began to urge the adoption of Protestant virtues.

Trevor-Roper's second point is the same as Luethy's: it was the Counter-Reformation that prevented the emergence of industrial capitalism in Catholic Europe, not Protestantism that produced it in northern Europe. But if we put the evidence cited by Luethy and Trevor-Roper in a larger comparative framework, as Weber tried to do, we can perhaps see that Weber was justified in concentrating on the creative role of Protestantism rather than the destructive one of Catholicism. In his books on South Asia and China he tried to show that in spite of the 'ascendant curve of development' apparent in both civilizations, neither could have led to a breakthrough to industrial society. The frustration of urban economic growth by ruling but non-productive strata is the norm, not the exception, in agrarian society.[10] Hence the stress that Weber laid on the necessity for the development of capitalism of the existence of rational law and a rational bureaucratic state. It seems to have been evident to Weber that mere technological growth and population increase are not enough to produce capitalism, and he therefore concentrated on the potential these civilizations had for the production of a capitalist spirit. This is why he says that he was 'necessarily dealing with the religious ethics of the classes which were the culture-bearers of their respective countries' (PESC: 30). The implication is that, but for Protestantism, or some equivalent, producing a capitalist spirit, Europe would have gone the way of South Asia or China.

The Chinese case

The Chinese case is particularly important for the Weberian approach because here many of the conditions for the development of modern capitalism seem to have been satisfied, but there was no capitalist spirit. 'Rational entrepreneurial capitalism, which in the Occident found its specific locus in industry, has been handicapped not only by the lack of a formally guaranteed law, a rational administration and judiciary, and by the ramifications of a system of prebends, but also, basically, by the lack of a particular mentality' (Weber 1951: 104). This crucial lack, which Weber calls his 'central theme', is tackled in Part 2 of *The Religion of China*, which attempts to show why a capitalist spirit did not, and indeed could not, given its cultural resources, develop in China.

Clearly Weber's explanation is a negative one: the absence of a capitalist spirit meant that China could not develop modern capitalism, even though in the early Medieval period it was the most advanced society in the world, in terms of agricultural, economic, commercial, and technological development. Weber does not provide a detailed answer to the question why this development should not be self-sustaining, i.e. sufficient to produce modern capitalism, though he gives a couple of hints in *Economy and Society* (henceforth *ES*):

> It would be a mistake to assume that the development of capitalistic enterprises must occur proportionally to the growth of want satisfaction in the monetary economy, and an even larger mistake to believe that this development must take the form it has assumed in the Western world. In fact, the contrary is true. The extension of money economy might well go hand in hand with the increasing monopolization of the larger sources of profit by the *oikos* economy of a prince. Ptolemaic Egypt is an outstanding example ... It is also possible that with the extension of a money economy could go a process of 'feudalization' (*Verpfründung*) of fiscal advantages resulting in a traditionalistic stabilization of the economic system. This happened in China ... (*ES*: 113)

> [A]s always in the area of 'techniques'—we find that the advance proceeded most slowly wherever older, structural forms were in their own way technically highly developed and functionally particularly well adapted to the requirements at hand. (*ES*: 987)

A detailed theory of what happens under these conditions has been elaborated by Mark Elvin for the Chinese case, which he calls the high-level equilibrium trap. I shall quote his summary.

> In China, demand and the supply of materials were increasingly constrained by a special combination of circumstances that gradually spread across the country until, by about 1820, they held all of the eighteen provinces within the Wall in their grip. These circumstances were: (1) the rapidly falling quality, and hence rapidly falling returns to labor and other inputs, of the small remaining quantity of new land not yet opened to cultivation and capable of being opened under the existing technology; (2) the continuing increase of the population, reducing the surplus per head available above subsistence for the creation of concentrated mass markets for new goods, and also (though less significantly) for investment; (3) the impossibility of improving productivity per hectare in agriculture under a pre-modern technology that was the most refined in the world in terms of manuring, rotations, etc., without the modern inputs such as chemical fertilizers

and petrol or diesel pumps that presuppose a scientific and industrial revolution for their production; and (4) the great size of China (close to twice the population of Europe), and its relatively good commercial integration, which made it impossible for pre-modern foreign trade to substitute for internal inadequacies, by providing either the stimulus of a large volume of new demand or the support of large quantitites of cheap raw materials. The trap could only be broken by the introduction of new technology exogenous to the Chinese world. (Elvin 1984: 383–4)

Rational strategy [therefore] for peasant and merchant alike tended in the direction not so much of labour-saving machinery as of economizing on resources and fixed capital ... When temporary shortages arose, mercantile versatility, based on cheap transport, was a faster and surer remedy than the contrivance of machines. (Elvin 1973: 314)

It is clearly a weakness in Weber that he provided no such analysis. Nevertheless Elvin's ecological explanation in terms of the high-level equilibrium trap and Weber's cultural explanation do not necessarily compete as Elvin assumes. Indeed one might even say that they imply each other or some equivalent: because China had no capitalist spirit, it was caught in the high-level equilibrium trap; because Europe produced a capitalist spirit it avoided the high-level equilibrium trap to which its 'ascendant curve of development' would otherwise have led it.[11]

From this point of view Elvin's term 'trap' is a misnomer, which only makes sense from the distinctive perspective of the modern world: the 'high-level equilibrium trap' describes the *normal* relationship between population, resources, and development in pre-industrial agrarian society. It is the development of the West, in spite of the fact that it is widely taken for granted, which is abnormal and in particular need of explanation. It is the development of the West that Weber was particularly concerned to explain.

The South Asian case

The South Asian case is different from the Chinese. For one thing, among the multifarious religious doctrines to be found in South Asia, one, Jainism, showed great potential for the production of a capitalist spirit. Thus the explanation for South Asia's failure to produce industrial capitalism rests on other factors, to do with the general Hindu caste context and the way that it overrode any particular ethic. It is to be presumed on this Weberian perspective that, if South Asian civilization had taken its course uninterrupted by the introduction of industrialism, it would have encountered some equivalent of Elvin's high-level

equilibrium trap, though probably at a technically lower leve.
short, South Asian society could develop a minority capitalisn
the Jains, or an emulative capitalism, as in the modern world, t
Weber claimed, an endogenous capitalism capable of transforming ⌄uth
Asia from an agrarian to an industrial society.

For the sake of clarity in the following discussion of South Asian
religions, it is worth making a distinction, due to Schluchter, of three
senses which rationality had for Weber: (i) scientific-technological
rationalism: control of the world on the basis of empirical laws, or means-
end rationality; (ii) metaphysical-ethical rationalism: systematization of
an ethos, or the application of logic to a world-view; (iii) practical
rationalism: a methodical way of life, or rational asceticism (Roth and
Schluchter 1979: 14–15). Although South Asia was advanced in
mathematics and grammar, it failed to develop (i). (ii) it certainly had:
Weber was very impressed by the karma doctrine as a solution to theodicy.
(iii) developed in the West thanks first to the monasteries, and then to
the Reformation. Its failure to develop in South Asia was what Weber
wished to explain.

Jainism

Weber was struck by the similarities between Jainism and Protestantism:

As with Protestantism, 'joy in possessions' (*parigraha*) was the objectional thing,
but not possession or gain in itself ... The Jains believed in absolute honesty in
business life ... [which] excluded the sect, on the one side, from typical oriental
participation in 'political capitalism' (accumulation of wealth by officials, tax
farmers, state purveyors) and, on the other, it worked among them and among
the Parsees, just as for the Quakers in the Occident, in terms of the dictum (of
early capitalism) 'honesty is the best policy'. (*ROI*: 200)

This was so even though Jainism was based on a quite different theology,
in which God, in so far as he is admitted to exist, is irrelevant to the
concerns of human beings. The Jain community was led by monks, and
the laity, far more than in Buddhism, were integrated into the ascetic
values, and to a certain extent the practices, of their monasticism.
However the Jains remained a minority within Hindu society to which
they increasingly accommodated themselves. They became in effect a
caste or several castes, and could not escape the general consequences of
caste society. 'That they remained confined to commercial capitalism
and failed to create an industrial organization was again due to their
ritualistically determined exclusion from industry and as with the Jews
their ritualistic isolation in general. To this must be added the by now

familiar barriers that their Hindu surroundings with its traditionalism and the patrimonial character of kingship put in their way' (*ROI: 200; Weber 1917: 424).[12]

Caste and status group

Weber explains the different types of religion to be found in South Asia principally with reference to two strata: 'the social world was divided into the strata of the wise and educated and the uncultivated plebeian masses' (ROI: 343). As we approach the present he also posits the category of the 'illiterate middle classes'. He does not discuss what he thinks is the relation between these strata and caste; the very use of the word 'stratum' is perhaps a sign of vagueness. Caste on the other hand Weber takes to be a 'closed status group':

What is a 'status group'? 'Classes' are groups of people who, from the standpoint of specific interests, have the same economic position ... 'Status', however, is a quality of social honor or lack of it, and is in the main conditioned as well as expressed through a specific style of life ... All the obligations and barriers that membership in a status group entails also exist in a caste, in which they are intensified to the utmost degree. (ROI: 39–40)

Louis Dumont takes Weber to task for this definition of caste: to understand caste as a form of something found in the West (a) is ethnocentric, and (b) necessarily makes the religious aspect of caste secondary (Dumont 1980: 26). Weber is aware of the importance of the religious aspect and that it is this which makes a crucial difference between caste among Hindus and caste among Muslims or Buddhists, but he does not see caste as different in kind from the status groups found in other societies, as Dumont does.

Without going further into theories of caste,[13] it is clear that Weber's approach seems to have blinded him to an important fact, viz. that although all brahmans to be considered as such had, in the traditional situation, to maintain a certain way of life (like the members of a status group), it was by no means the case that all brahmans could be said to belong to the class of cultured intellectuals. The same applies *mutatis mutandis* to kshatriyas ('rulers', 'nobles'). 'In India', Weber says, 'the Brahmans represent a status group of literati partly comprising princely chaplains, partly counsellors, theological teachers, and jurists, priests and pastors', though he immediately concedes: 'In both cases [i.e. South Asia and China] only a portion of the status group occupied the characteristic positions' (ROI: 139–40). In fact, although many of the twice-born would comply with brahmanical customs, and even learn Sanskrit, and thus maintain 'the specific style of life' of a brahman or kshatriya, the extent and the manner of this compliance varied enormously; consequently the meaning of this allegiance cannot be explained in terms of their all belonging to a stratum of cultured intellectuals, but only in caste terms— which is presumably Dumont's point. It was therefore possible for brahmans to participate, and indeed take leading positions, in what Weber saw as uncultured forms of saviour religion or Tantric 'orgiasticism'. Hence the Medieval formula: a Vaidika [i.e. conservative follower of the orthodox Vedas] for *samskaras* (life-cycle rituals), a Shaiva [a devotional adherent of the great god, Shiva] in the market-place, and a Kaula [a practitioner of antinomian Tantric rituals] in secret. Thus, in short, the questions of status groups and the types of religion which grew from them, and of the relation of orthodox brahmanism to Tantric forms of religion, were considerably more complex than Weber realized. Weber's crucial mistake was to argue back from religious texts to the motivations of those who gave allegiance to them; there is a long tradition of this in Indology to which he merely gave sociological formulation. Nevertheless Weber was acquainted with all the types of religion to be found in South Asia. The fact that they could be combined in this way, in disregard of their 'original' meaning, does not of itself invalidate his conclusions about the 'spirit' of Hinduism and its consequences for economic activity.

Caste did not prevent the division of labour in the workshop, but the existence of caste ritualism, Weber argued, made it inherently unlikely that capitalism could develop. It was 'as if none but different guest peoples, like the Jews, ritually exclusive towards one another and toward third parties, were to follow their trades in one economic area' (*ROI:* 112). Further, it was the increasing strength of caste, encouraged by Hindu kings, that undermined independent guilds and independent cities. Thus 'individual acceptance for apprenticeship, participation in market deals, or citizenship—all these phenomena of the West either failed to develop in the first place or were crushed under the weight of ethnic, later of caste fetters' (*ROI:* 131).

Weber emphasizes the 'religious promise' of the caste system:

No Hindu denies two basic principles: the *samsara* belief in the transmigration of souls and the related *karman* doctrine of compensation. These alone are the truly 'dogmatic' doctrines of all Hinduism, and in their very interrelatedness they represent the unique Hindu theodicy of the existing social, that is to say caste system. (*ROI:* 118; Weber 1916: 728/1996: 202)

These views reveal Weber's textual bias, as does his remark that in consequence of these beliefs the Untouchables had most to gain from ritual correctness, which, he thinks, explains their hostility to innovation (*ROI*: 123). The work of anthropologists shows that considerations of purity and impurity/sin, which impose themselves or are imposed on the individual, are far more pervasive, 'dogmatic', and built into the social structure than beliefs about karma or samsara. The evidence is that these beliefs are invoked in an *ad hoc* and retrospective way and do not guide the lives of caste Hindus (e.g. Srinivas 1976: 317).

Weber was on much firmer ground when he deduced this consequence of the caste order: universalist humanism and individualism similar to that of the West is only to be found outside it.

In this eternal caste world, the very gods in truth constituted a mere caste ... Anyone who wished to emancipate himself from this world and the inescapable cycle of recurrent births and deaths had to leave it altogether—to set out for that unseen realm (*Hinterwelt*) to which Hindu 'salvation' leads. (**ROI*: 123; Weber 1916: 733/1996: 207–8)

Such literature of the Indians as arguably parallels the philosophical ethical systems of the West [i.e. in their universalism] was—or more correctly, became in the course of its development—something altogether different, namely, a metaphysically and cosmologically grounded teaching (*Kunstlehre*) of the methods of achieving salvation from this world ... A religious eschatology of the world was as little possible here as in Confucianism. Only a (practical) eschatology of single individuals could develop ... (**ROI*: 147; Weber 1917: 358/1996: 236–7)

Here in essence is the theory later elaborated by Louis Dumont in his famous essay on world renunciation in South Asian religion (Dumont 1960).

Brahmanical religion

Weber's remarks on brahmanical religion were extremely perceptive. Even if today they would have to be supplemented, his conclusions as to the social implications of the most orthodox part of Hinduism remain valid:

For the character of official Indian religiosity it was decisive that its bearer, the Brahmanical priestly aristocracy, was a genteel educated stratum, later simply a stratum of genteel literati. This had above all one consequence, ... that orgiastic and emotional-ecstatic elements of the ancient magic rites were not taken over and for long periods either completely atrophied or continued and were tolerated [only] as unofficial folk magic. (***ROI*: 137; Weber 1917: 345/1996: 221)

As noted above, this may be taken as correct if read as referring to brahmanical religion, above all to what is known as Smarta brahmanism; brahmans themselves by no means always kept to 'genteel' (*vornehm*) religiosity. The similarities and differences with Confucian intellectuals are extremely enlightening:

In both we find a status group of genteel literati whose magical charisma rests on 'knowledge'. Such knowledge was magical and ritualistic in character, deposited in a holy literature, written in a holy language, remote from that of everyday speech. In both appears the same pride in education and unshakable trust in this special knowledge as the cardinal virtue determining all good. Ignorance of this knowledge was the cardinal vice and the source of all evil. They developed a similar 'rationalism'—concerned with the rejection of all irrational forms of holy seeking. (*ROI:* 139)

However, whereas the Confucian literati were paradigmatically office-holders and guardians of a universalistic ethic, the brahmans were 'by background and nature priests' (*ROI:* 148) and the guardians of a relativistic ethic.

The view that brahmans are paradigmatically priests has been contested by Heesterman (1964, 1971). Certainly the evidence is unambiguous that the brahman who can avoid priestly activity and devote himself to knowledge and teaching, has higher status than the practising priest, especially the temple priest (see, e.g., Parry 1980, Fuller 1984: 62–4). Nevertheless, brahmans remained guardians of a relativistic caste ethic, whatever their occupation, so long as they gave allegiance to the Vedas (i.e. did not become Buddhists or Jains). Weber quite rightly noted that 'contemplative mysticism as a type of gnosis remains the crown of the classical Brahmanical style of life, the goal of every well-educated Brahman though the number of those who actually pursue it was as small in the medieval past as today' (*ROI:* 148).

Weber is equally good when he deduces the *aim* of brahmanical religion from the social position of its adherents:

The status pride of cultured men resisted undignified demands of ecstatic therapeutic practices and the exhibition of neuropathic states ... [but] could take a quite different stand toward the forms of apathetic ecstasy ... and all ascetic practices capable of rationalization. (*ROI:* 149)[14]

[Thus] the development of such salvation doctrines signified essentially, as is to be expected of intellectuals, a rationalization and sublimation of the magical holy states. This proceeded in three directions: first, one strove increasingly for personal holy status, for 'bliss' in this sense of the word, instead of for magical secret power useful for professional sorcery. Secondly, this state acquired a definitely formal character, and indeed, as was to be expected, that of a gnosis ... All religious holy seeking on such a foundation had to take the form of mystical seeking of god, mystical possession of god, or finally, mystical communion with the godhead. All three forms, pre-eminently however, the last named, actually appeared ... The rational interpretation of the world with respect to its natural, social and ritual orders then was the third aspect of the rationalization process, which the Brahmanical intellectual stratum consummated in reworking the religio-magical material ... (*ROI*: 152–3)

Once again, this is an excellent characterization of brahmanism, but misses the way in which even its adherents interpreted it in terms of magical powers. Crucial to the way in which anti-magical or anti-deistic doctrines would resurface in magical or deistic interpretations was the fact that texts were learned by heart in Sanskrit, not learned by reading, so that even many of those who could recite them needed explanations.[15] Also, Weber perhaps overestimates the importance of communion with a 'depersonalized' godhead: the other two forms of mysticism he mentions became increasingly important with the rise of the monotheistic sects.

Weber saw very clearly that the development of this mysticism posed certain problems for brahmanical thought: how to reconcile the ideal of renunciation with caste duty?

For one thing, from such mysticism no ethic for life within the world could be deduced. The Upanishads contain nothing or almost nothing of what we call ethics. For another, salvation through gnostic wisdom alone came into sharpest tension with the traditional content of holy texts. The gnostic doctrines led to the devaluation not only of the world of the gods, but, above all, of ritual ... [T]he orthodox remedied the situation through 'organic' relativism. (*ROI*: 172; Weber 1917: 389/1996: 275)

Thus although this 'denial of the world' was extremely 'radical', it 'did not reject the suffering, or sin, or uncharitableness, or imperfection of the world, but rather it rejected its transitory nature' (*ROI*: 167; Weber 1917: 383). So, as Dumont has also been at pains to stress, brahmanical soteriology is accommodated to brahmanical social teaching: the ideal of the renouncer is absorbed into Hinduism in such a way as to pose no threat to it, and in such a way that it excluded the possibility of a rational this-worldly asceticism. This was because on the one hand, the ideal was relativized and, on the other, because it was, in its dominant strains, conceptualized as opposed to all activity.

Buddhism

As with brahmanism, Weber is not a reliable guide to the practice of Buddhists. Nevertheless, he has some very perceptive remarks to make about Buddhist doctrine which are surely correct in their assessment of the limitations it placed on the action of its adherents. Weber's well-known summary is particularly misleading:

Ancient Buddhism ... is a specifically unpolitical and anti-political status religion, more precisely, a religious 'technology' of wandering and of intellectually-schooled mendicant monks ... Its salvation is a solely personal act of the single individual. There is no recourse to a deity or saviour. From Buddha himself we know no prayer. There is no religious grace. There is, moreover, no predestination either. (*ROI: 206*)

This picture is based on the doctrinal texts of the Pali canon, and if it was ever true of Buddhism it can only have been so for a short period while the Buddha was alive. A similar picture of 'true Buddhism' was arrived at by nineteenth-century commentators in Sri Lanka and elsewhere who then went on to condemn what they saw of Sinhalese or other Buddhism as corrupt, degenerate, animistic, superstitious, and so on.[16] By paying no attention to the Vinaya (monastic discipline) texts, Weber underestimated the all-important role of the Sangha (monastic community) in the life of the monk. He also underestimated the degree to which early Buddhism had already accommodated itself to lay religious interests and therefore included elements of prayer, deification of the Buddha, and so on.[17]

The urban origin of Buddhism, its original appeal to the middle classes, its universalism, and soteriological egalitarianism, its rejection of magical means to salvation, and its ethical stress on carefulness (Gombrich 1974) might make one think that Buddhism was a South Asian Protestantism. Weber's conclusions on this count are surely valid:

[A]ll rational action ('goal directed action') is ... expressly rejected. Thus there is lacking the tendency which in occidental monasticism developed increasingly with time and was so important for its specific character, namely, the impulse toward rational method in the conduct of life in all spheres, except that of the pure intellectual systemization of concentrated meditation and pure contemplation. The latter, on the other hand, was increasingly developed [within Buddhism] to that level of sophistication usually striven for in India. (**ROI**: 222; Weber 1917: 451/1996: 356)

Not only was Buddhism not rationalistic in Weber's sense, it was also not ascetic, as indeed the Jains charged:

In principle Buddhistic salvation is anti-ascetic if one conceptualizes, as we wish to do here, asceticism as a rational method of living. Certainly Buddhism prescribes a definite way ... However, this way is neither through rationalistic insight into the principles on which it metaphysically rests, in themselves, indeed, timelessly simple, nor a gradual training for ever higher moral perfection.

Liberation is ... a sudden 'leap' into the psychic states of the several stages of enlightenment, for which methodical contemplation is only a preparation. The nature of this leap is such that it puts the seeker in his innermost active dispositions in harmony with his theoretical insights, and grants him thereby the Buddhist *perseverantia gratiae* and *certitudo salutis* ... As all traditions indicate, this was the Buddha's own self-conscious state of grace. (**ROI*: 220; Weber 1917: 449/1996: 353)

[In short] just as every rational asceticism does not constitute flight from the world so not every flight from the world represents rational asceticism—as convincingly shown by this example. (*ROI:* 219)

Buddhism was therefore a 'genteel' or 'elite' (*vornehm*) 'soteriology': 'That it was such a genteel soteriology of intellectuals was precisely the basis of all its differences with ancient Christianity. Opposition to all genteel intellectuality ... was fundamentally important to the latter.' (**ROI*: 371; Weber 1917: 687/1996: 369n).

For the laity Buddhism offered the Five Precepts 'as an inferior substitute ethic of the weak (*Unzulänglichkeitsethik der Schwache*) who do not wish to seek complete salvation' (**ROI*: 215; Weber 1917: 443). This would seem to mean, not that Weber thinks these are 'paltry stuff' as Gombrich (1971: 245) interprets him, but that the ethic is necessarily inferior to the path of becoming a monk. Thus although

the later Buddhist suttas ... deal more thoroughly with lay problems ... [they] seek to treat lay morality as a preliminary step to the higher spiritual ethic ... This 'higher' morality does not lead—this is the decisive point—to increasingly rational asceticism (this- or other-worldly) or to a positive life method. Every idea of the sanctity of work ... is and remains heretical. Rather the opposite holds; active virtue in conduct recedes more and more into the background as against ... the ethic of non-action ... in the interest of pure contemplation. (*ROI:* 217; Weber 1917: 446/1996: 349–50)

This inability to produce a 'positive life method' was legitimated by the Buddhist theological principle of 'skill in means', i.e. 'the Buddhist belief in meeting the audience on their own level' (Gombrich 1971: 247). Thus on the one hand Buddhist monasticism could not produce rational asceticism out of its conceptual inheritance, but nor could Buddhist lay ethics on the other, because they were tied in, as an inferior partner, to those same values.[18]

The religion of the masses

The mass of South Asian people, and this included for the most part the Buddhist laity in its religious dealings with this world, in no way bound itself to a single faith. Rather, the simple Hindu who has not been specifically initiated into a sect treats the [different] cults and deities [of Hinduism] just as the ancient Greek worshipped Apollo and Dionysus according to the occasion, and as the Chinese devotedly attends Buddhist masses, Taoistic magic, and Confucian temple cults. (**ROI: 327; Weber 1917: 797/1996: 524)

Not the 'miracle' but the 'magical spell' remained ... the core substance of mass religiosity. This was true above all for peasants and laborers, but also for the middle classes ... This was either in the gross form of compulsive magic or in the refined form of persuading a functional god or demon through gifts. With such means the great mass of the illiterate and even the literate Asiatics sought to master everyday life. (*ROI: 335–6; Weber 1917: 806/1996: 533)

This most highly anti-rational world of universal magic also affected everyday economics. There is no way from it to rational, this-worldly conduct. (ROI: 336)

From the viewpoint of Weber's interests, these judgements are fair. He was not interested, as an anthropologist would be, in showing how these beliefs formed a system, and therefore possessed their own rationality. It should not be necessary to repeat that Weber was interested in the origins of a particular type of rationality, one which from other points of view might appear quite irrational.

Saviour religion (i.e. the Vaishnava sects) Weber interprets as being originally the preserve of the 'illiterate middle classes' (ROI: 307, 309, 335). In fact it was often the urban lower classes who turned to this form of religion. Its potential for creating a rational asceticism was negated by two facts: its nature which followed from the 'orgiastic and indeed sexual-orgiastic origin of bhakti ecstasy' (ROI: 307).[19] Secondly, there was the position of the guru: 'adoration of the living savior was the last word of Hindu religious development' (ROI: 324). The influence of the gurus was wholly traditionalistic and anti-rational:

Instead of a drive toward the rational economic accumulation of property and the utilization of capital, Hinduism created irrational accumulation opportunities for magicians and spiritual counsellors, and prebends for mystagogues and ritualistically or soteriologically oriented intellectual strata. (*ROI: 328; Weber 1917: 798/1996: 525)[20]

It is worth mentioning here Weber's conclusions on the ethical conse-quences of the doctrine of the Bhagavad Gita that one should fulfil one's caste duty while remaining unattached to the 'fruit' or results of the ac-tion. Milton Singer has claimed that Weber's 'emphasis on its organismic relativistic character and on its "world indifference" led him, I think, to slight a major parallel with the "Protestant ethic" in Hindu thought' (Singer 1961: 147). But Weber was surely correct to say that

[The professional fulfilment taught by the Bhagavad Gita] was rigidly traditionalistic in character and thereby mystically oriented as an activity in the world but not yet of the world. At any rate, it would occur to no Hindu to see in the course of his economic professional integrity the signs of his state of grace—or what is more important—to evaluate and undertake the rational constitution of the world according to empirical principles as a realization of God's will. (*ROI*: 326)

In any case, in spite of the Bhagavad Gita's universal popularity, no sect which has survived into modern South Asia has based its ethical doctrine principally on that text. The inspiration of the Vaishnava sects has come rather from the Bhagavata Purana with its emphasis on the need for emotional abandonment in one's relationship to God. Thus even when Vaishnava sectarianism has represented values of hard work and self-improvement (see, e.g., Pocock 1973: 141), it does not make those values imperative in the way that interested Weber.

Religion, as it developed in South Asia, was incapable of imposing on the masses new sorts of social action, as Protestantism did in the West. The same religion offered different ideals to, and made different demands upon, different social strata. Furthermore,

with very few exceptions Asiatic soteriology knew only an exemplary promise. Most of these were only accessible to those living monastically but some were valid for the laity ... The bases of both phenomena were similar. Two above all were closely interrelated. In the first place [there was] the gap which set the person of literary cultivation above the non-literate masses of philistines. Then [there was] the associated fact that in the final analysis all philosophies and soteriologies of Asia shared a common presupposition: that knowledge, be it literary knowledge or mystical gnosis, is ultimately the only absolute path to the highest spiritual good both here and in the world beyond. (**ROI*: 330; Weber 1917: 800/1996: 528)

[The mystical character of this gnosis] had two important consequences. First was the formation by the soteriology of a redemption aristocracy, for the capacity for mystical gnosis is a charisma and not by a long chalk accessible to all. Then, however, and correlated therewith, it acquired an asocial and apolitical character ... (**ROI*: 331; Weber 1917: 802/1996: 529)

But [Asia's] goals of self-discipline—in some cases purely mystical, in others purely worldly and aesthetic [i.e. especially in China]—could in any case be pursued only by emptying experience of the real forces of life. These goals were remote from the interests of the 'masses' and their day-to-day activities, who were therefore left in undisturbed magical bondage. (**ROI*: 342; Weber 1917: 814/1996: 543)

It was this 'emptying' nature of the road to salvation which Weber thinks is the crucial 'spiritual' factor, to be placed alongside caste and the power of the guru, in prolonging the 'enchantment' of the Hindu, i.e. the prevalence of magic as opposed to rationality. It meant that religious means were always, in one way or another, irrational: 'Either they were of an orgiastic character and led directly into anti-rational paths which were inimical to a rational way of life, or they were admittedly rational in method but irrational in aim'. (**ROI*: 326; Weber 1917: 796/1996: 521).

Conclusion

Weber's sociology of Hinduism and Buddhism is a marvel of condensation and, in spite of a superficial appearance to the contrary due to the mass of details, it displays an impressively unitary theme. In order to try and bring out that theme, I have presented and commented on only the most general and prominent points of *ROI*. To discuss and assess it in all its detail would require another book at least. To ignore Weber's book on South Asia because many of the details are wrong is to ignore also three virtues it conspicuously displays, from which the study of South Asian religion and society could well benefit: (i) comparative range, from China, to Europe, to Ancient Greece, which no single scholar will probably ever again possess; (ii) a genuine historical depth, which is only approached even by the best sociologists and anthropologists; (iii) an impressive theoretical apparatus: (a) he treats society as a whole whose parts are interdependent, unlike even so distinguished a Sanskritist as A.L. Basham, whose otherwise excellent *Wonder That Was India* has one chapter on politics, one on everyday life, one on religion, and so on, with little indication of the extent to which they are interrelated; (b) Weber tries to understand and explain the functioning and development of Hinduism and Buddhism in terms of a few basic categories, which are the same as those used to explain other societies. In this, as in much else, the foremost disciple of Weber, in the study of South Asia, is clearly Louis Dumont.[21]

Notes

1. Much of the stimulus for writing the original version of this paper, published in 1982, came from discussions with Mark Elvin (see below, and Elvin 1984). It would be impossible to cover all the literature that continues to

pour forth on Weber, or even on Weber and South Asia, but mention should be made of the work of Kantowsky, Marshall, and Schluchter (see references). *The Religion of India* is in fact a translation, and in many places a mistranslation, of part (Weber 1916–17) of Weber's series of long articles entitled 'The Economic Ethics of the World Religions'. (Ghosh 1994 demonstrates that even the more trustworthy Talcott Parsons translation of *PESC* is frequently misleading.) It would have been more accurate to call the translation of *ROI The Religions of Asia*. Kantowsky (1986: 214–16) describes how such a poor translation came to be published. I have checked the translation of *ROI* where I have quoted it, and indicated with an asterisk (*ROI*) where I have changed a word or two, and with two asterisks (**ROI*) where I have changed more. I am grateful to Nick Allen, Professor T.J. Reed, and Wolfgang Schwentker for advice on this. The new critical German edition (Weber 1996) should now be consulted, and a new translation of *ROI* is clearly a scholarly necessity.

2. I use the term 'India' in the title since it appears in the title of *ROI* and was used by Weber; but the region is today generally referred to as South Asia to differentiate it from the modern political unit called India.

3. For example, Fuller 1977 has traced some of the drawbacks in anthropologists' accounts of caste to the division of labour between them and historians.

4. For an important discussion of the Scottish case, scholarly both in its analysis of Weber and in its presentation of the historical evidence, see Marshall 1980. I shall argue that in fact South Asia (India) was closer to Scotland than to China: i.e., it had an analogue of neo-Calvinism (namely, Jainism), but lacked other ('material') conditions for 'take-off' (cf. Marshall 1980: 272–3). As discussed below, Elvin 1984 argues against Weber that even in the Chinese case the explanation must hinge on ecological and technical factors, not on the absence of functional equivalents of Protestantism.

5. Thus Singer's long analysis of present-day Hindu entrepreneurs in Madras (1972: Chapter 8), although interesting enough in itself, fails to attack Weber's main thesis. A similar criticism can be made of Munshi's (1988) otherwise very useful and detailed critique. Marshall (1980: 11–12, 30; 1982) lists numerous other, even more elementary misinterpretations springing from lack of attention to Weber's text.

6. Thus I claim that for Weber Protestantism was what J.L. Mackie (1965) has called an INUS condition of the capitalist spirit, i.e. it was an insufficient but necessary part of a collection of conditions which together were/are unnecessary but sufficient for the production of the capitalist spirit. According to Mackie this is, in fact, what we generally mean by 'cause'. Marshall (1980; 1982: 58–9) argues that Weber's initial problem was a search for the origins of the capitalist *spirit*, and that this only subsequently came to encompass the separate question of the origin of capitalism itself. The formulation given here is compatible, I believe, but more precise.

7. Turner (1974: 172–3, 1993: Chapter 3) argues that in the Muslim case also

Weber's position was that the main burden of explanation lay with 'material' factors, i.e. with the patrimonial nature of Muslim states.

8. Many commentators and critics, even those of Weber's own time, have ignored the context of his writing, e.g. the fact that PESC was first composed, and later revised, as part of debate with Sombart. On this background, see Marshall (1980: 1–35; 1982).

9. As Schluchter (1981: 4) puts it, 'Weber's work can be viewed as the gigantic effort to refute the basic assumptions of evolutionism'. He rightly criticizes Tenbruck's (1980) evolutionist interpretation of Weber as one-sided.

10. In this context Hall 1985 has traced the consequences of Europe's multi-state system as opposed to China's single imperial state. Cf. R. Collins (1986: 49).

11. In an approach similar to Elvin's, R. Collins (1986: Chapter 3) emphasizes technological innovations, both in Medieval Europe and in China from the eighth to the twelfth century, and the similar economic dynamism of Christian and Buddhist monasteries (a parallel Weber missed).

12. The Jains seem to have had closer connections to industry and to kings than Weber realized. On Jainism one should consult Jaini 1979, Carrithers and Humphrey (eds) 1991, Banks 1992, and Laidlaw 1995. The last is the only one to engage with Weber and concludes, 'In so far, which is quite far, as the Jains have been one of India's major cadres of entrepreneurs, there is no compelling reason to attribute this to the asceticism of their monks and nuns, or to the laity's respect for and emulation of this' (Laidlaw 1995: 363).

13. For a longer discussion of Weber on caste, see Stern 1971. For some characteristic critiques, see Marriott 1976, Appadurai 1986, Raheja 1988, and Quigley 1993. Some South Asianists, tired of the emphasis on caste, for which they hold Weber partly responsible, have in recent times rejected the notion that caste was important in South Asian history. For a representative critique, see Inden (1990: Chapter 2), and for a counterblast to an earlier version of the same argument, see Quigley 1988.

14. For reflections in a very Weberian mode on the place of spirit-possession in South Asian religions, see Höfer 1974.

15. See Staal 1979 and Heesterman 1974 for attempts to grapple with the problem of the effects on South Asian Great Traditions of the methods by which they were passed on.

16. The most impassioned critique of these sorts of views is by Southwold 1983. For the Christian model which dominated nineteenth-century observers' views on Buddhism, and for a typology of modern anthropologists' views, see Chapter 2 below.

17. On these issues, see Gombrich 1971, 1988. On early Buddhist monasticism, see Wijayaratna 1990.

18. For discussion of Weber's remarks on Mahayana Buddhism, see chapter 4. Randall Collins believes that Chinese monasteries did form a significant parallel to the Benedictine monasteries of Medieval Europe (see n. 11 above).

19. Munshi (1988: 24) is surely right that Weber's repeated use of the terms 'orgiastic' and 'sexual-orgiastic' is likely to mislead. Turner (1974: 183) goes so far as to say that 'Weber's mistakes about Islam are closely bound up with his whole attitude towards the relationship between religion and sex'.
20. For a discussion of Weber's use of the term 'prebend', see Turner 1981: Chapter 7.
21. See Dumont 1980, 1977. Others have noticed this debt also. See Burghart 1985: 6, Buss 1985: 13–14, 24 n. 2, 61–2, Conrad 1986: 172, and Holton and Turner 1989: 86–7; and in a more hostile manner, Appadurai 1986: 745 and Dirks 1987: 9. For interesting personal background to Dumont's study of South Asia, see S. Collins 1989.

2

What is the Anthropology of Buddhism About?

Introduction

Buddhism today can be broadly divided into the Theravada (found in Sri Lanka, Burma, Thailand, Laos, and Cambodia) and the Mahayana (found in Nepal, Tibet, China, Japan, Korea, and Vietnam). For various reasons most of the early work in the anthropology of Buddhism focused on Theravada Buddhism, and this included the classic works of Obeyesekere, Tambiah, Gombrich, and Spiro.[1] In the 1980s and 1990s much more ethnography was carried out on Mahayana Buddhism than before, but the imbalance remains.

'Theravada' means 'the doctrine of the elders'. Of all the schools of pre-Mahayana Buddhism—traditionally there were thought to be eighteen, a conventional number—the Theravada prided itself on being the most conservative. It is the only one to survive into the modern world. Certain texts and doctrines associated with other pre-Mahayana schools have survived within the Mahayana tradition. Thus the Tibetans preserve the Sarvastivadin monastic code, but among them it is merely an optional, supererogatory practice within Mahayana Buddhism. It does not define an institutionally separate kind of Buddhism. There is no group of Buddhists today whose primary allegiance is to Sarvastivada Buddhism.[2]

Of these early schools, Theravada Buddhism alone survived due to a fortunate geographical accident. It happened to be dominant in Sri

Lanka and in Southeast Asia, and therefore it avoided most of the factors which led to the eventual disappearance of Buddhism within India itself. Scholars disagree on what exactly these factors were, but the rise of new forms of Hinduism, the loss of royal patronage, and Muslim invasions and conquests were all important.[3]

Mahayana ('Great Vehicle' or 'Great Way') Buddhism appeared in India around the turn of the common era. The monks who adhered to it coexisted, often within the same monastery and sharing the same monastic discipline, with those who did not accept the new Mahayana scriptures, until they were all destroyed by Muslim invaders between the eleventh and the thirteenth centuries. By that time the Mahayana had long since been taken up in China (and from there continued to the other countries of East Asia), and was already becoming firmly established in Tibet. Within South and Southeast Asia, Indian Mahayana Buddhism survived only in the Kathmandu Valley, Nepal, and, very minimally, in Bali. Elsewhere all scriptures were translated from their original Sanskrit into Chinese or Tibetan.

The Protestant/Catholic model

A common comparison likens Theravada Buddhism to Protestantism and Mahayana Buddhism to Catholicism. Nineteenth- and early twentieth-century western scholars and observers, whether explicitly or implicitly, certainly viewed Buddhism in this light. Many of them were attracted to Theravada Buddhism and were keen to reform it. With one or two exceptions (such as Alexandra David-Neel) who were precisely drawn by its 'magic and mystery', they tended to dismiss the Mahayana Buddhism of Nepal and Tibet as superstition, idolatry, wizardry, and depravity.[4] In a much-quoted passage Stcherbatsky ([1923] 1977: 42) drew a sharp contrast between the two types of Buddhism:

When we see an atheistic, soul-denying philosophic teaching of a path to personal Final Deliverance, consisting in an absolute extinction of life, and a simple worship of the memory of its human founder,—when we see it superseded by a magnificent High Church with a Supreme God, surrounded by a numerous pantheon and a host of Saints, a religion highly devotional, highly ceremonious and clerical, with an ideal of Universal Salvation of all living creatures, a Salvation by the divine grace of Buddhas and the Bodhisattvas, a Salvation not in annihilation, but in eternal life,—we are fully justified in maintaining that the history of religions has scarcely witnessed such a break between new and old within the pale of what nevertheless continues to claim common descent from the same religious founder.

Stcherbatsky drew attention to a real problem—what, if anything, do the different forms of Buddhism have in common?—but he made its solution sound more difficult than it is. Pre-Mahayana Buddhism was not just a philosophy (as modernists frequently present it) and it did not teach the extinction or annihilation of the self, but of desires. Stcherbatsky's Protestant-Catholic model is very clear, since he continued in a footnote: 'The two churches co-existed peacefully in the same monasteries, because the Buddhists very wisely always made allowance for human nature which sometimes feels inclination towards a simple rationalistic Low Church and sometimes is attracted towards a devotional and magnificent High Church.'

In fact the parallel between Protestantism and traditional Theravada Buddhism quickly breaks down, for at least six reasons.

(i) *Chronology*. Theravada Buddhism came first and is a representative of the earlier Buddhism against which Mahayana Buddhism reacted. It was Mahayana Buddhism which claimed to be returning to the true spirit of the Buddha's original message. Unlike Protestantism, Mahayana Buddhism did so, not by returning to original texts, but by composing new ones and attributing them to the Buddha. In some cases they were said to have been hidden by him under the sea until a sage capable of understanding them (Nagarjuna) would retrieve them.

(ii) *The role of monasticism*. Theravada Buddhism was certainly a religious individualism (Gombrich 1988: 72f.) but it was never egalitarian. Nor did it impose its individualism on 'life in the world', i.e. on the social arrangements of the laity. Spiritual hierarchy was built into it from the beginning. At the very least this consists of two stages, monk and lay, but in practice other levels of attainment are recognized too. Thus, there is spiritual equality of opportunity, but not equality of result. It is not a question of sheep and goats, but of a large number of gradations, in short, of hierarchy.

(iii) *The language of the scriptures*. Originally preserved orally, later written down, the Pali of the Theravada scriptures is incomprehensible both to the laity and to many of the monks who recite it. Unlike Protestantism, with its stress on literacy and reading the Bible for oneself, traditionally lay Theravada Buddhists have had no access to the scriptures, unless they have themselves spent time as monks.

(iv) *The extent of the scriptures*. Whereas Protestantism is based on one (relatively) short book, the Theravada scriptures, although in principle limited, are very much more extensive. Few monks can have been acquainted with more than a part of them.

(v) *The worship of relics*. In spite of its individualist and rationalizing tendencies, Theravada Buddhism has always given a large place to the worship of relics, which, within Christianity, is characteristic of Catholicism, not Protestantism.

(vi) *The doctrine of rebirth.* Since life is presumed to continue through innumerable rebirths, and since many Theravada Buddhists believe that at present, unlike the time of the Buddha, no one can attain nirvana, the quest for salvation has rather less urgency than in Protestantism.

In the modern period a new type of Theravada Buddhism has arisen which is indeed closer to Protestantism. It rejects spiritual hierarchy and has direct access to the scriptures (due to increased literacy and the existence of translations into English and the vernaculars). It has parallels in Japan in the new religious movements there; in Nepal imported Theravada Buddhism, present there only since the 1930s, is the primary vehicle for Buddhist modernism of this sort. Heinz Bechert first coined the term 'Buddhist modernism'; Gombrich and Obeyesekere (1988) call this new form Protestant Buddhism. Houtman (1990: 125) suggests in a striking phrase that we see this new form of Buddhism not, as is conventionally done, as laicization, but rather as the 'monasticization' of the religion.

Mahayana less studied by anthropologists

One reason why Theravada Buddhism has received greater anthropological attention than Mahayana Buddhism, and was studied ethnographically at an earlier period, is simply that it is easier to get to grips with. In particular, it has a more or less clearly defined canon, all of which has been translated into English. Mahayana Buddhist scriptures have not even all been edited, let alone translated. Furthermore, if the relationship of precept and practice, text and context, is always problematic, it is arguable that the relationship of Mahayana scriptures to practice is even more than usually problematic. Within Mahayana Buddhism there are many local variants, laying very different stress on different parts of the scriptural corpus. The single most important development was the emergence of Vajrayana ('Diamond Vehicle'/ 'Way') or Tantric Buddhism. This is based on an even later set of esoteric scriptures, known as Tantras, and it represented a specialized path within the Mahayana, for priests, monks, and other virtuosi. The process of scripture-innovation begun by the Mahayana was therefore much imitated, and remained controversial. Not all Mahayana Buddhists accept the Tantras, and the Tantric Buddhists of Japan accept one class of Tantras, but reject those of a later historical period which have become the highest and most secret teachings for Buddhists in Nepal and Tibet. In Tibet itself the Nyingma sect has its own Tantric scriptures (*terma*) which are not accepted by other schools.

In addition to the baroque complexity of the religion itself, two other factors help to explain the relative lack of anthropological work on Mahayana Buddhism. First, Buddhism is not, in most of East Asia, the overwhelmingly dominant ideological force that it is in Tibet or Theravada countries. Anthropologists working there have not been forced to confront the issues outlined below by their sheer salience in the culture. Second, the political situation in Mahayana countries such as Tibet and China has meant that overall they have been less intensively studied by anthropologists than, say, Thailand or Sri Lanka.

Basic questions in the study of Theravada Buddhism

The anthropology of Theravada Buddhism has tended to focus on a series of questions which derive from the agenda set by the Theravada/ Protestant and Buddhism/Christianity comparisons. These questions have been posed in their sharpest form by Spiro (1982: 7–9). How can a religion which is materialistic (the doctrine of no soul), atheistic (no creator God), nihilistic (all real things are impermanent), pessimistic (everything is suffering), and renunciatory (the only answer is to abandon one's self, family, and possessions), be the official religion of so many countries? Do—can—Theravada Buddhists really believe in Theravada Buddhism? As Spiro goes on to note, some of these characterizations of Theravada Buddhism are exaggerated. For example, Buddhist schools have differed radically over which aspects of existence are to be considered real; and there are ways of being a good Buddhist which do not necessarily involve complete renunciation.

Despite these exaggerations, such presuppositions and expectations informed the early European and scholarly encounter with Buddhism, and ultimately influenced many Buddhists themselves. Reared on accounts of Buddhism which managed to derive from the scriptures a picture of the Buddha as a humanist reformer and a rationalist, many observers of actual Buddhist practice were alarmed and sometimes shocked by what they found. None of the laity and very few monks meditated; the Buddha seemed to be worshipped as if he were a God; Buddhists often worshipped Hindu gods and local spirits and demons, and shrines to the gods were often found within monastery precincts; Buddhists simultaneously believed in systems such as astrology and therefore explained misfortune in those terms as well as by the doctrine of karma; there were rituals which seemed to imply the transference of merit to others and the magical efficacy of sacred objects, in contradiction of the strict individualism, and the moral and psychological rationalism, of the scriptures; most Buddhists seemed to be aiming not at nirvana but at achieving rebirth as a god or rich human being.

These gaps between the outsiders' expectations and actual Buddhists' practice led many researchers to ask the question which Spencer (1990: 131) characterizes as odd: Are these people really Buddhist? Many answered with a resounding 'No'. A similar, though more downbeat, concern to separate specifically Christian elements from pagan ones within the Christianity practised by Mediterranean peasants can be discerned in the relevant ethnographies (e.g. W. Christian's excellent *Person and God in a Spanish Valley*); such a concern is still more evident in many accounts of Latin American or African Christianity. As Ames (1964a: 37) remarks, 'This is the whitewash theory of syncretism; the high religion forms only a thin veneer covering a rich jungle of pagan cults.' The extraordinary persistence of the question, 'Are these people really X?', and the emphatic force of the response, almost certainly derive from western rather than Asian conceptual priorities.

It is no doubt true that westerners are more ready to resort to the whitewash theory, the more 'other' or exotic the culture appears to them.[5] It would be a mistake, however, to think that before western influence there were no movements for a return to more authentic practice, i.e. away from un-Buddhist corruption. In exactly the same way, the concern to recover practice based on 'original' scriptures is not entirely a modern innovation: Carrithers (1990) describes just such reform movements in both Theravada Buddhism and Jainism. It is true that the western Orientalist is more concerned to tar *all* Buddhists as inauthentic, whereas the traditional reforming Buddhist is likely to be more concerned with criticizing *monks*. Nevertheless there is an overlap between their views. The explanation of the overlap lies, I believe, in the hierarchical nature of the religion.

A spectrum of anthropologists

Both Buddhism and Catholicism presuppose a spiritual hierarchy, which Protestantism rejects. Those at higher levels of the religion frequently regard ordinary lay practice as 'not really Buddhist/Christian' or 'only minimally Buddhist/Christian'. The laity themselves may often agree with these judgements, without intending to convey the same condemnatory force as the Protestant-influenced western observer or Buddhist modernist.

Such modernists tend to describe actual Buddhism as 'mixed up' or, since this inevitably sounds pejorative in English, as syncretic (e.g. Bechert 1978). Some anthropologists have also taken this line, for instance Terwiel, who spent six of his eleven months in a Thai village as a temporary monk. However, in one way or another, most anthropologists have taken issue with this judgement. These different positions can be represented, without too much artificiality, on a spectrum as in Chart 2.1.[6]

Chart 2.1: A representation of the spectrum of views taken up by anthropological observers of Theravada Buddhism

Modernist/'Protestant Buddhist' position	'Anthropological' position	Populist position
Buddhism is the practice of an elite, necessarily misunderstood by the people	Buddhism contains a hierarchy of teachings and roles and coexists with other systems in a structured hierarchy	Buddhism is the practice of the masses, which has been distorted by the middle class
e.g. Terwiel	e.g. Obeyesekere, Tambiah	e.g. Southwold

Seen by others, such as Tambiah (1984a: 315), as occupying the modernist end of the spectrum, Spiro nonetheless has moved away from it. He distinguished three different forms or modes of Buddhism: nibbanic, kammatic, and apotropaic, oriented respectively towards attaining nirvana, improving one's chances of a good rebirth, and using Buddhist ritual for apotropaic purposes (Spiro 1982). Only the first, he claimed, is fully canonical.[7] Gombrich (1971: 49) argued that Theravada Buddhism never aspired to be more than a religion of salvation, so that it was inevitably 'accretive', always coexisting with other systems which satisfied Buddhists' this-worldly needs. Thus, the worship of gods derived from Hinduism, or other spirits, could hardly be called syncretic, unless it were done for salvation. Furthermore, those features of contemporary Sinhala Buddhism which led modernist observers to deny that the Sinhalese were true Buddhists seem in fact to have been part of Buddhist practice as far back as the evidence goes.

Ames (1964a, 1964b, 1966), Obeyesekere (1963), and Tambiah (1970) emphasize how Buddhism as practised forms one part of a single religious system which includes opposed or countervailing strands. (Samuel 1978 takes up similar position on Tibetan Buddhism.) They treat as one Sinhalese or Thai religion that which Buddhists themselves normally see as distinct systems. Thus Tambiah (1970: 42) describes his task as the delineation of 'distinctions, oppositions, complementarities, linkages and hierarchy' within the total system. There can be no doubt that these holistic approaches have been extremely fruitful in contrasting and relating the types of language, ritual, prestation, and behaviour appropriate in each sphere. Village Buddhists themselves may say, as Davis (1984: 181) reports from Thailand, that the opposed systems (in the Thai case, of Buddhism and brahmanism) are inseparable. For the people themselves, however, this inseparability does *not* extend to systems of exorcism. Tambiah's criticism (1984a: 315) of Spiro for breaking Burmese religion down into Buddhism and animism could only have force for those entirely and unreservedly committed to the holistic approach.

Most extreme of all is the position taken up by Southwold.[8] For him it is not enough to recognize that the Buddhism of ordinary Sinhalese villagers is 'surprisingly orthodox' (Gombrich 1971: 40). Nor is it enough to see Buddhism as one part—albeit the dominant part—of a pantheon and ritual heritage containing other, opposed values, as Obeyesekere and Tambiah do. Southwold sets out to show that what village Buddhists do is and must be orthodox Buddhism, and that what he calls middle-class Buddhism—the kind of Buddhism which is identical with or has been strongly influenced by modernist or 'Protestant' Buddhism—is in error. He makes a considerable number of cogent points along the way, both about Buddhism and about religion in general, but his determination to find the villagers right in all things eventually leads to absurdity. As examples one can cite the suggestion that celibacy for monks has entered Theravada Buddhism only as a late and inappropriate clerical addition (Southwold 1983: 40), or the argument that village Buddhists' everyday experience 'without knowing what it is they experience, is very plainly nirvanic ... [T]he nirvanic is the fellowship of the world' (ibid.: 69). Southwold has to find villagers wrong when they assert the existence of a spiritual hierarchy which puts themselves at the bottom.

No doubt there could be debate on where in this spectrum different authors should be placed. Calling the central part of the spectrum anthropological is of course to take sides. For Southwold his is the truly anthropological viewpoint which other anthropologists have been unable to attain due to various biases. However one chooses to label the spectrum, some general points about it can be hazarded. Those towards the populist end are more likely to see Buddhism as a this-worldly religion. Max Weber is frequently criticized for describing early Buddhism as 'unpolitical and antipolitical'.[9] This is one of the strands in Tambiah's work on the relationship of Theravada Buddhism to kingship, a field to which he has made a large but controversial contribution.[10] At the other end of the spectrum Buddhism is seen as essentially otherworldly, so that the actual practice of ordinary Buddhists is then a falling away, or 'animism in all but name'. There is an irony in that the modernist end of the spectrum is also the elitist end—and therefore corresponds in some moods to what a traditionalist monk might say. The reason for this irony is that the modernists have taken the values of the old elitists and made them mandatory for the mass of monks and lay Buddhists, so that what ordinary Buddhists actually do is seen by them as not really Buddhism at all.

It is the populist end of the spectrum which is uniquely modern. Anthropologists' views do not exist in a vacuum, sealed off from the societies they study. Thus I think it valid to suggest that two of the basic positions shown in Chart 2.1—the modernist and the anthropological—correspond, very roughly, to indigenous views. However, the two-dimensional spectrum shown there is meant primarily to capture some aspects of anthropologists' stances, and to show the two principal ways (the modernist and the populist) in which the hierarchies of traditional Buddhism can be ignored. It would be surprising if the model were adequate to the task of representing the full complexity of views taken up by Buddhists themselves within a given social context.

The analysis of Buddhist ritual

The analysis of Buddhist ritual has been an important sphere of debate. Those at the modernist or rationalist end of the spectrum tend to see ritual as instrumental—and thus not really Buddhist—whereas those towards the other end of the spectrum are more likely to emphasize its expressive nature. Thus the rationalist approach taken by Terwiel is criticized by Wijeyewardene (1986: 72): there is 'a significant, non-instrumental component [the attainment of peace of mind] to even the most popular of Thai religious practice.' Spiro (1982: 411 fn.), on the other hand, criticizes Ames' (1966) contrast of expressive Buddhist ritual with the instrumental, exchange-oriented rituals directed at the gods. He considers that exchange is fundamental to Buddhist ritual, pointing out that 'The layman provides the monks with all physical requirements—and more!—necessary to pursue his salvation-oriented goal, while the monk in turn provides the layman with the spiritual requirements (merit) necessary for *his* salvation-oriented goal' (Spiro 1982: 412).

Just as modernistically inclined scholars tend to see Buddhist ritual as an un-Buddhist departure from the original or true religion, Buddhist modernists themselves reject the use of thread and water which has been empowered by chanting monks. They deny that any particular power, other than psychological benefits and religious merit, accrues from the presence or chanting of monks. But as Wijeyewardene remarks (1986: 47), 'watching [Thai Buddhist] rituals, there are many occasions when the only interpretation one can give is that the participants are grabbing for power ... quite literally.' He gives the example of young men ripping out the teeth of a dead monk as he lay on the funeral pyre. This obvious belief in such ritual efficacy led Terwiel to describe Thai village Buddhism as basically animist. However Gombrich (1971: 204) demonstrates that the use of thread and water is as old as the Pali commentaries, and he argues that belief in magic does not make one any less a Buddhist, since Buddhism defines itself in terms of right action and good intentions.

A monk who practises black magic is doctrinally on a par with a man who drinks; a bad Buddhist, if you like, but bad in the sense of wicked, not of inconsistent. A monk who says *pirit* [Pali verses] to cure sickness, whatever may be his theory to explain its efficacy, is a good Buddhist in every sense. (ibid.: 209)

Similar conclusions, without the supporting scholarship, had already been reached by Ames. Spiro (1982: 153) also noted that although monks were much more likely than lay people to denigrate rituals, three-quarters of his sample of monks still believed that the recitation of Pali texts was efficacious in itself.

Related to this question is the question of whether or not, or in what sense, merit can be transferred from one person to another (or to a god) in Theravada Buddhism. Theravada doctrine is clear that one cannot give merit to others, but Buddhists have naturally wanted to be able to do this. Gombrich (1971: 266ff) plots several historical stages in the justification of this need. When a Buddhist merit-making ritual is held either to benefit ancestors or to benefit gods who will then provide some specific worldly protection, what is strictly supposed to be happening is that the ancestors or gods (as the case may be) are being given the opportunity to rejoice in merit. Should they happen not to be present or not to be in a form in which they can be present, strictly speaking they cannot benefit, and only the performers of the ritual will acquire merit.

The cognitive/affective distinction

Gombrich's solution on the question of merit-transfer, as on the question of whether or not the Buddha is considered alive or dead, is to invoke a distinction between cognitive and affective beliefs. The former are the avowed, canonical beliefs; the latter are beliefs which can be deduced from behaviour, but which conflict with the former and therefore remain unexpressed. Cognitively Theravada Buddhists know, and usually say, that the Buddha is dead and that people cannot transfer merit to one another. None the less it is possible for the observer to infer that affectively they feel otherwise. The initial response of Spiro's (1982: 149) Burmese villagers was indeed that the Buddha is dead and gone. However when he asked them who then assists them during protection ceremonies, they changed their mind and decided he must be alive.

This distinction, between cognitive and affective beliefs, suggests one way around the instrumental/expressive dichotomy: cognitively Theravada Buddhists know that their attitude to Buddhist ritual should be expressive and that ideally they should not be motivated even by the desire to obtain merit; but in fact, on many occasions, their affective attitude is instrumental. However, the cognitive/affective distinction has had a mixed reception. Tambiah (1984a: 375 n. 11) dismisses it out of hand. Obeyesekere, whose early article (1966: 5, 8) made a similar distinction, presumably accepts it, but all his subsequent work has dealt with very different psychological attitudes. Spiro (1982: 153-4) makes a similar distinction between belief and motivation. Steven Collins (1982: 152) suggests that the distinction is presupposed by the Theravada tradition itself and is essential to its reproduction: on the doctrinal level Theravada Buddhism firmly preaches the doctrine of non-self, but in the Rebirth stories of the Buddha's previous lives, which are the main staple of monks' preaching to the laity, lay people are encouraged in an affective acceptance of continuing personal existence across many rebirths. *transferal of merit.*

The most interesting response to the cognitive/affective suggestion, is perhaps that of Southwold (1983: Chapters 12–13). He considers it seriously but rejects it on the grounds that it implies that Buddhists only really believe what we deduce them to believe affectively; but, he objects, any course of observed action is compatible with more than one set of inferred beliefs. His proposed alternative interpretation of Buddhist ritual hinges on an approach he opposes to instrumentalism: he calls it sapientalism. He defines sapientalism as 'a rational strategy for ameliorating experience by altering the mind and the self, rather than the environing world; it is parallel to, and alternative to, the instrumental strategy ...' (Southwold 1983: 188). We do not have to follow him in associating sapientalism with the right sphere of the brain and instrumentalism with the left, to see that this is a felicitous term for describing Buddhist attitudes. (Wijeyewardene has already been quoted saying something similar.)

The ethnography of Mahayana Buddhism

In recent years the study of Mahayana Buddhism has begun to catch up with that of Theravada Buddhism. For the reasons alluded to above the material available on Buddhism in East Asia is rarely put in a comparative Buddhological framework, but much of what has been written about Tibetan Buddhism does indeed engage with the themes I have been discussing. Tibetan Buddhists living within Nepal, particularly but by no means only Sherpas, have received considerable ethnographic attention. Holmberg (1989), writing on the Tamangs, might be said to follow Tambiah's lead, in that he outlines the contrasting spheres and interlocking competencies of the three crucial ritual specialists, the Buddhist lama, the lambu or earth priest, and the bombo or shaman. All three positions are largely hereditary, though the shamanic calling the least so.

The contrast between lama and shaman lies at the heart of other studies of Tibetan Buddhism as well. Mumford's (1989) classic study evocatively describes the competition between Tibetan lamas and Gurung shamans at the northern edge of Gurung territory. In this case the relationship is more conflictual and dynamic than the Tamang situation as described by Holmberg. The Tibetan lamas are celibate, highly literate new arrivals in the area, and they actively missionize and campaign against shamanic animal sacrifice (unlike the Tamang lamas). Mumford borrows heavily from Bakhtin to elaborate a 'dialogic' framework in which to explain the dynamic and evolving mutual self-definition of the lama and shaman: both offer help in the afterlife, and both accept the lama's superiority—for all that some shamans are not willing to face the dire consequences (as they see it) of giving up animal sacrifice.

A further step is taken by Samuel in his *Civilized Shamans* (1993). This is not an ethnography but rather a massive synthesis of his own and others' ethnography along with history and textual studies across the whole range of Tibetan societies. It offers, furthermore, a very specific framework for understanding Buddhism which—far from seeing it as fundamentally opposed to shamanism—puts shamanism at its very heart. Samuel is well aware of the paradox in this.

At one level the key distinction that Samuel uses to explain the variety of Tibetan Buddhism is between 'clerical Buddhism' and 'shamanic Buddhism'. Clerical Buddhism—exemplified by the Gelukpa—stresses celibacy, hierarchy, long study, and control; it flourished in, and quickly became, the centre of state power in Lhasa. Shamanic Buddhism, on the other hand, puts much greater stress on Tantric teachings (thus de-emphasizing celibacy), and stresses much faster ways to spiritual progress through ritual, meditation, or ascetic practices; it has an 'elective affinity' with peripheral places where state control was weak or non-existent. Tibetan specialists have, of course, critiqued Samuel's model. Many qualifications are no doubt required; crossovers between different forms of Tibetan Buddhism occurred frequently. But that there was some kind of basic distinction of this sort and that different forms of Buddhism were associated with different socio-political contexts seems to me highly likely. This could be put in terms of the affinity of celibacy, book-learning, and discipline with temporal and spiritual hierarchy, on the one hand, and of more charismatic, freelance forms of religion with resistance to political control, on the other.[11]

So far, for Samuel, clerical and shamanic Buddhism are in opposition to each other. However, at another level, Samuel advances a theory which is responsible for the paradox. At this level, the clerical form of Buddhism is simultaneously a *transformation* of the shamanic (a sublimation perhaps), just as Weber saw that brahmanism was a transformation of an original shamanic religion (see above, pp. 34–6). Samuel goes further than this, however, and sees the shamanic form of Buddhism as more authentic precisely because it stays closer to its origins. This final step in Samuel's argument, though pleasingly unconventional and anti-modernist, cannot really be upheld. Are we to say that it is just an accident that animal sacrifice is associated with shamanism? Are the calming meditative states sought by the Buddha really to be equated with ecstatic trance and possession by a spirit familiar?

Sherry Ortner has written on the theme of lama–shaman relations in response to some of this literature. Her first book (1978: 157–9) compared the Sherpas' Buddhism briefly to Thai Buddhism as described by Tambiah (1970). Mahayana Buddhism reinforced the Sherpas' individualist tendencies, whereas Theravada Buddhism, 'supposedly the more individualist form', had evolved a communal religion. Ortner subsequently examined the history of the founding of monasteries in recent generations among the Sherpas (Ortner 1989). All the while she was reflecting on the communal–individualist opposition, and wondering whether the institution of shamanism, now moribund among the Sherpas, was really to be seen as representing a collectivist ('relationalist') form of religion, and the lamas a more individualist form. As she describes, her essay on this (Ortner 1998) was twenty years in the writing. Her final conclusion is explicitly comparative: contrary to what both Mumford and she had previously assumed, Sherpa Buddhists sometimes present Buddhism as the more socially responsible and relationalist form of religion, and disparage shamanism precisely because of its egotistical focus on the needs and desires (often illicit) of the individual:

> Shamanism may be opposed to Buddhism as relationalism is to individualism in some contexts, or for some purposes, or within some ideological framework, but we must never imagine that shamanism is essentially and eternally relational, or that Buddhism is essentially and eternally individualistic ... the shamanism/Buddhism opposition [is] just too simple ... (Ortner 1998: 261)

Ortner might have cited here the work of Graham Clarke (1980, 1983), who showed how the people of Yolmo (Helambu), just a few valleys from 'her' Sherpas, use priestly Buddhist status precisely to assert a collective identity as 'Lama' and 'Sherpa' and 'not Tamang'. Ortner ends with a denunciation of modernization narratives which would predict the inevitable decline of shamanism (while simultaneously acknowledging that in a sense shamanism clearly did die among the Sherpas). The problem remains, however, that Sherpas themselves share a developmentalist view of the world which sees Buddhism as higher and more civilized than shamanism, a view that nowadays is no doubt fused with modernist understandings of Buddhism.

Conclusion

Despite the various sophisticated anthropological critiques which have been outlined above—ranging from the historically and textually informed Popperianism of Gombrich to the structuralism of Tambiah, the populism of Southwold, and the deconstructions of Ortner—the modernist view of Buddhism is unlikely to go away. It is fed by presuppositions of equality and context-free self-definition which are deeply embedded in modern culture, a modernism which is now a part of all the contexts in which Buddhism is practised.

Most of this chapter has focused on the question: What *has* the anthropology of Buddhism been about? It has, I have tried to show, focused on the question of Buddhist identity: What kind of religion is Buddhism? How does it coexist with other systems? Given its radical individualism, how can one help others? If the Buddha is dead, how are worship and ritual to be legitimated?

It would be remiss, however, not to raise explicitly the question: What *should* the anthropology of Buddhism be about? Lurking behind the anthropological critique of modernist approaches that dismiss the practice of ordinary Buddhists as inauthentic is the suspicion that the very question of Buddhist identity is artificial: it has been raised entirely by outsiders, even if it has now become an essential part of Buddhists' own internal cultural debate. I cannot myself accept that, in different ways, Buddhists never thought about what Buddhism is, and should be, before they had contact with Europeans. In fact, defining the boundary between what counts as Buddhism and what is not Buddhism, has necessarily been a concern for Buddhist monks throughout history. It is also true, however, that the anthropology of Buddhism will have attained maturity only when it can focus equally on other questions and only when it can analyse and compare Buddhism in different contexts without immediately becoming embroiled in issues of identity and authenticity.

Notes

1. See also Ames 1964a, 1964b, 1966; Bunnag 1973; Carrithers 1979, 1983, 1984; Evers 1972; Y. Ishii 1986; Leach 1972; Mendelson 1975; Southwold 1983; and Strenski 1983. See Zelliott 1992 and Fitzgerald 1997 on the adoption of Ambedkarite Theravada Buddhism by Indian Untouchables.

2. An exception to this generalization about non-Mahayana groups may be the tiny Risshu sect in Japan (with about fifty members in two monasteries), who claim that their entire monastic practice is based on one of the old monastic codes. Since it has 250 rules it is presumably that of the Dharmaguptakas (R.F. Gombrich, personal communication).

3. Jaini 1979 argues that these all affected Jainism equally, but Jainism survived where Buddhism did not because its monks had closer links with the laity. This is perhaps another way of saying that Jainism was not dependent on large monastic centres, as Buddhism seems to have been (at least by the end of the first millennium).

4. For the history of views of Tibet, see Lopez 1998: Chapter 1 deals specifically with the equation of Tibetan Buddhism and Roman Catholicism.

5. For attempts to get away from this in the study of Christianity, see the various essays in James and Johnson 1988.

6. Wijeyewardene (1986: 9) calls the problem of Buddhism's coexistence with other systems 'the Theravada problem'. He implies the existence of some such spectrum as that proposed here when he remarks that 'in recent times the most extreme views on the problem have been on the one hand, the thesis that Theravada Buddhists subscribe to two quite contradictory systems of belief, and on the other, that no problem exists which has not been created by anthropologists, and before them by missionaries.' Historians of Buddhism, as well as other Buddhologists, could also in many cases be placed on this spectrum.

7. But see the qualifications made by Gombrich 1972.
8. Southwold 1982, 1983, 1985. Wijeyewardene 1986 is probably to be placed somewhere towards populist end of the spectrum. Both he and Southwold have been influenced by Ling's (1973) depiction of Buddhism as a this-worldly religion.
9. Weber 1958: 206. Both Southwold (1983: 173) and Ling (1968: 95) criticize Weber for this remark.
10. Tambiah 1976, 1984a. The debate is too complex to summarize here. See, i.a., Seneviratne 1987; Carrithers 1987; and Tambiah 1987, all in the special issue of *Contributions to Indian Sociology* devoted to the work of Tambiah and Obeyesekere; see also Spiro's 1977 review of Tambiah 1976 and the subsequent exchange between them (Tambiah 1978; Spiro 1978). More recently, see Tambiah 1989; Lingat 1989; and Carrithers 1992: Chapter 7.
11. On this, see further Chapters 4 and 8 below.

3

Religion, Politics, and Ritual:
Remarks on Geertz and Bloch

Introduction[1]

Most people would allow—recalling Remembrance Day parades and royal coronations—that even in modern societies religious rituals may sometimes serve political purposes. Anthropologists today would want to go much further than this, however, and argue that politics and social life everywhere have—to put it at its mildest—a fundamental ritual and symbolic aspect. Thus there has in recent years been a revival of interest in the study of ritual both among anthropologists and among scholars sympathetic to anthropology.[2] In addition, there has been a more ethnographically based revival of interest, from a variety of theoretical perspectives, in studying the political aspects of ritual.[3] In this essay I wish to consider ritual—taken in the more or less conventional sense as formal, significant, symbolically intended, and complex action[4]—and to ask whether there can be a global theory of how it works.

I shall begin by contrasting two eminent theorists of ritual, Clifford Geertz (in particular the Geertz of *Negara*, 1982) and Maurice Bloch. I shall try to draw out how far they differ and what they share. I will then attempt to illustrate how one might progress further, using some material from Nepal, the area of my own ethnographic competence, such as it is.

It is worth emphasizing at the beginning that I choose to concentrate on these two authors because I admire them, both as ethnographers and as theorists. I believe that both of them repay detailed attention.[5] It is because their work is valuable and lasting that I think it worth attempting to criticize it. Both have attempted to deal with the political and social implications of ritual and to do so by means of detailed ethnographic and historical work. Against Geertz, I shall argue that his interpretivist stance undermines the attempt to draw general lessons from his single case. Against Bloch, I shall argue that his monistic theory cannot work as it stands and needs to be supplemented by a theory of kinds of ritual, in other words, a typology. With Bloch, I shall be arguing for a historically grounded and generalizing theory, however ambitious and premature that may seem.

Clifford Geertz

Of my two emblematic authors, Geertz is certainly the better known and has already been the subject of many interesting critiques.[6] One reason to focus on Geertz is the sheer weight of his influence. This influence can be measured both by the prominence to which his students have risen and by the pervasiveness of his ideas (which in turn can be measured, if you want quantitative precision rather than interpretative understanding, by that quintessentially modern invention, the citation index). I focus on *Negara* because it combines Geertz's mature understanding of culture with a full-length ethnographic monograph on the role of ritual in politics—indeed on ritual *as* politics.

Geertz, it is hardly necessary to say, stands for the idea of interpretation or hermeneutics. The task of the anthropologist is not to count lineages or measure fields in an attempt to come up with causal hypotheses. Nor is it to pretend to 'get inside people's heads' or to seek for historical processes or to impose supposedly scientific order. It is to *interpret* cultures, understood as systems of symbols. Anthropologists are specialists in other people's meanings. There are better and worse interpretations, but interpretations can never be final. There can be no natural-scientific, right-for-all-time answers. In Geertz's own words (1973: 29), 'Cultural analysis is intrinsically incomplete ... Anthropology, or at least interpretive anthropology, is a science whose progress is marked less by a perfection of consensus than by a refinement of debate. What gets better is the precision with which we vex each other.'

When Geertz started out, in Harvard, under the influence of Talcott Parsons, anthropology was viewed as one part of an inter-disciplinary team (Kuper 1999: 70–1). Biology, psychology, and sociology were equally necessary to understand human behaviour; anthropology was there to deal with 'culture'. By the time of *The Interpretation of Cultures* Geertz had left this notion behind. Anthropology as interpretive quest could on its own cope with any field of human action. Just because it was 'symbolic' in its *method* did not mean that it was not equally appropriate to apply it to *subject-matter* that is conventionally defined as the opposite of 'symbolic', e.g. violence, economics, urbanization, or agriculture (Geertz 1973: 30), an idea that has been extremely influential in north American cultural anthropology.

Geertz came to the study of the Balinese politics only after a long apprenticeship in Indonesian anthropology. In *Negara* he is concerned both to advance his theory of how the traditional Balinese state worked and simultaneously to argue for a more symbolic or expressive view of politics *everywhere*. It is to Geertz's great credit that before beginning to consider the details of royal ritual, he devotes two substantial chapters to considering kinship and political alliance, including material on local government, the 'feudal' links between villagers and lords, and the politics of irrigation and trade.

He gives a detailed description of the social organization of Balinese villages, focusing on the relationship between the ordinary villagers and their overlords, as the context in which the state operated. What he shows is that the regulation of everyday life was handled at the village level: 'Perhaps the bulk ... of Balinese government, in the strict sense of the authoritative regulation of social life, was carried out by the hamlet, leaving the state free to dramatize power rather than to administer it' (Geertz 1982: 49). Villagers, in fact, had just two duties to their lords: to pay taxes and contribute labour or resources for rituals or fighting. Ties of organization were cross-cutting and fragmented, so that any concentration of power was necessarily fragile and short-lived.

The Balinese courts may not have controlled much politically in the villages they dominated, but they were the unambiguous *cultural* centres of the country. The continual elaborate ceremony,

was an argument, made over and over again in the insistent vocabulary of ritual, that worldly status has a cosmic base, that hierarchy is the governing principle of the universe, and that the arrangements of human life are but approximations, more close or less, to those of the divine. (ibid.: 102)

Thus,

The stupendous cremations, tooth filings, temple dedications, pilgrimages, and blood sacrifices, mobilizing hundreds and even thousands of people and great quantities of wealth, were not means to political ends; they were the ends themselves, they were what the state was for .... [M]ass ritual was not a device to shore up the state, but rather the state, even in its final gasp, was a device for the enactment of mass ritual. Power served pomp, not pomp power. (ibid.: 13)

It was, in short, a 'theatre state'.

Despite the powerful and compelling rhetoric, there is unfortunately an ambiguity in Geertz's argument, which he never completely faces up to. Are the Balinese typical or are they an extreme case? Is politics always and everywhere equally about symbols? Or is it *more* symbolic in Bali than in, say, modern Switzerland?

None the less, there is an important lesson, which Geertz drives home. Modern political science, obsessed with economic models of voting patterns and other scientistic paraphernalia, has completely missed the extent to which ritual of various sorts is still a central concern, both of political leaders today, and of the people who vote them into power. That Ronald Reagan agreed with Geertz can perhaps be deduced from the comment he is supposed to have made shortly after he was elected President: his aides weren't leaving him enough time to *be* President. The idea that politics is essentially about ritual and symbolism—despite the difficulty we have in perceiving our own actions as symbolic—has been eloquently taken up and illustrated with numerous historical and anthropological examples by David Kertzer (1988). Kertzer goes beyond Geertz in two ways: first, in the genuinely global reach of his comparisons and, second, because he emphasizes the fact that ritual is equally important both to those who dominate and to those who resist domination.[7]

Maurice Bloch

Maurice Bloch is less well known than Clifford Geertz and certainly does not occupy the powerful position within British or European anthropology that Geertz did in the USA. None the less, he is a highly interesting writer and in some ways is typical of British social anthropology, for all that he has an unusual interest in Marxism. His fieldwork has been almost entirely on the island of Madagascar, beginning with his Ph.D. on kinship and ancestor rituals (Bloch 1971). He subsequently wrote an introductory book, *Marxism and Anthropology* (1983), and there is a collection of his influential essays, *Ritual, History and Power* (1989). What I wish to concentrate on here is the monograph *From Blessing to Violence: History and Ideology in the Circumcision Ritual of the Merina of Madagascar* (1986) and his short work *Prey into Hunter: The Politics of Religious Experience* (1992).

Bloch has long been known as a Marxist, or at least as an anthropologist sympathetic to Marxism. One might think that this would lead him to be diametrically opposed to Geertz. Where Geertz concentrates on the interpretation of symbolic meanings, Bloch would surely cut through these, seeing them as mere mystification, and focus instead on structures of power. But in fact Bloch is far from being a crude Marxist in this sense. He is as interested as other anthropologists, perhaps more so, in the analysis of ritual and symbolism. The difference is that he has always sought to show how these work to maintain structures of power and inequality. His Marxist inclinations are also apparent in the position he took up in his celebrated essay, 'The Past and the Present in the Present':[8] he argued that there is, on the one hand, ritual communication which obscures and legitimates hierarchy and, on the other hand, everyday practical communication which gets closer to how things 're-ally are'.

In *From Blessing to Violence* Bloch examines, rather like Geertz in *Negara*, the rituals of the Malagasy royal state and the way in which they legitimated social and political hierarchy. Bloch provides rather less information on the social organization that underlay the state than Geertz, but he gives more detail on the ritual itself and in particular on the way it was transformed between approximately 1780 and 1970. The ritual of circumcision started as a private, small-scale, and irregular affair which involved only the immediate relatives of the boys going through it. Then, with the expansion of the Merina kingdom in the middle of the nineteenth century, the circumcision of royal princes became a seven-yearly ritual involving the whole country, and became more and more elaborate. The army was given a prominent role as a celebration of Merina conquests. A clear symbolic link was made between the violence of the ritual and the domination of neighbouring peoples. At the same time the circumcision of commoner boys was linked to the royal circumcision ritual; being circumcised became simultaneously an act of allegiance to the throne. With the adoption of Christianity in 1869 the ritual was driven underground and reverted to being a small-scale familial affair. After independence from France in 1960 the ritual started to be performed more openly and began to be seen as an anti-elite and anti-Christian rite.

The important point here is that through all these changes, modifications, and reversals, there was a central core of ritual acts and meanings which did not change. Contrary to what a simplistic functionalist approach might suggest, different social needs did not generate different rituals; the same ritual satisfied very different needs at different periods, and even within the same period. Bloch's explanation of this is intended simultaneously to be an answer to the question of how ritual can serve to legitimate domination, not just in the eyes of the rulers, but in the eyes of the ruled as well.

The first thing Bloch has to do is reject certain crude reductionisms in the interpretation of ritual. Ritual should not be seen simply as *doing* something social (the functionalist position). Nor should it be seen either as *expressing* something (the symbolicist position) or as *saying* something (the intellectualist position). Rituals, he remarks, lie 'somewhere between an action and a statement' (1986: 10); thus they cannot be reduced either to the one or to the other. Rituals certainly do 'do', 'express', and 'say' things, but they do so ambiguously, and this ambiguity is of the essence. The ambiguity permits different and opposed levels of understanding among those who share allegiance to the same ritual.

It is precisely because rituals do not simply say things that they acquire their power to persuade and legitimate. There is a gap between everyday communication and ritual communication but it is not, and cannot be, an insuperable gap (which Bloch takes to be Geertz's position in *Negara*). There has to be *some* connection between what is implied in ritual, on the one hand, and everyday life, on the other, for the ritual to work as a legitimating device. Bloch concludes (1986: 191) that '[t]he ritual is a vague, weakly propositional, construction of timelessness built on an antithesis that will do for any domination ... It offers [the Merina] order in exchange for submission.' The very complexity of the symbolism, and the fact that the ritual offers them incorporation within a descent group, explains why women are as enthusiastic participants as anyone else, even though the ritual they participate in legitimates their secondary status.[9]

Bloch's second book, *Prey into Hunter*, based on the Morgan Lectures given in 1987, is explicitly an attempt to take the argument further by means of considering global examples. Bloch certainly deserves praise for attempting to do this, in a way that Geertz, consistently, one might say, with his interpretive and anti-generalizing view of anthropology, has never done.[10] In *Prey into Hunter* Bloch argues that all religious rituals have a common core; they all share a similar symbolic structure of 'rebounding violence' (a term introduced here for the first time).

As in van Gennep's and Turner's theories, rituals for Bloch consist of three stages. In the initial stage they are about the aggressive domination of the forces of life (or 'vitality' as Bloch calls it). During this stage violence is directed at individuals or at animals identified with them. In the next stage of the ritual the principal actors are separated from the forces of life and acquire a transcendent quality. In the final stage, with this transcendence incorporated, the actors return to life empowered and revivified.

Bloch recognizes that this common structure can be used in a variety of ways and in his conclusion he attempts a typology of such uses:

> The symbolism of rebounding violence offers at least three alternative avenues of legitimate practice and in addition any mixture of the three: (1) the assertion of reproduction; (2) the legitimation of expansionism, which itself takes one of two forms: (a) it may be internally directed, in which case it legitimates social hierarchy, or (b) it may be externally directed and become an encouragement to aggression against neighbours; (3) the abandonment of earthly existence ... Which particular alternative dominates and informs action is largely, though not exclusively, determined by people's evaluation of their politico-economic circumstances ... (Bloch 1992: 98)

Clearly these are intended to be 'ideal types' in the Weberian sense, though Bloch avoids the latter term. He illustrates type (1) with the religious symbolism of the Orokaiva of Papua New Guinea. In fact Bloch begins his analysis with the Orokaiva because the initiation of Orokaiva children—first chased out of the village like pigs and later returning in triumph as hunters and distributors of pig meat—illustrates the 'prey into hunter' theme particularly well and gives him the title of his book. Bloch sees cattle sacrifice among the Dinka of the Sudan, even though performed for what I call instrumental reasons (as explained below), in much the same way. Likewise, despite some symbolic difficulties, spirit mediumship among the Buid of the Philippines is also interpreted as being about 'the assertion of reproduction'. Type (2a)—internally directed expansionism—is used to explain the subordination of women and is illustrated with Maria Phylactou's (1989) material on marriage by capture in her unpublished Ph.D. on Ladakh. Type (2b)—the legitimation of expansionism directed externally—is advanced with the example of Hindu India and Japan. The traditional Hindu idea of kingship, Bloch claims, 'implies exactly that image of the consuming conqueror' (p. 49) which is also found in the other rituals he analyses. In the Japanese case he tries to connect the symbolic violence of Shinto ritual (itself not always obvious) with the militarism of the 1930s. Bloch's own material on the Merina of Madagascar, as outlined in *From Blessing to Violence*, also clearly falls into this type, as well as into type (2a). Bloch's type (3) stands for millenarianism and is illustrated both by material from Madagascar and the history of early Christianity. In a final chapter he looks at the Ma'Betisek aborigines of Malaysia who, when their normal healing rituals fail, invoke the commonality of human beings and plant and animal life. This is to 'conjure up a truly radical rejection of rebounding violence in ritual' (ibid.: 104). Bloch recognizes, then, that in extreme situations the symbolism of violence can be abandoned.

Geertz versus Bloch

Before moving to a critique of Bloch, it is worth considering what both Geertz and Bloch share, and where they differ. Both have been drawn to look at the historical background of the place where they did fieldwork (or in Geertz's case, one of the places). Both have been drawn to look at the symbolism and ritual of the pre-modern monarchical state, and at what happened in the encounter with colonialism. Surprisingly, Geertz, the interpretivist, includes more detail on trade, irrigation, landholding, and village-level organization than Bloch, the Marxist, does.[11] Perhaps equally surprisingly, Bloch provides far more ethnographic detail and much closer symbolic analysis of his chosen ritual. Geertz discusses the main themes and examines the main indigenous concepts, but he declines to get involved in the microscopic details of ritual. (He might have done so, despite the lack of elaborate court ritual today, in the way Bloch does, namely, by focusing on local-level equivalents that continue today.)

Whereas Geertz insists that the ritual has a clear message, viz. that the king is close to the gods, Bloch argues that the message can never be entirely clear: its fuzziness is of the essence. For Bloch, it is precisely because the message is not clear that the ritual has the power to legitimate social and political hierarchy. The medium is the message and the medium is somewhat opaque. Ritual is an act that asserts and has meaning but which cannot be argued with. Both Geertz and Bloch are working in an earlier tradition of anthropology which emphasizes the conservative power of ritual; neither pays much attention to the question, so important in contemporary North American cultural anthropology, of how far rituals may be used to contest established structures of power.

Both Geertz and Bloch have been criticized for not taking the effects of colonialism sufficiently into account. Thus Berg (1986) has suggested that in the eighteenth and nineteenth century in Madagascar the relationship of ritual and practical knowledge was very close: at this time 'the ritual expressed contractually the social hierarchy based on land and controlled by the descent group'. It was only later, with the decline in the importance of landholding as a source of power, that the gap Bloch claims to be universal, between the transcendent world of ritual and the real world of social relations, opened up. In a somewhat similar way several critiques of Geertz suggest that what he has described is the Balinese state at the period when the Dutch had removed much of its ability to coerce and wage war and when, therefore, there was a greater emphasis on timeless ritual.[12]

Bloch, unlike Geertz, looks at 'his' ritual *in* history, i.e. how it has changed over time, although while doing so he uses a disconcerting analogy from physics (1986: 183) which is probably best ignored. However the stress on history and process really only applies to the Bloch of *From Blessing to Violence* and not to the Bloch of *Prey into Hunter*. Finally, Geertz does not maintain that there is a core of symbolic meaning that can be found globally; he merely implies that the *role* of ritual in politics has been ignored on a global scale. Bloch, on the other hand, attempts in an extremely ambitious way to test the approach he worked out for Madagascar in a variety of worldwide contexts.

Three kinds of religion and ritual: A critique of Bloch

What are we to make of Bloch's theory? It is evident that it works better in some cases than others. It is no coincidence that Bloch begins with the Orokaiva and their frightening initiation rituals in which boys are hunted like pigs in order to become men. But as the book proceeds the strain in the argument increases. When he is discussing Shintoism he has to work very hard, and indulge in considerable ingenuity, to make the theory fit a religion in which there is no place for animal sacrifice. Thus, for example, he argues that Buddhism in Japan provides the first stage of rebounding violence, aimed at the self, in that it prepares the Japanese for death. Shintoism, on the other hand, mobilizes young people and symbols of violence for this-worldly purposes. He recognizes that the theme of violence is much less obvious than in the Orokaiva case. He coins the term 'piscivorous' (on the model of 'carnivorous'), since the Japanese are not much given to meat-eating, and he argues:

The piscivorous aspect of Shintoism links up with the strength-giving aspect of carnivorous activities and is a general, implict, but powerful theme of Japanese life ... [I]n modern Japan the eating of raw fish and meat also takes on the form of a kind of secular aggressive ritual in certain types of restaurants or bars mainly patronised by men. There the theme of violent consumption is expanded to the extent that the fish needs to be shown to be alive immediately before it is eaten. Sometimes slices of it are eaten while it is still wriggling on the dish and sometimes the whole fish is eaten alive. It is difficult not to see this type of activity as a celebration of the conquest of other forms of life, which brings us back to the Orokaiva concluding feasts. (ibid.: 60)

It would be easy to criticize such argument for ignoring the interpretations of the participants themselves, and for using the theory to explain the material, rather than the material to test the theory. But such problems are encountered by any attempt at a global theory, and I want to present a rather different critique.

In my opinion, no such theory of ritual can work unless it recognizes that the whole category of 'religion' is a question-begging western, or Judaeo-Christian-derived, term. Because of the exclusivist assumptions of Christianity there have been centuries of misunderstandings of Asian religions. The category of religion needs to be deconstructed; it should be replaced by a hierarchy of (at least) three types of religion. First comes soteriology or salvation religion. Second is social or communal religion, the kind about which Durkheim was concerned to theorize and for which his theory works well. Third, there is instrumental religion, the attempt to make specific things happen within the world. It will be noted that this approach does not define religion in terms of belief, but in terms of what is done; and it distinguishes between the different purposes for which different kinds of religious actions are done.[13]

Rituals may usually be ascribed predominantly to one or other type. Those concerned primarily with salvation from all the ills of this world are soteriological, those which express the solidarity of the group or incorporate individuals within it are social, and those which attempt to cure illness, ensure a successful business enterprise, or the passing of an examination, may be considered instrumental. Naturally enough there may well be many rituals which combine aspects of more than one type of ritual, or which are transformed over time from being predominantly of one type to predominantly one of the others. I shall illustrate such a movement when I describe a text-reading ritual below.

Not every religion possesses each type of ritual. There are 'tribal' religions which lack a soteriology. If I understand the material on the Kham Magar, a small group of remote mountain villagers in Nepal famous for their shamanism, there is in their ritual and social life a relative de-emphasis on both soteriology and social religion. The instrumental rituals of their shamans dominate the religious field (Oppitz 1986; de Sales 1991).

In many situations in Asia, which westerners have found so hard to understand, there are different religious systems serving different religious purposes. According to Tambiah's classic analysis of north-east Thailand (1970: 338), there were four related religious systems. Buddhism provided for the salvation and collective village merit-making rituals. The 'Sukhwan' ritual specialists known as *paahm* (Thai for 'brahman') took care of rites of passage. Local guardian spirits, worshipped through mediums, protected the village fields and their fertility. Finally, malevolent spirits causing illness were dealt with by diviners and exorcists. Each of the four systems had separate specialists, separate rituals, and its own characteristic ritual language. Each was defined by its position in the overall system. Soteriology was unambiguously the realm of Buddhism. Different aspects of social religion were dealt with by each of the first three systems. Instrumental religion is the sphere of the fourth. In Gombrich's account of Sri Lanka (1971) there is a simpler opposition between Buddhism and the gods of Hinduism, but a similar analysis could be attempted there too (cf. Ames 1966).

The main point is that Theravada Buddhist monks, until the modern period, never aspired to provide for *all* the laity's needs. Their respected status derived precisely from the fact that they were supposed to have nothing to do with mere worldly matters. They were concerned with salvation and, provided that Buddhism's overall ideological hegemony was not threatened, they did not mind what cults their lay people resorted to for purely worldly ends. Gombrich sums this up by saying that 'Buddhism in real life is *accretive*' (1971: 49; original emphasis). In other words, it must always coexist with some other religious system or systems which provide for the worldly needs of its adherents. This coexistence is not necessarily syncretic or improper.[14]

In practice, of course, many monks have always been involved in astrology, had mistresses, or ran businesses. But the significant point is that this was in spite of, not a consequence of, their religious role. The highest prestige went to those monks who carried out their role to the full. There is some evidence that forest-dwelling monks did not always have higher status than those involved in book-learning and servicing the laity (Gombrich 1988). But it seems likely that in the past as today (Carrithers 1983) the forest monks were the most attractive for the laity as recipients of their donations, if only because they were the most inaccessible.

What of the category 'world religions'? The very notion has been rightly attacked as nonsense, a collection of disparate phenomena classed together in order to satisfy the needs of religious studies classes where like must be compared with like (Fitzgerald 1990). Thus, the religions of Asia, such as Hinduism, Buddhism, and Shintoism are forced into the Procrustean bed of Judaeo-Christian categories. They must each have their ethics, doctrines, life-cycle rituals, festivals, prophets, and scriptures. In the terminology I have introduced, Buddhism started as a soteriology and in most of the countries it has spread to it has remained overwhelmingly so, although in Mahayana countries it has adapted to provide many instrumental rituals alongside its soteriological ones. In Nepal, among the Newars, as described below, it has adapted further than elsewhere: it provides for all the needs of social religion as well. Hinduism, by contrast, is essentially a social religion which has numerous alternative soteriologies within it, so that many have doubted whether it should be considered a single religion at all. Shintoism, on the other hand, is primarily a social and instrumental religion, with virtually no soteriology. Soteriology has, even post-Meiji, been left to Buddhism.

Despite these differences, there is one characteristic that all the world religious soteriologies have in common: a radical rejection or reordering of the world as such, based either on a jealous and all-demanding God, or on the necessity of taking a path away from all worldly things. It is not, as is sometimes claimed, that non-literate religions have no concept of the transcendent: this is an idea that Bloch criticizes convincingly. But in 'tribal' religions it is a transcendent that can be accessed only occasionally and contextually.

Soteriologies, at least at their outset, are based on the rejection of conventional religious thinking. In some cases old symbolism is retained but given new meaning, e.g. Christ's self-sacrifice as the Lamb of God. In Bloch's theory this can be seen as a transformation of rebounding violence. But in other cases, not even the symbolism is retained. It is hard to see pacifist rituals in terms of 'rebounding violence': hence the strained way in which Bloch interprets Buddhist pilgrimage in Japan as the first part of 'rebounding violence', namely as 'attacks on vitality' (Bloch 1992: 55). The rejection of animal sacrifice is central to Buddhism. The examples from Nepal discussed below go some way to illustrate this.

Furthermore, not only is Bloch's theory as applied to soteriological rituals problematic, it is even more difficult to see it applying to instrumental rituals. Sometimes the means by which instrumental rituals are understood to be effective, to bring about the desired change in the world, are in line with Bloch's ideas about sacrifice. At other times changes in the world are believed to be effected by strictly soteriological means (I shall give an example presently). At still other times a more old-fashioned Frazerian explanation, in terms of ritual as bastard science, is more appropriate.

What this shows is that Bloch's theory works best for social religion. His theory is really about how complex symbolism helps to construct social order. This suggests that, for all his residual Marxism, Bloch is equally, if not all the more, a Durkheimian.

Three Newar rituals

My three examples come from the Kathmandu Valley, Nepal, where I have myself done fieldwork, and can speak with some confidence about their interpretation. The three rituals are the *guru mandala puja*, the annual festival of Dasain, and the ritual of text-reading in the Kwa Bahah monastic temple complex known to foreigners as 'The Golden Temple'.

The Kathmandu Valley is a fertile bowl at 1000 metres in the foothills of the Himalayas. Before 1769 it housed three small competing kingdoms (Kathmandu, Lalitpur, and Bhaktapur) each based on a small city of about 60,000 people with its associated rural hinterland. The royal rituals of these cities, and the manner in which they fought each other endlessly, were not wholly dissimilar from Geertz's nineteenth-century Bali, or indeed Bloch's early-nineteenth-century Madagascar. In 1769 Prithvi Narayan Shah of Gorkha, the ancestor of the present king of Nepal, conquered the Kathmandu Valley, which paved the way for the creation of the present-day state of Nepal.

In this way the people of the Kathmandu Valley, the Newars, became an encapsulated minority (between 5 and 6 per cent) of the new country. Many Newars emigrated from the Valley to become the traders and shopkeepers of the new polity. Those who remained behind to a greater or lesser extent preserved their pre-unification language, social organization, religious traditions, and rituals. Some Newars are Buddhist, others Hindu. The prime means of differentiation is by priest. Those Newars whose domestic priest is a Vajracharya count as Buddhist; those who call a Brahman are Hindu. The Vajracharyas have been dubbed 'Buddhist brahmans': they are indeed, like brahmans, a married, hereditary priesthood. Together with a slightly lower subsection of the same caste, called Sakya, they control and preserve the temple complexes, called *vihara* (monastery) in Newari, which are the main sites for Buddhist worship. This coexistence of Buddhism and Hinduism is highly unusual in South Asia, but was once far more common. The great French Sanskritist, Sylvain Lévi, came to Nepal in 1898, and wrote a history of the country in three volumes (1905), because he felt that Nepal was 'India in the making', i.e. the coexistence of Buddhism and Hinduism in the Kathmandu Valley was typical of the situation in India a thousand years ago, before the Muslim invasions. The kind of Buddhism practised by the Newars is highly ritualized. There are no large monastic institutions as in Tibet or South-east Asia, so the level of scholarship is obviously much lower. All the same, just like Tibetan Buddhism, and in some respects more so, it is a direct lineal descendant of the Mahayana and

Vajrayana Buddhism practised in north India, and in what is now Bangladesh, seven to eight hundred years ago.

The guru mandala puja

The first ritual to be considered is the *guru mandala puja*. It is the most basic item of Newar Buddhist liturgy, i.e. it is the first complete ritual learned by a novice priest and in the past many lay people knew how to perform it too. All complex rituals, requiring the presence of a Vajracharya priest, begin and end with the *guru mandala* (see Plate 8). It acts as a kind of frame for the whole ritual. It may also be performed on its own, as part of one's personal daily ritual. On its own it takes about five minutes if known by heart, but it took me 36 pages when I wanted to publish a blow-by-blow account of every utterance and ritual act that make it up (Gellner 1991a). Briefly described, it consists of the following four stages:
1. building up the mandala (i.e. sacred enclosure) of Mount Meru (the cosmic mountain at the centre of the world) by making small offerings to each element of the mandala;
2. offering the mandala to Vajrasattva, the guru, who is a symbol of the Tantric Buddhist absolute;
3. various Mahayana Buddhist undertakings (e.g. to become a Buddha to save all beings and a confession of sins);
4. an offering to lower spirits to prevent obstacles.

When (as is usually the case) the guru mandala is used as the frame of a larger ritual, this final part is held over till the end.

This framing function means that the guru mandala is fundamental to all Newar Buddhist rituals. The only significant occasion when it is absent is in the daily worship of the main Buddha statue in monastic temple complexes, and even there many parts of it are often incorporated (Gellner 1991b; Sharkey 1995). Mothers perform the guru mandala on behalf of their five- or six-month-old babies at the First Ricefeeding. Married couples perform it together on to a single shared mandala during the wedding ceremony. In terms of my three types of religion, the guru mandala, taken on its own, is clearly soteriological in intent; but *the way it is used* varies from the soteriological (e.g. as part of a pious Buddhist practitioner's daily devotions) to the social (e.g. when part of a larger life-cycle ritual).

There is a considerable range of understandings of this ritual. The least sophisticated parishioners or patrons of Vajracharya priests do not even know its name. They simply perform the rite under the instructions of their priest. As far as they are concerned, both understanding it and ensuring its success are the priest's work and duty; they neither want nor need to know its details. For the priest's part, he sees no need to explain what he is doing to his parishioners, especially if they are lower caste, unless they particularly want to know.

Others know the name of the ritual, and know that the mandala is offered to Vajrasattva, but cannot perform it themselves without the guidance of a priest. Still others, including priests themselves and many pious lay people, perform it daily as part of their regular devotions and do so by heart and fluently.

The ritual has remained essentially unchanged since the twelfth century, but it may be several hundred years older than that. The ritual appears, virtually as it is today, and in exactly the context in which it would be used today, in the *Kriya Samuccaya* by Jagaddarpana Acarya, which dates from the twelfth century. Today minor parts of the ritual are performed in slightly variant orders by different priests. This is because there are different ritual traditions within each city, and in Lalitpur (and perhaps elsewhere too) within the city as well. Despite such variations, it is, in its essentials, the same ritual everywhere.

The explanation for this standardization and fixity must lie in the specialized training of Vajracharya priests, and in the fact that it is a ritual they perform so often that it becomes second nature to them. No Vajracharya who carries on the priesthood can fail to know it by heart. At the same time it is a purely Buddhist liturgy, with the recitations chanted incomprehensibly in Sanskrit. It is therefore of no concern to outsiders and is opaque to many, perhaps most, of the Buddhist laity. Consequently there has been no incentive to elaborate it, or control it, on the part of the (Hindu) powers that be. It has neither grown nor shrunk in the years in which it is possible to trace its history.

Dasain

Dasain is a very different kind of ritual. It is the biggest public holiday in Nepal. It is the one festival for which Nepalese everywhere try to be at home. Everyone is supposed to receive a blessing in the form of a vermilion spot on the forehead (*tika*) on the tenth day of the month, the climax of the festival, from their household head, from the elders of their lineage, and ideally from the King himself. Even Muslims participate in this, stopping short only at receiving a red spot of vermilion, substituting colourless cooking oil (Gaborieau 1996). The main divinity worshipped is the goddess Durga, and the principal means by which she is worshipped is the sacrifice of buffaloes and goats. Pumpkins, cucumbers, and other gourds are also often substituted. The close connection between the worship of Durga and the successful maintenance of power may be illustrated by the fact that every police station in Nepal has a small Durga shrine outside it.[15]

In the Malla period the main ritual act seems to have been the parade of swords, empowered by the goddess. This gave it its Newar name, *payah* or *khadgajatra*, literally 'the sword festival'. In this form it seems to go back at least to the thirteenth century (Petech 1984: 95). The parade of swords is still practised today: several high-caste Shrestha lineages still go in procession with ancient swords draped in the barley shoots which are planted on the first day of the month in their lineage's secret goddess shrine. These swords are frequently used to 'sacrifice' a pumpkin: all the initiated men of the lineage line up and slash it as they pass. Possession by the goddess is indicated when the man or youth holding the sword shakes and trembles.

With the advent of the Shah dynasty in the eighteenth century, the procession with swords from the royal palace, in which the Malla kings had themselves participated (G.V. Vajracharya 1976: 187), receded in importance. A further change introduced was that barley seeds were planted in Nuwakot, outside the Kathmandu Valley, from where its conquest was planned, and then brought on the seventh day (Phulpati) to the royal palace, a clear recapitulation of the conquest of the Valley from the north-west. But in most other respects the traditions of the Malla rulers of the three cities of the Kathmandu Valley were maintained by the new dynasty. Still today the rituals of Dasain unfold in parallel in the three old royal palaces of Kathmandu, Lalitpur, and Bhaktapur, supported by the Guthi Samsthan, the government office that oversees religious activities funded by (mainly royal) land grants of the past.

The Rana Prime Ministers who ruled Nepal from 1854 to 1951 never actually replaced the kings of Nepal, who remained as symbolic figureheads, rather like the Emperor in pre-Meiji Japan. The Ranas did systematize the reappointment of government servants, called *pajani*, by holding it annually during the Dasain festivities (Pfaff-Czarnecka 1993: 277). Government servants had to attend in full ceremonial dress, never knowing whether they would be reappointed for the next year. If they were not, they had to walk away without the turban which the ruler gave them as a sign of their position, a very public humiliation. It seems also to have been the Ranas who added the military parades and the worshipping of regimental colours (ibid.: 274–5). Perhaps Jang Bahadur was influenced by what he had seen in England.[16]

Today civil servants have more secure tenure and no longer have to parade at Dasain, though before 1990 there were many occasions, including Dasain, when gazetted officers were expected to demonstrate their support of the regime and the throne. Military parades continue alongside the more traditional animal sacrifices and masked dances. The king still gives *tika*, in order of precedence to his priests, family, leading figures of the government, and to the general public (Lecomte-Tilouine and Shrestha 1996). At the same time as these large-scale public events, there is also a small reduplication at the level of the family. Household heads give *tika* within the house just as the king and headman do within their respective political domains.

Dasain is therefore the prime calendrical festival of Nepal. It symbolizes the harvest, fertility, royal power, and the power of the patrilineage, including the dominance of males over females (Bennett 1983). As such, it does what Bloch claims of the circumcision ritual for the Merina in the nineteenth century: it legitimates and symbolizes worldly order. Like the circumcision ritual it is highly susceptible to the accretion of new elements added by new dynasties or new political regimes, as well as to being publicly contested. Thus, since 1990 in particular, it has begun to be contested by the activists of many 'ex-tribal' ethnic groups who now wish to define themselves as non-Hindu.[17] There is also an older tradition of Tibetan Buddhist practitioners carrying out rituals to compensate for the sin of so many sacrificed animals. Even before 1990, as Toffin (1996b: 89) shows, there seem to have been disputes between different priests over the right to control specific rituals.

Does the ritual of Dasain achieve its effects through the 'construction of timelessness', as Bloch claims for the Merina circumcision ritual? It is arguable that in the Hindu world it is above all the high Hindu god, Shiva or Pashupati, or perhaps Vishnu, who stands for this, whereas the symbolic force of the goddess—her ability to stand for fertility, power, and control—comes from her location *within* the world. In other words, the more timeless a divinity is, the less useful for this-worldly purposes. It is the relatively *less* transcendent nature of the goddess that makes her appropriate for the acquisition of worldly power.

Despite this split within the Hindu divine universe, between male otherworldliness symbolized by the high gods Shiva and Vishnu, and the more worldly power of the Goddess which is the symbolic centre of the rituals of Dasain, in other respects it must be allowed that the messages of Dasain fit rather well with Bloch's analysis in *Prey into Hunter*. Fertility, regeneration, royal power and conquest, national unity, and the domination of lineage elders (and of men over women) are all tied together and guaranteed by animal sacrifice. It seems like a perfect illustration of 'rebounding violence'.

Text-reading in Kwa Bahah

My third example is a ritual called *pā thyākegu* (or *pāth yākegu*), 'having the text read', which is frequently held in the monastic temple complex of Kwa Bahah, Lalitpur (see Chapter 7). The text that is read is called 'The Perfection of Wisdom in Eight Thousand Lines' and may be as much as 1900 years old (though this copy is more like 700 years old). There is more to the ritual, however, than just having the text read. The local people believe that reading *this* copy of the text, in the manner specified by tradition, guarantees the fulfilment of one's wishes. Ten Vajracharya priests each take a share of the text, perform the guru mandala ritual, and then read through, either silently or nearly so, the Sanskrit of the text, simultaneously with all the others. It is a common practice to vow to have the text read if one is in danger, either from disease, from travel, at work, or in any other way. The equivalent practice in Kathmandu is to worship the goddess of smallpox, Hariti, in her temple on the north-west side of the Svayambhu *stūpa*. The local people in Lalitpur believe that the goddess, the Perfection of Wisdom, has really become present in this text and that she answers the petitions of her worshippers. Many of them also have the text read when not in dire need, e.g. for weddings or initiations.

The historical evidence, so far as I have been able to reconstruct it, suggests that the ritual as it is today dates from the eighteenth century, or possibly only from the mid-nineteenth century. At the moment it is read about two days out of three. Present-day officiants remember having to introduce a rule that it could only be read twice a day.

This ritual is clearly *instrumental* in nature, for all that it is cast in an unimpeachably Mahayana Buddhist *soteriological* idiom.[18] Of 184 Sakya and Vajracharya households living in the vicinity of Kwa Bahah, 114 (62 per cent) had had the text read at least once for one reason or another in the last ten years. The most common reason was illness, cited explicitly by just over 30 per cent. It is probable that many of the 28 per cent who simply said that they wished to have the text read also had it done for reasons of illness. Five per cent mentioned fears to do with jobs, 3.5 per cent long-distance travel, another 3.5 per cent misfortune or inauspiciousness at home, 2.6 per cent mentioned rites to do with death. Nearly 17 per cent mentioned an auspicious occasion at home, such as a wedding.

Recapitulation

Of these three Newar rituals, the first is clearly soteriological, although it is used as a basic building block of Newar Buddhist liturgy and is therefore found in social and instrumental ritual contexts as well. The second ritual, Dasain, as a calendrical festival, is primarily social. The third ritual is predominantly instrumental, though the form in which it is cast is soteriological.

Conclusion

It should be clear from these three examples, described very schematically, that there are many different types of ritual. Bloch's central argument is that (1) in a 'weakly propositional' manner (1986: 191) rituals construct order—a timeless, unchanging world—and legitimate dominance; and (2) they do this through the symbolism, and to differing degrees the enactment, of 'rebounding violence' (1992). In *From Prey into Hunter* Bloch tries to show that this applies to a wide range of rituals. Inevitably he is forced to recognize the great heterogeneity of rituals and himself proposes a typology of the uses of ritual, which I have quoted above (p. 67). In my opinion this does not go nearly far enough and a more radical typology of ritual itself is required, with each type of ritual likely to have different characteristic symbolic structures.

Of the three types of ritual that I have proposed, Bloch's theory clearly works best for social rituals. He has in fact been criticized for leaving out of his account of the Merina circumcision ritual any consideration of the *sampy* cult, which was primarily instrumental in orientation (Berg 1986); it is noticeable that Christianity, which might be taken to be soteriological, plays only a small part in his analysis. I have illustrated social rituals with Dasain, and I have suggested that Bloch's account should really be seen as Durkheimian in intent, with its emphasis on ritual and symbolism producing order.

My second criticism of Bloch is that there is too much stress on the ritual itself and not enough on the institutions which enable it to be preserved over long periods. Surprisingly for a supposed Marxist, social history is introduced only as background. It is here that we can learn from Geertz, supposedly the more hermeneuticist author. For he, quite rightly, thinks that without knowing about the details of control over irrigation, the place and importance of the royal centre cannot be understood either. What is needed is the emphasis on history, ritual, and the impact of colonialism that both authors seek, combined with Bloch's interest in the sociological implications and micro-analysis of ritual detail, and Geertz's wide-angled awareness of context. Geertz, on the other hand, has been criticized for a bias in his application of such contextual considerations: for restricting his symbolic analysis to the elite

level and implying that the ordinary people are concerned with technical rationality alone.[19] I have already noted that Geertz in particular is
also open to the charge of not going far enough in including the colonial
context in his analysis.

Thus I side with Bloch against Geertz in seeking a universal theory,
but I reject Bloch's monistic assumption that all ritual must fit a single
framework: at least three fundamentally different kinds of ritual and
religious orientation must be recognized. All three types of ritual share
the features of redundancy, stereotypy, and formalization that have been
identified by many authors (e.g. Tambiah 1985a); but different purposes
lead them to be inflected symbolically in very different ways. Bloch's
assumption that 'rebounding violence' is a structural feature of all rituals
is inappropriate for soteriological and liturgical rituals like the guru
mandala puja and it is equally inappropriate for an instrumental ritual
like the text reading I have described. Although both 'posit timelessness',
neither is violent in any way, unless Bloch is going to construe the purity
rules that have to be observed to carry them out as some kind of violence.
By contrast, his framework seems to work very well for the major
calendrical festival of Dasain. Even here, I wonder whether it is wise to
exclude the possibility of annual festivals based on some other kind of
symbolic nexus.

What both the authors I have discussed agree upon—as well as many
others I have not mentioned—is that if we want to understand why
people perform rituals and what it means when they do so, we have to
take into account their political aspect. And furthermore both Geertz
and Bloch exemplify a wholly necessary and admirable rapprochement
between anthropology and history. To Bloch's aspiration for a systematic
theory I have added the rider that we need a typology of religion and
ritual to make that plausible. The idea that there is a single 'thing' called
religion or a single kind of ritual is an outmoded and too frequently
unexamined part the Judaeo-Christian inheritance of the human
sciences—an idea we should abandon forthwith.

Notes

1. I would like to thank A. Kuper, J. Pfaff-Czarnecka, D. Quigley, and C.
   Toren, as well as participants in discussion at Zurich University (April
   1997), for helpful comments on earlier versions of this paper.
2. See, for example, Bell 1992; Humphrey and Laidlaw 1994; Boyer 1994.
3. In addition to the works discussed in this essay, I am thinking of Kertzer
   1988; Harrison 1995; Boholm (ed.), 1996; Peabody 1997; for a useful survey,
   see Kelly and Kaplan 1990.

4. See Tambiah 1985a. This means *not* extending 'ritual' to cover *any* formalized action, such as shaking hands, but rather restricting it to sets of actions that are recognized by the actors themselves as set apart from mundane activities.

5. As a small example of the fruitfulness of Bloch's theory, one could cite the way he uses it to throw new light on Paul's rejection of the circumcision ritual for early Christians. This was dictated, he shows, less by Paul's universalism, as is conventionally believed, than by his millenarianism (Bloch 1992: 91–4).

6. See Asad 1983; Shankman 1984; Munson 1986; Kuper 1999: Chapter 5, to cite only a few.

7. Kertzer also links his argument to developments in cognitive psychology (1988: 179). In a later passage he situates himself with respect to both Geertz and Bloch: against Geertz, he points out that 'the best that elites can hope to do is shore up a predominant symbolic construction of how society should work. They can never eliminate all loose ends ... nor all vestiges of alternative symbol systems' (1988: 176–7). Kertzer agrees with Bloch that there are universal processes of human cognition grounded in similar material conditions, but he rejects the claim that there are two distinct kinds of cognition and communication, the ritual and the everyday (Bloch 1977; Kertzer 1988: 203 n. 9).

8. Originally the Malinowski Memorial Lecture, it appeared in *Man* (n.s.) 1977, 12: 278–92. Republished in Bloch 1989.

9. For a similar discussion, see Kertzer 1988: 176.

10. Geertz has not argued against comparison as such. He could hardly do so, having published a distinguished comparative study of Islam in Morocco and Indonesia (Geertz 1968). However, the thrust of his interpretivism is certainly against attempts to construct global and/or systematic comparisons.

11. Berg (1986) notes that 'what is lacking [in Bloch's book] is historical information about changes in landownership, changes in the rights and obligations of initiates with regard to land and other forms of wealth, variation in the performance of circumcision rituals among outgroups such as slaves or hinterland demes far from power, and change in relation of urban to rural elites at the close of the 19th century.'

12. See Lansing 1991; Schulte Nordholdt 1993; Kuper 1999. For a similar analysis of the famous Swazi Ncwala ritual, showing how an appreciation of the colonial context is essential, see Lincoln 1987.

13. I used this typology in my monograph on Newar Buddhism (Gellner 1992a); see further Chapter 4 below.

14. For more on the question of Buddhism and syncretism, and for a comparison of the relationship between Buddhism and other religious systems in Nepal and Japan, see Chapters 14 and 15.

15. For an unrivalled collection of material on Dasain, see Krauskopff and Lecomte-Tilouine (eds) 1996. See also Levy 1990 (S.V. Mohani); Pfaff-Czarnecka 1993, 1996. For an equivalent in India, see Schnepel 1996.

16. On Jang Bahadur's trip to England and France, see Whelpton 1983. Of course, the worship of weapons was an integral part of Dasain even before this.
17. Pfaff-Czarnecka (1996) shows that in some local cases this was happening already before 1990.
18. I suspect that the increasing popularity of the ritual in recent years may have something to do with the decline of other traditional instrumental rituals performed by Vajracharyas (e.g. the worship of the Pancharaksha goddesses, and the *navagraha puja*).
19. Tambiah 1985b: 336; Valeri 1991: 135–6.

PART II

The Legitimation of Religious Specialists

4

Priesthood and Possession: Newar Religion in the Light of Some Weberian Concepts

The very existence, and influence, of the traditional higher, sanskritic, civilisation demonstrates without question the unity of India. One might even think that it does not only demonstrate, but actually constitutes it. But this last statement is too narrow, at any rate for the sociologist, because, as we shall see, the lower, or popular level of civilisation has not only to be recognized, but to be taken as being in some way homogeneous with the higher one.

Louis Dumont, 'For a Sociology of India', p. 9

Introduction[1]

It is, I think, unquestionable that the greatest post-war contribution to the study of South Asian society has been made by Louis Dumont. Not only has *Homo Hierarchicus* become a yardstick for all subsequent work in South Asian sociology and anthropology; it has also, as he hoped though not as much as he hoped, been influential far beyond the ranks of South Asianists, whose works non-specialists normally find esoteric.[2] The purpose of the present essay is to suggest, with the help of some data from Nepal, that South Asianists might benefit from paying more attention to the concepts and insights of another sociologist who has some important features in common with Dumont: Max Weber.

Weber's work on South Asia has recently begun to receive greater attention from South Asianists than in the past. But it seems to me that they still tend to associate the kind of approach Weber stood for with Dumont rather than with Weber himself. South Asianists have yet to discard their prejudices against Weber, prejudices which as often as not are based on a misunderstanding of Weber's project and on an acquaintance exclusively with *The Religion of India* (henceforth *ROI*).[3] Inden (1986: 405 n.1) claims that *ROI* 'has been crucial in setting the agenda for the sociological study of South Asia (and especially of "modernization" or "westernization") in the past twenty-five years.' It is my impression that it has been only partially read and rarely understood; and that, far from being crucial, development experts and theorists would have taken the same attitudes, *ROI* or no *ROI*. It was not *ROI* that set the agenda but the agenda which determined how *ROI* was read.[4]

The similarity between some of Weber's formulations and those of Dumont may perhaps be taken to indicate that Weber influenced Dumont more than the latter has cared to acknowledge. On two specific points—the distinction between power and status, and the analysis of the division of labour—Dumont does indeed acknowledge his debt.[5] The distinction between power and status is crucial to Dumont's definition of the caste system for comparative purposes (Dumont 1980: 259–60). Whatever may be the exact truth on the question of influence, others have also noticed the similarity. Several authors have noted that Dumont probably owes to Weber his seminal opposition of the social man-in-the-world and the individualistic renouncer, a point supported by Dumont's own references.[6] Burghart calls Dumont 'more a Weberian sociologist than a Lévi-Straussian structuralist, the Weberian nature of Dumont's project becoming even more apparent with the publication of *Homo Aequalis* as the companion piece of *Homo Hierarchicus*.'[7]

The reception of Weber's work on South Asia has not been helped by the slipshod translation of *ROI*, which Kantowsky (1986: 215) calls 'a transgression'. Not only is the translation well below the generally undistinguished standard of Weber translations, it was done with no consideration whatever of the subject matter. South Asian words appear in confusingly variant and frequently incorrect spellings (Golzio 1984: 369–70). As Kantowsky has been at pains to impress on Anglophone audiences, *ROI* was never intended as a separate study, but was very much part of Weber's overall project, namely, a comparison of world religions to see if they had the potential to evolve an ethic similar to the

Protestant from their own resources. Weber has valuable things to say about South Asia in places other than *ROI*, and conversely, *ROI* presupposes the general ideas expounded elsewhere (see Chapter 1 above).

The present essay looks at what Weber said about Nepal and about the nature of South Asian religion in general; it then asks what Weber's general concepts can contribute to an understanding of religion among the Newars. It is hoped that conclusions valid for them will be applicable to other parts of South Asia also, and therefore give some pointers to how Weber's work can be used by South Asianists. Of course, it is frequently necessary to point out where Weber is wrong; but I hope to be able to show that he has much to offer all the same.

Weber on Nepal

In *ROI* Weber devoted just under a page to Nepal as an introduction to his discussion of Buddhism in Tibet (*ROI*: 282–3). 'Nepal' here means the Kathmandu Valley, as it did traditionally and still does for many Nepalis.[8] His only cited source of information on Nepal was the 1901 Census of Bengal which itself summarized information culled from Hodgson, Hara Prasad Shastri, Oldfield, and Wright. There are two mistakes in Weber's text which seem to be due to sloppy reading on his part. Weber writes that the *banhar* (= Sakyas and Vajracharyas, the sacerdotal caste of Newar Buddhism) cannot take water from the Udas (= Uday/Uray, i.e. Tuladhar and others), where the Census has food, not water; he also writes that 'Buddha was united into a trinity with Shiva and Vishnu' (*ROI*: 283), which does not appear in the Census at all.

These factual inaccuracies, and others due to his source, are surely unimportant. *ROI* is full of them. Weber should be read—and is perhaps at last being read—for his insights and conceptual formulations. From this perspective there are three points about Nepal that need to be considered. First, Weber considers Nepal as separate from India, as being, like Tibet, the object of a mission to the north. Second, he writes that Buddhism 'underwent the typical prebendalizing process in the course of which it was penetrated by Tantric magic and its blood sacrifices.'[9] Third, he continues, Buddhism 'had to compete with the Hindu propaganda of the Shivaists and was in the Mahayanistic North Indian fashion amalgamated with the Hindu caste system' (*ROI*: 282).

On the first point Weber was mistaken, as many others have been. Culturally and socially, the Kathmandu Valley has been an outpost of

South Asian urban civilization for more than 1600 years. Its political independence is irrelevant. Much confusion is created by the fact that 'India' refers to three different things. In ascending size they are: a modern political unit, a colonial entity, and the subcontinent as a whole. To respect the feelings of the Nepalese (who reject the last usage) and in order to emphasize the cultural affinity of Nepal with its southern neighbour, I refer to the subcontinent as South Asia.

On the second and third points Weber is largely right, although his phrasing could be improved. The Buddhism of Nepal did consist of stable and hereditary institutions supported by religiously endowed land. Its sacerdotal order, the Vajracharyas and Sakyas, are a hereditary caste of priests and part-time monks. Newar Buddhism did become predominantly Tantric. Its popular festivals do occasionally include blood sacrifices (but only to low, protective deities) and Buddhist priests tolerate such sacrifices when desired by their patrons. It did and does coexist with Hinduism, predominantly Shaivism, and accommodated itself to the caste system, and this was indeed typical of north India in the heyday of Mahayana Buddhism.

This last point—the fact that the Kathmandu Valley represents something of India in the late first millennium—is a thesis particularly associated with Sylvain Lévi, the great French Sanskritist and historian of Buddhism. In his history of Nepal (1905) he wrote that Nepal allowed one to observe 'in a limited space as in a laboratory' an essential stage in South Asia's history, that stage where brahmanism took over from Buddhism. He went on to give a brilliant outline sketch of the dynamics of this process and of subsequent history.[10]

Unfortunately Weber seems not to have known or used Lévi's work, except for a single article on the history of the use of Sanskrit and Prakrit (ROI: 379; cf. Kulke 1986: 99). Lévi's work on Nepal would have been grist to his mill. Weber was principally interested in analysing various forms of South Asian religion with a view to understanding how far they might have been able to promote a capitalist spirit. As a non-specialist he was not primarily concerned to explain the rise and decline of particular types of South Asian religion or to give an explanatory narrative of crucial events in South Asian history. None the less he was aware that the preference of kings for brahmanism was crucial for what he called 'the orthodox restoration' and the consequent decline of the 'heterodoxies' (Buddhism and Jainism) (ROI: 292–4). The work of Lévi would have supplied him with a more reliable picture of Nepal and also with a plausible sociological account of the rise of brahmanism at the expense of Buddhism.[11]

Weber on the general characteristics of South Asian religion: Buddhist history as an example

For Weber, South Asian religions, and in particular Hinduism, represented in many ways the polar opposite of the Judaeo-Christian tendencies which came to a head in Protestantism. This opposition can be summed up as shown in Chart 4.1. The concepts and ideal types listed in the Chart are expounded by Weber in *Economy and Society* (henceforth *ES*).[12] They have been usefully and systematically brought into relation with each other in several works by Wolfgang Schluchter.[13]

Chart 4.1: Opposed characteristics of Judaeo-Christian religion and South Asian religion, according to Max Weber

Hinduism	Christianity, especially Protestantism
immanent god	transcendent god
prophet as vessel, filled with the divine	prophet as instrument of god
exemplary prophecy	ethical prophecy
self-deification	self-perfection
soteriological elitism: lay devotion to the attained few	church in which all believers are equally capable of salvation
consistent theodicy: rebirth in accordance with one's actions	consistent theodicy: predestination
leads to other-worldly mysticism which if rational in means is irrational in ends (i.e. flight from the world)	culminates in active, rational *this-worldly* asceticism (i.e. mastery of the world)

Whether Weber was right to oppose these ideal types in this way is quite properly the subject of sociological debate. It is certainly possible to refine them. Schluchter, for example, distinguishes cases where the followers of a religion emphasize the message of a religion from those where they focus on the personage of the messiah: this would capture the difference between the Buddha, at least as he intended himself to be conceived, and other Indian gurus (Schluchter 1989: 516 n. 68). One might also argue that more precisely the distinction is between religions in which prophecy is both ethical and exemplary (the Judaeo-Christian) and those in which it is merely exemplary (the South Asian). Similarly one could argue that the distinction is between religions that aim only at self-perfection (the Judaeo-Christian) and those that aim both at self-perfection and at self-deification. Many other such refinements or criticisms are certainly possible.

For present purposes, it is only necessary to agree that some such characterization is valid. That South Asian religions share certain presuppositions which are not shared by Judaeo-Christian religions would appear to be undeniable.[14] One should remember, though, that these are ideal types. Consequently they are not refuted by single cases; indeed they are unlikely to be found in pure form in any actual case. Thus they are not refuted by what people do. It is not enough to respond that 'South Asians aren't like that' or even 'South Asians don't think like that'. Neither in *ROI* nor in his general characterization of South Asian religion was Weber attempting to describe directly the whole life or the whole history of South Asia. He was attempting to analyse South Asian religion in order to find out what its effects on the actions of its adherents would be if and when they attempted to act systematically in accordance with their religious doctrines or prescribed practices. He was not propagating an Orientalist stereotype ('South Asians are otherworldly'); he was arguing that those South Asians who chose to act consistently in accordance with a South Asian religious vocation *ipso facto* could not be active this-worldly ascetics of the Protestant type. Nothing follows from his analysis about the usual behaviour of most South Asians who have a more normal and relaxed attitude to their religion. Indeed he stated explicitly that 'the masses' remained 'undisturbed'.

One further point needs to be made about Chart 4.1. Weber did not believe that this was a global contrast. Judaeo-Christian and South Asian religions by no means exhaust between them all possibilities. They are all salvation religions and as such are different both from magic and from religions such as Confucianism which do not exist in tension with the world. (In this respect it could well be argued that Weber's thought is richer and more complex than Dumont's, because Dumont *is* open to the charge that a single comparison—between South Asia and Europe—is given too much weight in his theories.) If one keeps these points in mind it is possible to avoid irrelevant criticisms of Weber. That said, many of his characterizations of South Asian religion require modification. One possible example of many is his picture of the development of Buddhism in South Asia.

Buddhism, as Weber recognized, was the purest soteriology the world has known (*ROI*: 206, *ES*: 627–8). Its most conservative form, Theravada Buddhism, has less involvement in this-worldly religion—life-cycle rituals, calendrical festivals, magical rites—than any other major religion in the pre-modern world. Weber considered that Buddhism arose simply from 'the metaphysical needs of the human mind as it is driven to reflect on ethical and religious questions, driven not by material need but by an inner compulsion to understand the world as a meaningful cosmos and take up a position to it' (*ES:* 499). Unlike other soteriologies it arose neither from the social condition of the underprivileged nor from the 'rationalism of the middle classes'. For Weber it stands 'at the opposite extreme from systems of religious ethics preoccupied with the control of economic affairs in the world' (*ES:* 627).

However, Weber failed to appreciate the extent to which Buddhism accommodated itself, even at an early period, to lay interests in prayer, worship of the Buddha, use of Buddhist sacra for protection, and so on.[15] This led him to exaggerate the contrast between ancient Buddhism and Mahayana Buddhism. Thus he contrasted 'authentic ancient Buddhism' with 'the completely altered manifestations Buddhism assumed in Tibetan, Chinese, and Japanese popular religions' (*ES:* 627):

As soon as Buddhism became a missionizing popular religion, it duly transformed itself into a savior religion based on karma compensation, with hopes for the world beyond guaranteed by devotional techniques, cultic and sacramental grace, and deeds of mercy. Naturally, Buddhism also tended to welcome purely magical notions. (*ES:* 628–9)

The process Weber describes certainly took place. Mahayana Buddhism did develop a battery of methods for transferring merit, as well as goods and even salvation, to the dead departed, methods which, in that form, were unknown to ancient Buddhism; but it would be wrong to assume that no such techniques existed in ancient or in Theravada Buddhism, and it is a common mistake to assume that the Buddhism found in Tibet, China, or Japan is radically changed from its original forms in South Asia. Weber was not aware of the way in which later Buddhism, alongside much that was new, preserved attitudes and practices which had always been part of Buddhism. This is true even of Tantric (Vajrayana) Buddhism, though in it the older teachings are relegated to the most exoteric, junior level of a complex hierarchy (cf. Chapter 5, below).

Weber revealed the poverty and bias of his sources on Mahayana Buddhism when he wrote: 'In comparison with the superior intellectual contemplativeness of ancient Buddhism, which had achieved the highest peaks of sublimity, the Mahayana religion was essentially a popularization that increasingly tended to approach pure wizardry or sacramental ritualism' (*ES:* 466; cf. *ROI:* 255, 289). What Tucci says in a recent authoritative study applies equally to all forms of Mahayana Buddhism: 'It would be a grave error, and reveal an insufficient understanding of the special nature of Tibetan Buddhism, if one were to disregard the soteriological goals permeating and dominating it' (Tucci 1980: 93).

Underlying the development of new forms of Buddhism (the Mahayana and Vajrayana) Weber saw an institutional development, already mentioned above in his description of Nepal, from individual monks wandering alone through monastic landlordism to what he called 'prebendalization', in which 'a monk married and made his place hereditary' (*ROI*: 356 n. 38). Weber rightly sees the Mahayana as adapting in three principal ways: to ownership of land, to lay religious needs, and to the requirements of 'brahmanically schooled intellectuals' (*ROI*: 247–50). In doing so it also preserved its original ideas, although Weber seems to recognize this only in the case of Japan.[16]

Weber's overdrawn contrast between ancient Buddhism as the 'religious "technology" of wandering and intellectually schooled mendicant monks' and the 'immense magical garden' created by Mahayana Buddhism (*ROI*: 206, 255) led him to a false problem:

Buddhism became one of the greatest missionary religions on earth. That must seem baffling. Viewed rationally, there is no motive to be discovered which should have destined Buddhism for this. What could cause a monk who was seeking only his own salvation and therefore was utterly self-dependent to trouble himself with saving the souls of others and engaging in missionary work? (*ROI*: 228)

Weber's answer was that 'the peculiar euphoria of god-possessed tranquillity' drew them 'on the road towards saving souls' (*ROI*: 229).

In fact the proselytizing ideal was present in Buddhism from the beginning and has remained a part of all forms of Buddhism till today. As Gombrich has argued (1971: 320–7), love or compassion has in practice always been as important as self-restraint in Theravada Buddhism. But it is not stressed in its canonical formulations, from which Weber wrongly deduced what the ancient Buddhist monks' state of mind must be.[17] Hence also the Mahayana charge of selfishness against the pre-Mahayana schools (of which the Theravada was one, and the only one to survive into the modern world). With its concept of the *bodhisattva* the Mahayana not only provided saviour figures for the masses (as Weber stressed), it also introduced a heavy emphasis on altruism on the part of all serious Buddhists, since they should strive to be bodhisattvas and thus to help and save others. This then kept Buddhist other-directed ideals alive in spite of the ever-present 'prebendalizing' tendency.

Although his portrayal of the historical development of Buddhism was overdrawn, Weber was right, I believe, in thinking that Buddhism shared the general characteristics of South Asian religion outlined in Chart 4.1. Buddhism is indeed universalist but in a logically distinct sense from Christianity. In common with other universalist doctrines in South Asia, Buddhists consider that any person can achieve enlightenment but it has never been thought possible—even in the Mahayana— that all could do so at one time. In practice, therefore, even when Buddhism seemed to make enlightenment more easily available, it remained soteriologically elitist. It remained an exemplary and never became an ethical prophecy imposing its full demands on all its followers.

Newar religion in the light of some Weberian concepts

The Newars are the traditional inhabitants of the Kathmandu Valley. As indicated above, some of them are Hindus, others Buddhists, and yet others—perhaps the majority—have some kind of allegiance to both religions. For the present discussion it is enough to note that the two Great Traditions have separate but parallel organization: sometimes they share a single practice but give alternative explanations for it, in other cases they provide two parallel, alternative, and competing practices. Nowadays the Newars are barely a majority of the population in the Valley and are very much a part of the wider Nepali society, just as, in a more distant but still very real sense, they have been a part of the South Asian world for over 1500 years. None the less, their social and religious life retains a sufficient degree of autonomy for it to be valid to consider it alone.

Types of religion

Newars think of religion primarily in terms of ritual practices. The word 'dharma' can mean religion in the sense that Buddhism, Hinduism, and Christianity are religions. It also means 'ritual' and 'religious merit', i.e. what one gains through ritual and other prescribed action. All Newars make a fundamental distinction between those rituals which are obligatory and those that are optional. Broadly speaking, obligatory rituals are those they are obliged to undertake or participate in by virtue of belonging to a given group (lineage, sub-caste, or caste), whereas optional rituals are those they undertake as an individual. (It is in the religious sphere that, in Dumont's sense, the man- or woman-in-the-world has the greatest freedom to act as an individual.) There is a slight complication in that certain individually chosen religious acts, such as taking Tantric Initiation, or some other vow of devotion, may subsequently entail obligatory rituals. These distinctions can be represented as in Chart 4.2.

These same distinctions are rearranged to bring out what they imply for a theory of religion in Chart 4.3. Since the 'Regular obligatory rites ...' and the 'Supererogatory rites' of Chart 4.2 are the principal components of soteriology (i.e. salvation religion) for the Newars, it will be seen that the Newar distinctions reproduce, albeit in a different order, the sociological ones between soteriology, social religion, and instrumental religion. These sociological distinctions, which begin from the Weberian definition of soteriology, are given in Chart 4.3.

As already noted, the distinction between soteriology and other types of religion is fundamental also to the self-definition of Buddhism (Gombrich 1988: Chapter 3). Although the boundary between soteriology and worldly religion is less sharp in Mahayana than Theravada Buddhism, the distinction retains its conceptual importance. In Hinduism the same distinctions are made. It should be noted that Charts 4.2 and 4.3 list ideal types; these are conceptual distinctions, models if you like, which are used by Newars themselves. They focus on rites, not beliefs, and are distinguished according to the motive for which they are performed: for merit or salvation (soteriology), to express group solidarity (social religion), or for a specific benefit (instrumental religion). In practice of course motives are often mixed. A rite designed to be soteriological may often in fact be used for social or instrumental purposes.

Chart 4.2: Types of religion from the Newar point of view

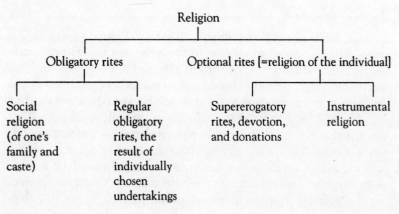

Religion

Obligatory rites

Optional rites [=religion of the individual]

Social religion (of one's family and caste)

Regular obligatory rites, the result of individually chosen undertakings

Supererogatory rites, devotion, and donations

Instrumental religion

Chart 4.3: Types of religion sociologically viewed

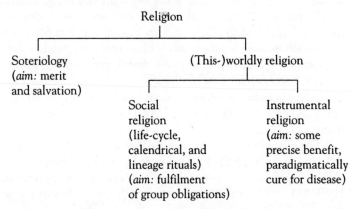

Weber, unlike Durkheim, was not interested in analysing the category of social religion. But the idea that soteriology had to be distinguished from other types of religion was central to his thought (*ES: 526f.*). It is precisely because the Judaeo-Christian tradition runs together all three types as 'religion' that he coined the term soteriology. Dumont, for his part, certainly recognized the types of religion distinguished here. The contrast between a 'discipline' of salvation and the religion of the group is indeed basic to the analysis of his famous essay on world renunciation (Dumont 1980: Appendix B). A formal analysis, such as that given here, would surely have strengthened his case.

Types of priest

Newars encounter various different types of priest, taking 'priest' to refer to any necessary religious intermediary or specialist, 'religious' being understood in any of the senses distinguished above. They may be listed as follows:

(i) temple priests/god-guardians (*pūjārī* or *dyaḥpāhlā*),
(ii) domestic priests (*purohita*),
(iii) personal gurus (e.g. *dīkṣā-guru*),
(iv) healers of various types (*vaidya* and *dyaḥ waipī*).

Temple priests are those who are the regular guardians of the cult of a given deity. In Newar society these roles are widely distributed and there is a rough homology between the caste hierarchy and the pantheon.[18] Sakyas and Vajracharyas are the temple priests of specifically Buddhist divinities. Brahmans are the temple priests of pure Hindu deities. Hindu Tantric priests called Karmacharyas are often the temple priests of Hindu goddesses who accept blood sacrifice. Middle-ranking peasant farmers are usually the temple priests of the elephant-headed god Ganesh. The temple priests of aniconic shrines located within the city, which are identified as one of the Eight Mother Goddesses or as Bhairava, as well as Bhimsen shrines (another form of Bhairava), are often low-caste death-specialists (Kapali/Jogi). The same shrines located outside the city, which encircle it and protect it and are often associated with a cremation ground, have Untouchable Sweepers as their temple priests. In all these cases, rights and duties rotate among specified members of the caste entitled to them.

The second type of priesthood relates above all to the sphere of social religion, as outlined above. Domestic priests have hereditary relationships to given families, who must all have one domestic priest (see Plates 1, 10, 14). (This means that even though many Newars participate in both Hindu and Buddhist activities they can have only one domestic priest and he must be either Buddhist, i.e. a Vajracharya, or Hindu, i.e. a Brahman.) The families in question must call 'their' priest to perform life-cycle rituals and any other obligatory rite (they may, if they wish, invite someone else to perform optional rituals). Domestic priests inherit, sell, and lease their rights in patrons like any other property right. Vajracharyas are the domestic priests for the majority of Newars in Kathmandu and Lalitpur; in Bhaktapur, the third large city of the Valley, Hinduism is far more dominant and Brahmans and Karmacharyas share between them the duties of domestic priest for most castes.

Other specialists—barbers, death-specialists, Karmacharyas in the case of high-caste Hindus and some middle-ranking ones—may be considered as types of domestic priest who carry on a lower, and therefore separate, aspect of priesthood. This was stressed by Hocart, but he went too far in saying that in the caste system 'every occupation is a priesthood'.[19] In fact the Newars distinguish specialists with hereditary links to patrons (jajmān) from those who lack such links. The former are paid in kind (stipulated traditional prestations) and with dakṣiṇā, a prestation of money according to the patron's desire, over which the specialist is not supposed to haggle. The latter fix their own charges and have no hereditary patrons; they operate in a competitive market.

The third type of priest is associated particularly with the sphere of soteriology. He may be chosen by the individual concerned. Included in this category are the priests from whom individuals receive Tantric Initiation, which is open only to the higher castes. As a type however it is much wider, and includes any teacher dispensing salvation of an established sort. Those outside the regular priestly framework would count, in Weberian terminology, as prophets, that is, holy men, or women, who rely on their personal charisma, not their office (*ES*: 440). Personal gurus, as priests, in some cases may end up having hereditary relations with their disciples, i.e. personal guruhood comes to be organized like domestic priesthood. This has happened among the Newar (Rajopadhyaya) Brahmans (Toffin 1989).

The fourth type of priest should not, in the Weberian perspective, be called priests at all. They answer only to Newars' instrumental needs. Domestic priests and occasionally also temple priests also have instrumental rituals at their disposal which they will perform if requested, but this is not their prime function. An example of this is the rite of reading the Buddhist text, the 'Perfection of Wisdom', at Kwa Bahah temple-monastery in Lalitpur (see Chapter 7).

In Newari two sub-types are distinguished within the fourth category of 'priest'. The first sub-type is referred to as *vaidya*, a word which covers any type of healer who is not directly possessed, and includes apothecaries. It thus includes Ayurvedic doctors but also Tantric healers who combine ritual and medical methods, and may diagnose astrological conjuncture or demonic possession as the cause of an illness (see Plate 13). The second sub-type is formed by the numerous mediums who are possessed by deities (*dyaḥ waipī*). They diagnose illnesses and other social problems; they often suggest that worship of a particular deity will cure or solve them. These mediums are more often women than men and more often low-caste than high (see Chapter 8 and Plate 14 below).

The first two types of priest correspond to the two halves of Weber's definition of priest: 'The crucial feature of priesthood [is] the specialization of a particular group of persons in the continuous operation of a cultic enterprise, permanently associated with particular norms, places and times, and related to specific social groups.' (*ES*: 426).

Clearly temple priests are those who specialize in maintaining cults. Domestic priests carry on sets of rituals associated with given norms and related to specified groups of people. The two sets do not correspond. In the extremely diversified urban culture of the Newars both types are widely distributed in different ways. It remains true that Brahmans and Vajracharyas, principal Hindu and Buddhist domestic priests, respectively, fill more, and more types of temple-priest roles than anyone else.

Weber wished to exclude soteriology as a defining characteristic of priesthood because of those priesthoods (e.g. in China and Japan) which lack a doctrine of salvation. But we may acknowledge that where one exists, spiritual teachers may evolve as a separate type of priest, as in the third category above. In the Newar case, where soteriologies are ritual disciplines, spiritual teachers are as much ritualists as any other priest. Weber would have called them mystagogues (*ES*: 446–7, *ROI*: 328, quoted above, p. 39).

The final type of priest is not a priest at all on the Weberian definition but rather a magician. Although some of their methods may be magical it is better to use the terms 'healer'—covering Ayurvedic doctor, Tantric healer, and folk healer—and 'medium'. In discussing possession, Dumont and Pocock (1959c: 56–7) rightly distinguish oracles, i.e. regular institutionalized possession occuring at festivals and complementing the role of priests, from demonic possession. They also distinguish the oracle from the healer, whom they guess to be an urban phenomenon. It is certainly true that the oracle is rare but healers and mediums extremely common in Newar cities (see Chapter 8).

Types of legitimation

Weber's three types of legitimation—tradition, charisma, and rationality—are often invoked in discussions of politics but rarely, if ever, in discussing religion in South Asia. This is surprising because religious roles equally demand justification. No distribution of religious roles is natural and all need to appear so.

Social religion is the sphere of traditionalist justifications. I have given the 'aim' of social religion above as maintaining group solidarity, but this is an anthropological observation, though not one wholly beyond the perception of Newars themselves. In fact Newars themselves usually justify this category of ritual in terms of tradition. It is done because it always has been done. It is the inherited duty of the group, their *kuldharma*.

Tradition as a legitimating idea has sometimes been ridiculed by commentators on Weber as an empty term, useful only as filling a gap. However no one who has studied a genuinely traditional society could fail to be impressed with the way in which tradition is a legitimating, if not *the* legitimating, idea. In a society such as that of the Newars an enormous array of social and religious practices are kept going, in the first analysis, by the power of ordinary people's belief in tradition. Ortner has put this very well for the Sherpas, in rejecting the idea that theirs is a religion of fear:

> The Sherpas perform most of their rituals because, although this may sound pedestrian, it is traditional to perform those rituals, and because disorder might ensue if they don't. The world is not a continuously threatening place; the point is to insure that it doesn't become so. (Ortner 1978: xii)

The most immediate reason for doing most of what is done in the name of religion (excluding the instrumental sphere) is this positive intention we name tradition. Other justifications—local myths, soteriological explanations—may also be forthcoming for the curious, but the first and most basic reason for doing things is that this is the way in which this particular group has always done them.

Charismatic legitimation is found among the healers, discussed above, who specialize in satisfying the demands of instrumental religion. This is especially true of the mediums who claim that their tutelary deity (and often other deities as well) is speaking through their mouth. There is much anecdotal evidence that this type of religion has become more pervasive in the last fifty years. One can speculate that social change has created a greater demand for such mediums, because it has produced more of the psychosomatic disorders which they seem to be successful in treating, while at the same time markedly reducing the respect which is accorded to other types of priest. In any case there is now at least one (and often more than one) such freelance healer or medium in each locality of every Newar city.

Tantric healers (usually Vajracharyas) and folk healers (often low-caste) also depend on personal charisma for success, although they have a greater store of traditional ritual means than mediums with which to legitimate their practices. By contrast Ayurvedic doctors claim a purely rational justification in terms of a medical theory and their knowledge of it.

In general, rational procedures or justifications are hardly to be found in Newar religion. As Weber remarked, 'In prerationalistic periods, tradition and charisma between them have almost exhausted the whole of the orientation of action' (*ES*: 245). But in so far as rational legitimation is present, it can be discerned in the 'disciplines of salvation' taught by spiritual preceptors. As mentioned above, the method is heavily ritualized and traditional justifications are also important. Furthermore, controlled possession—i.e. a routinized charismatic justification—is a crucial part of the rituals by which Tantric Initiation is imparted. None the less, there remains the idea that this is a sphere in which rational procedures (techniques for producing a given result) are important. What Weber wrote of South Asian religion as such applies equally to Newar soteriologies:

Either they [Indian religious means] were of an orgiastic character and led directly into anti-rational paths which were inimical to a rational way of life, or they were admittedly rational in method but irrational in aim.[20]

Even here there is no question of rationality in Weber's fullest sense being intended. Schluchter has usefully analysed Weber's rationality into three components: (i) scientific-technological rationality directed at controlling the world; (ii) metaphysical-ethical rationality, viz. systemization of a world-view; (iii) practical rationality, viz. this-worldly active asceticism (Schluchter 1979: 14–15). It is only the second which has any role in soteriological endeavour in Newar Buddhism: that is, systematic understanding of the world is thought to be appropriate here as not elsewhere in religious contexts. But even here this is mediated by a guru and is, in practice, thoroughly ritualized and traditionalistic. Furthermore the goal is mystical: this fits with Weber's view that ritualism and mysticism go naturally together in one system (*ES*: 531).

With these qualifications, then, there is a very rough correlation between Weber's three types of legitimation (rationality, tradition, and charisma), the three types of religion (soteriology, social religion, and instrumental religion) and three of the four types of priest (spiritual teacher, domestic priest, and healer). The rights and practices of the fourth type of priest, the temple priest, are justified in terms of caste and kinship, both of which are in turn justified primarily in traditionalistic terms.

In the Newar context the three-way opposition can often be reduced to a single bipolar one between tradition and charisma, priesthood and possession. It must be emphasized, however, that these are ideal types. In reality, as examined in the next section, the two types of legitimation are often found together.

The Great Tradition as a sublimation of the 'orgiasticism' of the masses

One of the problems that has rightly exercised students of South Asian society is how to conceptualize the relationship between the 'high' culture or Great Tradition of Sanskrit texts and the 'low' or Little Tradition of Hindu villages. Dumont and Pocock (1959b) criticized the terminology of Great and Little Tradition, since it tends to make the Little Tradition into a residual category: it comprises whatever local practices appear to lack textual justification.[21] For this reason it is probably better to talk only of Great Traditions, which certainly exist, and to contrast them with 'popular religion'. To call the latter a Little Tradition either appears to imply that it is organized in the same way as the Great Traditions (which it is not) or that it constitutes a pool of survivals of pre-Hindu or pre-textual practices (which is doubtful).

From his sociological viewpoint, Weber saw popular religion as an autonomous field, not as a residue; and he saw the scriptural religions of South Asia as reactions to it. He saw the 'Great Traditions' of South Asia as different sublimations and rationalized reworkings of South

Asian 'popular' religion. The latter he often characterized as orgiastic. By 'orgiasticism' Weber meant the use of intoxicants, music, and dance as the means to altered states of consciousness, particularly ecstasy. It did not necessarily include sexual elements; where it did, Weber called it 'sexual orgiasticism' (*ES:* 401–2, 535).

In his description of Medieval Hinduism, late Buddhism, and Tantrism Weber over-emphasized the role of orgiasticism. This was due to the lurid and strongly disapproving Victorian accounts on which he relied.[22] There is a natural tendency for scholars to reach for their Freud and begin speculating about Weber's own sexual repressions when they see him repeatedly using the term 'orgiasticism'. For the purposes of the present argument, however, this would be a red herring. The crucial point is Weber's insight that the holy states prescribed by the various Great Traditional soteriologies of South Asia represented a reworking and sublimation of 'orgiastic' religion, and that this can be understood sociologically. Thus Weber wrote:

the Brahmanhood turned into a status group of genteel experts, resting its claims on knowledge and genteel cultivation. The more this was the case the less was Brahmanhood able to encompass all forms of magical asceticism ... [T]he status pride of cultured men resisted undignified demands of ecstatic therapeutic practices and the exhibition of neuropathic states. (*ROI:* 149; cf. 152)

What Weber says of South Asian religion in general is true of Newar religion in particular. The phenomenon of possession is widespread. Yet high castes are hostile to it and are frequently sceptical about the claims of its practitioners. Men of the Brahman and Vajracharya-Sakya castes are rarely if ever possessed. During the largest festival of the year, Dasain, there is a procession in Lalitpur around the city. Brahmans (the priests of the royal tutelary deity, Taleju), kshatriya-caste Hindus (Chathariya Shresthas) who live near the palace, and peasants from the village of Thecho all participate. The peasants come as dancers wearing the costumes and masks of the Mother Goddesses. The kshatriyas carry swords from their lineage's esoteric (Tantric) shrine and the Brahmans carry swords from Taleju's shrine. The peasants and occasionally the kshatriyas show signs of possession (principally shaking), but the Brahmans never do. They walk in a calm and matter-of-fact manner.

However, in secret, esoteric contexts, forbidden to middle and low castes, these same priestly castes who consider public possession beneath them, often are and must be possessed. In Buddhist Tantric Initiation all those who come to receive it—male and female—must be possessed, in a stylized fashion, by the Tantric deities whose mantras they receive. In more regular Tantric rituals, the priest's wife or the most senior woman of the sponsoring lineage is possessed by the Tantric goddess and distributes the deity's blessing—here alcohol in a skull-cup—to the participants. In esoteric rituals meat, alcohol, song, and dance are offered to the Buddhist deities, whereas in exoteric contexts these things are forbidden and may not be part of offerings to the pure, ascetic Buddhas and bodhisattvas. Esoteric dance, indeed, seems often to be a substitute for possession on the part of the Buddhist priests, whereas it is more acceptable for their womenfolk to be possessed directly in esoteric contexts. Hindu Tantric rites are now much on the decline, but similar considerations apply there too.[23] In short, in these examples, the direct charismatic inspiration of holy states is hardly sublimated at all. It is merely transferred from a public to a secret context.

In addition to this, high-caste ('genteel') religiosity among the Newars is indeed sublimated, in the way described by Weber. Admired salvific states are controlled and rule-bound. The theory on which nearly all Tantric rituals requiring the presence of a priest are constructed is that the priest visualizes the deity as emerging from his own body. The priest deifies himself in the introduction of the ritual and thereby acquires the authority and the power to make deities present for the laity to worship (see Chapter 5, pp. 125–6). This theory is particularly true of Buddhist ritual, and applies also to a large part of Hindu ritual. From the lay point of view the priest merely summons the deities and is not identical with them. But from the textual and Great Traditional point of view the priest or other high-caste practitioner is made divine—a ritualized, exclusive, and hierarchically valorized version of 'low-class' possession.

Finally, there is another sense in which Newars can be said to participate in the divine, a sense that needs to be distinguished from the foregoing. It has already been mentioned that there is a rough homology between the divine and social hierarchies. It is often observed that the Nepalese king is considered to be an incarnation of Vishnu. But, as Toffin has argued, the king was never worshipped *as* Vishnu (as in the god-king cults of South-east Asia). He was considered to be *like* Vishnu and to be possessed by him in ritual contexts (Toffin 1986, 1993). Here it is possible to suggest that Dumont was wrong to insist so strongly on the secularization of Hindu kingship (1980: Appendix C). In fact, Hindu kings found many ways to sacralize their position through Tantric ritual and public enactments of divine myths.

Toffin's argument can be generalized to other castes. Buddhist priests are like the Buddha in exoteric contexts and like the Tantric Buddhist divinities in secret. Peasants who specialize in cremation are believed 'to have something of Bhairava [the fierce form of Shiva]'. Untouchables likewise have frightening powers because of their associations with blood-drinking dangerous divinities.

In all these ways, the religion of the high castes, which is close to—and indeed, for locals, comprises—Great Traditional models, may be seen to be homogeneous with that of middle and low castes and to share a common idiom. This does not mean that Newar religion is a mere function of the caste hierarchy. I agree with Fuller when he says that

the world of the gods is not simply an 'upward' projection of the world of human beings, as defined by the caste system, and the relation between god and man is not merely a transposition of those relations of hierarchy pertaining between men. The religion of gods must first be understood in its own right. (Fuller 1979: 474)

There is perhaps in this an implicit (and just) criticism of Dumont and Pocock's claim (1959a: 37) that 'the religion of gods is secondary; the religion of caste is fundamental ...'

Conclusion

I have attempted to show that there are important similarities between the visions of Weber and Dumont. To some extent the similarity may be due to an insufficiently acknowledged influence. But it may also be the result of similar preoccupations. What Henri Stern wrote about Weber applies equally to Dumont: his writings on religion derive 'from the combination of two concerns that unfortunately are rarely found together: the construction of a general sociological theory and the use of a comparative method' (Stern 1971: 70). I have tried to suggest that South Asianists ought to combine an awareness of where Weber went wrong, largely because of his sources, with a greater recognition of the general theory underlying his study of Hinduism and Buddhism, from which there is still much to be learned. In particular, a Weberian analysis of the concepts of religion, priesthood, and legitimacy provides insights which a Dumontian emphasis on caste tends to obscure.

Notes

1. For valuable comments on earlier versions of this paper, I am grateful to members of seminars at the World Congress of Sociology (Delhi 1986), at LSE, and at All Souls, Oxford, as well as to N.J. Allen, D. Quigley, T.J. Reed, and J. Urry.

2. See Dumont (1980: xiif) for his reactions to the initial reception of *Homo Hierarchicus*. See Barnes, de Coppet, and Parkin (eds), (1985) for some non-South Asianist views.

3. *ROI* was a translation of one part of a series of long articles on the economic ethics of world religions (Weber 1916–17, 1996).

4. I have argued against the understanding of Weber as a development theorist and tried to place *ROI* in its proper context elsewhere (see Chapter 1); see also Buss (1985) and Kantowsky's essays (1982a, 1982b, 1984, 1985), the last three of which are reprinted in Kantowsky (ed.) 1986. Both Kantowsky and Buss, in addition to pointing out that Weber was only interested in explaining the first, endogenous appearance of capitalism in the West, also take the line that Weber was deeply hostile to the values of capitalism and, if alive today, would have looked to Asian societies for values with which to resist its 'iron cage'. Schluchter (1979: 51–9) is not so sure. Many of the works which attempt to engage with Weber still attack a straw man (e.g. Singer 1972: chapter 8; Puthusseril 1986); even Munshi's long and sophisticated critique (1988) sometimes seems to make this mistake. For some qualifications to specific interpretations of Weber on India see Schluchter (ed.) 1984; Kantowsky (ed.) 1986, and *International Sociology* 2 (3) (September 1987); cf. Bayly 1983: 188–9 and Munshi 1988.

5. See Dumont 1980: 30; also (p. 256) on power and status, and (pp. 374–5 n. 421) on the division of labour.

6. Dumont 1980: 401 n.92a. See also Chapter 1 above, Tambiah 1984b: 212, and Burghart 1985: 12 n.7; for Weber's observation, *ROI*: 147. Conrad (1986: 172) writes that Weber's 'conception of kingship ... contains in a nutshell the essential elements later elaborated in Louis Dumont's famous essay.' For other references, see p. 44, n. 21.

7. Burghart 1985: 6. Cf. Buss 1985: 13–14, 61–2. Dumont (1980: 394 n. 75d) seems to think that his viewpoint escapes Weber's Eurocentricity.

8. For a discussion of the word's changing reference, and the political and sociological implications of these changes, see Gellner 1986: 117, 123.

9. I have substituted the normal 'Tantric' for the '*tantristic*' of *ROI* 282. The original reads 'tantrische'.

10. Lévi 1905 I: 28f. I agree with Höfer (1979b) that Lévi's work has been 'more often quoted than really read' and that it deserves greater attention from social scientists.

11. I have attempted to sketch the outlines of this elsewhere (Gellner 1992: 98–104).

12. *ES*: 399ff. For Weber's own discussion of ideal types, see Weber 1949: 89ff. For a recent attempt to persuade anthropologists of the usefulness of Weber's thought, and for the point that his ideal types represent 'tendencies or orientations of actions', not political institutions, see Schnepel 1987.

13. Schluchter 1979: 26–45; 1981: Chapter 6; 1984; 1989. He follows Habermas in calling the Judaeo-Christian view theocentric and the Indian

cosmocentric (Schluchter 1981: 157). For an earlier discussion of the same set of oppositions, see Parsons 1965.

14. For an excellent analysis of the shared assumptions of Indian philosophical and theological systems, see Potter 1963.

15. See Gombrich 1971; 1988: chapter 5. See also Chapter 1, above.

16. *ROI*: 276. For a brief historical survey of Buddhism in Sri Lanka, written in terms of the adaptation of the Monastic Community to its roles as landlord, political actor, and ceremonial specialist for the laity, while still retaining its original ideal, see Carrithers 1984; cf. Gombrich 1988: Chapter 6.

17. Parkin (1982: 45–6) has criticized Weber for making the same methodological error in *PESC*.

18. See Toffin 1984a: 598; Gellner 1992: 78–9.

19. Hocart 1950: 16. Judging from the context, Hocart understood 'occupation' to refer to specialized occupations, not agriculture. He seems to have thought that this remark summed up three separate propositions: (i) that all occupations have their own rituals; (ii) that they are normally hereditary and therefore—even though ultimately depending on initiation—cannot be performed by anybody else; and (iii) that they all are necessary ritual specialists for patrons (paradigmatically kings or farmers). In fact it is clear that there is a *spectrum* of specialists, with brahmans, barbers, and funeral priests at one end, and, say, carpenters at the other (cf. Parry 1979: 58–83). If all occupations are priesthoods, some are more so than others.

20. **ROI* 326/Weber 1917: 796/1996: 521. The English of *ROI* has so mistranslated the German original as to produce nonsense; it reads: '... were linked quite immediately in an anti-rational manner to the course of each alien life methodology' for 'led directly into anti-rational paths which were inimical to a rational way of life'.

21. For similar criticism, see Das 1982: 109–10. For a critique of Dumont and Pocock which argues that they reproduced the same distinction under another name, see Tambiah 1970: 369–70.

22. See Kulke 1984 and Lutt 1987. Lutt points out the importance of the 1862 Maharaja libel case for the development of modern Hinduism. The leader of the Vallabhacharis filed a libel case against one of his followers, who had attacked the 'sexual immoralities and other evils' of the sect. Unfortunately Weber followed his sources in restricting himself to the tabloid revelations of this case.

23. Levy (1990: 306) notes that Brahmans must consume alcohol and perform animal sacrifice as part of secret rituals: 'All this involves a genuine risk for the Brahman, not only in the usual Tantric sense that what is clearly a violation and a sin in an ordinary context must somehow become transmuted into a proper religious act but also because their behavior (like all Tantric behavior, but the Brahman has most to risk) can be used as an attack against the status of the participants by those who discount the validity of the Tantric ritual.'

5

Monkhood and Priesthood in Newar Buddhism

The problem

Can there be priests in Buddhism? It is clear that in Theravada Buddhism there are none:

the *bhikkhu* [Theravada monk] is most certainly not a priest ... [H]e is not an intermediary between man and the supernatural; he administers no sacraments; he does not minister to a congregation, whether as the celebrant of a divine service or as a pastor. Although when requested he performs rituals on behalf of laymen, this is not his essential function, which, so far as laymen are concerned, is to serve as a 'field of merit', i.e. as a means by which (through offerings they make to him) they can acquire merit. (Spiro 1982: 280)

The Theravada Buddhist monk has another function not included in Spiro's summary: he preserves the Buddhist tradition and teaches it to laymen (Gombrich 1971: 271). In fact some of the monks Spiro asked included teaching Buddhism or performing religious ritual as a function (purpose) of a monk. However those who mentioned these functions thought them secondary; all agreed that 'the main function of Buddhist monasticism is to promote the monk's spiritual welfare' (Spiro 1982: 285). This is the origin of the Mahayana charge that the pre-Mahayana type of Buddhism is selfish, a charge repeated to me both by Buddhist priests and by Brahmans in Nepal. From the Theravada point of view, however, the monk's primary pursuit of his own salvation is precisely the point: it is this which makes him worthy of respect and generosity.

Theravada monks are then more learned than laymen and they are defined as monks by the fact that they keep more rules than laymen (Gombrich 1971: 64–7), but they are not intermediaries. The reason for this is that in Theravada Buddhist doctrine an individual can advance spiritually only by his or her own efforts.[1] What is extremely surprising in comparison with other religions or other forms of Buddhism is that even unsophisticated Theravada Buddhists recognize a strict division between otherworldly religion (religion proper, Buddhism) and this-worldly activities which westerners tend to think of as religion also. The latter include festivals and life-cycle rituals, the self-interested bribing of gods, godlings, or other supernaturals, and apotropaic rituals. None of these count as religion (*dharma* or *śāsana*) in Theravada Buddhism. Since Theravada Buddhism always refrained from evolving this-worldly rituals or justifications for those deviant monks who indulge in or encourage such activities, it necessarily always coexists with some other system which provides for this-worldly needs:

The Buddha's teaching was limited to what he thought conducive to enlightenment. Most people have broader interests, so Buddhists are almost bound to have other beliefs besides those of Buddhist doctrine. To sum this up in a word, Buddhism in real life is *accretive*. (Gombrich 1971: 49; emphasis in original)

This explains the coexistence of Buddhism with Hindu gods in Sri Lanka and with spirit cults in Burma and Thailand.[2] It is in these other systems which coexist with Theravada Buddhism and provide for the this-worldly needs of Theravada Buddhists, that priests are to be found. As ministers to lower ends they receive much less respect than monks.

The traditional Buddhism of the Newars of the Kathmandu Valley, Nepal, is not Theravada,[3] but Mahayana ('the Great Way') Buddhism. There are important, and usually unappreciated, continuities between Theravada, the last surviving representative of the pre-Mahayana schools of Buddhism, and Mahayana Buddhism; but of course there are also certain important differences. One of these is the philosophical doctrine of emptiness (*śūnyatā*) that underlies all Mahayana soteriology. I discuss the relevance of this to Newar Buddhists below. Another difference is the complex pantheon of divine beings evolved by Mahayana Buddhism: at the top are numerous Buddhas, below them saints called bodhisattvas who are so compassionate that they do not advance to ultimate enlightenment but turn over their vast merit to suffering beings, even to those who appeal to them for worldly goods; below the bodhisattvas come other protective gods. The bodhisattva represents the moral ideal of the Mahayana: all good Buddhists should strive to become bodhisattvas, that is, they should devote themselves to uplifting all sentient beings and bringing them to enlightenment.

One consequence of the bodhisattva doctrine was to shift the emphasis away from the monastic ideal and away from a rigid interpretation of monastic vows.[4] The Buddha himself had been a bodhisattva dedicated to attaining enlightenment for the sake of all beings in many lives before his final rebirth, and in all of them he had lived as a layman, not as a monk.

A second important consequence was to provide a justification for a Buddhist priesthood. In the Nepalese context, the bodhisattva doctrine is combined with the practices of Vajrayana ('Diamond Way') Buddhism, also known as Tantric Buddhism. The Diamond Way is not an alternative to the Great Way, but a specialized, privileged, and esoteric set of ritual and yogic practices within it. By making use of these practices, the priest is supposed to realize emptiness, which is inseparable from compassion in Buddhist doctrine. He makes use of this power, therefore, in line with his bodhisattva vow, to visualize the manifold divine beings of the Mahayana pantheon on behalf of others (his patrons or parishioners).

The Buddhism of the Newars of the Kathmandu Valley is indeed an ideal testing ground if one wishes to see how a Buddhist priesthood can exist within Mahayana Buddhism. Newar Buddhists are in effect the last surviving South Asian Mahayana Buddhists. They are the last Buddhists whose scriptural and ritual language is Sanskrit. This is why Sylvain Lévi came to Nepal and wrote its history as a first step in writing the history of the whole of South Asia. Newar Buddhism goes back in an unbroken line to the late Mahayana and Vajrayana Buddhism evolved in the great monastic universities of north India (Nalanda, Odantapuri, and others) which were destroyed by Muslim incursions from the twelfth century onwards. The Kathmandu Valley is a small place and its medieval kings were always inclined to Hinduism not Buddhism. Consequently there were no great scholastic monasteries as had existed in India and grew up later in Tibet. Until the thirteenth century Tibetans came to the Kathmandu Valley for instruction from Indian or Nepalese teachers. Thereafter scholarship declined and Newar Buddhists became convinced, as their myths show (Gellner 1992a: 86), that Tibetan Buddhism preserved a level of understanding, practice, and orthodoxy from which they had fallen away.

It is hard to avoid the conclusion, also expressed in these local myths, that this decline was connected to the disappearance of celibacy within the holy order of Newar Buddhism. It would be wrong however to follow the myths in representing this transformation of a celibate monastic order into a caste of married monks and Tantric preceptor-priests as a single cataclysmic event. It seems far more likely that married priests appeared (perhaps in the tenth or eleventh century) along with the rise of Vajrayana Buddhism, and coexisted with celibate monks until the latter dwindled, finally to disappear some time in the middle of the Malla period (1200–1768).

It is the task of this essay to explain how Vajrayana Buddhism legitimates a Buddhist priesthood very similar to that of the brahmans in Hinduism, while at the same time maintaining continuity with Mahayana and pre-Mahayana Buddhism. Looking at the priesthood in this way enables one to avoid the naïve and/or moralizing approaches which, judging Vajrayana Buddhism by the canons of the Theravada, or by those of the modern West, ignore the views of Newar Buddhists themselves.[5]

Sakyas and Vajracharyas: Types of priest

The holy order of Newar Buddhism is a caste: it is made up of two subsections or status groups,[6] the Vajracharyas ('Master of the Diamond [Way]', i.e. Tantric preceptor) and the Sakyas, formerly called Sakyabhikshu ('Buddhist monk') or Sakyavamsa ('of the Sakya, i.e. the Buddha's, lineage').[7] The majority of Sakyas and Vajracharyas live in the old royal cities of the Kathmandu Valley, Kathmandu itself, Lalitpur, and Bhaktapur. Others live in outlying towns and villages but most of them maintain an urban and high-caste style of life. Only Vajracharyas may act as domestic priests (*purohit*) for Buddhists, just as Brahmans must be the domestic priests of (clean-caste) Hindus. In Lalitpur and Kathmandu the majority of Newars have Vajracharya and not Brahman domestic priests. In Lalitpur priestly roles in most festivals and religious practices are filled by Vajracharyas, and thus one can say that Lalitpur is predominantly Buddhist. At the same time one must remember that the rituals of the royal palace at the city's centre are in Brahman hands, and the domestic priests of the socially most prestigious families (the Chathariya Shresthas) are Brahmans. Furthermore, the majority of the population—when faced with the census-question of either/or—declare themselves to be, or are declared, Hindus.[8]

Vajracharyas are superior in status to Sakyas because only they may act as domestic priests for others. The traditional self-images of Vajracharyas and Sakyas—as Tantric priests and married monks, respectively—differ, and this is why I call them separate status groups, but the

Plate 1: *Asha Ratna Bajracharya, domestic priest, reads out the 'story'* (bākhā) *accompanying the performance of the Observance* (vrata) *of Vasundhara (Buddhist goddess of wealth), sponsored annually by a Sakya guthī. Jog Maya Sakya sits to his left as the 'sponsor'* (jajmān, jaymā) *and seniormost participant.*

distinction is not one of caste (though outsiders, particularly Hindus, may see it as such) since they interdine freely and frequently intermarry. During the 1920s and 30s there was a long and bitter dispute between Vajracharyas and Uday (Uray) in Kathmandu, which is still keenly remembered. The Uday are a highly educated and often wealthy lay Buddhist caste (found only in Kathmandu) ranking just below the Sakyas and Vajracharyas. The dispute arose over the claim of the majority of Vajracharyas that they were superior in caste to the Uday and ought not therefore to accept cooked rice from them; the Uday themselves, and the minority of Vajracharyas who sided with them, claimed that the superiority of the Vajracharyas was not based on caste and that therefore they ought to continue to accept cooked rice in their clients' homes (Rosser 1966). At no time did the Vajracharyas claim that they could not eat rice cooked by Sakyas, even though most of the Sakyas ultimately sided with the Uday. In short, the Vajracharyas never publicly claimed higher caste status than the Sakyas. The Kathmandu Vajracharyas did however begin to break off marriage with them (ibid.: 124–6).

I would interpret this as an accentuation, possibly prompted by caste feelings on the part of some, of a tendency of Vajracharyas everywhere to be reluctant to accept Sakya wives, while willing to give their daughters to Sakya husbands (Gellner 1995b: 218–19). Newar Buddhists say that for ritual reasons Vajracharyas do not like to accept Sakya brides: parishioners (*jajmān, jaymā*) prefer to have a Vajracharya woman as the priest's wife (*gurumā*) who must (unlike a brahman's wife) always accompany her husband to important rituals, and to whom patrons must pay one half of whatever they give to her husband; on the practical level a Sakya girl is less likely to be well acquainted with rituals; and if a Vajracharya is ever to give Tantric Initiation his wife must be a Vajracharya.

As far as their monastic identity is concerned there is no difference between Sakyas and Vajracharyas. Sakya and Vajracharya males are distinguished from all other Newar men by the fact that instead of the puberty/caste-initiation ceremony of *kaytā pūjā* or *vratabandha* they undergo a four-day Monastic Initiation (*cūḍākarma* or *bare chuyegu*).[9] By this rite they become members of their father's monastery, with all the rights and duties which that entails.[10] For this reason the son of a Vajracharya or Sakya by a lower-caste wife is not allowed to go through Monastic Initiation in his father's monastery, but must do it outside at a *caitya*, which confers no membership of a monastic community (*saṃgha, sā*).

The principal duty of monastery members is to take turns to be the guardian (*dyaḥpāḥlā*) of the monastery's main non-Tantric deity (*kwābāju, kwāḥpāḥdyaḥ*): the guardian is responsible for performing the daily rituals and for the security of the images and ornaments in the shrine; and during his tenure (which varies from monastery to monastery: it may be one or two weeks, a month, or even, in some cases, a year) he receives the offerings of devotees and keeps them for himself. He is therefore a temple priest of a sort, though in many small monasteries he performs the ritual on his own, and the offerings are negligible. Kwa Bahah in Lalitpur (Plate 2) is the largest and most impressive monastic temple complex of this kind and until recently the volume of offerings there ensured that the chance to be guardian (which comes only once in a lifetime because the Monastic Community of Kwa Bahah is so large) was a jealously guarded privilege.[11]

In some monasteries there are only Sakyas, in others only Vajracharyas, and in yet others there are both. As members of the same monastery Vajracharyas have no advantage over Sakyas: rights, duties, and positions of authority are determined by simple seniority. The only exception to this is that the seniormost Vajracharya is called the Chakreshvara and is responsible for the regular worship of the monastery's principal Tantric deity; he has an assistant, called a Betaju, who must also be a Vajracharya and not yet an elder of the monastery, chosen for his knowledge of ritual, who oversees the whole round of ritual in the monastery.

Plate 2: The façade of Kwa Bahah (the 'Golden Temple'), Lalitpur.

All Vajracharyas and Sakyas undergo Monastic Initiation and thereby gain membership of a monastery. Vajracharyas differ from Sakyas in that only they may subsequently undergo the rite of Consecration as a Master (of the Diamond Way) (ācāryābhiṣeka, ācāḥ luyegu).[12] This rite gives Vajracharyas, on top of the monastic identity conferred by Monastic Initiation, the status of priests and preceptors for all Newar Buddhists.

Most Vajracharyas perform the rite immediately or shortly after Monastic Initiation, although there is another pattern, followed in Bu Bahah, whereby it is performed only after marriage. It is in fact an abbreviated version of Tantric Initiation (*dīkṣā*), followed by the neophyte performing his first fire sacrifice (*homa, yajña,* or—most colloquially—*jog*). In Kathmandu Sakyas and Uday are also entitled to Tantric Initiation; in Lalitpur, Sakyas, Shresthas, and also, in a less elaborate form, Tamrakars, Rajkarnikars, Barahi, and Sthapits. Logically, then, in terms of the textual tradition, these castes—or at least those who receive the same initiation as Vajracharyas—ought also to be able to take up the priesthood. It is here that the practice of Newar Buddhism is most in conflict with its own canon: not in abandoning celibacy (which is justified in the Tantras) but in making the highest spiritual role, that of the Vajracharya, an exclusive and hereditary status group. For this there is no scriptural justification, only the legitimating power (which is still for the most part accepted) of tradition.

The practical significance of the different religiously defined identities of Sakya and Vajracharya can be clearly seen when we consider the forms of priesthood encountered by Newar Buddhists. As a matter of empirical observation (and as discussed above, p. 95ff), Newar Buddhists interact regularly with ritual specialists of the following four broad types:[13]

   (i)   temple priests/god-guardians (*dyaḥpāḥlā*);
   (ii) domestic priests (*purohit*);
   (iii) initiation priests (*dīkṣā-guru*);
   (iv) various types of healer and medium (*vaidya* and *dyaḥ waipī*).

The third type is a relatively obscure role; most Newars do not encounter them, as they do not take Tantric Initiation. The initiation priest for Buddhist Tantric Initiation must be a learned Vajracharya whose wife is still living. Whoever organizes the initiation and therefore fills the role of principal sponsor and senior initiand (*dhahmū thakāli*) chooses the priest and he does not have to choose his own domestic priest. The many others who come to receive the initiation at the same time (it is expensive and therefore occurs infrequently) effectively have their initiation priest chosen for them.

The fourth category of specialist is very heterogeneous.[14] It includes Ayurvedic doctors, healers who use mantras, blowing and brushing (*jhārphuke vaidya*), and midwives (*didi aji*) with hereditary relationships to given families. There are also Vajracharya healers who combine various methods eclectically: they may describe the cause of an ailment in terms of the Ayurvedic system of humours, astrological conjunctures, divine anger, or witchcraft. Vajracharyas of this sort often take a special Tantric

Initiation of the deity Chandamaharoshana (*acaladīkṣā*). This is appropriate because the final section of the Chandamaharoshana Tantra, unlike most other Buddhist Tantras, contains much information on medical matters.[15] All of these healers so far described are called *vaidya*, a category which also includes those such as apothecaries (*baniyā*) and Ayurvedic doctors who make no use of religious symbols and cannot be considered ritual specialists at all.

Also in the fourth category of ritual specialist are the numerous 'faith-healers', literally 'those to whom a god/gods come(s)' (*dyaḥ waipī*). One might add to this category those who dance as deities (sometimes known as *dhāmī* as, for instance, in Naradevi, Kathmandu); also the shamans, *jhākri*, of other ethnic groups, whom Newars know about but do not normally use. Although the 'faith-healers' are most often possessed by Hariti (usually written 'Hāratī' by Newars), the Buddhist goddess of smallpox, they are not part of organized Buddhism. The healer may be a Buddhist, but need not be. So this kind of religion is not specifically Buddhist but belongs rather to the ambiguous 'folk' religion which is neither Buddhist nor Hindu, but can be articulated in the idiom and using the symbols of either religion.

Thus the whole fourth category of ritual specialist belongs exclusively to the sphere of purely 'practical' religion. Practitioners of this category are chosen primarily by their own volition. Traditionally their roles were often inherited, but they need not be. Although Newar Buddhism has evolved many practices to help in this-worldly affliction, it has retained its primary orientation to salvation. By contrast the activities of healers are very obviously worldly, of advantage to the practitioners themselves and to their self-interested clients. Consequently people are often sceptical about these freelance healers, whereas they are never sceptical about the activities of other types of priests and never doubt the existence of the gods they worship. (The complaint *there* is that their rituals are expensive and burdensome.) The fact that most of the 'faith-healers' are women no doubt also tells against them.

The first three types of specialist are associated with the sphere of religion which is soteriological and/or symbolic in aim and is often expressive of social relations. By contrast, the fourth type belongs to that aspect of religion which is this-worldly, instrumental, and practical. There is the same conceptual distinction between this- and otherworldly practices as in Theravada Buddhism, but the boundary between the two is no longer sharp. Priests now have the highest religious status and teach the path to salvation; their rites include magical elements to an extent quite foreign to the sober spirit of Theravada Buddhism.

In talking of priesthood in Newar Buddhism, rather than of ritual specialists in Newar society as such, we must mean priests of the first three types. Of these it is the first two which are really important. They correspond to the two halves of Max Weber's definition: 'The crucial feature of priesthood [is] the specialization of a particular group of persons in the continuous operation of a cultic enterprise, permanently associated with particular norms, places, and times, and related to specific social groups'.[16] Weber (1968: 424–5) wanted to set up an ideal of type of priest that distinguished them from magicians. He rejected definitions of 'priest' as a specialist employed by an organization rather than self-employed, as a specialist legitimated by doctrine and vocational qualifications rather than by miracles, and as a specialist practising worship rather than magic. In assessing these putative definitions Weber often illustrated their shortcomings with the case of Catholic priests: some are not office-holders, some are not at all learned, and, most significantly for our present discussion, 'the concept of the priest includes ... a magical qualification' (ibid.). What Weber says of Catholic priests and of priests as such applies fully to Vajracharya priests. Vajracharya priests are not, and are not regarded as, magicians, even though they are often believed to be able to perform magical acts, and the more spiritually advanced they are, the more capable. In the Newar, as in the Weberian view, some of them may perform magic, but this is not their prime function, which is to carry on a permanent cult associated with given norms and social groups. Furthermore, in the Nepalese context they are defined as priests rather than magicians because the doctrine they are associated with is a soteriology (*mārga*). (Weber avoided this in his definition because of the priesthoods, e.g. the Shintoist, which lack a doctrine of salvation.)

Newar Buddhism presents the observer with an analytical distinction between two main types of priest, and, as indicated, these correspond, roughly, to the two halves of the Weberian definition. The first kind of specialist listed above, the god-guardian, serves the continuous cult of the public Buddhist deities. Domestic priesthood, by contrast, is associated with the sacralization of life stages (a type of religion in which Weber, unlike Durkheim, was not particularly interested): that is, the perpetuation of ritual ties and norms of given social groups (those with Buddhist priests). Vajracharyas have the right to carry on both types of priesthood, whereas Sakyas may carry on only the former. Thus B.R. and R.K. Vajracharya (1963: 9) define a Vajracharya as 'a monk who has received the consecrations of *vajra* [ritual implement symbolizing the absolute] and bell [i.e. passed through the Consecration as a Master ritual mentioned above], which are the entitlement (sarvādhikāra) to perform the fire sacrifice and so on'. Thus, doctrinally Vajracharyas are defined as a kind of Sakya (i.e. monk), who have, in addition, the right to be a priest. Interestingly, the uninformed popular view, in which Vajracharyas are more prominent, reverses this, and sees Sakyas as a kind of Vajracharya who lack the right to serve others as domestic priests. (I have heard this expressed jocularly as their not being allowed to ring the priest's bell.)

Domestic priesthood is, then, the monopoly of the Vajracharyas. Under this heading we might also wish to include other religious specialists who inherit their clientele (jajmān), viz. Barbers and Kapali (death specialists).[17] Vajracharyas do not merely have a monopoly on performing life-cycle rites for families: only they may perform the fire sacrifice, and in practice only they may direct complex, occasional rituals (e.g. vrata), since only they are sufficiently knowledgeable.

The other type of priesthood, god-guardianship, is much more widely distributed in Newar society. Almost every caste has at least some members who take turns as guardians of certain gods. The shrines of Ganesh are usually tended by Maharjans. Mother Goddess shrines outside the city gates are tended by Untouchables (hence their honorific caste name 'Dyahla' from dyahpahla). The guardians of Bhimsen shrines are usually Kapali. However, purely Buddhist divinities—the main Sakyamuni images of monasteries, Tara shrines, and Avalokiteshvara cults such as the famous Matsyendranaths—must have Sakyas and/or Vajracharyas as their god-guardians. This kind of Buddhist priesthood is justified in terms of Sakyas' and Vajracharyas' common status as monks, as 'sons' of the Buddha. Only they go through the Monastic Initiation rite, and while performing the rites for the god, the guardian must keep monastic rules: celibacy, food restrictions, and purity taboos.

The god-guardian type of priesthood does in fact have considerable antiquity within Buddhism. Here it is necessary to qualify an impression given at the outset. In general, Theravada Buddhism lacks priests. But Theravada monks may, as a secondary feature, take on priestly activities in a limited way. In particular, they may act in effect as a kind of god-guardian of the monasteries in which they live. Only rarely however, at large monasteries, often with royal connections, does this role seem to acquire any importance (Evers 1972: Chapter 4). The monastic god-guardian role of Sakyas and Vajracharyas is directly descended from the elaborate Buddha-worship conducted in such monasteries. Here however, due to changes legitimated by the Vajrayana, as discussed below, the food and other offerings made are considered to be imbued with the deity's blessing (prasād) and are returned to devotees. From the Theravada point of view this is the Hindu, not the Buddhist, view of offerings.[18]

The cult of the esoteric (Tantric) Buddhist deities differs from that of exoteric deities: usually only Vajracharyas may carry on their cult. Thus, as mentioned, the seniormost Vajracharya of a monastery in which there are both Sakyas and Vajracharyas performs the daily ritual of the monastery's principal Tantric deity.[19] Vajrasattva is a Tantric deity of a more exoteric sort (his image may be displayed in public) and his cult is also in the hands of Vajracharyas alone: in Kwa Bahah there is a separate shrine to him in which the Vajracharya members of the monastery take fortnightly turns as guardian.

The legitimation of the Vajracharyas' monopoly of the domestic priesthood and of their pre-eminence in the cult of Tantric deities is rather a complex matter in contrast to the monastic practices and symbols which legitimate the god-guardianship that they share with Sakyas. To this legitimation we must now turn.

The hierarchy of the Three Ways (*yāna*) in Newar Buddhism

Two other anthropologists, Stephen Greenwold and Michael Allen, have addressed the question of how the Vajracharya priesthood is legitimated, and it makes a useful starting point to recapitulate their findings. The main points of Greenwold's article (1974a) 'Buddhist Brahmans' (a description of Vajracharyas going back to Lévi 1905 I: 226) may be listed as follows:

(i) The ideal Vajracharya is a Realized One (*siddha*) who lives in the world, not a monk who renounces caste and family.[20]

(ii) The ritual of Monastic Initiation is used to maintain control of monasteries and exclude outsiders: 'the very basis of the Newar priesthood is prior ordination as a monk' (Greenwold 1974a: 110).

(iii) Since only Vajracharyas may perform the fire sacrifice for Buddhists, only they may act as domestic priests for parishioners.

(iv) Only 28 per cent of Greenwold's sample of working Vajracharyas in Kathmandu served as priests and only 11.9 per cent had no other job but the priesthood.[21] It is the ritual status of priest, not the actual practice of priesthood, which is essential to being a Vajracharya.

(v) There is a close parallel with the position of the brahmans, whose high status in a hierarchy of purity, and whose ability to act as priests for others, depend on their incarnating ascetic values.

To these five points made by Greenwold, three others may be added, taken from M. Allen's article (1973) 'Buddhism without Monks':

(vi) The Three Ways (or Vehicles) of Buddhism represent a hierarchy through which the Buddhist neophyte ascends, thereby recapitulating the history of Buddhism itself.

(vii) The highest, Tantric Way is based on inversions of the first, monastic one: 'sex in place of celibacy, long hair instead of shaven pates, indulgence instead of abstinence, drunkenness instead of sobriety' (Allen 1973: 13).

(viii)A crucial factor in the preservation of the income and identity of Buddhist priests has been the development of popular cults, such that of Karunamaya-Matsyendranath, which appeal equally to all Newars.[22]

Greenwold ignored the sixth point above, the ideological framework used by Newar Buddhists themselves, and was led therefore (particularly in 1974b) to see the ideal of the priest as straightforwardly opposed to that of the monk.[23] By following La Vallée Poussin and translating *siddha* as 'magician' rather than as 'accomplished' or 'realized person', he perpetuated an oversimple, and partial, opposition between otherworldly monks and this-worldly Vajracharyas. Furthermore, strictly speaking, in contrasting the *siddha* with the monk he was not comparing like with like: the former is a soteriological ideal and the latter a socio-religious role (see Chart 5.3).

These confusions can be sorted out if we distinguish, as Newar Buddhists do themselves, between three levels in their traditional Buddhism: the Shravakayana (Way of the Disciples), the Mahayana (Great Way), and the Vajrayana (Diamond Way).[24] In the texts of Mahayana Buddhism the term 'Shravakayana' is used to refer to the pre-Mahayana schools in order to contrast their limited and selfish goal with the more noble and altruistic aim of the hero of the Great Way, the bodhisattva. This usage continues among Newar Buddhists today: the newly introduced Theravada Buddhism is referred to, especially by the older generation, as Shravakayana. At the same time the monastic practices *within* traditional Newar Buddhism are also referred to by the same term, in particular the keeping of the Eight Precepts in the context of Observances (*vrata*) (of which Monastic Initiation is one).[25]

The cardinal virtue of the Great Way is the altruism of the bodhisattva, intent on the spiritual good of all beings, not just his own enlightenment. For Newar Buddhists this means carrying out all the religious duties of a Buddhist householder as they have been handed down to them. Vajrayana, the Diamond Way, is closely associated with Vajracharyas, so that for most Newars 'Vajrayana' tends to mean 'what Vajracharyas do'. It also has the popular connotation of the practice of supernatural and magical powers gained by advanced spiritual states and (to this end) frequenting frightening places such as cremation grounds. At the same time the Diamond Way includes the practice of rites and daily exercises to which one has access only through Tantric Initiation.

These three levels are arranged in a hierarchy running from the Disciples' Way to the Great Way, and to the Diamond Way at the highest level. They are not practised sequentially however: attainment of the highest level through Tantric Initiation does not mean that the practices of the other levels are abandoned. Higher levels contain the lower within themselves. Nor is the relationship of the levels, each to the other, symmetrical. The Great Way has displaced the Disciples' Way as the proper Buddhist path in Newar Buddhism, while continuing its rites and practices within prescribed contexts. The Diamond Way, on the other hand, represents a means *within* the Great Way whereby its aims can be attained with greater efficiency within this life.[26] In order to convey what this means in practice, I present in Chart 5.1 a summary of the different kinds of religious practice that tend to be associated with the different levels of Newar Buddhism.

Chart 5.1: Summary of the different religious practices in the Three Ways (*yāna*) in Newar Buddhism

The Way of the Disciples (*śrāvakayāna*)	monasticism worship of the Buddha ascetic rule-observance

The Great Way (*mahāyāna*)	worship of all the gods
	fulfilment of hereditary householder duties
	    including festivals and life-cycle rituals
	    acquiring merit through donations
	cultivation of moral perfections in accordance
	    with the ideal of the bodhisattva

The Diamond Way (*vajrayāna*)	worship of Tantric deities
	taking Tantric Initiation (*dīkṣā*)
	acquiring magical powers and advanced spiritual
	    states by strict rule-bound devotion to powerful
	    secret deities or their exoteric manifestations

The different deities of Newar Buddhism can be assigned to different Ways: the Buddha Sakyamuni belongs to the Shravakayana, the bodhisattvas to the Great Way, and 'Great Buddha' Vajrasattva and the esoteric deities to the Diamond Way. Similarly the architecture of the Buddhist monastery was several times explained to me as reflecting this same hierarchy (see Chapter 6, p. 149). The Three Ways also provide a model of Buddhist history: as a matter of historical fact the types of Buddhism represented by the Three Ways did arise in that order, and the texts of the later forms reveal an awareness of this. However, these later texts claim that they were taught by the Buddha himself, but were hidden by him, since the Disciples at that time were not ready for their teachings. The majority of Newar Buddhists do not have a first-hand acquaintance with their texts; all the same, some of them do see the Great Way and Diamond Way as a later adaptation of the Way of the Disciples, that is, they understand the conceptual levels as a chronological development. This may be due to the influence of the Theravada monks and nuns now active in Nepal, or it may be due to the fact that this structure is built into the rite of Monastic Initiation in which the neophyte passes from being a monk to becoming a householder.

The structure of Newar Buddhism determined by ritual, not doctrine

It would be wrong to interpret this conceptual structure of the Three Ways as a rigid framework into which every aspect of Newar Buddhism can or should be fitted. Newar Buddhists may define themselves by caste (Sakyas, Vajracharyas, and others), by priest (all those with Vajracharya domestic priests), or by personal devotion (to the Buddha and Buddhist deities); they would never think to define Buddhists as those who believe a specific doctrine.[27] There is no organization whose role or duty it is to propound doctrine. Consequently the application of well-known doctrines or concepts, such as the hierarchy of the Three Ways, to particular cases can be and is interpreted in different ways. Newar Buddhists, especially elderly men, often discuss these issues, but the discussion, although lively, is carried on in a tolerant spirit: all readily admit that their understanding is deficient and they readily defer to others considered more learned; no one would accuse another of heretical opinions.[28] The only organization even remotely resembling a church is the Acharya Guthi (Association of Vajracharyas) in Kathmandu.[29] In Lalitpur there is no association of all the Vajracharyas of the city, but in Kwa Bahah and other large monasteries all the Vajracharyas of the monastery have their own association. These associations are less important nowadays, but in the past they were supposed to ensure uniformity of rituals among their members.

As far as doctrine is concerned, there are a few informal groups meeting to study under the guidance of a more learned guru. But for the vast mass of Newar Buddhists the only teaching they receive is contained—often only implicitly—in the stories of the previous lives of the Buddha or other saints occasionally recounted in public by learned Vajracharyas. One of the reasons for the popularity of the new Theravada movement is the fact that preaching by monks occupies the central place that ritual holds in traditional Newar Buddhism. Thus there is an enormous variation in doctrinal knowledge between the learned pundit and the illiterate farmer who is his hereditary parishioner, and there are innumerable degrees of knowledge between the two. And it is an essential part of the religion that there should be such hierarchy—of two levels at least—since it is forbidden for the teachings given at Tantric Initiation to be mentioned to the uninitiated.

Traditional Newar religion—whether Buddhist or Hindu—consists for the most part of ritual and ritualized devotion. However the simple act of making an offering is in itself ambiguous: nothing has been said about what the devotee thinks is happening, and most Newars are happy to leave it that way. Even complex sets of ritual determined by tradition can be interpreted in different ways. For instance, Sakyas and Vajracharyas claim that the Maharjans are Buddhist since their priests are Vajracharyas and their rites are, therefore, mostly directed at Buddhist deities and use Buddhist mantras. Maharjans themselves often say they are Hindus. The life-cycle rituals of the Maharjans are indeed Hindu in origin, but they have been adapted for Buddhist householders. Within both religions most worshippers believe that it is in the power of the gods to grant protection and success, but others, a sophisticated minority, denounce, in certain contexts, this self-interested orientation; they none the less continue to worship, but reinterpret it as custom, disinterested piety, or a kind of psychological therapy.

The rites of the Vajracharyas can be divided into exoteric and esoteric forms. The differences between are summarized in Chart 5.2. These differences are very clear to Newars who have taken Tantric Initiation. Even those who have not are aware that substances required in one context are forbidden in another. Contrary to what M. Allen implied (1973: 13), rites of the Diamond Way do not require drunkenness or orgies: alcohol, meat, and sexual symbolism are used in a highly ritualized way as a controlled infraction of exoteric taboos. Vajrayana Buddhism is as hostile as other forms of Buddhism to licentiousness.

Chart 5.2: Shravakayana and Mahayana rites, contrasted with Vajrayana rites

Rites of the Shravakayana (Disciples' Way) and Mahayana (Great Way)	Vajrayana (Diamond Way) rites
Worship using only pure substances	Worship must include impure substances, in particular meat and alcohol
Dance and song forbidden	Dance and song essential parts of worship
Celibacy required	Sexual imagery central
Calmness required; hostility to possession	Controlled possession by deity required of women, permitted of men
Observance (*vrata*)	Yogic visualization (*sādhana*)
Aim: merit and blessing of deity	Aim: power, liberation through identification with the deity
Access open to all clean castes	Access only to the initiated

There are inevitably certain overlaps and exceptions to the distinctions outlined in Chart 5.2. Thus, the opposition between Observance (*vrata*) of a deity's rules and yogic visualization is not absolute: for instance the monthly ritual for the main Tantric deity of a monastery performed by its ten elders is in practice like an Observance but makes use of Tantric substances. The dividing line between the esoteric and the exoteric may be laid down differently in different contexts and interpreted slightly differently by different groups. In spite of these qualifications, however, the opposition between the exoteric (*bāhya*) and esoteric (*guhya*) is fundamental in Newar religion as others have already observed.[30]

This opposition between exoteric and esoteric corresponds to that between the Great Way and the Diamond Way, since the Great Way, when not itself opposed to the Disciples' Way, can be understood also to include it. All Newars, even those who have never heard of the doctrine of Three Ways, understand the distinction between esoteric and exoteric rites. In the simplest terms it is expressed as an opposition between rites one may see (*swaye jyū*) and those one may not (*swaye ma jyū*). Even those castes which may not receive Tantric Initiation, either Buddhist or Hindu, hold fast to this distinction.[31]

Theravada Buddhism by contrast is not a system of ritual. There are a very few, extremely simple, Theravada rituals, but they can hardly be said to form a system. This is tacitly recognized in Newar Buddhism, in which 'Shravakayana' connotes practices of restraint, particularly celibacy in a monk-like idiom.

The Vajracharya as *siddha* and bodhisattva

With this background understood we can now see in what sense Vajracharyas are *siddhas* and how they are also monks, although this latter status is incorporated and transcended in the role of Vajra-Master. This is summarized in Chart 5.3. Newar Buddhists sometimes assert that these Three Ways differ only in means, that the end result is the same; at other times they emphasize the differences between the Ways. Both ways of speaking have scriptural precedent. Vajracharyas have to combine all three Ways, while being most clearly identified with the third, the Vajrayana.

Chart 5.3: Soteriological ideals and social roles of the Three Ways

Religious Level	Soteriological Ideal	Social Role
Disciples' Way (Shravakayana)	*arhat* (noble one)	monk (i.e. during Initiation, Samyak, etc.)
Great Way (Mahayana)	bodhisattva (wisdom-being)	Practising Mahayana Buddhists; Vajracharyas in their purely exoteric aspect
Diamond Way (Vajrayana)	*siddha* (Realized One)	Vajracharya priest

Vajracharyas put monastic ideals into practice at various times: during the Monastic Initiation ritual, whenever they act as god-guardian, and, in a sense, whenever they perform a ritual. Until a ritual is completed the priest, as well as the sponsor (*jajmān*) and other participants (e.g. *dhalā dāpī*[32] in an Observance), must maintain a state of ritual purity: this includes bathing, fasting, and avoiding contact with impure substances. When the ritual lasts more than one day it also includes celibacy. One can see that the practice of restraint characteristic of the Disciples' Way is interpreted primarily in ritual terms. The members of Kwa Bahah, Lalitpur, refer proudly to the fact that more rules i.e. more rules designed to maintain purity, are kept there than in any other monastery. It is no accident that this is the monastery in Lalitpur most frequented by high-caste Hindus. All Newars who participate in Buddhist rituals take a vow to become a Buddha for the good of all beings, that is, the bodhisattva vow, as part of the guru mandala rite (Gellner 1991a). The vast majority are not aware that they are doing this. Unlike the Eight or Ten Precepts in an Observance (*vrata*) which are read out in a singsong and archaic—but comprehensible[33]—Newari, the bodhisattva vow is read in Sanskrit and in such a way as to be wholly incomprehensible. Knowledge of the bodhisattva vow is confined therefore to the pious, mostly men, and mostly Vajracharyas and Sakyas. Most Newar Buddhists are equally unaware that the great compassionate deity Karunamaya (Matsyendranath) is a bodhisattva: to the unlearned he is simply 'Bungadyah' (god of Bunga village), 'Karunamaya', or 'Matsyendranath'. For most Newar Buddhists 'bodhisattva' refers only to the Buddha in his previous lives and to one other divine being, Maitri (= Maitreya) bodhisattva, the future Buddha.[34] A few knowledgeable Buddhists assert that Vajracharya priests are supposed to be bodhisattvas, wise beings who help others: this is usually followed by the assertion that no such exist today. Paradoxically those who are sophisticated enough to be acquainted with the bodhisattva concept are also sophisticated enough to despise actual practising Vajracharyas, whereas those who genuinely respect their Vajracharya priest and believe in his powers are almost invariably peasants of the older generation who regard him simply as 'their Gubhaju'.

Compared to the bodhisattva the ideal of the siddha is much more widely known. Vajracharya Realized Ones are the heroes of many popular folktales in which they put out fire at their home in Kathmandu by pouring tea on the floor in Lhasa, walk across rivers by singing Tantric songs, defeat Indian jugglers or Tibetan lamas, and turn into animals at will.[35] Very few non-Vajracharyas identify Vajracharyas as bodhisattvas; all know stories about powerful Vajracharyas who attained success/powers (*siddhi*). The popular stories focus on the magical powers of the Realized One, but they are also aware that these depend on an advanced spiritual state expressed and obtained through strict observance of purity rules and devotion to the gods: a loss of singlemindedness, for instance deception by a woman, can lead to the holy man's downfall. Although these ideal Vajracharyas are capable of impressive magical feats, it would be a mistake to see them purely as magicians. This applies *a fortiori* to ordinary practising Vajracharyas, whose main *raison d'être* as far as lay people are concerned is as ritual technician and religious expert. That they also may have a reputation for magical knowledge is due in part to the theory underlying the rituals they perform for their patrons, a theory which we must now briefly examine.

Vajracharya practice: Control of deities, self-divinization, or the realization of emptiness?

Vergati (1975: 315) criticized Greenwold for ignoring 'the social consequences of the [Mahayana Buddhist] belief in non-duality. If everything is empty there is no difference between good and evil. There is therefore nothing surprising in the fact that the Vajracharyas chose to compromise with worldly values.' Is it true then that the doctrine of emptiness (*śūnyatā*) plays a direct role in legitimating the Vajracharya priesthood either in their own eyes or in those of their clients? Superficially it does not do so. It is the power to control deities (plus the sanction of tradition) which legitimates Vajracharya priests as far as the laity is concerned, and it is the altruism of the bodhisattva which is most often invoked by Vajracharyas themselves.

One theme which recurs in the folktales referred to is the control of deities (or other supernatural beings) by a Realized One: he can force them to come and stay in a particular place. One of the best-known stories, which is in fact an important myth since it legitimates and gives the origin of the cult of Matsyendranath, tells how the Vajracharya Bandhudatta brings back the god Karunamaya from Kamarupa (Assam) in order to end a twelve-year drought. This myth also expresses another facet of Vajracharyas' power, which is called upon by Buddhists and Hindus alike: their ability to control holy serpents (*nāga*) and cause rain during a drought.[36]

Whenever a Vajracharya priest performs a complex ritual he likewise controls deities: he begins by setting up a holy waterpot (*kalaśa*) and various other ritual objects and containers on a row of unhusked rice (the throne, *āsan*), and he then summons (*sādhan yāye*) various deities into the pot and objects by a process of ritualized meditation (Plates 1 and 10). Once the deities are present the complex worship, performed by the sponsor (*jajmān, jaymā*) of the ritual under the Vajracharya's direction, may begin.

In accordance with these popular perceptions the ritual texts of the Vajracharyas do indeed talk of summoning (Sanskrit *ākṛṣ* or *āhve*) deities and then offering them worship (*pūjā*). Equally important however is the fact that certain forms of the deity are summoned out of the Vajracharya himself (Sanskrit *bhāv* or *vibhāv*) and that he identifies himself with the deity.[37] If one asks a Newar Buddhist directly, 'Is a Vajracharya priest identical with the deities he summons down for a ritual?' the answer is likely to be 'No, of course not'.[38] On the commonsense level— which includes the understanding of many Vajracharya priests who recite their texts by heart without being able to analyse or explain them—the officiant summons deities but he is not identical with them. His power to do so derives from knowing the prescribed form of Sanskrit utterance, and in particular the personal mantras of the deity to be summoned. The term *sādhan yāye* in Newari refers to the meditation on the deity performed by the Vajracharya priest in which he holds the five-coloured thread (*pañcasūtrakā, pasūkā*) and *vajra* in his right hand and counts his rosary with the left. Most Newars who know this term understand it as a technical term to refer to the 'pulling down' and installing (*sālāḥ taye*) of a deity. What this 'folk' understanding omits is the priest's identification with the visualized deity which is part of *sādhana* according to the texts.

Ordinary Newars would acknowledge that Vajracharyas have to imitate the deities they worship: they carry bell and vajra like Vajrasattva, and hold them like him; they wear a crown of the same sort with the Five Buddhas on it. In this they are no different from other holy orders: monks imitate the Lord Buddha, Shaivite ascetics dress like Lord Shiva, and so on. However, imitating the deity is one thing, identity another. Popularly a kind of identity is thought to occur at death: those who are 'saved' (*taray juyāḥ wane*) are sometimes thought to become one with (*līn juye*, literally 'merge into') the deity.[39] This is rather a theistic Hindu conception: it is expressed at the end of the Buddhist story, already referred to, of bringing Karunamaya to Nepal: Bandhudatta, the Buddhist priest, merges into the right foot of Karunamaya's image, the king Narendradeva into the left, and the farmer into the deity's seat (Locke 1973: 48).

So far as the 'commonsense' view is concerned, identity with the deity in this life is obtained in secret—not by mystic meditation but by controlled possession. Newar Buddhists who have taken Tantric Initiation have dressed in the bone ornaments of the secret Tantric deities (Chakrasamvara and Vajravarahi) and been possessed by them, even if only in a ritualized manner. During the Tantric Initiation ritual, and at many other regular esoteric rites, the identification of the main priest with Vajrasattva is made clear in dance; and even more so, the identification of his wife with Vajravarahi. In secret rites she (or, if not she, the senior unwidowed woman of the household or lineage sponsoring the ritual) must be possessed by Vajravarahi in order to distribute to all the participants the goddess' blessing (here: rice beer in a skull-bowl). The modernizing apologist for Tantric Buddhism tends to see the identity of practitioner and deity as a therapeutic metaphor: the tradition presents it more as controlled possession by the deity induced by mantras.[40]

In short, the identification of Vajracharya and deity is only very indirectly an important element in the legitimation of priesthood, whereas the power of the priest to force the deity to be present is directly and cognitively so.[41] The mystical teaching of emptiness—that ultimately everything is empty of essence, and all conceptual distinctions are void—was certainly a crucial philosophical legitimation of the new developments in Buddhism which took place in the first millennium CE. It is also an essential part of the doctrinal teachings given in Tantric Initiation, and the small minority of Newar Buddhists who are philosophically inclined understand its importance and discuss it. All Newars would allow that a Realized One must understand mystical truths. But the concept of emptiness is too remote, even for those who know of it, to play any active role in legitimating the Vajracharya priesthood. In the eyes of Newar Buddhists it is rather the set of *attitudes* and *actions*—which in canonical texts are justified by reference to the emptiness and mind-only doctrines[42]— that legitimate Vajracharya pre-eminence: treating all the universe alike, thus being able to frequent dangerous and impure places, archetypically cremation grounds; consequently possessing power over deities and other forces which can be used for good or evil.[43] At the same time, paradoxically, the Vajracharya has to observe purity taboos very strictly. The texts explain this as following the rules so as not to frighten 'the world', i.e. ordinary people. Vajracharyas themselves see it as part of their religious vocation. The paradox of following purity rules more strictly than others while understanding—unlike them—that they are unimportant, is only dimly perceived, if at all, in common parlance.

For the laity then it is primarily the symbol of the *siddha*, plus the restraint associated with a ritualized, Tantric version of monasticism, that legitimate the superior status and hereditary vocation of the Vajracharya. The Vajracharyas themselves however, though equally believing in the importance of these two ideals, often stress the altruism of the bodhisattva, their vocation to help others, as their *raison d'être*. Thus in a local text, the Manjushri-Parajika (Rules of Conduct expounded by the Buddha to Manjushri), the Vajracharya is defined thus:

If one is a Vajracharya he must act for all the world, that is to say, for the good of all beings. Whoever, being a Vajracharya, acts thus in accordance with scripture, will obtain both release and worldly enjoyment. [translated from the Newari rendering of M.R. Vajracharya 1985: 9]

Although acting for all beings, the Vajracharya cannot save them himself, but can only help them to help themselves. Spiro contrasts the monk and the priest:

As the Burmese see it ... the monk's duty is to save himself: and the layman's duty is to provide him with the physical requirements by which he can devote his energies to that end ... Whereas in Christianity, for example, it is the duty of the priest, by his sacramental functions, to assist the layman to achieve salvation, in Buddhism it is the recognized duty of the layman to assist the monk to achieve salvation. (Spiro 1982: 287)

Certainly in this respect the Vajracharya is closer to the Catholic priest than to the Theravada monk. Yet he cannot distribute grace in the way that the Catholic priest can. In Vajrayana Buddhism, as in Theravada Buddhism, each person's salvation is in his or her own hands. Like the Theravada monk, the Vajracharya has a duty to teach, but above all to use his superior ritual knowledge and entitlement for the good of others. Whether they profit from his services depends, most Newar Buddhists would agree, on their own devotion, sincerity, and application.

Conclusion

I have attempted to show that, in order to understand how a Buddhist priesthood is possible, one must first consider the ideological hierarchy which integrates and makes sense of the many different rites and practices that Newar Buddhists call dharma. Once this hierarchy is given its due weight, it can be seen how Vajracharya priests are at once monks, householders, and priests. The images of the altruistic bodhisattva and, on the other hand, of the siddha who uses his power for the good of his parishioners, are both essential elements which tie the whole together. This is notwithstanding the fact that, because of the emphasis in Newar religion on tradition and ritual as opposed to doctrine and catechism, most of the parishioners of Vajracharya priests are only dimly aware of, and cannot themselves expound, the doctrines associated with the three images. Greenwold was right to say that 'the very basis of the Newar [Buddhist] priesthood is prior ordination as a monk' (1974a: 110) but wrong to see monkhood and priesthood as always and systematically set in opposition to each other (1974b).

Newar Buddhism was well adapted to its pre-modern context. It preserved Buddhist ideals in a society founded on caste hierarchy, close kin ties, and respect for traditions. It survived in a situation of Hindu dominance as other forms of Buddhism did not. To many of the young and educated today, however, it has come to seem too ritualistic, too time-consuming, and too expensive. In the face of modernity it appears to lack the intellectual and institutional resourcefulness shown by the Theravada and the Tibetan Mahayana forms of Buddhism. Many adherents of Newar Buddhism, particularly practising priests, wonder if it can survive the continuous decline of lay patronage and priestly application that they have witnessed in their lifetime. At the very least one must say that Newar Buddhism is in crisis. The social hierarchy preserved, and gave meaning to, the divine and ideological hierarchies. Now that the social hierarchy is rapidly metamorphosing, and new ideological models are being propagated, the hierarchy of monk, householder, and Tantric priest is indeed beginning to seem to reflective Newars like a contradiction. Nor is it realistic to expect traditional Newar Buddhists to adapt by sloughing off the Tantric element in the overall religion, as Newar Brahmans and most high-caste Hindus are doing. The Diamond Way is the very heart of Newar Buddhism: even though hidden from many of those it serves, without it all else collapses.

Notes

1. This doctrine is maintained even in the face of the (hardly surprising) desire of Theravada Buddhists to be able to perform rites to improve the lot of their deceased parents. The Theravada Buddhist technique, here as in other contexts, is to permit simple rituals which on a straightforward literal interpretation seem to imply a transfer of goods or food, but which on the canonical and cognitively accepted interpretation maintain the individualist doctrine. See Gombrich (1971: 226–40) for a brilliant dissection of the doctrinal gymnastics required in the case of death rites.

2. Hence the title of Tambiah's classic study, *Buddhism and the Spirit Cults in Northeast Thailand* (1970), and Spiro's equally classic two books, *Buddhism and Society* (1982 [1970]) and *Burmese Supernaturalism* (1967).

3. In this century Theravada Buddhism has been introduced to Nepal from India (via the Maha Bodhi Society), Burma, Sri Lanka, and latterly Thailand. See Kloppenberg 1977 and Gellner 1986: 128–37; 1992a: 321–8.

4. Tucci (1980: 11) gives a good example of the latter from a thirteenth-century Tibetan text: 'It is forbidden for the monk of the Small Vehicle [i.e. non-Mahayana Buddhism] to possess gold or silver, but for the monk who is a Bodhisattva, that is who has renounced *nirvana*, it is no sin, for he is striving for the good of his fellow men.'

5. This was the approach pioneered by Greenwold 1974b: 131. I have appropriated and adopted his title in a conscious attempt to go further in the same direction. To the hostile judgements of Hodgson, Lévi, Oldfield, and Snellgrove cited by Greenwold, one could now add the unsympathetic remarks of Slusser 1982: 296b, 298a.

6. I have coined the term 'caste subgroup' for intermarrying subsections of an endogamous caste which maintain separate socio-religious statuses (Gellner 1995a: 19–22).

7. On the history of these older titles, abandoned only in the 1950s, see Gellner (1989). Archaic tradition also recognizes various other titles, e.g. Brahmacharya Bhikshu ('celibate monk') of the *bahi* monasteries, the Chailaka ('robe-clad') initiated at a *caitya*, and the Buddha- or Bauddhacharya ('Buddhist master') of certain monasteries in Bhaktapur and elsewhere. Only the latter is still in use. All of these may be considered Sakyas for the purposes of the present discussion.

8. This was true in the early 1980s, but after 1990 there was a definite trend for middle-ranking castes who had previously allowed themselves to be recorded as Hindu to assert a Buddhist identity.

9. On this ritual, see Locke 1975, 1980: 42–7 and Gellner 1988.

10. For types of monastery, see Chapter 6. Locke (1985) is an encyclopaedic survey of all the monasteries of the Kathmandu Valley.

11. This is no longer the case because (a) people offer less than in the past; (b) it is believed that there is a much greater risk of theft, for which the guardian will be held responsible; (c) taking one's turn as guardian automatically entails further duties in the following years, culminating in the organization of the annual feast for all members (Plate 4): as there is a shortfall in monastery income, the organizers currently (1984) have to contribute about 2000 rupees each from their own pocket. Consequently there is an increasing trend to refuse one's turn as god-guardian and thereby avoid all these problems; this worries the members of Kwa Bahah, who discuss the issue frequently.

12. On this ritual, see Locke 1975; 1980: 47–50 and Gellner 1992a: 266–8; 1997b.

13. I omit from this typology Theravada and Tibetan monks, whose presence complicates the description of present-day Newar Buddhist practice considerably.

14. See further Chapters 8 and 9, below.

15. I owe this point to Alexis Sanderson, who kindly provided me with a summary of the contents of the last nine chapters (*paṭala*) of the Tantra based on the manuscript 'Hodgson 2' in the Bodleian Library, Oxford: chapters 17–21 provide herbal recipes for, i.a. indigestion, lice, sexual feats (invisibility and so on); chapter 22 gives material on the use of breath control (*vāyuyoga*) for magical acts; chapter 23 gives the signs of approaching death; chapter 24 analyses the body as made of moon (= semen) and sun (= female blood); finally, chapter 25 gives forms of the deity to be visualized so as to achieve the ultimate aim of identity with him.

16. Weber 1968 II: 426. Weber continued: 'There can be no priesthood without a cult, although there may well be a cult without a specialized priesthood. The latter was in the case in China ...'

17. For a summary of what is known about these specialists, see Gellner 1995c.

18. In Theravada Buddhism offerings made to a Buddha statue are equivalent to offerings made to the Monastic Community, which it is sinful for lay people to consume (Gombrich 1971: 119–20).

19. The only exception occurs in some monasteries which are exclusively Sakya,

e.g. Uku Bahah. Here the senior elder may carry on the cult of the Tantric deity.

20. In this connection it is interesting to note that the personal name of Sakyamuni Buddha in traditional Newar Buddhism was not, as in Theravada Buddhism, Siddhartha ('he whose aim has been achieved'), but Sarvarthasiddha ('he who has achieved all aims').

21. In my sample of 115 Vajracharyas from ward 15, Lalitpur, 22 per cent were practising priests and only 4 per cent had no other job. The discrepancies in the figures for the two cities may be due to the fact that those for Lalitpur were collected in 1984, whereas Greenwold's for Kathmandu date from 1971–2. Informants say that it has become increasingly difficult to live from the priesthood alone.

22. Material amplifying these points has since been published by others, notably by Locke (1975, 1980).

23. Vergati (1975) rightly criticized him for this. There were also two mistakes of fact not pointed out by Vergati: it is not true that only Vajracharyas take Tantric Initiation, and the initiation is of Chakrasamvara not Vajrasattva (Greenwold 1974a: 120).

24. There is a competing usage (particularly common, it seems to me, in Kathmandu) whereby Newar Buddhism is called 'Vajrayan' and Tibetan Buddhism 'Mahayan': in fact, as knowledgeable Newars are aware, both Newar and Tibetan Buddhism are equally both Mahayana and Vajrayana.

25. On the Five, Eight, and Ten Precepts in Theravada Buddhism, see Gombrich 1971: 65–6. The participants in a Newar Buddhist Observance do not utter the precepts themselves but have them read out by the officiating priest. Although the participants may not be fully aware that they have taken the precepts, they do follow them, and they are fully aware that the point of an Observance is to keep such rules. The precept about not eating at the wrong time is taken to mean that one should eat only one meal of pure food (in the case of a long ritual this may occur only at 3 p.m., and then one fasts until the next day).

26. Cf. Katz 1982: 282: 'The mahasiddha is not anithetical to the bodhisattva, just as the bodhisattva is not anithetical to the arahant; in fact, the mahasiddha is understood, within the tantric tradition, as a special case of bodhisattvas who are distinguishable by method alone.'

27. Cf. Weber 1968 II: 461: 'Asiatic religions ... knew practically nothing of dogma as an instrumentality of differentiation.'

28. The followers of the modern Theravada movement are an exception. They have a more western concept of what a religion should be, and denounce traditional Newar Buddhism as corrupt, not real Buddhism, etc. They make frequent use of the non-traditional word *andhaviśvās* (literally 'blind trust'), invented by Dayananda Sarasvati to translate the English 'superstition' (Bharati 1970: 45). The word is now an active part of the hortatory neo-Hindu, and here neo-Buddhist, vocabulary of the north Indian vernaculars, except Bengali.

29. See Locke 1980: 23–9; for the role of the Kathmandu Acharya Guthi in the dispute between Vajracharyas and Uday, see Rosser 1966: 116ff.
30. See M. Allen 1975: 56; Vergati 1979: 127; Lienhard 1996.
31. Indeed, perhaps because they do not have a more strictly *religious* sphere in which such exclusivism is practised, middle and low castes are often much fiercer in excluding outsiders from their socio-religious (*guthi*) rites and feasts.
32. This derives from *dharma dane* and means 'those carrying out á religious act'. *Dhalā dane* is nowadays a technical term and the derivation from dharma is not obvious. 'To do dharma' is used for any religiously meritorious act; and 'dharma' is used also for the merit itself (rather than *punya*) in the common phrase *dharma lāye*, to gain merit.
33. Although the 'explanation' (*khā*) of an Observance is clearly meant to be comprehensible, few participants appear to make a concerted effort to understand, and they are never made to feel that they ought to. Invariably they are tired from feasting, and, in any case, merit derives from participating and from keeping the rules, not from mentally asserting a canonical dogma. This does not mean that one's attitude of mind is irrelevant: a selfish and/ or aggressive attitude would negate any benefits to be had. On these 'explanations', see Gellner 1988: 52, 97 n. 28; 1992a: 222–4.
34. The language none the less maintains the distinction between god (Sanskrit *deva*, Newari *dyaḥ*) and bodhisattva. The great gods of Hinduism are called Mahadyah and Naraindyah. *Dyaḥ* is never appended to the Sanskritic names of the bodhisattvas: they are simply called 'Karunamaya', 'Manjusri', etc. Note that ordinary usage, in confining the term bodhisattva to the Buddha in previous lives and to Maitri Bodhisattva is extraordinarily conservative: this is exactly how the term was used in pre-Mahayana Buddhism.
35. See Sakya and Griffith 1980: 31–4 for Jamana Gubhaju defeating the Indian juggler, and ibid.: 38–41 for Surat Vajra putting out the fire and crossing the Brahmaputra river.
36. See N.J. Allen (1986) for a comparative survey of the myth and Vergati (1985) for an early version of the myth before the accretion of Hindu elements due to the changed political situation after 1769. The basic source in English is Locke 1973.
37. See Gellner 1992a: 287–92. In an exoteric rite such as the guru mandala there is meditation that one is of the form of emptiness, and summoning of the deity, but no explicit identification with the deity (Gellner 1991a). Identification with the deity worshipped is a key feature of Tantric worship in Hinduism also (Goudriaan 1979: 8; Gupta 1979: 129; Fuller 1985: 107; Sanderson 1986).
38. Partly due to the unnaturalness of the question, and partly because I failed to see its importance during fieldwork, I did not put this question to a cross-section of Newar Buddhists. The following answers, to questions sent by post, given by an elderly Tuladhar lady from Kathmandu are probably representative. What is a bodhisattva? 'A bodhisattva is someone with the

thought of enlightenment who helps everyone and has good thoughts (*citta*). *Bodhisattvas* are men, but men with thirty-two special qualities (*lakṣaṇa*).' What is a siddha? 'All gods are siddhas. They are also men. They are called *siddha* because of their great accomplishments (*tataḥdhāgu jyā*) while alive.' Can Buddhist priest (*guruju*) and god be considered identical? 'Priest and god are not identical. Priests are the gurus of men. Without them no great worship of the gods can be successful. Gods, on the other hand, are those who are already saved (*taray juye*) and now try to uplift (*uddhār yāye*) the world.'

39. Opinions on this, as on other topics, are varied. Many others refer to it simply as *nirvāṇ* (or *nirmāṇ*, sic) *juye*; or as attaining the abode of Amitabha, Sukhavati.

40. This was also the way Shaivite Tantric rites were understood in Medieval Kashmir (Sanderson 1986: 169 n.2).

41. In the same way, the Tantric Initiation of the Shaivite priests of Minaksi in Madurai clearly 'identifies priest and god ... [But] I do not mean to suggest by this that anyone actually believes that an ordinary priest is identical with the Lord of the Universe. No one does...' (Fuller 1985: 127).

42. See, e.g., Dasgupta 1974: 180–4, 193.

43. This lay belief is well expressed in a quotation given by Greenwold 1974a: 117–18. See also Chapters 8 and 9 below.

6

The Newar Buddhist Monastery:
An Anthropological and Historical Typology

•

> ... there is for historiography of any kind no more important proposition
> than [this] ...: the cause of the origin of a thing and its eventual utility,
> its actual employment and place in a system of purposes, lie worlds
> apart; whatever exists, having somehow come into being, is again and
> again reinterpreted to new ends ...
>
> Nietzsche, *The Genealogy of Morals* 2.12

Introduction

Can there be Buddhism without monks?[1] The title of M.R. Allen's article
('Buddhism without monks: the Vajrayana Religion of the Newars of
Kathmandu Valley') implies that there can, and that this is an example.
Outside South Asia, notably in Japan, Buddhism did indeed develop
non-monastic forms (Heinemann 1984). And in the modern world new
types of Buddhism have arisen which require neither monks nor monasteries and blur the monk-layman divide.[2] However, for traditional South
Asia, of which Kathmandu Valley is unquestionably a part, I would maintain against Allen that Buddhism cannot exist without monks, and that
the Sakyas and Vajracharyas of the Kathmandu Valley are monks, albeit
married householder monks.

The issue here is not the scientific one of what type of institutions should be recognized in some universal schema as monastic, but simply this: should we not start by using the concepts given in the culture to explain the way it functions (even if we then go on to show their limitations)? By this criterion the institutions and traditions of the Sakyas and Vajracharyas do indeed define them as monks. Every Sakya and Vajracharya must be a member of a Monastic Community (*saṃgha, sā*) based on a monastery (*bāhāḥ, bahī*; Skt. *vihāra*). He becomes a member by going through Monastic Initiation (*bare chuyegu*) in that monastery, a rite in which he spends four days as a monk (Locke 1975; Gellner 1988). This gives him membership, that is, the right and duty to participate in the monastery's recurrent functions, in particular to take turns as guardian (*dyahpahla*) of the principal deity. Eventually, by seniority according to time of initiation, he may become one of the five or ten elders (*sthavir, āju*) of the monastery, for which it is necessary to have taken Tantric Initiation (*dikṣa*). He is then responsible, with the other elders, for the regular worship of the monastery's Tantric deities, and will also have various other ceremonial functions. Elders are often invited to receive gifts (*pañcadān*) on auspicious occasions, particularly at weddings. The idea here (though it usually remains implicit) is that they stand for the whole Monastic Community (who would in many monasteries be too numerous to invite). At the ordination of young boys, the five most senior elders must be present and pour the consecrating waters over the new members; for this, and on certain other occasions, the elders bare their right shoulder in monastic fashion.[3] Once I asked a Vajracharya, a practising priest, if he had ever invited Theravada monks to his house. He replied: 'We ourselves are monks (*jimi he bhikṣuta*) [i.e. we don't need to].'

As monks, Sakyas and Vajracharyas have control of monastery deities, since only they may perform the daily worship (*nitya pūjā*) in monasteries. The members of other castes occasionally found a small monastery but either they turn it over entirely to Sakyas and/or Vajracharyas, or they have them come to perform the required daily ritual. A striking partial exception to this, from Kathmandu, proves (or at least illustrates) the rule: at Than Bahi in Thamel, which is owned, exceptionally for such an ancient and sizeable establishment, by Buddhist Shresthas (the Thamel Pradhans), the main shrine receives its daily worship from a Vajracharya, and for the shrine of Sinhala Sartha Bahu, a Panchthariya Shrestha is appointed: in order to be able to do this he has to go through Monastic Initiation so that he becomes an honorary Sakya for the purposes of his office.

Plate 3: The annual feast (sambhway) of all the members of Kwa Bahah, held in three sittings in Ila Nani, just behind Kwa Bahah.

In this paper it is not my intention to focus on the monastic identity of Sakyas and Vajracharyas as such but on the essential adjunct of that identity, the monastery. I shall not treat exhaustively all the details of the monastery as an institution but only introduce as much as is necessary to understand the monastery as a religious monument. For instance, Hemraj Sakya lists 167 monasteries in Lalitpur (Sakya 1956). How are we to understand this list? What types of monastery are there and what is their history? The material presented relates to Lalitpur (Np. Patan, Nw. Yala) but, I believe, my argument applies broadly to Kathmandu, Bhaktapur, and other Newar settlements as well. It should become clear that Newar monasteries, that is, all the institutions which the Newars themselves call *bahah* or *bahi*, can be understood as something more than a historical residue.

The monastery and its types

The casual observer can easily tell a Buddhist monastery from a Hindu temple. This is so, even though the principal shrine of the monastery may itself be a free-standing 'pagoda' temple similar in style to a Hindu temple. Monasteries are always set back from the road in a courtyard, so that one has to pass through a door to get to them. Hindu temples by contrast are sited in the street, or at crossroads, at points of maximum exposure. Tantric shrines of both religions, being private affairs, are secluded on the first floor of monasteries, of special god-houses (*āgāchē*), or in private houses. Their presence can usually be detected from the outside from elements of temple architecture (e.g. a small pagoda roof, *puco*).

Architecturally the Newar Buddhist monastery is defined by its possession of the following three elements:

(i) A *principal deity* (*kwābāju/kwāpādyaḥ*). This is nearly always Sakyamuni Buddha with the earth-touching gesture; occasionally he may be a form of Avalokiteshvara. He faces either east, west, or north, and the main entrance to the monastery is opposite his shrine.

(ii) A *caitya* (the most basic and ancient Buddhist cult object) in front of the main deity, in the middle of the courtyard.

(iii) A *Tantric shrine*: Upstairs in an enclosed room on the first floor (*āgā*), a secret, Tantric deity (*āgamadevatā, āgādyaḥ*), most commonly Chakrasamvara and his consort Vajravarahi.

The different types of Buddhist monastery, and their logical relationships one to the other, are represented in Chart 6.1. A word of

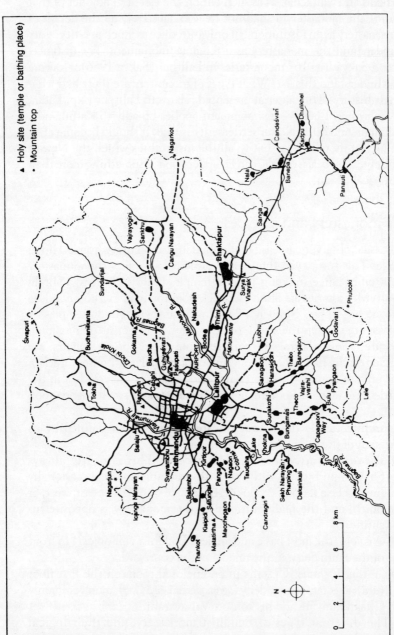

Map 6.1: Map of the Kathmandu and Banepa Valleys, showing the main Newar settlements.
Source: N. Gutschow.

caution is required, however, on the interpretation of the typology. The chart does not describe relations between particular institutions but only shows the different species within the genus 'monastery'. It shows, for instance, that lineage monasteries are a kind of branch monastery, and that branch monasteries are a type of *bahah*. It does not show, and it is not in fact the case, that all branch monasteries are branches of bahah. Some branches are independent of all other monasteries and some lineage monasteries are owned by members of *bahi*, i.e. they are branches of a bahi.

The concepts shown in Chart 6.1 have three sources. The genus 'monastery' (Skt *vihāra* or *mahāvihāra*) derives from the Buddhist Great Tradition. All the monasteries considered here count as monasteries in this sense (with the possible exception of monasteries-by-extension). From the point of view of religion and ritual no distinctions are recognized between any of them: the same ritual and the same devotion are appropriate in all of them, even though some are huge and popular shrines while others are so small that almost no one knows of their existence. The next level down shows the local concepts which have evolved to describe the different types of monastery (with different functions and identities) that actually exist on the ground. This does not mean that the different types are found only here in Nepal: I shall argue below that the distinctions may actually reflect differences found elsewhere too. Nevertheless from the strictly religious point of view, these types are irrelevant, and so the vocabulary used to describe these types is essentially local. Finally, the rest of the chart represents sub-species identified by the researcher, which make up for one important inadequacy in the local terminology, and introduce some elaborations that Newars themselves would recognize but which are not sufficiently significant to be reflected in everyday speech. A checklist of the most important characteristics serving to distinguish the different types of monastery is provided in Chart 6.2.

The three main types of monastery distinguished by local usage are, then, in order of importance:

(a) *Main monasteries* (*mū bāhāḥ*). Tradition lists eighteen of these in each of Kathmandu and Lalitpur, although in Lalitpur they are confusingly known as the Fifteen Bahah (*jhīnyāgu bāhāḥ*).[4] A few of these are small and have no more than the three elements listed above, but the rest possess other shrines as well, and some are spectacular religious complexes, having been enriched by numerous donations over the years (see Plate 2). Some of them have only Vajracharya members (e.g. Dhum Bahah), others have only Sakya members (e.g. Uku Bahah, Si Bahah,

Chart 6.1. A typology of Newar Buddhist monasteries with examples from Lalitpur

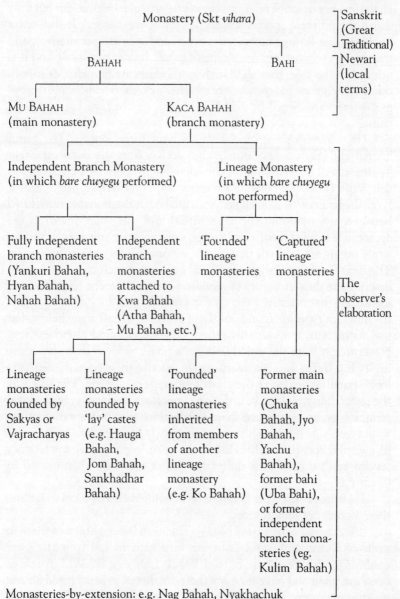

Monastery (Skt *vihara*) — Sanskrit (Great Traditional)

BAHAH   BAHI — Newari (local terms)

MU BAHAH (main monastery)   KACA BAHAH (branch monastery)

Independent Branch Monastery (in which *bare chuyegu* performed)   Lineage Monastery (in which *bare chuyegu* not performed)

Fully independent branch monasteries (Yankuri Bahah, Hyan Bahah, Nahah Bahah)

Independent branch monasteries attached to Kwa Bahah (Atha Bahah, Mu Bahah, etc.)

'Founded' lineage monasteries

'Captured' lineage monasteries

The observer's elaboration

Lineage monasteries founded by Sakyas or Vajracharyas

Lineage monasteries founded by 'lay' castes (e.g. Hauga Bahah, Jom Bahah, Sankhadhar Bahah)

'Founded' lineage monasteries inherited from members of another lineage monastery (e.g. Ko Bahah)

Former main monasteries (Chuka Bahah, Jyo Bahah, Yachu Bahah), former bahi (Uba Bahi), or former independent branch mona- steries (eg. Kulim Bahah)

Monasteries-by-extension: e.g. Nag Bahah, Nyakhachuk

Note: Newari/Nepal Bhasa terms are given in capitals. Sources of the distinctions are shown in the right-hand margin.

Chart 6.2: Principal characteristics serving to distinguish different types of the Newar Buddhist monastery

	Main monastery	Bahi of today	17th century bahi	Fully independent branch monastery	Independent branch monastery of Kwa Bahah	Lineage monastery	Monastery-by-extension	Monastery in the hills
Caitya and main deity	√	√	√	√	√	√	×	√
Tantric shrine	√	√	×	√	√	√	×	×
May have Vajracharya members	√	×	×	√	√	√	√[a]	√
Ritually established as a monastery	√	√	√	√	√	√	×	×
Has a system of god-guardians	√	√	√	√	√	√	×	×
Number of elders	10	5	?[b]	5	5	X[c]	×	×

(Chart 6.2 contd...)

(Chart 6.2 contd...)

	Main monastery	Bahi of today	17th century bahi	Fully independent branch monastery	Independent branch monastery of Kwa Bahah	Lineage monastery	Monastery-by-extension	Monastery in the hills
Has a Monastic Community (saṃgha)	√	√	√	√	√	×	×	×
Bare chuyegu performed there	√	√	√	√	√d	×e	×	√f
Can be a focus of devotion by non-members and lay castes	√	√	√	√	√	×	×	√

Notes:

'√' indicates that the type shown possesses the characteristic, 'X' that it lacks it.

(a) These 'monasteries' have no membership as such, but Vajracaryas may live there as much as Sakyas.

(b) BV does not make it clear whether there was a formal system of elders or not, but seems to imply that there was not.

(c) There are no elders (*sthavir*, *āju*), but only (*thakāli*), as in any *guthi*.

(d) Half of the ceremony takes place in Kwa Bahah (Gellner 1987: 400–1).

(e) This is only performed exceptionally, for the sons of Sakya or Vajracharya fathers by lower-caste mothers.

(f) *Bare chuyegu* has only been performed in these monasteries in recent times (since 1951).

Plate 4: Three of the ten senior elders of Kwa Bahah, a Vajracharya flanked by two Sakyas (note the different caps) (1986).

Guji Bahah), and the rest have both. Nearly two-fifths of the members of the main monasteries are Vajracharyas and the rest are Sakyas.[5] I shall refer to all monasteries using their Newari name, even though this will have a colloquial and non-honorific ring to Nepali ears. (The Sanskrit titles are long and unwieldy, and even locals often do not remember them.)

(b) The bahī. In Lalitpur there are twenty-five bahi and in Kathmandu sixteen. They are distinguished by the fact that they have only Sakyas and no Vajracharyas. (This is how it is explained today: traditionally the members of the Lalitpur bahi called themselves Brahmacharya Bhikshu, not Sakya.) The bahi are also architecturally distinct, and they have very few members compared to bahah. None the less some of the bahi possessed much guthi land until recently.

(c) Branch Monasteries (kacā bāhāḥ). There are two distinct types of branch monastery:

(c)[†] Lineage Monasteries. This is the most common, though least conspicuous, type of monastery. In Lalitpur there are over 130 lineage monasteries. They are branch monasteries founded by individual members of (a), (b), or (c)[††]as an act of religious merit, and endowed with land for their upkeep and the performance of annual ceremonies in the name of the founder. They are modelled on the main monasteries, but are usually much smaller. Many consist of no more than a *caitya* and a diminutive shrine of the Buddha, the Tantric shrine being merely a locked room in one of the adjacent houses; in a few cases the Tantric shrine has been omitted, and in others it is now abandoned. Often they have been built at the same time as, and as an integral part of, the founder's home. The monastery and its lands belong to the descendants of the founder, and this may comprise many households if he is genealogically distant. I have called them lineage monasteries because they usually belong to a single lineage. Many of them now belong to a single family, however, as lands are lost and members abandon the duties associated with the monastery.

Anyone may found a lineage monastery—it is thought of simply as founding a monastery—be he a member of a main monastery, of a bahi, or of an independent branch monastery, be he Vajracharya, Sakya, or other caste. The only problem is the expense. The founder's descendants, so long as they are prepared to keep up the ritual obligations, will constitute the membership. But membership of a lineage monastery is not essential to the identity of Sakyas and Vajracharyas: many do not have one; those who do simply see it as similar to any religious association (guthi) they belong to, that is, as a worthy thing, but one which may depend on one's means and religiosity. It is quite otherwise with the main monastery, bahi, or independent branch monastery where a Sakya or Vajracharya is initiated (takes *bare chuyegu*). He can renounce his membership of the lineage monastery if he finds its duties onerous or if he quarrels with the rest of the clan, but he must maintain membership in his main monastery, bahi, or independent branch monastery on pain of outcasting. Monastic Initiation is never performed in lineage monasteries, except that sons of a Vajracharya or a Sakya father by a lower-caste mother, who will not be accepted by the father's Monastic Community, are sometimes made to go through the ritual at a nearby *caitya*, which is likely to be in the father's lineage monastery if he has one.

(c)[††] *Independent Branch Monasteries*. For the second and distinct type of branch monastery (*kacā bāhāḥ*) the term 'branch' is in fact something of a misnomer: though known as branches, these monasteries are actually independent and initiate their own members. In their case the term 'branch' simply expresses the fact that they are not included in the set of eighteen main monasteries, and not the fact that they were founded, as a supererogatory act of merit, by individual members of main monasteries. In Lalitpur these independent branches are small and, like bahi, have only five elders, not ten as in the main monasteries.[6] In Kathmandu, by contrast, independent branches are both more numerous and have larger Monastic Communities than in Lalitpur; the refusal to grant them the title 'main monastery' looks in Kathmandu like a Vajracharya prejudice against exclusively Sakya monasteries.

A glance at Chart 6.1 will show that, whereas bahi and main monasteries are homogeneous categories, the branch monasteries form a heterogeneous group. The reason for this is that, of the three terms used in Newari, 'branch monastery' is, to a certain extent, a residual category. That is, a branch monastery is a monastery which is not either a main monastery or a bahi. Hence 'kaca bahah' is used to cover two distinct types of institution: lineage monasteries and independent branch monasteries.

Within these, further sub-types can be distinguished, but the schema is my own elaboration. I have not given Newari equivalents of the sub-types, because there are none in common use. The failure of the language to distinguish between lineage monasteries and independent branch monasteries is admittedly a confusion. But the lack of names for the further internal differentiation of lineage monasteries shown in Chart 6.1 is not: they all function alike, and what I have distinguished, in order to help the reader are merely the different historical routes by which lineage monasteries have reached the present. For example, the membership of one bahi evidently died out many years ago, and now-adays, though still called Uba Bahi, it functions as a lineage monastery belonging to members of Uku Bahah. Similarly, three main monasteries, though still treated as such by non-members on certain ritual occasions have become no more than lineage monasteries; evidently their original membership died out, and they were inherited by Sakyas or Vajracharyas belonging to other main monasteries. The chronicle, BV,[7] records that King Siddhi Narasingh granted Chuka Bahah to a Vajracharya from Nyakhachuk who was a member of Kwa Bahah (BV: 129b–130a). His descendants still live there today. According to them he was called Kulapad and received Chuka Bahah for helping the king complete a fire sacrifice in front of the Krishna temple in Mangal Bazaar.

A final type to be included is the monastery-by-extension. In Newari *bāhāḥ* (and in Nepali *bāhāl*) has come to mean any courtyard with Buddhist associations. Thus Nag Bahah/Nag Bahal is the modern name for a large and well-known courtyard inhabited by members of Kwa Bahah. To locals and especially to the older generation it is known as

'Ilanhe'. 'Nag Bahah', locals insist, is a name only recently given to it by outsiders because of the holy serpents (*nāg*) painted on the wall of the two shelters there. Now it has won general acceptance and is the official and more widely known name.[8]

One further category, not included in the typology since it is a modern development, is constituted by the monasteries to be found in the bazaar towns of the Nepalese hills where there are concentrations of Newar Buddhists. I have visited myself Suvarnavarna Mahavihara (Arughat), Mahachaitya Vihara and Ananda Vihara (Tansen) (Plate 6), and Padmachaitya Vihara (Butwol). Except for the first, which was founded in 1921 on the initiative of a Newar Mahayana monk,[9] the others only recently came to be considered as monasteries, though they are holy sites, with *caityas* of 100 years' standing or more. Indeed, by the traditional criteria of the Valley they are not monasteries: they lack a Tantric shrine, they have none of the institutional structure of the traditional Newar monastery (elders, god-guardians), and the deities there were established separately, not together as a monastery.[10] Nowadays they are often also used for Theravada rituals and Theravada monks and nuns often live in them.

Plate 5: The seniormost elder of Kwa Bahah is carried in a duli to invite other monasteries of Lalitpur to the Samyak festival (photo by Mark Felsenthal, 1984).

Main monasteries

The main monasteries include the most conspicuous and well-known Buddhist monuments of Lalitpur. A few main monasteries are small, nothing distinguishing them architecturally from the larger branch monasteries. But most of them are large and imposing shrines, made more and more ornate by votive offerings over the years. The larger ones are important landmarks for Buddhist and non-Buddhist alike, which seems to have been the case in the past as well: two localities (*twāḥ*) in Lalitpur are called after monasteries which no longer exist: Ko Bahah and Ga Bahah.[11]

Most of the main monasteries are built around a courtyard 10 or 15 metres square, and in those of them with a large and well-organized membership, this courtyard is wholly given over to religion. Kwa Bahah, Uku Bahah, Ha Bahah, Cho Bahah, and Guji Bahah are of this type. Others were probably once complete courtyards like this, but nowadays part of the court is owned and lived in by individual members of the monastery. Ten of the eighteen main monasteries fall into this category. In yet others the main shrine of the monastery is a free-standing temple, and there probably never was a complete courtyard of the type found in Kwa Bahah. Bu Bahah with its giant residential courtyard is of this sort, and so is Bhinche Bahah. Kipu Bahi in Kirtipur also has a freestanding shrine: it was founded in 1514 by Vajracharyas from Lalitpur on an ancient Buddhist site: it faces a *stūpa* attributed, like those in Lalitpur, to Ashoka. It is therefore an exception to the rule that Buddhist monasteries are always found in an enclosed courtyard. The suitability of the site in other ways evidently overruled the convention in this case.

In all the main monasteries, whatever the type of courtyard they occupy, the focus is the principal deity (*kwābāju*). In front of him there is always an ancient *caitya* belonging to the monastery: in Kwa Bahah there is room only for one, and this has been enshrined, with a complete and elaborate temple built around it (its roof is visible bottom left in Plate 2). Elsewhere individual members have established *caityas* beside the original one, as well as other statues, and a particular cultic form, dedicated to Manjushri, known as *dharmadhātu*.[12] In monasteries such as Bu Bahah, where there is plenty of room, there is a veritable forest of *caityas* and other cult objects in front of the principal deity.

The principal Tantric deity of the monastery is always on the first floor in a small enclosed room; sometimes this is found directly above the main (non-Tantric) deity, but it can also be to one side, or on the side of the courtyard facing the main deity. This is known as the *āgā*; the deity is usually known simply as *āgādyaḥ*, 'god of the *āgā*' (Skt *āgamade-vatā*). Most adult members of the monastery will be aware of the deity's Sanskritic identity (usually Chakrasamvara and his consort Vajravarahi), but outsiders (except for Vajracharyas who are professionally concerned with such things) will not.

All main monasteries have the three necessary elements listed above: (i) principal deity, (ii) *caitya*, and (iii) Tantric shrine on the first floor. Most main monasteries also have the following features:

(iv) *digi*: this is a long antechamber outside the Tantric shrine in which various rituals relating to the Tantric deity are performed. It usually covers all of one side of the monastery courtyard.

 (v) *gumpā* (Tibetan for monastery): This is a long room on the first floor of the north wing where the principal deity is east-facing, or of the west wing where he is north-facing. It is used for the performance of the monthly fast to Amoghapasha Lokeshvara (the *aṣṭamī vrata*) and the main shrine there is to him. This room is known as the *gumpa* because in Kwa Bahah and Uku Bahah it has been done up in the Tibetan style for the use of (Newar) monks of the Tibetan tradition; traditionally it seems to have been called *dharmāgāra* (Skt 'religion room'), but except in learned circles this word is now obsolete.

(vi) *Vajrasattva shrine*: Those main monasteries with Vajracharya members always have a shrine to the Buddha Vajrasattva, in which they alone may serve as guardian (*dyahpahla*). Possession of such a shrine is one of the marks and duties of the association of monastery Vajracharyas (*ācārya guthi, ācā gu*). Theologically Vajrasattva is identified with Adibuddha ('Original Buddha'), the absolute. But the idea of him which most Newars, and most Vajracharyas, have, though not inconsistent with this, is that he is the archetypal Vajracharya, the teacher (guru) of all Vajracaryas. Like the Vajracharya when he performs rituals for his parishioners, Vajrasattva sits cross-legged with his feet tucked up on his thighs (Skt *padmāsana*); like them, he holds the bell (*ghaṇṭā, gā*) in his left hand and the vajra, symbol of Tantric Buddhism, in his right hand.

In addition to this, the large monasteries may have numerous other shrines, established collectively, as well as the icons offered and consecrated by individuals. At Kwa Bahah there has clearly been a conscious attempt to turn the whole courtyard into a series of shrines, all of which can be visited one after the other as the pious make their morning rounds.

The structure of the monastery was explained to me on several occasions as follows. The shrine of the main deity, and the ground floor of the monastery in general, is (the sphere of) the Disciples' Way/Vehicle (Shravakayana); upstairs in the gumpa where all [clean-caste] devotees are also admitted and fasts to Lokeshvara are performed is (the sphere of) the Great Way (Mahayana); and the Tantric shrine, into which access is restricted, is (the sphere of) the Diamond Way (Vajrayana). The pattern is implicit in the organization of the monastery, the types of ritual performed in each place, and the degree of access permitted. Most Buddhists would not be capable of expounding this schema—they leave that to Vajracharyas—but it is a sound and authoritative representation all the same.

The bahi or 'outer' monasteries

Opposed to the class of bahah is the class of bahi. In both are found the principal deity, *caitya*, and Tantric shrine, the three defining characteristics of the Newar Buddhist monastery. Whereas the main monasteries (*mū bāhāḥ*) often have an extremely large membership, some of whom are wealthy men, the bahi almost invariably have few members and they are all poor.[13] Only 8.75 per cent of the total Vajracharya-and-Sakya population of Lalitpur belong to bahi.[14]

A folk etymology sometimes given for bahi and recorded in Wright's history (1972: 237) derives it from Skt *bahis*, outside, the point being that the members of the bahi 'did not live in cities but in forests'. The Sanskrit form of both bahah and bahi, is *vihāra* as used by Newars today and in all historical records. Some western commentators have explained the term bahi as meaning 'minor' or 'lesser monastery'.[15] While this has no justification in present Newari usage, it has some claim to represent the Newar idea of the bahi.

Whether or not the etymology from Skt 'outside' is correct, it is certainly not, or not principally, *physical* exteriority which is expressed. Most of the bahi are in fact well within the city and their members do not live, and probably never have lived, in forests, as claimed by the chronicle. By calling them 'outside' or 'outer monasteries', the lower status of the bahi is expressed, that is, from the point view of the bahah they represent only the lowest, exoteric teachings of Buddhism. The fact that they have only five elders, whereas the main monasteries have ten, may also have been intended to express their peripheral nature: the monastic code (*vinaya*) of early Buddhism relates how the Buddha permitted five monks to initiate new members in outlying areas, although

Plate 6: Ananda Vihar in Tansen (1983). It combines elements from both traditional Newar Buddhism (the caitya, dharmadhātu, and vajra) and the modern Theravāda movement (the modern Buddha image in the background); it lacks the institutional framework of a traditional monastery.

ten were necessary in the metropolis (Frauwallner 1956: 90–1). It is tempting to assume that the old tradition of the monastic code was consciously used to translate into a spatial idiom the hierarchical relationship between different institutions and the levels of doctrine they represent.

Whatever the correct analysis of the term bahi may be, the bahah represent, and have for long represented, the culturally and numerically dominant form. When someone establishes a new lineage monastery, it is always called bahah in the vernacular, even when it is founded by the member of a bahi. The bahi form a category which cannot be added to. They are treated in the culture as a leftover, whose time has passed; or, from the viewpoint of the bahi themselves, as the proud reminder of purer though irrecoverable past.

It is therefore impossible to explain the nature of the bahi without invoking their history. The main reason for this is that Newar Buddhists themselves traditionally explain the differences between bahah and bahi in historical terms; but a further twist is given by the fact that many of these differences have been eroded in the last sixty years. For many young Sakyas there is left only the feeling that the bahi are poorer, more dilapidated, and less desirable places to belong to. Locke records the following learned view of the bahi:

One informant gave me the following explanation ... [I]n the days when all of these communities were open to any qualified candidate, the *bahis* were a lower class of *vihara* where the *bhiksu* would receive his first training. After completing his training he would become an *upasampradaya* [sic] *bhiksu* and join a *baha* where he would study further and receive further training which would eventually entitle him to become a Vajracarya ... It might well be [Locke concludes] that the *bahis* were the last surviving communities of celibate monks (true *brahmacarya bhiksus*) which lost many of their members by 'graduation' to the married Vajrayana communities of the later *bahas*. Finally, they too succumbed to the new trend in order to survive, but maintained their separate identity and traditions.[16]

There are certainly many characteristics of the bahi differentiating them from bahah which suggest (or rather, as I shall argue, were meant to suggest) that the bahi are survivals from the time of genuine monastic practice, though it must be added that for most members of the bahi these differences are no longer important. It is none the less possible to reconstruct what the traditional bahi-identity was and thereby to understand how the bahi made skilful use of ritual and architecture to assert a 'purer-than-thou' superiority to the bahah-mainstream which so greatly outnumbered them.

Characteristics of bahi not found in bahah

Architecture

1. Open halls on the ground floor of the bahi and semi-open verandas on the first floor.[17]
2. A walkway around the back of the main deity, so that it can be circumambulated.
3. A flight of steps leading up to the main entrance.[18] This follows from the fact that, unlike bahah, bahi are often situated on higher ground (Becker-Ritterspach 1982: 310).
4. The Tantric deity of a bahi is enclosed in a small windowless room on the first floor, sometimes above the main deity, sometimes to one side. This contrasts with bahah in which the Tantric shrine is completely incorporated into the overall structure of the building: its position is shown by the fivefold window (*pañcajhyā, pasukājhyā*) which is an external symbol of Tantric shrines in both Buddhism and Hinduism.

Social

5. In Lalitpur (but not in Kathmandu) the members of bahi take the Sanskrit title Brahmacharya Bhikshu, 'celibate monk'. (Nowadays they prefer to call themselves Sakya, and the older title is today found only in inscriptions and in ritual contexts.) This title implies real monasticism and expresses a claim to descent from the last real monks of Nepal. It is tacitly opposed to 'Sakyavamsha' and 'Sakyabhikshu' (traditional titles of all other Sakyas) who are, by implication, monks only in virtue of descent from Lord Buddha. The colloquial Newari equivalent of Brahmacharya Bhikshu is 'Bhikkhu Bare', 'monk Bare';[19] it is recognized but is disrespectful, and I did not hear it used spontaneously: the normal way to refer to them in Lalitpur today is simply as *bahīpī*, 'those of the bahi'.

In the Malla period the members of bahi in Lalitpur seem in most cases to have been called simply *bhikṣu*, 'monk'. Thus in Cikā Bahi (Plate 7) the first inscription to use the title 'Brahmacharya Bhikshu' occurs in 1850 (NS 970): all those from the eighteenth century and before refer simply to Bhikshu so-and-so. However the title 'Brahmacharya Bhikshu' of a member of Guita Bahi does occur already in an inscription of 1516 (D.R. Regmi 1965 III: 104) and in some other documents thereafter.[20]

6. There are no Vajracharyas in the bahi (with the partial exception cited below under (7)).

Plate 7: Cikā Bahi, viewed from the east (1984). The temples of Taleju and Degutale, which form part of the royal palace at the city centre, can be seen in the background. Both the side wings have since been rebuilt using modern techniques and corrugated iron roofs.

Organization

7. Unlike the main monasteries, each of which has its own Monastic Community (*samgha*), the bahi of Lalitpur were traditionally divided into two samghas, that of the Ten Bahi and that of the Fifteen.[21] All the members of the bahi of each group formed a single Monastic Community with a single set of five elders[22] and held a single annual feast (*samghabhojan, sambhway*) which took place in each bahi of the group by turn. This system broke down among the Ten Bahi around 1930. By contrast, although five bahi broke away earlier, the ten remaining of the group of Fifteen maintained a single Monastic Community until 1972. Now, except where there are too few members,[23] each bahi constitutes a separate association. What follows is due to informants from Cikā Bahi, one of the Fifteen. Most of it probably applies *pari passu* to the group of Ten Bahi, though I was unable to find a sufficiently aged informant to confirm or confute this assumption.

The group of Fifteen Bahi had five elders (*sthavir, āju*) and one assistant (*upādhyāya*—usually pronounced, and often written, *upādhyā*) who were the six most senior men of the Monastic Community. Below them in order of seniority came four *karṇi*, made up as follows: one *bhalī* (feast-preparer), responsible for making the buffalo-meat pieces (*chwaylā*) served at the end of rituals, who used always to come from Nhaykan Bahi; two assistants to the monastery priest who, like him, came from Na Bahi; finally, a *ṭikādhārī* from Pucho Bahi Chway, who placed the golden spot (*lūcī*, Skt *tilaka*) on the forehead of boys taking Monastic Initiation. In Cikā Bahi these roles (except the two assistants to the monastery priest) have been preserved, though now of course they are filled by members of Cikā Bahi itself (Plate 8).

8. Each of the two Monastic Communities, the Ten Bahi and the Fifteen, has its own hereditary priest (*sā gubhāju*) who is one of their own number. The group of Fifteen is served by a man from Na Bahi (Np. Naka Bahil), and the group of Ten by a man from Jyaba Bahi. The monastery priest comes at Monastic Initiation, the annual feast, and at the festival of Panchadan; he also came traditionally to read scriptural stories (*bākhā*) at death. At the same time each bahi household also has its own hereditary domestic priest (*purohit*), a Vajracharya from a bahah and therefore not a member of the bahi association: he performs life-cycle rites (including ancestor worship) and any other rituals in the home or lineage monastery.

Thus there is or was a clear division of labour, with no parallel in the bahah between the monastery priest, performing all rituals to do with the bahi and its members' monastic identity, on the one hand, and the ordinary Vajracharya, performing all the rites relating to their life as householders, on the other. This system of monastery priests still operated in the 1980s in Cikā Bahi, Nhaykan Bahi, I Bahi, Bunga Bahi, Way Bahi, Kipu Bahi, Pucho Bahi, and Na Bahi itself. Among the Ten Bahi only Iba Bahi, Khway Bahi, and Jyaba Bahi maintain the old system. Elsewhere bahi-members had started to call their domestic priests even for monastic rituals, as bahah-members do.

9. Whenever any member of the Monastic Community died, the current god-guardian (*dyahpahla*) of each bahi of the samgha had to come to carry the corpse in the funeral procession. This custom was onerous because it

Plate 8: A performance of nāyaḥ luyegu, *the consecration of a new elder, in Cikā Bahi (28/4/84). The elders and other officers of the bahi are performing the guru mandala rite, with which all complex rituals begin. The far row comprises the new monastery priest and the four elders in order of seniority. The near row comprises the new elder (who is to 'become Amoghasiddhi', the fifth Buddha), the Upadhayaya (with the text, the Pancaraksa, in front of him), the Tikadhari, and, last, the current god-guardian of the bahi. The Bhali was absent. In front of the seniormost elder is the new elder's son who acted as sponsor (jajmān, jaymā) of the ceremony. The helmets (mukuṭ, mukhaḥ) of the monastery priest and the four elders can be seen on the left in order of seniority from right to left. The helmet of the new elder is just out of the picture beyond them.*

Plate 9: The sponsor of the rite (see Plate 8) anoints the feet (licāykegu) of one of the elders of Cikā Bahi.

meant that whenever a Sakya died belonging, say, to Way Bahi in Way (Chapagaon), seven kilometres south of Lalitpur, the god-guardians of all the Lalitpur bahi of the group of Fifteen had to go there immediately.

Ritual

10. When Monastic Initiation is performed by the monastery priest, unlike in bahah of Lalitpur, there is no fire sacrifice (*yajña, jog*) and the whole ritual is performed in the open. On the fourth day, when the boy abandons his monk's robes, the rite is performed before the Tantric deity of bahi, not in the boy's home. Moreover it is performed by the monastery priest and not by the boy's domestic priest, whereas in most bahah the rite of returning to lay life is wholly in the hands of the latter.

11. Since most bahi-members live in the immediate vicinity of the bahi

Plate 10: *A member of Cikā Bahi, whose father died seven days previously, sits in front of the principal deity of the bahi while his domestic priest (purohit) prepares for him to perform the first of two purifying fire sacrifices. The second will take place in the ground floor of his own home (1983).*

or even, if very poor, in the bahi itself, when someone dies the bahi must also be purified on the seventh day. The fire sacrifice ritual (*gṛhaśuddhi, ghaḥsū*) has therefore to be performed twice, first in front of the main deity of the bahi and subsequently in the ground floor of the deceased person's home. Actually this also occasionally occurs in bahah too in the case of those who live right next to it, but the vast majority of bahah-members, even when living in adjacent courtyards, perform ghahsu only once, in their own homes. Similarly, bahi-members throw rice balls (*piṇḍa, pyā*) and other remains of the ancestor worship ceremony in their bahi, a practice rarely found in the bahah.

Iconography

12. The Tantric deity of the bahi is always referred to as *ajidyaḥ,* grandmother goddess, and is therefore thought of as female; she is identified as Vajravarahi. In bahah, by contrast, the Tantric deity is always called *āgādyaḥ* and thought of as predominantly male. This, however, is popular usage: from the doctrinal point view, since they are both Tantric deities, they are always in the company of their consort, i.e. Vajravarahi

is accompanied by Chakrasamvara and vice versa. So far as I know, the rituals performed to the Tantric deity of a bahi are no different to those performed in a bahah.

13. It is popularly believed (though not in fact universally true) that every bahi has a square stone with nine circles on it, called a *guphā manda* (ninefold mandala). Folk mythology has it that Ashoka put them there for Buddhists to use as a Gaya-stone (*gayālhwā*),[24] i.e. a place to throw the rice offerings from ancestor worship, instead of taking them to the nearest sacred river (in Lalitpur, the Bagmati). It does seem be the case that every bahi has a Gaya-stone, even if not in the form of a *guphā manda*.

14. As Hemraj Sakya (1979: 98) was the first to point out, the term *gandhurīdyaḥ* is used in inscriptions only of the main deity of a bahi, never of a bahah. The most likely etymology seems to me to be from *gandhakuṭī*, Skt 'perfumed hut', an ancient honorific originally used to describe the place, wherever it was, that the Buddha happened to be staying. In Theravada Buddhism *kuti* is still the term used for the room in which a monk lives (Bunnag 1973: 86). Strong (1977) has summarized the evidence and shows that in India, Tibet, and elsewhere the term came to mean the shrine-room housing a Buddha image. Particularly evocative in the Nepalese context is the Divyavadana story of Sangharakshita descending to the palace of the Nagas under the ocean and being shown the gandhakuṭī of Sakyamuni and the six previous Buddhas. He is then told to sweep the *maṇḍalaka* of the Blessed One, make salutation to the *caitya*, eat, and prepare his bed (ibid.: 402). As I have described, the principal deity of a Newar monastery always has a *caitya* before his shrine. There is also a *dhāmanda* or mandala for sprinkling water and rice during the daily ritual immediately in front of the doorway of the shrine, and this must be what is referred to as maṇḍalaka. It looks as if the Divyavadana is here describing the duties of a god-guardian (*dyahpahla*).[25]

Folk history/mythology

15. According to local tradition, now largely forgotten, the present incumbents of the bahi are the descendants of the last monks among the Newars. The ninety-year-old senior (*thakāli*) of Cikā Bahi told me:

When the bahi were inhabited by married Sakyabhikshus who worked for their living, there were still Brahmacharya Bhikshus, unmarried monks, who did no work, in the bahi. In the bahah they did Tantric rituals, had guthis [i.e. annual ritual obligations] but in the bahi all they had to do was keep the rule of celibacy (*brahmacarya pālay yāye*). Then one day the king decided that the 1200 *ropani* of land belonging to Konti Bahi was too much, and he took the land to feed his soldiers. "Since you live by begging," he said, "go ahead and beg!" Eventually they had to marry and find work, although the sixty-four kinds of work had already been given out to the sixty-four castes. So they did as the Sakyavamsha were doing.

This account claims to be history but is really myth, since it is not placed in any period. With economy and conciseness it expresses the present-day distinctiveness of the bahi while at the same time explaining why they are no longer celibate.

I overheard the same elder explain to the new and inexperienced monastery priest (who had only recently taken over from his deceased father) that their traditions in the bahi were a higher way (*yāna*) than that of the Vajracharyas: he should call himself a Bhikshu-Acharya, not a Vajracharya, as he did not need the Vajracharya's bell and vajra. (In fact he does make use of these implements, though he does not perform fire sacrifice.)

Significance of the differences between bahah and bahi

Nearly all of these differences between the bahi and the bahah can be interpreted as illustrating or meant to illustrate the closer proximity of the former to the genuine monasticism of the past. The architecture of the bahi is indeed clearly monastic, and the circumambulatory passage around the main deity goes back to the rock chapels of western India of the last century BCE, in which the main cult object was a *caitya*, not a statue of the Buddha.[26] However architecture is one thing, and social rules and customs are another. Several of the most striking differences between bahah and bahi in fact date only from the reforms of Siddhi Narasingh in the seventeenth century (see below).[27] It would seem that the members of the bahi deliberately constructed an archaic identity for themselves by not changing the architecture of their monasteries, and by calling themselves 'celibate monks' (though they were married) in opposition to the 'Sakya lineage' monks of the bahah.

Unfortunately most of this is a matter of historical reconstruction. Nowadays very few members of the bahi care, or can afford to care, about the special traditions which they have inherited. Even if only partially understood, they were kept up until recently as tradition. But bahi-members are too few in number for their traditions to survive the shock of the modern world; many are so poor that they find the family rituals required simply to keep up their caste status an increasingly difficult burden. The tradition has declined to such a point that, for example, most members of Cikā Bahi believe that the term *brahmacarya* refers to their putative brahman origin and that only those bahi whose eponymous founder was a brahman (Cikā Bahi, I Bahi, Konti Bahi, Pintu Bahi, and Duntu Bahi) have a right to the title 'Brahmacharya Bhikshu'. In this connection I was frequently told the story of Sunaya Shri Mishra, the brahman who founded I Bahi and whose pupils, according to them, founded the other bahi listed.[28] The historically and semantically correct explanation of *brahmacarya* was given to me only by the senior elder quoted above.

For the present therefore I think it is fair to say of the distinctive traditions of the bahi, as it is not of Newar Buddhism as such, that they are moribund. Differences betweeen bahi and bahah are fast disappearing. What is left is a slight prejudice on the part of those living in bahah that the bahi are somehow inferior and that it is less desirable to marry into bahi families. Partly this is explained by the fact that, since the population of the bahi is small, they inevitably live in areas dominated by other castes.[29]

Was it so in the past? It seems certain that the bahah have always looked down on the bahi. At the same time, as stated, their members do intermarry and there is a basic unity of values. The following may serve as an illustration of this. During the Rana period the members of Cikā Bahi became rich and landed, working as doctors (*vaidya*) in the palaces of the powerful. Much of their money went into religion: three lineage monasteries and numerous guthis were founded, and many donations were made to their bahi. The forms of worship which they chose to sponsor were exactly those which would have been sponsored by members of bahah in a similar situation. Indeed it would be very surprising if the tiny bahi population had managed to maintain real differences in religious values between themselves and other Sakyas and Vajracharyas with whom they intermarried. Nevertheless, in spite of the basic unity which existed between them and other Buddhists, the members of Cikā Bahi simultaneously kept up a separate set of traditions relating to the monastic part of their identity. These traditions represented a kind of Buddhist 'left-wing', claiming a closer relationship to all earlier, 'purer' Buddhism.

As an example of the way this superiority was asserted, here are the words of Dharma Aditya Dharmacharyya (1928: 215), Newar Buddhist reformer and cultural nationalist, himself a member of Cikā Bahi, who wrote at a time when these traditions were better preserved:

Those [Buddhists] who settled earlier belonged to the banaprastha bhikshu class and lived in the forests outside the cities [he probably got this from Wright] ... The latter have their own Sangha and hold their annual assembly every year on the Falgun or eleventh month of the Indian calendar. Whereas the present

Buddhism [of the bahah] represents the latest stages of Buddhism and sacred literature, they [the bahi] claim to follow the pure Mahayana Buddhism.

Thanks to their monastic traditions, which they knew how to justify in this way in terms of a separate history, and how to explain in religious, and not merely mythological, terms, the members of the bahi were in a position (if and when they felt like it) to turn the tables, and assert the superiority of the bahi to the bahah. This they can no longer do.

The history of the bahi and their relation to the bahah according to Wright's *History of Nepal*

There are nowadays few significant differences between the bahi and the bahah. The interesting question about the bahi is therefore historical: What can they teach about the history of Newar Buddhism? They appear as a leftover now, but what was their role in the past?

It could be true, as Locke's informant claimed (above, p. 151), that the bahi were the lower schools, in which monks were first ordained and that when they had progressed sufficiently they moved on to a bahah where they settled and married. This theory is neat enough, and could describe correctly the period preceding the Malla dynasty (eleventh to thirteenth centuries CE). Unfortunately this is precisely the period of Nepalese history for which the records are least satisfactory. Some of the bahah were founded only much later, some were already in existence (e.g. Uku Bahah), and others were probably founded at this time (e.g. Kwa Bahah). Whether or not the bahah and bahi were ever related in this way, and if so, during which historical periods, is impossible to say with any certainty on present evidence.

In the Malla period, however, it seems that something like the present situation obtained. The chronicle BV calls the bahi-inhabitants *nirvāṇik vānaprastha*, which was explained to Wright as meaning that 'the inhabitants did not marry' though the manuscript makes it plain that they did. The term *vāṇaprastha* (correctly *vānaprastha*) seems be a *vṛddhi* form of *vanaprastha*, which usually denotes a Hindu forest ascetic, the third of the classic four stages (*āśrama*) of a Hindu's life. It would also be a natural way to refer to that well-known Buddhist figure, the forest monk (Carrithers 1983). BV does indeed seem to use *vāṇaprastha* as a synonym for Skt *vanavāsin*, living in a forest (Wright 1972: 185; BV: 108a), which is precisely the term used for Theravada forest monks. BV contrasts the *nirvāṇik vāṇaprastha vihār*, i.e. the bahi, with the *saṃsārik tāṃtrik vihār*, i.e. the bahah (BV: 133b): that is, the bahi were otherworldly and forest-dwelling, the bahah were this-worldly and Tantric. When King Siddhi Narasingh (reigned 1620–61) tried to reform them, the members of the bahi claimed that since they followed the otherworldly forest-dwelling dharma they could not take Tantric Initiation (BV: 132b).[30]

The chronicle begins its account of the reform of the bahi with I Bahi. Its members were assigned a Vajracharya from Dhum Bahah to perform their life-crisis rites, which till then they had been performing 'for each other'. Why I Bahi was treated differently is not clear: perhaps because its members were believed to be descendants of a brahman. Subsequently they were evidently absorbed into the group of Fifteen Bahi. Siddhi Narasingh then summoned all the other bahi, but only fifteen of them came, those which lay on the left side of the main road called 'Cāgālākwa' (perhaps 'below the road leading to Changu') (BV: 132a).[31] The chronicle continues:

He [Siddhi Narasingh] made the five oldest of the monks into elders (sthavir) and he made arrangements for the maintenance of their ceremonial association (guṭhi). He established rules so that the different monasteries were responsible for different tasks in every rite from Monastic Initiation (bhikṣu hunyā) through to death. As for the priest (pūjārī), up until then whoever of the elders knew best used to perform the ritual in each monastery separately. Henceforth there was to be a single arrangement for all fifteen monasteries: one monastery had to provide the priest for all the others. Now the monks objected: 'We may be following the householder dharma but we are monks of an otherworldly (nirvāṇik) monastery. It is not permitted for a householder master (grhastha ācārya) who is living in a worldly (sāṃsārik) monastery and following the 'family' path (kulāyan) to perform our rites.' Since it was forbidden in the otherworldly forest-dwelling dharma to take the initiation (abhiṣek dīkṣā) of the Tantric family (kul) dharma, the son of the eldest of them all was given the fivefold initiation (pañcābhiṣek) and made a monk-master (bhikṣu ācāryya), and he became their priest (pūjārī). The problem arose: what should happen if he became one of the five elders? How then could he go around doing rituals for everyone? The rule was laid down that, since everyone would have accepted one person to do their rituals, if he became an elder, his son should carry them on. With this the monks of the Fifteen Monasteries were in agreement.

After this, consultation was made with the monks of the ten monasteries remaining of the twenty-five, viz. those which lay on the right side of the main road used in Machiṃdranāth's chariot festival (called 'Cāgalatha'). Arrangements were made, all ten agreed, rites were carried out to make five elders, and all other arrangements were set in motion.

Before this, whenever the people of Lalitpur did respectful worship (mān pūjā) of the otherworldly forest-dwelling monks, they did it to many of them at once. Now they began to worship only two, the eldest of the group of monasteries above the main road [i.e. the Ten Bahi] and the eldest of those below [i.e. the Fifteen Bahi]; there was also a *guthi* for this.

In this way the rules were established both for the worldly Tantric (*sāṃsārik tāṃtrik*) monasteries and for the otherworldly forest-dwelling (*nirvāṇik vānaprastha*) monasteries. Some people called the forest-dwelling monasteries *vahī* [= *bahī*] because they were built outside (*vāhīra*) in the forest (*vanāṃtara*) and were inhabited by monks (*bhikṣu*). (BV: 132a–134a)

It is clear from the chronicle that Siddhi Narasingh was anxious to make the inhabitants of the bahi conform to Hindu social norms: their death rituals were made to include a purifying fire sacrifice, and this, and other rites, had to be performed by a properly qualified priest. We may compare this, as Locke has done, to the detailed regulations which Siddhi Narasingh's son, Shri Nivas, established for the cult of Matsyendranath, excluding low castes from the temple area and making arrangements for the feeding of Kanphata Yogis there (Locke 1980: 308–12, 339–40). Siddhi Narasingh had already himself established the custom of having two Brahmans ride on the front of the chariot although the cult of Matsyendranath was, and is, in other respects entirely in the hands of Buddhist priests (ibid.: 303). Sylvain Lévi saw these reforms of the monasteries as 'one of the most crucial moments of the crisis [of Buddhism]' (Lévi 1905 II: 32). Siddhi Narasingh, he wrote,

began by destroying the appearance of anarchy which safeguarded [the monasteries'] independence; he made them responsible to the crown ... The [main] monasteries of Patan [= Lalitpur], Kirtipur, and Chobahal [Chobhar] had to accept a hierarchical classification based partly on seniority, partly on mere chance, as if the better to demonstrate royal indifference ... A purification ceremony was made obligatory for these Buddhist Newars who had been to or resided in Tibet ... [and] the required fee reverted to the king. The monasteries which still observed the rule of celibacy tried to avoid the rules; summoned to hear the royal decree, ten out of twenty-five sent no delegates ... (ibid.: 33–4)

The chronicle does indeed describe in detail the reorganization of the main monasteries that Lévi refers to, and the imposition of the purification tax (Gellner 1996: 144–6). But the hierarchy of main monasteries outlined in the chronicle seems to have no practical relevance today, and the chronicle itself contradicts Lévi's assumption (1905 II: 29) that the members of the twenty-five 'otherworldly' monasteries were still celibate monks. Nor does the text, either in BV or in Wright's translation, warrant the inference that the Ten Bahi were celibate but the Fifteen were not.

Certain elements of Siddhi Narasingh's regulation of the bahi do not correspond to the present situation. I Bahi was treated separately and given a Vajracharya priest. In the other bahi all rituals were to be performed by one of their own number. As we have seen this is no longer the case: those rituals relating to the monastery and monasticism are indeed performed by the bahi-priest, but all rituals of the family, including those after death, are performed by a Vajracharya. This present arrangement is one which makes sense, but, if we accept the chronicle's account, it must have been the result of a later compromise. In BV the bahi are shown defending strongly their 'otherworldly forest-dwelling' identity against any encroachment by the 'this-worldly Tantric' monasteries. Nowadays, and certainly as far back as those alive today can remember, Tantric Initiation, far from being forbidden to the members of bahi is positively required in order to become an elder. Nowadays the explanation of the three parts of the monastery—the main deity, the *gumpa*, and the Tantric shrine—as representing Shravakayana, Mahayana, and Vajrayana, respectively, applies equally to the bahi. By contrast the bahi at the time of Siddhi Narasingh must have lacked a Tantric shrine (since they were proud of being forbidden to take Tantric Initiation) and they surely would have rejected this schema.

The decline of the bahi was evidently already under way when Siddhi Narasingh made his reforms, since the chronicle tells us that certain bahi were empty, their inhabitants having moved on after taking up the householder dharma. The members of the bahi made a virtue of their being the descendants of the last truly celibate monks, but this was not enough to stop a steady decline in population. Wherever possible members must have transferred to bahah; but precisely because such practice is in theory not allowed it is extremely difficult to trace it or prove it. The lower prestige of the bahi is due to the fact that the traditional Buddhism of the Newars is Tantric: celibate monastic Buddhism (the Shravakayana), with which the bahi are associated and previously associated themselves, is given a place, but only the lowest one. The bahi themselves have been less and less able, and less and less interested, to combat this assessment. Their ideology is in any case now rendered anachronistic by the presence in Nepal of the newly introduced and dynamic Theravada Buddhist movement.[32]

Lineage monasteries

Lineage monasteries are usually small inconspicuous establishments incorporated into the structure of the houses which adjoin them. Wana Bahah, which belongs to a large lineage of Bu Bahah Vajracharyas, is unusual in being well known outside its immediate area. A lineage monastery must not only possess the three defining characteristics of a monastery—*caitya*, main deity, and Tantric shrine—it must also, like any other monastery, be ritually established *as* a monastery. There are several sites— e.g. Sarasvati Nani mentioned in note 8—which could be considered to possess all three but are not monasteries, because not founded as such. The rituals for the foundation involve considerable expense and last a full year; they have rarely been performed in recent times.[33]

Most lineage monasteries founded by lay castes function in a way similar to those of Sakyas and Vajracharyas, that is, as a kind of private lineage guthi. But a partial exception to this is provided by Hauga Bahah and Jom Bahah in Lalitpur, and Yatkha Bahah and Than Bahi in Kathmandu. These four monasteries are 'owned' by particular occupational status groups (*thar*) of the adjoining area: Rajkarnikar (sweetmakers), Shilpakar (carpenters), Sthapit (carpenters), and Pradhan (nobles), respectively. In these cases the monastery provides a focus for, and defines the unity of, a group of lineages, in the same way that main monasteries do for Sakyas and Vajracharyas, and Hindu temples sometimes do for other groups (e.g. the Joshi Agan in Solimha for Lalitpur Joshis).

Attitudes to lineage monasteries differ from those towards all other monasteries. Newar Buddhists do not speak of lineage monasteries having a Monastic Community (*saṃgha, sā*) since no one is initiated there. Rather they speak of the monastery 'belonging to' the lineage. Others are not encouraged to bring offerings to the shrine and are not invited to participate in, and would not be welcome at, any of the annual rituals (except where it is laid down that daughters given out of the lineage in marriage, their children, and their husbands must be invited to a given feast). Lineage monasteries are private shrines even when owned by many families.

It is quite otherwise at even the smallest monastery with an initiated Monastic Community. All those living in the locality are expected to feel, and normally do feel, some identification with it, even if they are not Vajracharyas or Sakyas. Thus Duntu Bahi in Ikhachen, with only two surviving members, was renovated in 1980 with money collected from all the inhabitants of Ikhachen. Similarly, in 1976, the main deity of Cikā Bahi was plated with gold: twenty-six individuals contributed gold or money, of whom half were members of Cikā Bahi; of the others, eight were Sakyas, three Awales, and two Vajracharyas. These bahi attract the support of non-members even though they are quiet, secluded shrines rarely visited for religious purposes. The large main monasteries by contrast receive a steady stream of offerings every morning; they are therefore *a fortiori* a focus of Buddhist devotion, and local people, whether members or not, are proud to be associated with them.

The way in which lineage monasteries develop can be briefly illustrated with the example of Cikā Bahi. The members of Cikā Bahi established four separate lineage monasteries in the residential courtyards surrounding their bahi in the years 1868, 1871, 1878, and at some time after that, probably around the turn of the century. Clearly there was a sense of competition between the leading families of Cikā Bahi in those years. Sometimes the founder of a lineage monastery names it after himself; sometimes also, though more rarely, an effigy of the founder is kept in the Tantric shrine and 'worshipped' in the course of the main annual ritual. The first three lineage monasteries have *in situ* inscriptions which describe the founding, list all the members of the donor's family, and give details of land donated for the performance of annual rituals. Two of the donors performed *bāhāḥ pūjā*, i.e. visiting and making offerings at all the main monasteries of Lalitpur, in order 'to make famous' the name of their new monastery.

The fourth lineage monastery of Cikā Bahi was founded by the eldest son of the man who had established the third. Their family tree is shown in Fig. 6.1. All main monasteries in Lalitpur with an extant Monastic Community have a list of members in order of seniority from time of ordination: duty as 'god-guardian' (*dyaḥpahla*) passes down the list, so that eventually everyone takes a turn.[34] In lineage monasteries, by contrast, duties are based on genealogical relation to the founder. This system is unavoidable in their case, since membership is not defined by individuals taking Monastic Initiation there. Even to talk of 'membership' of a lineage monastery is slightly forced: as I have pointed out, Newar Buddhists themselves speak rather of lineage monasteries belonging to them, as lineage property.

In the example shown in Fig. 6.1 there are two ways of determining god-guardians:

(i) *Rights vested in lineages:* The Bhaishajya Bahah lineage is made up of three 'families' (*kutū*, from Skt *kuṭumba*)[35] descended from brothers A, B, and C. (It is only through inscriptions that the existence of a fourth brother without offspring is revealed.) Duty passes to each 'family' in turn so that household 5 gets a turn every three months, whereas households 4 and 9 take a turn only once every six months, and households 1–3 and 6–8 only once every eighteen months. Similarly in Kul Ratna Bahah, family 4 takes half the turns, and families 1–3 one-sixth each. This is the old system.

Plate 11: A lineage monastery and shelter (phalcā) built in 1871 (this photograph taken 1998). The caitya *dates from the reign of King Shri Nivas Malla (1658–85) and 'belongs to' some Shresthas living in Mangal Bazaar, i.e. it is they who have the right to come and receive offerings during the annual procession-festival of Mataya. The monastery belongs to a lineage whose menfolk are members of Cikā Bahi. The 'pagoda' of Cikā Bahi is visible in the background. The monastery is known colloquially as cibhā cuk ('caitya courtyard'), and more formally as Triratna Vihar. The inscription recording the founding can be seen to the right of the main shrine door; it gives the name 'Triratna-vīra-vihar'. The inclusion of the word* vīra, *hero, was no doubt due to the fact that the three brothers who founded the monastery all had bīr (vīra) as the second element of their name.*

Fig. 6.1: *Structure of the lineage attached to Bhaishajya Bahah, Cikā Bahi.*

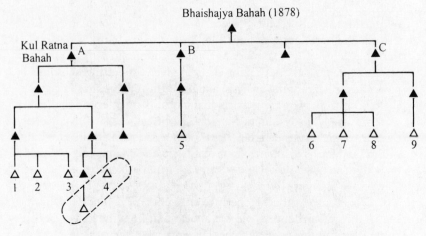

Note: Numbers 1 to 9 represent nine separate households.

(ii) *Households treated equally:* In this system each of the nine families of Bhaishajya Bahah takes a monthly turn every nine months. Likewise, in Kul Ratna Bahah, the four households nowadays share duties equally.

In the last twenty years numerous religious associations (guthi) have passed from system (i), rights vested in lineages, to system (ii), which treats all households alike. The reason is that the resources which used to support them have suffered drastically from the Land Reform in 1963–4 (which has much reduced the payments required from tenant farmers) and from the rapaciousness of many guthi-members. Consequently what used to be a jealously guarded right has become an increasingly difficult burden. The inscription describing the establishment of Bhaishajya Bahah lists all the rituals to be performed each year and the fields (12 *ropani* in seven different places) to pay for it. It ends by saying 'the remainder shall be enjoyed by the descendants of the founder'—which meant, of course, the descendant whose turn it was that year to run the guthi. Now that guthi income has declined, members have to make up the shortfall out of their own pocket. Consequently those households which have to take frequent turns (i.e. family 5, and to a lesser extent 4 and 9) press for the system to switch from system (i) to system (ii), or they threaten to leave the guthi.

The genealogical system which vests rights in lineages is less purely Buddhist than the list-system used to determine duties in most main monasteries because the latter treats members as separate individuals. The necessity of using the lineage system in lineage monasteries means that they are further away from the monastic realm and more in that of 'worldly Tantric' Buddhism, as the chronicle called it. Further, the lineage monastery, since it excludes all but the patrilineage and, by invitation, its affinal relatives, has moved beyond the universalist values which are embodied just as much in the main monasteries as in the bahi.

Since these lineage monasteries function just like a private guthi it would have been understandable if some term such as *niji bahah* (private monastery) had evolved as the name for this type. The fact that some such expression has not gained general acceptance shows the power of the formal and ritual sphere of Newar Buddhism in which the distinctions I have outlined between different types of monastery are not acknowledged. From the strictly religious point of view all Newar monasteries that are founded as such are equally *vihara* and the same rituals are appropriate in all them.[36]

Conclusion: a theory of architectural development

It should be clear that the bahi, if not always the oldest, are certainly the most archaic Buddhist foundations, and consciously so. Their architecture preserves most purely ancient Buddhist patterns. However I think it is possible to move beyond this and postulate the steps by which bahah architecture has developed away from the ancient model. This is shown in Chart 6.3.

Chart 6.3: The historical development of monastery architecture

1. bahi
   ↓

2. bahah   with courtyard intact, i.e. non-residential,
   ↓   communally owned, and used only for religious and/ or communal purposes.

3. bahah   where the courtyard has been partly taken over for
   ↓   private residential use.

4. bahah   in which the main deity inhabits a free-standing
   ↓   temple and the courtyard is, and was always intended to be, mostly residential.

5. bahah   (viz. most lineage monasteries) which are designed as an integral part of a residential unit.

The ultimate development of the bahah form was the lineage monastery constructed as part of a new house. Even this maintained it as part of a secluded courtyard, and retained the three elements—main deity, *caitya*, and first-floor Tantric shrine—outlined above. The architectural development shown in Chart 6.3 did not manifest itself only when new monasteries were founded: quite a few main monasteries now falling into category 3 must have developed piecemeal from category 2. And it seems likely also that some bahi were turned into bahah of type 2. This may well have occurred at Uku Bahah, for example.

The tendency towards type 4—a free-standing temple as the principal shrine of main monasteries—should be seen as the result of growing Tantric influence. It is perhaps no accident that the two main monasteries of this type in Lalitpur, Bu Bahah and Bhinche Bahah, are both dominated by Vajracharyas.[37] Snellgrove writes that the free-standing temple is primarily Hindu in conception (Snellgrove 1961: 106) but goes on to show how the square pagoda temple symbolizes the mandala from which the deity looks out in all four directions, an idea which is as fundamental to Tantric Buddhism as it is to Tantric Hinduism (ibid.: 107–9). Without broaching the complex question of the relation of Tantric Buddhism to Hinduism, suffice it to say that most Newar Buddhists would deny that their free-standing temples are in any way Hindu. Slusser has admirably summarized the architectural evidence that the 'Newar-style temple ... is a three-dimensional mandala' (Slusser 1982: 145). She too comes to the conclusion that 'the incorporated temple of the *vihara* is modelled after a free-standing temple, and represents an exotic to the quadrangle plan' (ibid.: 146).

Of course the bahi themselves have undergone certain changes as a result of the developments which have affected all religious tendencies in the Kathmandu Valley, but in their case the changes have been more in the nature of small accretions and not a systematic restructuring. Becker-Ritterspach (1982: 305) reckons that the 'pagoda' (*puco*) over the main shrine of a bahi was a late addition to bahi architecture, dating from the seventeenth or eighteenth century. Perhaps the same is true of entrance lions and a tympanum over the main doorway where these occur. The Tantric shrine must also have been introduced in bahi only after Siddhi Narasingh's reforms, as argued above.

It should be noted how architecture has come a full circle, neatly illustrating the changing values of Nepalese Buddhism. At the beginning, in traditional monastic style, celibate monks lived in the austere and open-plan bahi (taking bahi here to refer simply to a style of architecture). When they married they moved out of the bahi and lived out their householder status outside it, returning only for monastic rituals and obligations. New shrines, especially Tantric deities, were added and the typical bahah, ornate and enclosed, emerged. By the last stage of development (type 5 of Chart 6.3) the two statuses, householder and monk, have become so fused that houses can be monasteries, and family residential units are built with Buddhist monastic shrines as part of them.

The Newar Buddhist tradition is, in a vague and general way, aware of this historical development, and indeed builds it into its rituals. The historical development is understood as a logical one, in which later stages incorporate and transcend earlier ones. Locke has noted how the Monastic Initiation and *ācāḥ luyegu* ceremonies represent condensed history in this way:

The whole complexus of these initiation rites presents a summary of the history of Buddhism in India and Nepal and an outline of the social structure of the Newar Buddhist community. The young *vajracarya* is first ordained a *bhiksu* in a rite which dates to the earliest times of Buddhism. He is introduced, however briefly and perfunctorily, to a number of the principal Mahayana texts and to the rites and rituals performed in the ancient Hinayana and Mahayana monasteries of India and Nepal. Finally he is ordained a Vajracarya Buddhist priest. (Locke 1975: 18)

However, just because the structure of monastery and ritual recapitulates history and because this is consciously articulated, it would be wrong to take the schema implicit in them *as* history, except of the most sketchy sort. For example, when the history of Buddhism in the Thakuri period comes to be written, it may turn out that celibate monasticism and Tantric religion existed side by side, perhaps even in the same institution. It will probably turn out that 'earlier' and 'later' forms of Buddhism existed concurrently, as far back as our evidence goes.

The essence of my argument is summarized in three charts, 6.1, 6.2, and 6.3. It would be a misunderstanding however to put Charts 6.1 and 6.3 together, and interpret Chart 6.3 as explaining the historical development of the institutions of today. First and straightforwardly, Chart 6.1 is synchronic and depicts the relations between the concepts used to describe different monastic institutions today, whereas Chart 6.3 is diachronic and postulates relationships between architectural forms (whose relation to types of institution may have varied over time). Thus, for example, it would be a mistake to conclude on the basis of Chart 6.3 that the bahi-institution we know today was a precursor of the modern bahah-institution. Second, and more importantly, to ignore the different aims of the two tables would be to miss the subtle way in which the tradition makes use of, and to a certain extent distorts, its own history in order to explain itself.

If we accept the account of BV—and I see no reason to reject it— the members of the bahi at the time of Siddhi Narasingh saw the distinction between the bahah and the bahi as an opposition which we may represent thus:

bahah	bahi
samsara (this world)	nirvana (the beyond or other world)
Tantric family dharma of Vajracharyas	non-Tantric, forest-dwelling dharma of monks[38]

This opposition was, it seems to me, the local form of a tension present in almost all types of Buddhism, which was institutionalized in medieval Sri Lanka as the opposition between village- and forest-monks (Rahula 1956: 159–60; Carrithers 1983: 168). Arguably this tension, between mixing with the world to save the masses and retreating from it to save oneself, can be seen at the very origin of Buddhism, in that moment when the Buddha, on achieving enlightenment, hesitated between going out to teach the world and entering full nirvana immediately.

One of the ways of expressing this opposition was through the architecture of the two types of monastery. The bahi deliberately retained the ancient forms and resisted most of the modifications which even small and relatively impecunious bahah introduced. In so doing they claimed to represent an older and more rigorous standard than that of the bahah. But in fact they too were householders with families at the time of Siddhi Narasingh's reforms, and we have only the word of their tradition that they had a special connection to the last celibate Buddhist monks. Whereas many bahah are attested in historical records of the Thakuri period, there is virtually no evidence for the existence of the bahi. Bahi-architecture is certainly ancient but the bahi-institution has undergone important changes, even since Siddhi Narasingh's time. The modern bahi-institution is almost certainly no older than that of the main monasteries, and may even be a more recent development. To accept that the bahi are older institutions than the bahah would be to fall for the ideological claim deliberately advanced by the former's architecture, rituals, and myths. Nowadays the opposition bahah:bahi exists no more: the gradual laicization of Newar Buddhism and the small size of the bahi have meant that what was once a keenly maintained opposition has become merely a difference of custom such as is found between almost any two similar but distinct groups within Newar society.

De Jong (1979: 642) sees the whole history of South Asian Buddhism as comprising essentially the gradual lay appropriation of the original religion. The Newars have taken this process a long way, as illustrated by their lineage monasteries. Even here however caution is required in interpreting Chart 6.3. The architectural form of modern lineage monasteries is certainly the latest development, and most modern lineage monasteries are relatively late establishments. But can we be sure that such institutions did not exist in the Thakuri period? It may be that the lineage monastery as an institution is inherently likely to change its architectural form in the same way that the ideology of the bahi requires them to be architecturally conservative.

It seems likely therefore that the institutional development implied by Chart 6.3 (from celibate monasticism to Tantric householder monk/priest) was accomplished long before the architectural one. More than that, I have tried to suggest that what part of the Newar Buddhist tradition sees as a simple diachronic progression (or decline) from otherworldly monasticism to this-worldly Tantrism, is in fact better represented as a synchronic opposition present in almost all forms of Buddhism (and certainly predating the rise of Tantric ritual and iconography). In my view, then, the bahi and bahah are, at any given period, defined in terms of each other. The claims of each to be earlier than the other are simply part of an age-old debate about the true teachings of the Buddha. The bahi claim to be an historic leftover but, in the sense of innocently preserving ancient customs in isolation from changes elsewhere, they are certainly not: they have put much effort and ingenuity into establishing their archaic identity, and yet have themselves changed as one generation has succeeded the next.

One lesson of this is, I think, that the institutions of a given period should be explained in terms of each other, in terms of the system which, taken together, they comprise. Only then should history be invoked. Historical evidence is required for the fullest understanding; but it should be an understanding that explains not only origins but also changes, which explains the way in which old institutions have been reinterpreted to new ends and which avoids the local tendency to see history in terms of the survival, accretion, or decline of isolated elements. To the epigram from Nietzsche I would only add that each generation reinterprets its inheritance for itself even when it earnestly tries to preserve it, even when it believes it is *merely* preserving it, and even when it does indeed preserve it.

Notes

1. I am particularly indebted to John Locke for numerous discussions of the matters discussed herein. His monumental survey of monasteries in the Kathmandu Valley (Locke 1985) should be consulted by anyone who wants to go further into the subject as well as for details on all the monasteries mentioned in the text. I have also benefited from the comments of Niels Gutschow, H. Kulke, S. Lienhard, K.P. Malla, Dhanavajra Vajracharya, Gautamvajra Vajracharya, and Anne Vergati. Needless to say, I take responsibility for the use or misuse I have made of all suggestions and comments. I would also like to record my debt to, and admiration of, Hemraj Sakya, local Buddhist scholar: in spite of the fact that I have, on occasion, found it necessary to qualify or criticize his conclusions, I have learned a great deal from his many works, which represent an heroic attempt to synthesize traditional and modern scholarship. Much detailed etymological discussion, and one entire section on branch monasteries attached to Kwa Bahah, have been omitted from this version of the original paper (Gellner 1987).

2. See, e.g., Gombrich 1983.

3. Local tradition takes this back to the (mythical) time of Krakuchanda Buddha (Wright 1972: 80). Historically the rule that five monks may initiate a new monk in border areas, though ten are required elsewhere, goes back to the oldest stratum of Buddhist scripture, redacted no later than 100 years after the Buddha's death (Frauwallner 1956: 90–1).

4. The historical reason for this is explained below.

5. For details, see Locke 1985.

6. In Lalitpur there are just two small monasteries of this sort wholly unconnected to the 'Fifteen Bahah', namely Hyan Bahah and Yankuri Bahah. There are also seven 'branches' of Kwa Bahah, whose members carry out part of their Monastic Initiation ritual inside Kwa Bahah, but have no other rights of membership. For more on them, see the original version of this paper (Gellner 1987).

7. BV is short for Buddhist Vamsavali, the manuscript (Cambridge University Library, Add. 1952A) that Daniel Wright, surgeon at the British Residency, had translated (in some places rather inaccurately) and published as his *History of Nepal*.

8. The extension of the title 'monastery' to courtyards which are not monasteries by any of the criteria given above is an ancient practice. Thus an inscription of 1616 (NS 736) records a Samyak festival held in Nag Bahah, which is given the title 'Vasuvarddhana Mahivihara'. Later generations preferred the name 'Pasuvarna Mahavihara', which refers to the statue of a bull there (Skt *paśu*, domestic animal, cattle) associated with the festival of Dipankha. Similarly the large courtyard known colloquially as Nyakhachuk is given the title 'Bhaskaravarna Mahavihara', no doubt because, like Nag Bahah, its inhabitants are nearly all members

of Kwa Bahah, and the founder of Kwa Bahah was called Bhaskara. By the same token Sarasvati Nani is called Vagishvara Vihara in inscriptions there, though no one calls it a bahah today. The temple to the bodhisattva Manjushri might be thought to make it a lineage monastery, but it was evidently never established as such.

9. The inscription actually records the consecration of a *caitya* and an image of Manjushri, and the building of a wall, by Harkha Dev Sakya of Uku Bahah, Lalitpur. The people of Arughat remember him as 'Devadatta' and recall that he lived as a monk. This is confirmed by the autobiography of the 'Bauddha Rishi' Mahapragya: Harkha Dev was called Devadatta because he had played that part in a representation of the life of the Buddha (Mahapragya 1983: 21). Harkha Dev, Mahapragya himself, and Kancha Sakya had just been ordained as monks in Kyerong, Tibet. Harkha Dev went straight to Arughat while the other two proceeded to Kathmandu (ibid.: 25). Mahapragya and Kancha were reordained with others there, and eventually expelled from the country by the Ranas. Harkha Dev spent most of the later part of his life in Kindol, Swayambhu, where he was known as Dharma Guruju (Gellner 1992a: 298).

10. In 1989, after the original version of this paper was published, the Buddhists of Tansen did indeed establish a new, traditional-style monastery, so that their boys would have a proper place to go through initiation, which they called Dharmachakra Vihara (Chattra Raj Sakya, personal communication).

11. There is now a bahah called Ga Bahah, but this is a modern reconstruction dating from 1956 and not the ancient monastery of that name (Locke 1985: 232).

12. It is in fact the base of a *caitya* with the mandala of Manjushri inscribed on top, instead of the normal dome with Buddha statues. On Nepalese *caityas*, see Gutschow 1997 and von Rospatt 1999.

13. The bahi with the largest membership is Cikā Bahi in Chyasa, Lalitpur, which has around 140 members (c. forty households). In most others the membership is much lower.

14. Locke 1985: 515. Only 3.9 per cent of the Sakyas and Vajracharyas in Kathmandu are attached to bahi; the figure overall is 5.3 per cent.

15. Hodgson 1972: 53; Oldfield 1981 II: 282; Gutschow 1982: 151; cf. Lienhard 1996.

16. Locke 1980: 19. The local view reported by Locke is similar to, if not identical with, that of Hemraj Sakya. According to him, the branch monasteries are for lay people who simply keep the Five Precepts, the bahi are for those who have gone beyond this, become monks, and are learning and teaching Buddhism, and the main monasteries are for those monks with ordination (*upasampadā*) who have put aside book-learning and practise meditation (Sakya 1979: 4). Sakya reports this as fact though it is highly speculative. It is interesting that the terms he uses for book-learning and meditation, *granthādhūra* and *vipaśyanādhūra* respectively, relate the bahah–bahi opposition directly to that between forest monks (who do

meditation) and village monks (who preserve book-learning) in Sri Lanka. That is, according to him the bahah represent the 'higher' pursuit of meditation and the bahi the 'lower' one of book-learning. With due respect to Sakya's great learning, there is to my knowledge no evidence for these ascriptions but only the prejudice of the bahah against the bahi whereas there is historical evidence, given on p. 163, for precisely the opposite view, viz. that, in the seventeenth century at least, the bahi represented the forest monk polarity and the bahah the village monk one.

17. This feature makes the bahi well suited to house primary schools. At least four Lalitpur bahi have now been put to this use. One other (Dhapaga Bahi) has donated one wing to be rebuilt as a Theravada monastery. The open style of bahi, as well as their small membership, has also made them especially vulnerable to theft, so that few of the beautiful images they once possessed are left. Many of the bahi are in a very poor state of repair.

18. This was a distinguishing feature that locals often pointed out to me, though they did not attach any particular significance to it. There are in fact one or two minor exceptions (Kinu Bahi, Uba Bahi).

19. See M. R. Allen 1973: 7; Sakya 1973: 55; Rosser 1966: 126 n. 19.

20. For example in a land document of 1666 (Rajvamshi 1983: 100) and an inscription from I Bahi dated 1673 (Burleigh 1976: 39).

21. See Locke 1985 for details. These are conventional numbers. If additional shrines are included, e.g. those on the north side of I Bahi, the numbers are somewhat greater.

22. Independent branch monasteries and main monasteries which are de facto lineage monasteries also have only five elders. Main monasteries with extant Monastic Communities always have ten.

23. For example the two members of Duntu Bahi in Ikhachen form a single samgha with Pintu Bahi next door, and the single household in Guita Chidan Bahi forms one samgha with the five households of the adjacent Guita Bahi.

24. From Gaya in Bihar, where it is particularly meritorious to perform ancestor worship. In Kathmandu I have heard these places for throwing rice offerings called kāśīlhwā, from Kashi (i.e. Banaras), of which the same is true. The ninefold mandala stones are certainly ancient, as people believe; they symbolize the nine planets (navagraha) (cf. the diagram given by Pal and Bhattacharyya 1969: 39), and offerings are made on them to appease their bad influence.

25. The term gandhakuti was used in Nepal as early as the seventh century (D.V. Vajracharya 1973: 385). Gandhakuti is also used, evidently as the name of a Buddha shrine, in the Kriya-samgraha and in the Kriya-samuccaya (both texts being much used in Nepal). For examples see Kriya-samgraha, p. 233, and Kriya-samuccaya, p. 24, vols. 236 and 237 respectively in the Sata Pitaka series. Lienhard (1996: 254–6) has criticized the etymology proposed here, but his alternative strikes me as equally, if not more, speculative.

26. Lamotte 1958: 555. Becker-Ritterspach (1982: 305) points out that the bahi lack only cells along the side wings to correspond exactly with Indian monastic models.

27. Features dating from these reforms are: (7), the division into two Monastic Communities; (8), the role of the monastery priest; and (11), the rule about double-performance of the death purification ritual. Since the bahi lacked Tantric shrines at that time, (12), the female identity of the Tantric deity, is obviously a late feature also.

28. Cf. Wright 1972: 115–7. The chronicle mentions only Konti Bahi and Pintu Bahi however. One must remember that these myths occur in different versions depending on who is telling them. Thus the claim that I Bahi and the other monasteries founded by Sunaya Shri Mishra were the first to be established in Lalitpur (Joseph 1971: 121) is no doubt the gloss which I Bahi members themselves put on this legend.

29. Repeated enquiries failed to reveal any way in which this slight inferiority of status is institutionalized in Lalitpur. By contrast, in Itum Bahah, Kathmandu, if a member marries a girl from a bahi she will not be allowed into the Tantric shrine of the monastery; and if she has a son, although otherwise a full member of Itum Bahah, he may not become a senior (*thāypā*) of the monastery; *his* son, however, may do so, so that in the third generation the 'offence' of marrying into a bahi is wiped out. Other Kathmandu monasteries, like Lalitpur monasteries, have no such rules, but it does seem to be widely believed by members of Kathmandu bahah that the bahi house 'Buddhist mixed classes' (Lienhard 1984: 113) and were founded later than the bahah. Neither of these beliefs is very widely or strongly asserted in Lalitpur. I would suggest that they simply express the Kathmandu bahah-members' feeling that the bahi are lower in status, a feeling shared, though to a lesser degree, by their Lalitpur colleagues. Such feelings are on a par with the widely held (but erroneous) beliefs reported by other researchers that Dhulikhel Shresthas (Quigley 1984: 49) and Pyangaon Maharjans (Toffin 1984: 110) practise cross-cousin marriage: they are simply a legitimation of other groups' refusal to grant them equal status.

30. For more on the context of Siddhi Narasingh's reforms, see Gellner 1996.

31. Those who are interested can consult Wright (1972: 236–7) to see how I have improved on the translation given there. If, as I suggest, we take the road in question as being the east–west highway that divides Lalitpur in two, the lower half lying to the north and the upper half to the south, then with a few exceptions (the Guita Bahi, Nhaykan Bahi, Kinu Bahi, and those outside the city itself) it does indeed mark the boundary between the Fifteen Bahi (in the northern half, on the left as one goes towards Changu) and the Ten Bahi (in the southern half, on the right as one goes towards Changu).

32. See references in n. 3, p. 129.

33. The rituals are said to be in the Kriya-samgraha (see Mitra 1982: 103–6; D.R. Regmi 1965 III: 764–5; Slusser 1982: 130 n.9).

34. In Kathmandu, however, the genealogical or household systems are sometimes used even in main monasteries. See Locke 1985: 275b, 280b, 282, 286b, 310b, 315a, 327a, 340, 354a.
35. Elsewhere the term *kawaḥ* is more common for sub-lineages. It is also used to refer to the sections of a guthi where the members are related.
36. Newar Buddhism is by no means alone in developing kin-based ways of passing on property. Even in Theravada Buddhism the incumbent of a monastery can pass it on to his nephew by making sure that he chooses him as his principal pupil (Evers 1967). For other examples of the use of guthi land tenure for this purpose in Nepal, see M.C. Regmi 1976: 54–6 and D.R. Regmi 1965 I: 708.
37. Hemraj Sakya argues that Bhinche Bahah was once of a more monastic form; but he also says that the name derives from *bhinnachẽ*, 'separated from houses', which implies that the monastery was of style 4 from the beginning (Sakya 1973: 14–15, 26).
38. Lienhard (1996: 245–6) has suggested that from the point of view of the bahah this was also an opposition between the *abhyantara* (the internal) and the *bāhya* (the external), basing himself on Amritananda's replies to Hodgson (1972: 51–2). Lienhard interprets this as inside and outside of family life; I would see it rather as meaning 'inside' and 'outside' with reference to Tantric teachings.

7

'The Perfection of Wisdom':
A Text and its Uses in Kwa Bahah, Lalitpur

Introduction

Kwa Bahah, Hiranyavarna Mahavihara, or, as it is known in English, 'the Golden Temple' is the largest Buddhist monastery of Lalitpur and is one of the most important Buddhist shrines of the city (Plate 2).[1] Casual visitors to the monastery often see an old manuscript of the Perfection of Wisdom in Eight Thousand Lines (Astasahasrika-prajnaparamita) being read, though they often fail to comprehend the nature of the ritual they are observing.[2] During the year August 1985–August 1986 it was read 243 times according to Tusingh Sakya, a member of the guthi of Sakyas charged with the safekeeping of the manuscript.

Many other Buddhist monasteries possess old copies of this text but only in Kwa Bahah has a ritual grown up around it so that it is read frequently at the request of devotees. Having the text read is a very popular practice with members of Kwa Bahah as well as with other castes in the locality. Members of Kwa Bahah are proud of the fact that more rules (niyam) have to be kept in Kwa Bahah than in any other monastery; and they sometimes say that they have to be kept because the Perfection of Wisdom is here. Unlike other monasteries, which just have the text, in Kwa Bahah, they say, the goddess herself is present. Both as a physical object displayed in the monastery, and as a goddess in the minds of her devotees, The Perfection of Wisdom is the object of great reverence.

The ritual and the *guthi*

Having the text read is known locally as *pā thyākegu* or *thākegu*.[3] When a devotee decides to have the text read, he or she approaches one of the Vajracharya priests of Kwa Bahah who reads the text regularly and asks for a day to be set aside. The devotee is given a stencilled sheet entitled 'List of materials for the worship-reading of the blessed goddess Perfection of Wisdom' which is translated in Chart 7.1.

Chart 7.1: Instruction sheet for devotees having the Kwa Bahah 'Perfection of Wisdom' read (1983)

Worship plate incl. bowl of yoghurt	Broken beaten rice *(cwakā baji)*[a]
Flower garland, flowers	Red powder *(abhīr)*
Vermilion and sandalwood powder	5 *kisali*[b]
Thread in a circle *(jajākā)*	5 saucers of food[c]
Popped rice	Ghee
Ground rice [for drawing mandalas]	Molasses
Mustard oil for lamp	1 *pathi* of rice for *kibhū*[d]
Five-coloured thread	1 *pathi* of beaten rice for *nisalā*[f]
Half metre of red cloth[e]	18 bananas, 18 sweet pastries,
Fruits	8 pieces of ginger
Various pastries to offer to the god	16 × 2 rupees stipend *(pāth*
6 *manā* of rice for throne *(āsāki)* [of the god]	*dakṣiṇā)*, total 32 rupees

Give stipend to your domestic priest when he gives *tika* in accordance with your faith.

For worship *(kalā pūjā)* upstairs: *pañcāku* (buffalo meat), lentil cake or *jyeri*-sweet, spirits, rice-beer, feast expenses: 16 × 5 rupees, total 80 rupees.

May the fears and sufferings of those who have faith in the blessed goddess Perfection of Wisdom be destroyed.

Notes:
(a) for making rice cones.
(b) spelt *kislī* on the list. A small clay saucer with unpolished rice, a betel [areca] nut, and a coin. It is used for making a vow *(phyānāḥ taye)* to a deity and is also placed on the Flask *(kalaśa)* into which the main deity is summoned during all complex rituals.
(c) *naivedya*, here beaten rice, molasses, and ghee.
(d) spelt *kevu*; it is a prestation of rice given to priests after a ritual.
(e) to tear into ties *(kwakhāy)* to be put around the neck after the ritual.
(f) a prestation of beaten rice, rock salt, ginger, and one sweet pastry, always made to a Buddhist priest at the end of a ritual.

On any one day two readings of the text are permitted.[4] Until the reading is over all the participants must fast: this includes the sponsor of the ritual, the ten priests reading the text, and the member of the Sakya guthi who is responsible for returning the text safely to the shrine when the rite is over. This means that if in one day there are two sponsors,[5] one of whom elects to give money instead of a feast (because it is less work), he will be placed first, the other second.

There are seven Vajracharya families with the hereditary right to read the text, two in Nyakhachuk, two in Chuka Bahah, one in Ila Nani, one in Kwalakhu, and one in Ikhachen. All are members of Kwa Bahah.[6] In some of the families the right has been divided through inheritance and therefore alternates, year to year, between different branches. In other families only a single line survives and one man has the permanent right to read. However, many of those with a turn, including those with a permanent turn, send a substitute in their place, either because they cannot read the script, or because they are too old or too busy to attend. In such cases, as when a Vajracharya priest sends a substitute in his place to any other ritual, the substitute turns over half the stipend (*dakṣiṇā*) to the right-holder, but keeps the other prestations for himself.

Three other Vajracharyas also read the text. These are chosen by the domestic priest of the sponsor. Normally the domestic priest fills the role of the main priest (*mūlācārya*) who worships the text at the beginning of the ritual, but he may not be the main priest if he is not a member of Kwa Bahah. A Vajracharya who is not a member of Kwa Bahah may read the text as an occasional reader but may not be main priest. In this case the sponsor is likely to approach one of the regular readers who will happily fill in as main priest, since he will then receive five shares of most of the offerings: as main priest, as reader (he reads two shares if doubling up in this way), plus the share for the main priest's wife, the share for the text itself, and the share offered to the worship utensils (*thāpā*). When the main priest is not a regular reader (one of the seven) he takes four shares, while the regular reader receives one only.

The sixteen stipends and feasts or feast-expenses mentioned in Chart 7.1 are distributed as shown in Chart 7.2 and the destination of the eighteen prestations of rice (*kibhū*) and beaten rice (*nisalā*) are shown in Chart 7.3. Some try to give stipends or ritual prestations to the Sakya members of the guthi; the priests are quick to correct them. They are intended only for deities or for priestly services.

Chart 7.2: Recipients of stipend (*dakṣiṇā*) and feast (*bhway*) or feast-expenses (*bhwaykharca*)

> 10 to the readers of the text
>
> 2 to the Sakya members of the guthi
>
> 1 to the main deity (*kwābāju*), taken by the god-guardian
>
> 1 to the main priest's wife (*gurumā*)
>
> 1 to the worship utensils (*thāpā*)
>
> 1 to the text/goddess.[a]

Note: (a) The Sakya guthi takes the stipend offered to the text, the main priest the feast or feast-expenses.

Chart 7.3: Recipients of ritual prestations (*kibhū* and *nisalā*)

> 10 to the ten readers
>
> 1 to the main deity (*kwābāju*)
>
> 1 to the enshrined Svayambhu *caitya* (known as the *digudyaḥ* or lineage deity)
>
> 1 to Vajrasattva
>
> 1 to Yogambara, the main Tantric deity of the monastery
>
> 1 to the text/goddess Prajnaparamita
>
> 1 to the main priest
>
> 1 to the main priest's wife
>
> 1 to the worship utensils (*thāpā*).

The ritual itself is fairly simple. There is no Flask (*kalaśa*), only yoghurt pots (*sagā dhaupatti*), lamp (*sukundā*), and spirit-offering (*bali*). The five *kisalī* are offered to the main deity (Kwabaju, i.e. Sakyamuni Buddha), to Svayambhu, Vajrasattva, and Yogambara (considered the principal deities of the monastery), and to Prajnaparamita herself. In reciting the 'intention' (*saṃkalpa*) of the rite the words *pūrvasaṃkalpita* ('as previously intended') may be included if the text is being read in fulfilment of a vow; otherwise the term *yathāśraddhā* ('in accordance with the faith/devotion [of the devotee]') is used. A specific intention, e.g. for the prevention of fights, may also be included. The text is divided into ten equal parts which are then read simultaneously. Each priest performs the guru mandala rite before beginning and touches the text to his head in respectful obeisance at the end. Once the text has been read and put away, a brief Tantric rite is performed to Yogambara on the first floor of the monastic compound, including worship of the alcohol pot (*thyākā*) as Varuni-Guhyesvari-Mamaki (the Tantric identity of Prajnaparamita). Only after the Tantric rite is over do the participants break their fast with buffalo meat (*pañcāku*). Rich sponsors may add the communal snack *samay baji* before proceeding to the feast, but this is optional.

The Sakya guthi I have referred to has seventeen members. Originally it seems to have been organized in two halves (*kawaḥ*) descended from two different men; each half provided one man to carry out the duties of the guthi. With departures from the guthi and new members entering, the kawah structure is no longer clear. One member has inherited two membership places. All the members are however still Sakyas from Nag Bahah and its immediate surroundings. Two members still take turns per year. The first opens the box in which the text is kept and breaks the seal; he may then depart. The second has to be present, fasting (except for drinking tea) until the rite is over; he then checks that the text is all there and reseals the box.

The Sakya guthi has several ropanis of land and a bank account in which money offered to the text is kept (devotees often place money on the text's throne as they visit the monastery). The guthi organizes feasts for its seventeen members on five days a year. One feast is held on Mukhastami in the month of Kartik when the guthi itself sponsors a reading of the text. On this occasion the Pancavimsati-prajnaparamita (a longer version of the text, in twenty-five thousand lines) is also brought out of the shrine. This was the day, one member of the guthi told me, that the text was brought to Kwa Bahah from Bu Bahah (as described below). The other four feasts are held within nine days of each other during the holy month of Gunla. On the tenth day of Gunla turns of service in the guthi are handed over (*pā gwayegu*). Six days later on Sa Paru (Np. Gai Jatra) and two days after that (the day after Matayā) are two days of feasting called 'Mahakaruna' ('great compassion'). On these two days the seven regular Vajracharya readers of the text are also invited. On the first of these days the senior of the two new 'turners', and on the second the junior, is responsible for organizing the feast. The final day of feasting (called *samāpad*, 'conclusion') is the day after the second Mahakaruna day. The accounts are checked (*lyā swaye*). In the old days this was a feast with boiled rice (*jābhway*) (including leftovers from the previous day no doubt); nowadays beaten rice (*baji*), less susceptible to disputes over status, is eaten, as in the other feasts.

Background and motives of the sponsors

According to members of the guthi every year the number of devotees asking for the text to be read increases. One member of the guthi, Tusingh Shakya, kindly allowed me to copy a list he had kept during his turn of duty for the year 1985–6. As mentioned above, the text had been read a total of 243 times during the year. One of these occasions had been by the guthi itself (on Mukhastami) and for 22 occasions data were not available. The rest broke down as shown in Chart 7.4. However, if we subtract members of Kwa Bahah, who have a special regard for the text, and sponsor the reading on a wider variety of occasions than non-members, the figures are as shown in Chart 7.5.

These figures bear a rough resemblance to the caste distribution within the total population of Lalitpur, except that Vajracharyas and Sakyas are over-represented. This over-representation of Vajracharyas and Sakyas is to be expected (a) because of the specifically Buddhist nature of the rite, and (b) because Sakyas and Vajracharyas of Lalitpur are likely to be related by marriage to members of Kwa Bahah, and are therefore exposed, more than others, to accounts of its excellence. One should note that Shresthas, many of whom have Buddhist domestic priests in Lalitpur, even if they mostly prefer to consider themselves Hindus,

Chart 7.4: Distribution of sponsors by caste during 1985–6   (Information
            unavailable in 22 cases)

Caste	No. of readings	Per cent
Sakya	110	52.4
Maharjan and Dangol	40	19.0
Vajracharya	31	14.8
Shrestha (incl. 1 Joshi)	13	6.2
Shilpakar	3	1.4
Uday (Tuladhar *et al.*, Kathmandu)	3	1.4
Awale	3	1.4
Nakarmi	2	0.95
Khadgi	2	0.95
Chitrakar	1	0.5
Napit	1	0.5
Tibetan monk (Newar origin)	1	0.5
	210	100%

Chart 7.5: Distribution of sponsors by caste for 1985–6, excluding members of Kwa Bahah

Caste	No. of readings
Maharjan and Dangol	40
Vajracharya and Sakya	31[a]
Shrestha (incl. 1 Joshi)	13
Uday	3
Awale, Shilpakar	3 each
Nakarmi, Khadgi	2 each
Chitrakar, Napit, Tb. monk	1 each
	100

Note:
(a) This figure is approximate only, since monastic attachment was not recorded: in some cases it was known, but in others it had to be deduced from the twāḥ (neighbourhood) of the sponsor.

are represented; and also that it is not unknown for Joshis, whose own religious traditions are wholly Hindu, to sponsor a text-reading. With a few exceptions the sponsors all come from Lalitpur.[7]

The figures in Chart 7.5 suggest the hypothesis that, Sakyas and Vajracharyas and Brahmans apart,[8] other castes within Lalitpur are about equally likely to sponsor a text-reading. Figures for ward 15[9] given in Chart 7.6, certainly illustrate that Sakyas and Vajracharyas are far more likely than other castes to sponsor the rite; but they also show that members of the local peasant caste (Maharjan and Dangol) are not far behind. Roughly two-thirds of the Sakya and Vajracharya families in the ward (nearly all of whose male members belong to Kwa Bahah) have had the text read at least once during the last ten years. One in ten Sakya families have had it done more than four times. Indeed in this last group are many locally recognized 'rich men' (sāhu) who have the text read several times a year, or at least once a year, at any special religious occasion in the family, or when any member of the family particularly desires it. One other noteworthy fact is that members of the guthi, as well as Vajracharyas who frequently read the text, feel little need to have the text read themselves, since they believe that they benefit from frequent contact and receiving the goddess' blessing (prasād).

Chart 7.6: Households of ward 15, Lalitpur, by caste according to number of sponsorings of text-reading in Kwa Bahah in the last ten years

	Number of households (1984)	Sponsored at least once once	Sponsored more than once	Sponsored four times or more
Sakya (incl. Dhakhwa)	211	64.5% (136)	19.4% (41)	10.4% (22)
Vajracharya	66	66.7% (44)	18.2% (12)	3% (2)
Shrestha (incl. Joshi)	43	2.3% (1)[a]	/	/
Maharjan and Dangol	21	47.6% (10)	9.5% (2)	/
Napit	7	28.6% (2)	/	/
Total	348	(193)	(55)	(24)

Note:
(a) This figure may be an underestimate: some Shresthas are reluctant to admit to having sponsored a Buddhist ritual.

Why then do people have the text read? Assessing motives is a difficult business. I included a question asking the occasion (*upalakṣya*) for having the text read in the questionnaires which provided the data for Chart 7.6. For present purposes, in order to ensure that the responses are of a comparable value, I shall restrict myself to the 184 questionnaires I administered myself: all of them to Sakyas and Vajracharyas, and all of them within ward 15, or in its immediate environs. Of these 184, 114 (62 per cent) had had the text read in the last ten years. Of the 114, 30.7 per cent (35) mentioned illness as a reason for have the text read; 28.1 per cent (32) said simply that they desired to have it read;[10] 16.7 per cent (19) mentioned an auspicious occasion as the reason;[11] 2.6 per cent (3) mentioned a rite connected to death;[12] 5.3 per cent (6) mentioned their job;[13] 3.5 per cent (4) mentioned long-distance travel (the hope of a safe return); 3.5 per cent (4) mentioned ill fortune or bad luck at home;[14] 3.5 per cent (4) mentioned the duties of a guthi;[15] 1.7 per cent (2) mentioned buying or completing the building of a house. Where specific reasons are given, the predominance of illness is clear. I suspect that were one to ask other sponsors (i.e. non-members of Kwa Bahah) severe illness would loom even larger as the main reason for having the text read, and that among them it would more unusual to have the text read to celebrate an auspicious life-cycle rite.

These are all specific, personal, and self-interested reasons for having the text read. Fourteen per cent (16) used the terms *phyānāḥ taye* or (using the Nepali term) *bhākal yāye*, meaning that they made a vow to have the text read if the goddess fulfilled their desire.[16] Many of those who said simply that they wanted to have the text read may well have made a vow, but not wanted to say so; and some of those who gave illness as a reason—those who had the text read after the illness was cured—had almost certainly made a vow also. It is believed that if one vows to have the text read and then forgets, once the desired outcome is secured, the goddess will appear, in reality or in a dream, to remind the devotee.

One member of the guthi told me that the very moment one vows to have the text read, the ill person begins to get better. He listed various cases, including one of diabetes, where people had recovered thanks to the goddess. Another local had the text read three days in a row, he said, when he had won a court case.[17] Another was trading in Tibet in the old days and had a lot of gold which it was forbidden to bring out of the country. He vowed to the Perfection of Wisdom: somehow the border guards forgot to check his luggage at the frontier. Then in India he vowed a second time. When they finally returned safely to Nepal, he and his family had the text read three times in a row.

This kind of attitude towards a divinity represents, according to Weber (1968: 424), the '*do ut des* [I give so that you will give] ... [which] clings to the routine and the mass religious behavior of all people at all times and in all religions.' In Theravada Buddhism it is denied that Buddhism can give such worldly benefits, and Theravada Buddhists have to take recourse to gods which are defined locally as non-Buddhist. In Mahayana Buddhism by contrast worshippers are not forbidden, and are often encouraged, to see Buddhist divinities in this way. However this view of things, while authentically Buddhist, is only the lowest level of a path with many stages of understanding. Canonically, it is the merit derived from worship which is deemed capable of having immediate beneficial results. Furthermore, Newar Buddhists of any learning know that one is not supposed to desire things for oneself, or that at least one should wish well for others too, even (or especially) when carrying out a ritual, such as that being considered here, which is widely known as a frequent self-interested resort. Thus 19.3 per cent (22) gave a reason which seemed intended to accord with the scriptural teachings of Mahayana Buddhism. Three said that this was doing dharma, good religious work. Four said that it would bring peace (*śānti*) or prevent obstacles (*vighna*) or dangers (*bhaya*). One said that it was a way of showing devotion (*bhakti*) to the lord (*īśvara*). Five said that it would uplift beings or the world.[18] Finally two gave self-regarding, but more scripturally sound, reasons when they focused on the *psychological* consequences of the text-reading: one said that it would bring peace to his mind; the second that by bringing happiness (*ānanda*) to his mind, the illness would be cured.

Myth and history of the text and ritual

According to Hemraj Sakya (Sakya and Vaidya 1970: 19–20), the colophon of the text records that it was copied by Ananda Bhikshu of Kapitanagar in 345 NS (i.e. 1225 CE) in the reign of Abhaya Malla.[19] Because of the importance of the text, however, various myths have grown up around it. The story I heard in Nag Bahah is related to that given briefly in Wright's *History of Nepal* (1972: 159).[20] In Wright a brahman widow brings the book 'dated 245 Vikram Samvat'[21] when she flees, along with her son, from the village of Jhul. The account in Wright is abbreviated and does not explain how the text got from Bu Bahah to Kwa Bahah. This is a summary of the account I collected in Nag Bahah:

The Prajnaparamita was in the possession of a brahman of Vishalnagar [present-day Tangal]. He used to do the *aṣṭamī vrata* Observance regularly and, like every married brahman there, had a Fire Sacrifice pit (*yajñaśālā*) in the house. One day his daughter-in-law went and excreted in the pit in the night, and it all turned to gold. Others asked how he became so rich and he explained how it had happened. So they all had their daughters-in-law excrete in the night in their firepits and they all became rich with gold. But famine came to the country and there was nothing to eat. Then the Lord (Buddha) came in the form of a buffalo, thinking that he must feed the people. He allowed them to cut off bits of meat to eat, and there was enough for everyone. Now the wife of the brahman who had the Prajnaparamita and performed the *aṣṭamī vrata* was pregnant and she asked her husband to fetch her some meat. He tried to persuade her that it was not a buffalo but a god, but she insisted. He went and spoke to the buffalo who said, 'Don't stay in this country. It is about to be destroyed by fire. Take what you have in a worship basket (*kalācā*) and flee!' So they put the Prajnaparamita and other wealth in the basket and fled. As they looked back, the firepits in every house blazed up and consumed the whole city. They came finally to Bu Bahah in the area (*ilākā*) of Ga Bahah, and stayed in the *agniśālā* [the Brahman-run Vedic fire sacrifice shrine]. They were in fact two brothers, elder and younger, who then quarrelled over who should keep the Prajnaparamita. The pregnant wife said: 'Don't fight over it, you don't need it. Put it in Kwa Bahah.' (from Gellner 1984)

The reference to Kwa Bahah, and the introduction of a second brother, are tacked on as an addendum to the basic myth, which is about the brahman origin of (at least some of) the Vajracharyas of Bu Bahah.[22] In other versions I was told that a girl given in marriage from Bu Bahah to Kwa Bahah brought the book with her; and in another account, that a girl given in marriage from Kwa Bahah to Bu Bahah offered it in Kwa Bahah during a *bāhāḥ pūjā* (a procession with offerings to all the Lalitpur monasteries) because her husband was dead and she had no sons. In yet another version collected in Kwa Bahah by S. Rajbhandari (1978: 31), the brahman woman, called Yashodhara, of Kapitanagar, brought the book 'here' [presumably: Lalitpur] because of a vision and kept it 'in a secret hole'. She then gave it to Kwa Bahah as the best place to keep the strict rules it required. The Sakya guthi, according to this account, are supposed to be her relatives. It is because of the presence of Prajnapara-mita, Rajbhandari was told, that the main doors of Kwa Bahah, unlike other monasteries, have to be kept open all day long.

Clearly, then, there are many variant local accounts which have received little formalization or systematization. What they all share is the belief that the text was originally in Bu Bahah, brought there by a brahman. One final mythological element is that the members of Michu Bahah, immediately behind Kwa Bahah, say that their copy of the Prajnaparamita is the original and should be used to copy or replace the Kwa Bahah one.[23]

What of the history? This depends on the location of Kapitanagar, mentioned in the colophon. The colophon also reveals that the text has been restored (i.e. rewritten in gold) in the years NS 723, 748, 1032, 1063, and 1080 (Sakya and Vaidya 1970: 19). It was copied again in February 1983 (NS 1103) which corresponded to an extra intercalated month (*analā*), an inauspicious time when it was thought inappropriate to have the text read (Plate 12). The dates of restorations suggest that the text was read frequently in the seventeenth century but that afterwards there was a lull. The box in which the text is kept is dated NS 948 (1828) and refers to the eleven donors as a guthi. In NS 979 (1859) the box was washed with gold by several devotees. In NS 1020 (1900) the Dhakhwa family, according to an inscription in the monastery, donated a gold-plated throne for the box.

I suspect that the ritual of having the text read may date, in its present form, and with its present organization, only from the beginning of the nineteenth century or even later. The emergence of this ritual and its increasing popularity in the city of Lalitpur may well be associated with the rise of Kwa Bahah itself. The Kwa Bahah text-reading ritual should probably be intepreted as an example of religious innovation which is yet highly continuous with what went before and fits easily into established Buddhist notions.

Plate 12: The rewriting of the famous Kwa Bahah 'Perfection of Wisdom in Eight Thousand Lines' by Shukra Raj Bajracharya of Bu Bahal in the ornamental Ranjana script (27/2/83). The writer has to fast while writing, and the guthi member whose task it is to return the text to its casket must refrain from eating rice. Note the printed edition open on the table for checking. Offerings from the laity can be seen in the foreground.

Conclusion

The kind of text-reading rite considered here is common in all forms of Buddhism. What is unusual is the power attributed to this particular manuscript and, within Mahayana Buddhism, that it should be attributed specifically to 'The Perfection of Wisdom'. There is another text, the Pancaraksa, which in traditional Newar Buddhism is frequently read for apotropaic purposes. It is not surprising, however, and it is in accord with a Mahayana Buddhist outlook, that the Prajnaparamita, a text which when deified is considered a form of Tara, should be considered a means of resort when in dire straits.

The ritual and beliefs which surround this text can be compared (and some Lalitpur Newars do so compare it) to the cult of Hariti in Svayambhu. Both cults seem to be growing in popularity, and the reasons for worshipping Hariti would, if analysed, probably turn out to be very similar to those given here. None the less the two goddesses are, from a Buddhist point of view, on very different levels. Prajnaparamita is a personification of the ultimate salvific wisdom whereas Hariti is a once-evil spirit converted to Buddhism, the goddess of smallpox and small children.

In future one can perhaps expect the cult of Hariti to grow faster than that of Prajnaparamita for several reasons. First, because Kathmandu has a larger population; secondly because of Kathmandu's cultural dominance as the capital; thirdly because Hariti has—as Prajnaparamita has not—numerous ambassadors in every area of the big cities in the form of women (and occasionally men) who are possessed by Hariti (and/or her children Dhan Bhaju, Dhan Maiju, Lata Bhaju, Lata Maiju) and send their patients to the Hariti temple.[24] A final factor working in Hariti's favour is that as a lowly goddess she can, with less conceptual strain, be accepted by Hindus. Even strict Hindus do not mind making use of a Buddhist priest to deal with low spirits, as, for instance, in the rite of making safe the foundations of a new house. The method by which the Perfection of Wisdom must be worshipped—the reading of a holy text—makes the central Buddhist identity of the procedure much harder to ignore.

Notes

1. Other monasteries which are of city-wide importance are Ta Bahah, which houses the temple of Karunamaya (Matsyendranath), Tanga Bahah, with its temple of Cakubadyah (Minanath), and Ha Bahah, home of Lalitpur's royal Kumari.

2. See photos in Slusser 1982 II: No. 491 and Toffin 1984: 570.

3. From Skt *pāṭh/pāṭha yākegu*. Newars from Kathmandu recognize only this form, and correct *pā thyākegu*. However the latter deserves to be accepted as a dialect term; it has probably entered Lalitpur Newari through the influence of the ritual to be described. *Pā thyākegu* is similar to other Newari examples such as *pu jyāye* (from *pūjā yāye*) and *siddhayke* (from *siddha yāke*). I am grateful to Kashinath Tamot for pointing this out to me.

4. People remember a time when three were permitted.

5. If a 'casteless' (*bejāt*) person such as a foreigner, Butcher (Khadgi), or

Untouchable, wishes to have the text read, they have to appoint someone else as ritual sponsor (*jaymā*) in their place.

6. Pundit Asha Kaji Vajracharya called them 'the Seven *tathāgata*', but unlike the designation of the ten elders of a monastery as the Ten Moral Perfections (*daśapāramitā*) this identification is not well known.

7. These conclusions are borne out in the proportions revealed by 54 random observations of text reading by me between April 1983 and February 1984. By chance no Rajkarnikars sponsored a text-reading in 1985–6, although I observed three such cases in other years.

8. One should probably add the Tamrakars (who in Lalitpur are strongly Hindu) and Untouchables to this list.

9. In the early 1980s ward 15 included the Ashok Cinema Hall, Nyakhachuk, Nag Bahah, Sarasvati Nani, and Kwa Bahah. I surveyed approximately 170 households myself. The remaining Sakya and Vajracharya households were surveyed for me by Daya Ratna Sakya, and the others by S.P. Shrestha.

10. The most common expression used here was *lastā* (13), meaning simply that they desired to do so. Other expressions used were *pharmās* ('voluntary act') (3), *khusī* (3) and *mansubā* (2) (Nepali and Persian equivalents of *lastā*), *athē* ('I just did') (2), *lahar* ('for fun') (1), *śraddhā* ('out of faith/devotion') (1), *manay harṣa waye* (roughly 'for spiritual pleasure') (1), and *manyā kāmanā* (roughly 'I decided to') (1). The different percentages given here and below add up to more than 100 per cent because some respondents gave several reasons for having the text read.

11. Wedding (10), birthday (3), child's first rice-feeding (*macā jākwa*) (2), old-age initiation (*burā jākwa*) (2), Monastic Initiation (*bare chuyegu*) (2).

12. After a death in the family (2); at the one-year anniversary of a death (*dakhilā*) (1).

13. One man mentioned that he had done it once in the hope of obtaining a new job and on another occasion in the hope of promotion.

14. Expressions used: *chē śāntι* (1); *daśā ma bhinā* (1), *āpad* (1).

15. Taking up one's turn as god-guardian in Kwa Bahah (1), on leaving it (2); on completing subsequent duties connected with organizing the annual feast of Kwa Bahah (1).

16. One other respondent used an expression implying the same: *manovắchā puray yāyeta*.

17. Another Sakya man told me that there is no difference between this kind of text-reading and the *paritran* of the Theravada monks (cf. Vaidya 1986: Chapter 28), but that one ought not to do it to thank the goddess for defeating one's enemies, helping one to seize their land, etc.; nor should one do it to impress others with one's wealth.

18. Of these, three used the phrase *sattvaprāṇipī uddhār*, one said *saṃsār uddhār*, and one *parayāta uddhār*.

19. I have not been able to discover where Kapitanagar is.

20. I have published the account I was given by the late Gyan Ratna Sakya of Tahalcheli, Nag Bahah, in Gellner 1984.

21. Sakya and Vaidya (1970: 19) note that the original date must have been changed from 345 to 245 in one of the many restorations of the manuscript.

22. Other versions of the myth recount how, of two brothers, one became a Buddhist in Bu Bahah and the other remained a Hindu and tended the perpetual fire in the Agnimatha. The myth is cited to account for the existence of a guthi shared by brahmans attached to the Agnimatha and the Vajracharyas of Bu Bahah, in which in one year a Brahman sits at the head, the next year a Vajracharya.

23. The relative antiquity of the Michu Baha text is borne out by its colophon, dated NS 131 (Sakya and Vaidya 1970: 1–2). The story expresses a claim to priority on the part of Michu Baha also found in their myth of origin (see Gellner 1987: 402; Locke 1985: 52).

24. See Chapter 8 on these mediums. During the Dasain festival the famous manuscript of Prajnaparamita of Than Bahi, Kathmandu, is brought out (and held in the arms of a Vajracharya) to witness the celebration of the 'sword procession' (*khaḍgajātrā, pāyāḥ*), in which the Pradhan members of the monastery are possessed by 'the goddess' and hack a pumpkin to pieces (Ter Ellingson, personal communication). Here then the Prajnaparamita is—at least—associated with possession (whether she is actually considered to possess is not clear). I would however be inclined to regard this as an exceptional case, due to the unusual position of the Thamel Pradhans as Buddhist kshatriyas and members of a Buddhist monastery (bahi).

PART III

From Soteriology to Worldly Benefits

8

Priests, Healers, Mediums, and Witches: The Context of Possession in the Kathmandu Valley

Introduction

In his well-known theory of shamanism and spirit possession I.M. Lewis argues for a distinction between central and peripheral possession.[1] A central possession cult exists when ecstasy is a part of the dominant religion and possession is the preserve of those of high status; typically, the possessing spirits are highly moral. Peripheral possession is possession by amoral spirits (e.g. demons or witches). It is peripheral in two distinct senses: first, because the possessing spirits are frequently represented as coming from outside; second, because the victims of such possession are usually of low status, and are mostly, though not exclusively, women. Becoming possessed in this way is, Lewis argues, a kind of protest at, or compensation for, lack of power and status. This, he claims, explains why it is predominantly women who become possessed in a peripheral manner.

There has been a certain development in Lewis's writings. In his Malinowski Memorial Lecture his concern was explicitly with 'what in medical parlance would be called the epidemiology of possession, by which in this context I mean the examination of the categories of persons who are most readily prone to possession in different societies.'[2] He also briefly sketched a spectrum of four types of shamanistic religion or cult, moving from peripheral to central possession: (i) possession which is an occasional means for mainly women to seek redress without an elaborate cult; (ii) regular, institutionalized shamanistic cults with a leadership and complex pantheon, but still in opposition to the values of the dominant religion; (iii) prophetic movements which not only solve worldly problems but propose a spiritual and moral message; (iv) established religions such as those of the Old Testament, the Nuer, and the Dinka. However, in spite of this typology which hinted at a developmental theory, or in Weberian terms at the routinization of charisma, Lewis's early essay was primarily concerned with one limited and precise question: Why do some types of people (women, low-status men) seem to be more likely to become possessed than others? But since these two categories between them account for more than half the population, one might well suggest that the question should be turned around: Why do high-status men not become possessed?

In his later writings Lewis has broadened his theory in two principal ways. First, he has suggested that those who suffer possession often go through certain standardized stages (Lewis 1971: 123–6; 1986: Chapter 5). Secondly, he has argued that those societies with a central possession cult are responding, just as the possessed individual is responding, to outside pressures.

In the context to be examined in this essay, it will be seen that two elements of Lewis's theory have considerable cogency: (a) the distinction between central and peripheral possession and the prediction that those of lower status, usually women, tend to be subject to peripheral possession, whereas central possession is reserved for people of high status; and (b) the postulation of stages which the possessed pass through if they embark on a career as a shaman or a (spirit-) medium. The third part of his theory—that (c) societies characterized by a central possession cult are so because they are under external pressure and that there is a parallel here between individuals and societies—is more problematic. In the case of individuals, Lewis does not envisage that every low-status individual will become possessed; likewise, not every society under pressure must necessarily develop a central possession cult. But in the Nepalese case to be outlined below we have a society in which the central type of possession, albeit secret, plays an important part in legitimating a complex religious hierarchy, and it is not evident that when this form of religion was adopted, the society was under any particular pressure at all.

Lewis's theory has been the subject of considerable critical comment.[3] Much of it has unfortunately ignored the fact that the heart of Lewis's theory is the very specific 'epidemiological' question with which his Malinowski Memorial Lecture began. Often his critics have assumed that to label possession peripheral is necessarily to imply that it is

unimportant or inessential. In fact, in some societies peripheral possession, as defined by Lewis, is of great importance and cultural salience.[4]
But this, while certainly a valid and interesting point, is not a criticism
of Lewis, as I understand him. Furthermore, Lewis's theory has little to
say, and intentionally so, about the cultural form or meaning of spirit
experiences. Yet this very fact is frequently held against it, as if it invali-
dated it. In recent writing about spirit possession dissatisfaction is often
expressed with the functionalist or indeed any theory of possession.[5]
The alternative offered is a general anti-reductionism, sometimes digni-
fied with the label 'the interpretive approach'. This surely forecloses interesting questions, both about recruitment to the role of medium and
about the ideological implications of indigenous schemes of thought.

My own criticisms of Lewis are rather different from those mentioned
so far, and are much less hostile to his general approach. First, and this is
fairly trivial, a meaningful distinction between mediums and shamans
may be made in the Nepalese context, as will be seen below. Second,
and more importantly, his extension of the theory to the level of whole
societies is implausible and vague, as noted already. Third, in describing
what he calls the 'possession' or 'shamanic career' (Lewis 1989: 8), he
has laid insufficient stress on the process by which shamans and mediums
actively seek to become 'central' in the way they perform and in what
they stand for (this will be illustrated below). Finally, the spread of what
Lewis calls peripheral cults—but which in many cases might more
accurately be called 'half-way central cults'—is not necessarily a response
to a decline in the position of women (ibid.: 12), but can also come
about as a result of some women taking advantage of an *improvement* in
their status and opportunities. Thus, in my examination of the material
from the Kathmandu Valley, I stress precisely these two points: the process
whereby an individual, once possessed in a peripheral manner, then moves
away from it and towards central possession as she establishes herself as
a specialist; and, second, the longer-term historical processes in which
the spread of possession is a reaction to hierarchy. In particular, I interpret
the increase in the numbers of mediums in the Kathmandu Valley in
recent years as an aspect of the general democratization of Nepalese
culture.

The local context

In the wider context of Nepal, shamans, known in Nepali as *jhānkri*,
have attracted considerable scholarly attention.[6] In the traditions of the
Nepalese hill shamans, who are usually male, drumming and trance are

used to cure patients and carry out certain priestly functions.[7] Relatively little has been written on the same themes within the Kathmandu Valley where the relationship between gender, possession, and priesthood is rather different.[8]

This contrast between the Nepalese hills and the Kathmandu Valley can be explicated by reference to an article by Höfer (1974). Höfer distinguishes between a South Asian tradition in which mediums, drawn from the laity, are possessed by gods, ancestors, or ghosts, who are believed to *come to* them, and a Himalayan and Central Asian shamanic tradition (exemplified by *jhānkris* of various types) in which the specialist shaman is believed to *go to* the god. Höfer argues that lay possession spread with the development of Hinduism which reduced the distance between gods and men (mainly by means of iconographic representations), but simultaneously increased the distance between the religious elite and the laity. He continues:

The question is, whether the spread of possession in India may be seen also as a response to the situation, i.e., whether it was a process which took place in defiance *and* in default of the religious elite. In defiance, because possession represents an alternative to the distance-reducing techniques of meditation and asceticism. In default, because, firstly, the intellectualism and other-worldliness of the elite could not satisfy all the religious needs of the laity and/or because, secondly, a specific concept of status debars parts of this elite from serving as priests among certain groups of the population or on certain occasions during the life-cycle, from which impurity accrues. (Höfer 1974: 162–3; original emphasis)

The very long-term historical development that Höfer postulates will be seen to be important when attempting to explain the recent rise of mediums in the Kathmandu Valley. For present purposes the point to note is that the Kathmandu Valley belongs firmly in the South Asian part of Höfer's typology, and not with the shamanism of the Nepalese hills.

The cultural context of the Kathmandu Valley is largely Newar. The Newars, who are the original inhabitants of the Valley, nowadays comprise about half its population. They have their own language, Newari, which is Tibeto-Burman. Today nearly all of them are bilingual in Nepali and Newari, and some have begun to speak Nepali systematically to their children, much to the despair of Newar cultural nationalists. Most of the other inhabitants of the Valley are Parbatiyas (literally 'hill people'), the Nepali-speaking dominant ethnic group of Nepal. Another large group are the Tamangs, a Tibetanized hill 'tribe', who speak their own Tibeto-Burman language, and are settled in the hills around the edge of the Valley and in some cases inside it. Kathmandu city, with over 235,000 inhabitants in 1982, has, among other more recent arrivals, longstanding Marwari and Muslim minorities. There are three old royal cities in the Valley, Kathmandu itself, Lalitpur, and Bhaktapur. Kathmandu and Lalitpur are in the western half of the Valley, either side of the Bagmati river; Bhaktapur is east of the Valley. In the western part of the Valley, which is the main focus here, about half the Newars are Buddhist, i.e. have Buddhist domestic priests (Vajracharyas) and half are Hindu, i.e. have Hindu domestic priests (i.e. Brahmans). Only for the highest castes, however, is religious identity at all exclusive. Both Vajracharyas and Newar Brahmans have the right to go through Tantric initiations and perform Tantric rituals, but it is the former whom Newars and other Nepalese particularly associate with Tantric powers and healing magic. In Kathmandu city Muslim healers are also considered to be powerful exorcists. This is perhaps not surprising considering that the majority Hindu and Buddhist population conceive of Muslims as 'upside down' (*ultā*), reversing all normal social conventions. Untouchables are also often thought to be powerful healers because, people say, 'they are able to frequent cremation grounds'.

Despite these ethnic or caste associations, anyone from any background can be a healer or medium. Gender, as considered below, is arguably more important than ethnicity. Anyone may be a client or a patient. Low castes are not excluded. Having said that, figures given below in Chapter 8 show that even a highly successful healer, with a Valley-wide reputation, draws the majority of his clients from his own ethnic group; this is presumably so *a fortiori* of less successful ones.

Healers and mediums: specialists in misfortune

Among the Newars there are basically two types of practitioner specializing in the diagnosis and cure of supernaturally caused misfortune, or in problems which, while occurring naturally, require supernatural diagnosis: the healer and the medium. Similar distinctions are made elsewhere in South Asia.[9] *Jhānkris*, to whom the term 'shaman' will be restricted, are not of great importance. Newars and Parbatiyas of the Valley know about them, but do not generally visit them in my experience.[10] They are confined to the Tamang community. I refer to those who consult healers, mediums, or jhānkris as 'clients' or 'patients'. Neither word is entirely satisfactory: the former suggests a long-term relationship which usually does not exist and the latter is too narrow. In Newari they are referred to most economically as *kyā waipī*, 'those who come to show', i.e. those who come to present symptoms, horoscopes, or some other problem.

I use the term 'healer' to translate the Newari *vaidya*, and 'medium' to translate *dyaḥ waimha* (Np. *devatā āune*) or *dyaḥmā*, respectively 'one to whom the gods come' and 'god-mother'. Healers, who are always male, are never possessed, but rather acquire their powers by spiritual exercises and straightforward instruction. Some women specialists, namely midwives, do know how to use the technique of brushing and blowing used for healing by both mediums and (ritual) healers, but they do not set themselves up as general practitioners. For women, the only path to becoming a general practitioner is as a medium. Men do sometimes become mediums, but they are vastly outnumbered by women. Mediums are possessed, often on a daily basis, by a tutelary deity; occasionally they are possessed by other deities as well.

The word *vaidya* can refer to a wide variety of healers and apothecaries. A broad division can be made between those who stick exclusively to Ayurvedic methods and diagnoses, and those who make use of an eclectic mix of Ayurveda, astrology, and Tantric ritual.[11] The latter are called *jhārphuke vaidya*, i.e. vaidyas who use the technique of brush-

Plate 13: Krishna Maharjan, a healer (jhārphuke vaidya) in Kirtipur with two clients asking about money problems (9/9/89). His broom is on the table behind him.

ing and blowing. The brushing is believed to remove evil influences and the blowing to impart protective mantras. Both the term *jhārphuk* and the practice are common throughout Nepal and north India.[12] It is note-worthy that both strictly Ayurvedic practitioners and ritual healers are equally vaidya; thus they are not sharply distinguished in local usage.[13] However, in the rest of this chapter, when I refer to healers it is these jhārphuke vaidya or ritual healers who are intended.

For mediums the main possessing divinity is Hariti, the Buddhist goddess of smallpox, who is believed to be a spirit (*yakṣa*) converted to Buddhism and the guardian of young children. Other divinities I have encountered as the main possessing tutelary deity—one case each— are Krishna, Unmatta Bhairava, and Vajrayogini.[14] On occasion other gods may also temporarily possess the medium, particularly Hariti's eight children. In an exorcism observed in 1982 twenty different divinities entered a male medium's body one after the other, three of them occur-ring twice. Of the twenty, eight were the children of Hariti, four were locally identifiable forms of the Goddess, one was an Indian form (Sadasi-mata) of the Goddess, two were local forms of Bhairava, four were more general forms of the Goddess (Kali, Durga, Kumari, and Vajrayogini), and one was Hanuman, the monkey god. The exorcism was performed by Hanuman on his second appearance.[15] Hariti, the usual possessing deity, did not appear on this occasion. Both 'good' possession by a god (*dyaḥ*), such as Hariti, and 'bad' possession by a witch (*bwaksī*, Np. *boksī*) are described using the same verbs in Newari, 'to come' (*waye*) and 'to enter into' (*dubiye*), a similarity which will be seen to be signif-icant below.[16]

The same kind of problems are, it seems, brought to both healers and mediums. These problems are rarely straightforward medical ones. When people believe that they are suffering from a simple physical ailment, today at least they buy medicine, consult a pharmacist, or, if it is serious enough and they can afford it, a doctor. Both healers and mediums encourage people to come to them with physical complaints, referring to themselves as 'the doctors of the poor'. They are, however, more than just doctors. Many problems brought to them would be classified by biomedical practitioners as primarily social or psychological, and some have no physical component at all. The symptom specified is often a vague and general malaise.

The treatment offered by healers and mediums is also very similar. They both offer blessed and empowered powder, blessed and empowered water, brushing with a broom, and blowing. Different healers have different styles of brushing. Some do it vigorously, positively whacking the patient, others in a very genteel manner, barely touching them. Both healers and mediums recommend specific acts of worship and rituals for certain ills. Both tend to be conservative with regard to purity taboos. However, there are two means which mediums cannot make use of: astrology and Ayurvedic medicine. Both of these are bodies of expertise which require literate study and from which women are excluded.[17] The god who speaks through the medium's mouth may pronounce on the auspiciousness of certain times, and may venture a diagnosis which makes use of Ayurvedic concepts, but the medium cannot actually consult a person's horoscope, decide the cause of imbalances in the body by feeling a person's pulse, or sell Ayurvedic medicines as the healer can, and often does. A medium must accept whatever gift grateful clients may offer; so too must the healer, but he also has this option of selling medicines for a fixed price.

These healers and mediums, as well as the *jhānkris* (hill shamans), are part of what Kleinman (1980) would call a healthcare system, and others would probably be happier describing as a pluralistic, and in many aspects, syncretistic, cultural field. The situation in Nepal has much in common with that in Taiwan as described by Kleinman. Western biomedicine has the highest prestige. In and near Kathmandu a wide range of biomedical facilities are available, including many hospitals and private clinics. There are also both private and government-run Ayurvedic clinics, and a government Ayurvedic college. However, fewer resources are devoted to them than to biomedicine, and most Ayurvedic specialists hope their sons will become biomedical doctors. Terms derived from western medicine have entered the wider language (TB, typhoid, cancer) and are used by healers and mediums. Biomedicine is one further tradition—though one with certain unique characteristics—which has been added to, and has achieved a hegemonic position within, what was already a pluralistic situation including Ayurveda, astrology, herbal remedies, magic, and religion. Most Nepalese have a considerable (but very rarely exclusive) faith in the technology of biomedicine, particularly in injections and antibiotics (the latter often being self-administered as a prophylactic). A wide range of western medicines manufactured in India is freely available without prescription from 'compounders' (i.e. those in charge at pharmacies) who lack any formal training. Other relatively new elements in this pluralistic situation are the manufactured traditional Chinese remedies imported from Tibet; and the existence of Japanese healing cults, e.g. Seimeikyo, in Kathmandu.

Witches and their enemies

In a large number of cases (39 per cent of diagnoses in one Kirtipur healer's practice: see p. 229), the healer or medium identifies 'spoiling action' (*syākāḥ taḥgu*), by definition the action of a witch, as the cause of the complaint. Thus both healers and mediums see themselves as identifying and combating witchcraft. They are crucial to the process of confirming and legitimating people's suspicions on this score.

Local, and especially Newar, cultural ideas about the interrelations of these various roles can be represented without too much distortion as a series of oppositions, thus:

order : disorder ::
male : female ::
priest : healer ::
healer : medium ::
medium : witch.

This is not meant to be a generative structure determining the limits of all Newar thought. In fact, the different oppositions apply at somewhat different levels. The first three are to an extent analytical distillations of local ideas; the fourth, in its full sense, is an interpretation made mainly by healers; and the last represents the point of view of mediums and those who resort to them. In short, this set of oppositions is intended as a heuristic device, a representation of the framework within which Newars and others of the Valley tend to associate related ideas.

It will be noticed immediately that both healers and mediums appear on both sides of the list of oppositions. This suggests that there is a sliding scale, with priests at one end and witches at the other. Witches are known as *bwaksī* in the feminine, *bwaksā* in the masculine. While educated Nepalese often deny any validity to mediums, they are usually firmly convinced of the existence of witches.[18] This reflects greater cultural certainty about the latter, even traditionally.

Newars encounter witches in four distinct contexts. First, there are stories and sayings about them: that they come out at night (and especially on particular dates, such as Pishacha Chaturdashi, a minor festival usually falling in March), use their lighted forefinger as a lamp, and meet at frightening places, especially Mother Goddess temples outside of settlements and near cremation grounds; that they can turn into animals at will; and that they try out their harmful medicines on street dogs, turning them mad. Many believe that it is religiously wrong to discuss witches at all, and that doing so may attract their malign attention.

Second, there are specific misfortunes which are ascribed by mediums and healers to the 'spoiling' action of others. Anyone who harms others by magical means is considered a witch. This may be done by acting on an item of clothing or a hair of the victim. But one may also harm others simply by looking at them or, particularly, at the food they eat. Some Newars say that anyone can do this; others say it only does harm if the onlooker happens to be someone who, as a child, consumed excrement through the inattention of the caretakers, a view found also in Rajasthan (Lambert 1988: 197); and yet others deny that anyone can harm other people simply through jealousy or desire to harm. As Levine (1982) emphasizes for the Nyinba, a Tibetan group in the far north-west of Nepal, there is no consensus on these matters. Nor is there any obvious pattern in the distribution of these beliefs among the Newars. Unlike the Nyinba, and unlike many African societies, Newars do not generally believe that witchcraft is hereditary.

A typical example of the way witchcraft is used as an explanation of misfortune is the following account given by an informant I shall name P:

P's cousin (his father's half-sister's daughter) has for 15 or 20 years wandered distractedly in the street, wearing dreadful old clothes. She steals her family's money to buy duck eggs to offer to Hariti. They have to lock everything up. Everyone says she is mad (*wī*). However when P goes for Younger Brother Worship (*kijā pūjā*) (for which she invites him) she appears perfectly normal, and although some people tell him not to go, he does. One day she came running to his house as if running away from some terrible danger. She rattled the front door, calling his name, as if in fear of her life. They let her in. A man appeared who was chasing her. P asked him: 'Who are you? Why are you trying to catch her?' The man explained that she had stolen an egg. P gave him the money and he went away. Meanwhile his cousin was on the roof, ready to jump off. P brought her down, and finally asked her why she always has to offer eggs. She replied that the god comes and frightens her, forcing her to offer eggs; if she offers eggs the god doesn't come. She insisted it wasn't a dream. People say that she has been 'spoilt' by a witch.

A third context in which witches are encountered is that of witch attack or possession by a witch. This is far more extreme and much less common than simply being harmed by a witch, since the witch enters the victim's body (usually a woman) and speaks through her mouth. I have only once observed such possession myself, in a woman waiting to see a medium, but such cases are often discussed by Newars. The possessed person acts in a violent and bizarre way. Members of the family, sometimes under the instruction of a healer, threaten the woman or even beat her or twist her thumbs, believing that it is the witch who is being hurt, in order to persuade the witch to name herself, or at least to drive her out. In the past the possessed woman's cheek was branded with a red-hot rice spatula in the belief that the witch would be marked by this procedure and thereby identified. The law code of 1854 attempted strict regulation of such action, making any healer who prescribed it liable to heavy fines if it did not work. It also forbade the banishment of a suspected witch unless the branding test had already succeeded; and it banned ordeals (Macdonald 1976). This kind of possession is often a prelude to the benign possession by a divinity which makes one a medium.

The fourth and final context in which witches are encountered is the actual suspicion and naming of known people. (Clearly this context is the background to the naming of a culprit during witch exorcism.) In practice it is women, especially old women, and among them especially widows, who are suspected of being witches. Nowadays little is done to them beyond avoiding contact; often, however, outward politeness is maintained, in order to avoid offending them. A common response seems to be to throw a brick through their window at night (whether it has glass panes or not). As implied by the 1854 law code, much severer action was commonly taken in the past. What one does not find, though everyone believes they exist, are women who call themselves witches and practise black magic. Without a trace of irony, Louis Mahuzier (n.d.: Chapter 1) describes his attempts to find and film such a woman performing her rituals: she always seemed to remain just out of reach, and all the Newars Mahuzier requested to mime a witch's rituals refused with horror. In other words, unlike the African cases vividly described by Jackson (1989: 94–6), no one ever confesses to being a witch.[19] On the other hand, the gap between the witch stereotype and actual people accused of witchcraft, identified by Jackson, applies equally to the Newar case.

Two further examples will put ethnographic flesh on the postulated opposition of mediums to witches:

Near a female medium from Lalitpur lived a woman who did not get on with her mother-in-law. All her children had died and she believed her mother-in-law was a witch and was killing them. She came to the medium who told her that her mother-in-law was indeed a witch and that as long as she was in the house she, the daughter-in-law, would never be able to have offspring who survived. If the mother-in-law died, on the other hand, the children would be saved. The woman went and confronted her mother-in-law. The local people decided that the senior people of the neighbourhood should decide the case. In front of them all the mother-in-law declared that she was not a witch. 'Alright then,' said her daughter-in-law, 'Let's go and see the medium.' They went there, but as they were coming in to the room the medium cried out, 'Don't come in, you are a witch!' 'No, I'm not,' she replied. The medium raised her hand, and her *vajra* [a Tantric Buddhist ritual implement] touched the temple of the witch. Even though it barely touched her, a great stream of blood flowed forth. The woman went to hospital. Later she took the case to court, saying that she had been accused unjustly of being a witch. The court called the medium who said: 'I didn't do it. She is a witch. If she is a witch, she will die in nine days. If not, she won't.' And the woman died within nine days. The case was dismissed and the medium became famous.

Interestingly, when I visited this medium, she told me that after this case she had given up searching out witches, and restricted herself to treating illness, at the request of her husband and children (who were evidently afraid that she would provoke further hostility).

Another case (involving Tuladhars, high-caste Buddhist Newars, from Kathmandu) also illustrates the hostility which can easily arise between mother- and daughter-in-law in the Newar joint family. In this case my informant pointed out that the daughter-in-law's natal family was rich but her husband's was relatively poor and that the young man, encouraged by his family, had asked his wife's father to buy him a house. Rather than wait for trust to grow, he had done this at the very beginning of the marriage and this evidence of the husband's family's greed had sown seeds of mistrust at the outset. The wife's father was reluctant to buy the house, which angered the husband's family (he feared to buy it in his daughter's name in case her husband's family should kill her to acquire it). The account began with the following incident:

The mother-in-law suspected her daughter-in-law of putting ensorcelled substances in her vegetables. A nearby medium confirmed that the daughter-in-law was a witch, and this led to the daughter-in-law returning to her natal home with her two small children. The daughter-in-law's family rejected the charges indignantly and made a counter-accusation that the mother-in-law was a witch. And they refused to send their daughter back to her husband for fear that the mother-in-law would enlist the help of other witches to kill her. Shortly after this the daughter-in-law's father died, and then her mother got ill, dying slowly over a year. The mother ascribed her illness to the witches enlisted by her daughter's mother-in-law, because the doctor's treatment was doing no good and because a healer or medium she consulted said 'Someone who comes to your house and sits near you may have harmed you.' This confirmed her suspicion that a neighbour who came regularly to watch their television set was a witch. Finally she was taken to Vellore in south India where the doctors found that she had cancer, not the TB for which her Nepalese doctor had been treating her, but it was too late.

In prescribing rituals and recommending ritualistic purity, in identifying witches and suggesting counter measures, mediums appear as the guardians of order. From another point of view, however, the medium is assimilated to the witch and opposed to the healer. Healers themselves do not look kindly on mediums. No doubt it is partly a question of competition for business. Thus, healers tend to run mediums and witches together, implying that mediums are witches. One healer put it to me that healers, being men, have to worship fierce male gods, particularly Bhairava, in order to undo the harm women do through their worship of a goddess, Hariti.

Yet even the healer is not above suspicion of using his knowledge to harm others. In fact, he is more likely to be suspected of this than mediums, who are regarded either as fakes or as divinely inspired. Thus, people are careful not to offend healers. Many say that the knowledge of how to cause harm and that required to undo it are the same. When I asked if there could be male witches one healer replied: 'I'm a witch (*bwaksā*)!'[20] I think it is true to say, as Kleinman (1980: 240) does of attitudes to Taiwanese shamans, that, though people are grateful for the healer's cures, 'he also is envied and distrusted for his financial success and occasionally feared for his reputed power to engage in sorcery or otherwise cause individuals to become sick.' Certainly I know of no case of a devotional cult focused on a healer parallel to that described below for a medium.

Compared to the double-edged benefits of healers, the blessings handed out by the male priests who control the cults of high and pure divinities (Brahmans, Karmacharyas, Vajracharyas, Sakyas) are unambiguously good, and not harmful. Unfortunately such blessings are often not sufficient to keep misfortune away. Thus healers are opposed to priests in that the latter dispense otherworldly and/or generalized worldly blessings, whereas the former provide specific remedies for specific worldly ills.

Mediums on the central/peripheral spectrum

Having considered local representations as a series of oppositions, the consequences of conceptualizing these same ideas as a spectrum can now be analysed. At the same time it will be possible to address Lewis's question, why women are more likely to be possessed and become mediums than men. When dealing specifically with this question (and not taken as a general theory which accounts for the origins, existence, meaning, and cultural form of possession in all societies) Lewis's theory is very plausible. Contrary to what is sometimes claimed, his theory is not contradicted by the fact that peripheral possession frequently springs from genuine suffering.

I have suggested that Newar culture presupposes a kind of spectrum with high-caste, male priests handing out generalized, wholly beneficent blessings at one end, and witches, causing particular harm, at the other. The healer and the medium must go part of the way towards the 'witch' end of the spectrum in order to combat the witches' harm. Lewis himself (1971: 44) admits that his two types of possession are 'opposite extremes on a single continuum.' I would suggest that the spectrum of local representations identified above is how Newars and others in the Valley think about Lewis's 'continuum'. The 'central: peripheral' pair might therefore be added to the set of oppositions given above.

Furthermore, local conceptions can be represented in a manner consonant with Lewis's spatial metaphor as indicated in Fig. 8.1. That this is possible is perhaps not surprising in view of the importance of the mandala in traditional Newar culture: in essence a mandala is a sacred diagram, with a centre, a boundary, and four gates. For most Newars it

Fig. 8.1: A spatial representation of local ideas about the relation of priests, healers, mediums, and witches.

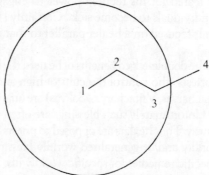

Key:
    1 = the central position, the moral 'high ground', occupied by the priests of high and pure deities
    2 = the position of healers
    3 = the position of mediums
    4 = the peripheral position of witches and demons

Note: The medium moves from 4 to 3 in the course of becoming a medium, when malign possession by a witch is replaced by benign possession by a divinity. Ritual healers, many of whom also occupy the central position in their role as priests, must spend the night in a witch-infested cremation ground (equivalent to position 4) as part of their training.

I owe to Nick Allen the suggestion that the spectrum's line should be jagged, not straight, to indicate that the oppositions which make it up are not all of exactly the same type.

refers primarily to the sacred diagrams drawn by priests during complex rituals, but it is also the model for the architecture of both Hindu and Buddhist temples, for the planning of Newar cities, and of the cosmos itself (see Chapter 12 below).

A typical medium's career traces a movement from the outside in. It usually begins with being attacked and possessed by witches—typical peripheral possession—until finally the woman agrees to be possessed benignly, usually by Hariti.[21] She must then worship Hariti on a daily basis, be possessed usually every day, and cure for the good of all beings. This is represented as the woman being chosen, against her will: it was her only option in order to prevent continuing maleficent possession by witches. She herself is usually the strongest advocate of this interpretation. She cannot therefore be blamed for undertaking what is in effect a career, one which is undoubtedly risky but may be relatively lucrative for her, if successful. It is the only career, as opposed to wage-labour or petty retailing, open to uneducated women. While possessed, she will be worshipped as a god. This is in stark contrast to women's normal position, which is symbolized by the daily obligation to bow down to the feet of their husbands and other senior affinal relatives. Possession can therefore be seen as giving some women, in some circumstances, the power within strict limits to determine their own fate.

By being possessed by a god, and no longer by a witch, the medium has moved away from the peripheral end of the spectrum. She tries, understandably, to get as near to the central end of the spectrum as she can. Being a woman, and considering the nature of the ills with which she deals, she can never be entirely successful in this. Even if the medium is no longer so peripheral in terms of the possessing agent, the divine possessor is rarely a very high god. The higher the god, the more likely it is that people will be sceptical of claims to possession by him or her. For instance, a Maharjan (Farmer) man from a village south of Lalitpur who appeared one day in Kwa Bahah (an important Buddhist sacred complex) and claimed to be possessed by Kwabaju, i.e. Sakyamuni Buddha, was met with polite but definite scepticism. Furthermore, a medium remains 'peripheral' in her origin (neither high-status nor rich), in the generally lower status of those who resort to her, and in her place in the overall hierarchy of religious specialists. The effort to move to a more prestigious, more 'central', position is none the less manifest in the fact that mediums often tell moral homilies in the middle of curing, and that they instruct clients to obey purity rules, and worship the gods. In religion they are traditionalists.[22] Mediums who attract a following of adherents tend to be those who appear continually benign. Newars find it puzzling that a medium should usually say entirely convincing things when possessed, but at other times seem to be full of petty jealousies, and their faith in such mediums is correspondingly weaker.

Local explanations for the predominance of women among mediums and witches fall into two types: those which invoke some religious myth or fact, and those which focus on stereotypes of the feminine. We have seen already that since the principal possessing deity is a goddess, Hariti, some consider it natural that women should be more often possessed. When asked why women are more often witches, some cite the following story. When Shiva was recounting all the wisdom of the world to his wife, Parvati, she fell asleep, but she woke up with a start when he got to the section on black magic (*kuvidyā*). Others say simply that women are weak, in particular morally weak, and are therefore more likely to wish harm on others and to succumb to the temptation to use magic to accomplish it. If asked why some women and not others become mediums, locals may say that it is a question of karma, i.e. that these women had the bad luck (determined by a previous birth) to be attacked by a witch, and that becoming a medium was the only remedy. Some are not above pointing out, in particular cases, the inadequacies of the woman's husband.

Ideas about the moral weakness and fickleness of women, a common theme of Newar folk tales, are confirmed for both men and women by the facts of everyday life in the joint family. Transported at marriage from her natal family to that of her husband, a young Newar woman must maintain multiple allegiances: to her parents, to her husband, and to her husband's household. She must repeatedly prove her allegiance to the latter by subservience to her mother-in-law, by hard work, by self-denial, and by producing children. It is at this most stressful point of a woman's life-cycle—transported to a new household, suffering a dramatic loss of status, and under pressure to give birth to sons—that peripheral possession often strikes. When households break up, women are frequently blamed for causing brothers to quarrel. Women, coming from outside, are not only essential to, but dangerous for, the stability of the household: they are essential for, but simultaneously threatening to, its ritual purity.[23]

Women, it is assumed, need to be controlled by men, and younger women need to be controlled by older women as well. Men perceived to be controlled by women are referred to by various unflattering and pejorative expressions (for instance, that they have disappeared up their wife's sari or vagina). In contrast to women, who are contextually impure, low castes are thought of as permanently impure. This is sometimes ascribed to their essential nature, but is perhaps more frequently explained as a consequence of the fact that they do not observe ritualistic rules (*niyam*) and perform few rituals. Traditionally low castes had to be controlled also, in order to prevent them adopting high-caste practices. Lack of control is evident in spirit possession. Thus one can see how both women and low castes are associated with spirit possession, and why high-caste males should shun it, except in closely defined esoteric contexts. This secret possession by the Tantric gods of Buddhism and Hinduism is part of Tantric Initiation in both religions (see above, Chapters 4 and 5). In both Hinduism and Buddhism such initiation is restricted (with a few, only partial exceptions) to high castes. High-caste Buddhist women repeat this possession in certain private, family, or lineage rituals during the year.[24] In fact, similar associations between the female, the low caste, and spirit possession are common throughout South Asia (Fuller 1992: 240).

In spite of these obstacles, a medium who combines a convincing teaching of religious truths with a reputation for curing people may under certain circumstances start a cult. A minor cult may be said to centre on one Lalitpur medium. She has been curing for over twenty years, and the new (though traditional-style) house into which she and her husband have moved is said to have been bought with her earnings as a medium. She has a loyal following of devotees who visit her regularly in gratitude for cures she has effected. A considerable number of these followers (between twenty and thirty) have themselves begun to be possessed regularly, and to cure, under her influence. On the anniversary of her first possession, she invites everyone to be present at an elaborate worship of Hariti performed by her Vajracharya domestic priest. The house is packed all day long. Women sing devotional hymns. The atmosphere is joyful and those present refer to the medium as 'mother'. Within the purified worship area all those who regularly become possessed sit in line, so that on the occasion when I was present (1989) there were about ten mediums all possessed simultaneously. When the worship is over, the principal medium offers gifts of cloth to her disciple mediums, and all the devotees come to pay obeisance first to her, and then to all the other mediums. The devotees are then invited to sit down together to a feast served by the medium's relatives, neighbours, and local devotees. This cult brings together Newars from a wide variety of class and caste backgrounds, as well as a few Parbatiyas. However, without the desire to expand, and lacking close disciples with expertise in the use of writing, bureaucracy, or the English language, it is unlikely that this very minor cult will grow as some others have done, such as some Japanese new

Plate 14: The anniversary celebration of the first possession of Chyasa Dyoma by the goddess Hariti (8/9/89). The barrier is erected to keep non-fasting lay devotees apart from the sacred area. The medium herself is out of the picture to the right. Her family's domestic Vajracharya priest can be seen leaning forward over the ritual offerings. To his right is the medium's husband who was the sponsor (jajmān, jaymā) of the Hariti worship. To his right is the first of a line of five disciples, one male, four female, all of whom have become mediums under the influence of Chyasa Dyoma. Some show signs of possession. The ritual, accompanied by hymn-singing, lasted all afternoon and was followed by a feast for all present.

religions, or the Sai Baba movement. As in Bengal (McDaniel 1988: 229–30), the fact that mediums deal every day with worldly problems is in itself an obstacle to establishing a spiritual movement. This is probably the case generally in South Asia, but is certainly not elsewhere.[25]

Mediums as beneficiaries of 'democracy'

I have stressed that both healers and mediums deal with the same kinds of complaint, but that mediums are unable to make use of two of the techniques, based on literate traditions, available to healers, namely Ayurvedic medicine and astrology. It may well be that mediums are, as far as they can, imitating healers. Many Nepalese say that the phenomenon of mediums is new; although possession occurred in the past, roughly some thirty or forty years ago, women did not establish themselves as regular mediums. In other words, the spread of mediums coincides with what the Nepalese refer to as the coming of 'democracy' (*prajātantra*) in 1951, i.e. the overthrow of the autocratic Rana regime. In the modern technical sense, i.e. rule through a national assembly elected on the basis of multi-party competition, democracy was stablished only in 1990 (apart from a brief interlude in the 1950s). In a larger sense, however, the popular perception is quite correct. The years after 1959 under King Mahendra's Partyless Panchayat Democracy, as it was called, did see the establishment of equality before the law, the principle of one person one vote, and in general a considerable decline in all spheres of life of the authoritarian and hierarchical values of the Rana period. The pace of social change has been especially rapid in the Kathmandu Valley. In the modern period, male priests and healers may disapprove of mediums, but there is nothing they can do to stop people patronizing them, and their disapproval now counts for little.

But is it in fact true that mediums never practised on a regular basis before 1951? Brinkhaus has translated a seventeenth-century Newari farce by Jagat Prakasha, king of Bhaktapur, which depicts one of the protagonists pretending to be a Buddhist female *siddhayoginī* who hands out charms and can perceive what is going on in Tibet while in Nepal (Brinkhaus 1987: 102ff). Perhaps this refers to a medium; perhaps it reflects the possible existence of female healers, not known today, at that time. Certainly, even today a local woman who set herself up as a medium in a Parbatiya village would rapidly find herself accused of witchcraft and—unlike the urban mediums described here—unable to practise.[26] Whether or not the medium phenomenon is entirely modern as many believe, it has undoubtedly grown and spread remarkably in the last few decades, so that every locality in the Newar cities and towns has at least one such medium.

In making use of possession, mediums are borrowing a technique that occurs in a number of traditional Newar contexts. R.L. Jones (1976: 5–6) has suggested that in general four, rather than Lewis's two, types of possession should be recognized: peripheral, tutelary, reincarnate, and oracular. The peripheral is, as in Lewis's terminology, that which can, in theory, happen to anyone, anywhere, at any time: possession by witches or other evil forces. Tutelary possession is the possession of the shaman or medium, which anyone can experience, but it is not permanent and only occurs at designated times. Reincarnate possession is that of the Tibetan reincarnate lama, who incarnates the spirit of a previous lama permanently at all times; this kind of possession is restricted to a few persons. Oracular possession is that which occurs to specified functionaries on specific ritual or festival occasions.

All four of Jones's types occur among the Newars. Peripheral possession has been discussed above, and tutelary possession refers to that of the mediums. Reincarnate possession is found in the institution of the 'living goddess' (Kumari) described by M.R. Allen (1975). One might also wish to identify a weak kind of reincarnate possession: that in which the king incarnates (or is believed to be a partial incarnation of) Vishnu, brahmans incarnate Brahma, Vajracharyas incarnate Vajrasattva, Kapalis (Jogis, low-caste Shaivite death specialists) incarnate Kapala Bhairava, and so on. Masked dances of the Mother Goddesses may be considered a form of oracular possession. Furthermore there is a kind of possession—that occurring during Tantric rituals, mentioned above—which fits none of Jones's types well. Unlike both oracular and tutelary possession it is not public; it is not restricted to functionaries as oracular possession is, nor it is open to all like tutelary possession. It can, however, be accommodated within Lewis's broad and vague category, 'central possession'.

Public possession occurs at certain festivals: for instance, in dances of the Eight Mother Goddesses at Dasain and other occasions. Such public possession is made manifest by shaking, just like both secret possession and the possession of the mediums. Usually it is fairly stylized and there is little prospect of the possessed person getting out of control. When middle and low farming castes incarnate goddesses in this way they sometimes receive blood sacrifice, and drink the blood directly from the animal's half-slit throat.

Against this background of controlled possession by traditionally specified personnel, the spread of freelance mediums can be seen to represent, in effect, a democratization of the means of religious authority. Mediums use possession to legitimate the pronouncements about daily life by means of which they act as arbitrators, doctors, priests, and moral preceptors. This parallels their use of ritual paraphernalia borrowed from the Great Traditions, for instance, the Vajracharya priest's vajra and dagger, symbols of his authority and Tantric power. The kind of group possession described above, which occurs at the annual celebration of a Lalitpur medium's first possession, recalls Tantric Initiation. But in this case participation is not restricted on grounds of caste and the possession is less routinized. At least one medium, who is permanently possessed, has adopted the 'reincarnate' possession of the 'living goddess', Kumari (see note 14).

In these ways, then, mediums appropriate the most prestigious religious means known to them. Furthermore, I would see this process as a rapid acceleration and expansion, under the conditions of modernization, of the very long-term historical tendencies of lay resistance to priest-ly prerogative within Hinduism postulated by Höfer. In other words, as priestly power has declined, both in terms of the deference afforded to priests, and in the extent to which political authorities are willing and able to act on their behalf, new religious opportunities have opened up to the laity. Thomas (1988) has made a similar argument for Pacific societies: that shamanism flourished where chiefs were weak and hierar-chy was undeveloped or in retreat; and that consequently shamanic practitioners expanded in numbers and significance with the initial disruptive impact of colonialism.

Conclusion

I have argued that the overwhelming predominance of women in the role of medium in the cities of the Kathmandu Valley should be interpreted in line with I.M. Lewis's theory of spirit possession. Yet, in order to understand what the medium role implies and how it is viewed we have to see it as part of a larger set which includes priests, healers, and mediums. We need to consider also, as Kapferer argues (1991: 139), 'the cultural constructs which men have of women and women have of themselves'. Thus the emergence of the medium role can only be understood in the light of (a) pre-existing cultural ideas about gender, priesthood, and witchcraft; (b) various pre-existing practices involving possession for both men and women; and (c) cultural and political changes in the Kathmandu Valley since 1951. These changes, far from implying a decline in women's position, as Lewis assumes, have, if anything, improved it. It is not yet acceptable for an unmarried woman over 35 to claim a share of her father's and brothers' joint family property, as a law of 1975 now entitles her to do. But some women have taken over religious techniques and symbols previously more firmly in the control of high-caste male priests. This democratization of the means of religious legitimacy is, however, only partial. The highest priestly roles remain the hereditary preserve of males of the highest castes. Possession in public remains a predominantly low-status activity. The existence of exactly the same technique in the secret rituals of those of high status paradoxically confirms its low status in the outer realm. I have suggested that it is right to see witch attack and spirit mediumship among the Newars as a kind of rebellion by some women and a few men against the circumstances in which they find themselves and, in the women's case, against the limitations of the female role expected of them, but it is a rebellion that calls into question neither the hierarchy of caste nor that of gender. The spirit medium role, addressing itself as it does to mundane problems, and beneficial though it may be both to incumbent and those who consult, tends to confirm stereotypes of gender and social lowness.

Notes

1. Lewis 1966, 1970, 1971, 1986, 1989. This essay has benefited greatly from the comments of the following, who have also done their best to get me to acknowledge its shortcomings: N.J. Allen, H. Donnan, J. Gray, H. Lambert, C. McDonaugh, B. Owens, A. Pach, D. Quigley, and P.R. Sharma.
2. Lewis 1966: 308, reprinted in 1986: 24.
3. See Giles 1987 for an excellent summary. For a general survey of works on shamanism, see Atkinson 1992.
4. For example, both Giles (1987: 245–7) on East Africa and Kapferer (1991: 153–4) on Sri Lanka have argued that women and their cults are symbolically central to the culture in question.
5. For two recent examples, both of which claim to be going beyond Lewis's theory but to my mind simply confirm it, see McClain 1989 and Kendall 1989.
6. See, for example, Hitchcock and Jones 1976. More recently, to cite only books, there have been studies by Miller (1979), Shrestha (1980), Peters (1981), Holmberg (1989), Mumford (1989), and Desjarlais (1992). See also Macdonald 1975 and *Himalayan Research Bulletin* Vol. 9 (1–2).
7. Some Tamang shamans are women, but most are men. None the less, shamanism is associated with femaleness, and opposed to the male domains of the other ritual specialists, territorial sacrificers, and Buddhist lamas (Holmberg 1983, 1989).
8. Particularly relevant here are Coon 1989, Okada 1976, Durkin-Longley 1982, and Dougherty 1986.
9. Thus Carstairs' and Kapur's (1976) study of a south Indian village mentions three types of specialist: the Vaid or pure Ayurvedic doctor, the Mantarwadi, using mantras or a mixture of methods, and the Patri, who becomes possessed by a spirit or godling. The Mantarwadi is the equivalent of the Newar healer, the Patri of the Newar medium. Unfortunately, though we are told that there are women Patris, we are not told what proportion of Patris are female. In the Malnad district of Karnataka, studied by Harper, the mediums appear to be exclusively male (Harper 1957: 268). In north India there appears to be a similar contrast between the Tantric healer (*siddh* or *sayānā*) and the medium (*bhopā* or *ojhā*), although it appears that the latter are usually male (Henry 1981: 303; Lambert 1988: 356).
10. On the one hand Levy (1990: 338) reports that the Newars of Bhaktapur mostly use 'hill shamans for spirit healers' but, on the other, he indicates that there are special *thars* (caste subgroups or clans) of Newar healers in Bhaktapur (ibid.: 362).

11. Kakar's chapter on 'Tantric healing' (Kakar 1982: chapter 6)—mostly a summary of inadequate secondary text-based sources—is much less convincing than those of his accounts which are based on fieldwork with practitioners. He does, however, rightly observe that 'it is difficult to get widespread agreement on any tantrik matter' (ibid.: 186).

12. Lambert 1992: 1073. In the Kathmandu Valley it is always an ordinary household broom that is used.

13. Durkin-Longley (1982: 162) listed the following types and numbers of Ayurvedic practitioner in Kathmandu in 1980–81: *kavirāj* (fully qualified Ayurvedic doctor): 50, *vaidya* (ordinary Ayurvedic doctor): 91, *gubhāju/gurumā* (Vajracharya healer): 16, *baniyā* (apothecary): 11, *nau vaidya* (traditional surgeon): 1, *aji* (midwife): 55 (estimate), *jhārphuke vaidya*: 26 (estimate). Two further types were obsolete, the *kai vaidya* (healer specializing in small-pox and other spots) and the *ānkhe vaidya* (healer for eyes). It would have been closer to local forms of expression to list these as types of vaidya. Furthermore, it is somewhat artificial to list 'Gubhaju' separately from jhārphuke vaidya; this may reflect the usage of Nepali-speaking Parbatiyas. It is true that Vajracharyas as a caste loom large within the category of such Tantric healers: they derive some prestige from their position as priests, and it is possible that people are more inclined to ascribe Tantric powers to them because of it.

14. One very unusual woman claimed not to be possessed, but simply to *be* Shivashakti, i.e. the Lord of the Universe and his consort; she never shook or showed any other signs of possession, and she refused to discuss the identity of the person who had inhabited her body before God took it over.

15. The complete list, identified by onlookers as they appeared, was as follows: Kali, Dhan Maiju, Nyata Ajima (Naradevi), Kal Bhairav, Kanka Ajima, Guhyeshvari, Bhadrakali, Akash Bhairav, Hanuman, Kumari, Vajrayogini, Bhagavati (Durga), Sadasimata, Dhan Bhaju, Wasi Bhaju, Wasi Maiju, Lati Maiju, Julum Bhaju, Julum Maiju, Lata Bhaju, Hanuman, Lati Maiju, Dhan Maiju, and finally Kali.

16. Joshi (1987: s.v.) glosses *dubiye* as 'to come into the body (as of a god, ghost (*bhūt-pret*), or witch etc.)'. As Gold (1988: 40) notes for Rajasthan, the physical symptoms, though very differently evaluated according to the nature of the possessing agent, are similar for both witch attack and divine possession.

17. Women are not excluded from literate study in modern medicine and there are a few women doctors, as well as numerous nurses and teachers.

18. See, for example, the story recounted by Dr B.P. Sharma (1986: 78–82), a psychiatrist at Bir Hospital.

19. In spite of the dramatic case described by Carstairs (1983) in which a suspected witch was beaten to death, normally in India, as in Nepal, public accusations are rare, and confessions unknown (Lambert 1988: 191; Fuller 1992: 237–8).

20. Greve (1989) notes that in much Himalayan shamanism the shaman is

thought to form a pact with a witch; this is represented mythically as taking her as his wife.

21. Among the Newars possession by a recently dead member of the family seems never to occur, as it does among Parbatiya Hindus (Höfer and Shrestha 1973; Stone 1983, 1988) and in both north and south India (Fuller 1992: 224–36).

22. Coon (1989: 2) also notes this.

23. In spite of their relatively higher status, greater freedom, and more extensive links with their natal home, Newar women ultimately share much with their neighbours, the Parbatiya women so well described by Bennett (1983).

24. In a rather technical sense, as discussed above, Chapter 5, Vajracharya priests could be said to be possessed whenever they perform complex rituals, but most lay people, and even many practising priests, are not aware of this and do not see the priests' ritual performances in this way.

25. See the many examples (there called 'thaumaturgical' movements) cited in Wilson 1975.

26. Al Pach and John Gray, personal communications.

9

Portrait of a Tantric Healer
[with *Uttam Sagar Shrestha*]

The man

Healing styles vary from the genteel to the ecstatic. Jitananda Joshi's is forceful, business-like, and frequently very earthy.[1] His consulting room is full every day of the week, except Sundays and Wednesdays when he does not see patients. The use of the word 'patient', and indeed the word 'healer', raises at the very outset the question of the most appropriate language in which to describe what Jitananda does. Many of the people who come to consult him are ill neither in body nor in mind; they wish rather to have information or ritual assistance which will help them to solve the problems of everyday life.

By his own account Jitananda was sent to 'Madras' in south India by 'Mahendra *sarkār*', i.e. by the king or the government, in order to learn how to cure madness by Tantric means. It was Vikram Samvat (VS) 2014 (1957–8) and Jitananda was eighteen or nineteen years old.[2] Before he left for India Jitananda had received both his sacred thread and Tantric Initiation (*dekhā*) from his family's Brahman priest. His father told him to leave his sacred thread on a tree at Guruju Dhara above Thankot as he walked out of the Kathmandu Valley. That way he would not have to worry about where he slept and what he ate while in India; and he would not have to do his daily worship every morning. When he returned five years later the thread was still hanging from the tree, but the string turned to dust when he picked it up. He went to Pashupati, performed the 'gift of a cow' (*sā dān*), and received another thread.

While in India he studied with two celibates (*brahmacārī*) called Santa Ba and Svasti who lived close to each other; Santa Ba was his main guru. Their students could wear what they liked below the waist, but above it they had to wear '*jogi* clothes', i.e. yellow. Wherever he goes Jitananda still carries with him three pieces of his guru's matted locks tied with copper wire. The teaching was primarily in Sanskrit; Jitananda did pick up some Tamil but has forgotten it. He stayed in south India for five years. On his return home he began to practise as a healer, but he found that his training was not complete, so he went back for a second stint of one year and nine months in VS 2028 (1971–2). At the end of this period there was a test in which he had to sit over a fire in meditation; thanks to the powers he had acquired the fire could not touch him.

Above the seat where Jitananda sees his clients and patients there is a picture of him going through the test (though no fire is visible): he is bare-chested and carries a trident. There are also old, standard pictures of King Mahendra and of his queen, Ratna, as well as the usual more recent ones of King Birendra and Queen Aiswarya. Down each side of the long consulting room are benches for those who wait, though many also squat or sit cross-legged on the floor as they patiently make their way to the front. There are three painted signboards (in Nepali) on the left-hand wall: one requests people not to take off their shoes; another announces that Jitananda is at people's service from 6 a.m. to 5 p.m.; and the third states that in life the greatest thing is to cause (others) to have faith and it concludes '(One should have) faith so that whatever is required (*kārya*) may be carried out successfully. (Your) servant Jitananda.' Although he thus describes himself as the servant of suffering humanity, his patients or clients address him respectfully as *gurubā* ('guru father'). On the opposite wall, with its two windows on to a small and unsalubrious courtyard, a sign states: 'It is in times of suffering that one gets to know what a person is really like.'[3] Other signs state that the service of suffering orphans is the worship of God and that in life one should work with the sweat of one's brow but not with tears.

Thanks to his success as a healer Jitananda possesses houses in Kirtipur, Kathmandu, and elsewhere. He has two wives, two sons, and a daughter. He lives in a frugal manner and a proportion of what he receives in donations (*dān*) from grateful clients he spends on religion, particularly on commissioning new statues of the gods and establishing them. Dharati Mata is a particular favourite of his, and he had an unusual icon of her made and consecrated in the compound of the Bagh Bhairav temple. Among others he has established a Ganesh image in Naya Bazaar and put a railing around Kirtipur's Chilancho *stūpa*. Once he cured the bewitched daughter of a rich Rana and was given 16- or 17,000 rupees. Thinking that he could not 'digest' so much *dān*, he bought five identical male buffaloes and had one sacrificed to each of five Bhairavs: Bagh Bhairav, Kal Bhairav and Akash Bhairav (both in Kathmandu), Unmatta Bhairav (in Cha Bahil), and Pachali Bhairav. (This ritual is called *Bhailadya śīkegu* and many local people formed a procession behind him with their own offerings.) He told Bagh Bhairav, 'This is the *kali* age. I cannot offer a human sacrifice (*narabali*). This buffalo's head is a substitute for my own.'

Usually clients are already waiting when Jitananda emerges in the morning. Before starting to see them he cleans his consulting board (cf. Plate 13) with pure water (*nīlaḥ*), lights incense, and performs a two- or three-minute worship of his guru in front of the waiting clients. He worships his guru in the form of two books tightly wrapped in red cloth with a peacock feather stuck in the bundle. One of the books is written in blood, he says. There is also a *bīr* inside (a powerful spirit, usually of a murdered man). Once this ritual obeisance is over, he begins with consultations. Although he takes occasional rests during the day to smoke a cigarette, he only eats rice after all the patients have gone, a remarkable feat of endurance to keep up on a regular basis. Such fasting generates great ritual purity (and power) for his curing sessions. However he does not supplement it with the other recognized method of acquiring purity, bathing. Rather, he admits to being afraid of water and that he bathes only when he has to, for instance before performing *śrāddha* on behalf of his father. When there are no more patients, he takes ritual leave of his guru; once completed, if more patients arrive, he refuses to see them.

The healing

In the Kathmandu Valley there are many *jhārphuke vaidya*, i.e. healers who cure by using the technique of brushing with a broom and blowing mantras on to the patient's body. They come from many castes; the most heavily represented caste is that of the Vajracharyas, Tantric Buddhist priests. Jitananda is somewhat unusual in being a Joshi, i.e. Astrologer. It does him no harm, however, because very many of the consultations have to do with astrological information. Not infrequently a woman will arrive with the horoscopes of all the family and ask for progress reports on all of them. If a more complex diagnosis is necessary Jitananda draws a diagram with a kind of chalk on his wooden consulting board, which is plastered with red clay. He then drops grains of rice on to it: their position tells him what he needs to know. The other main technique used in diagnosis (as will be seen from Table 9.2) is feeling the pulse, both on left and right wrists. Very occasionally he uses a stethoscope to listen to that part of the body where the patient's problem is located.

Jitananda has a vigorous manner of treating patients, often chatting and joking with those who have accompanied the patient he is treating, as well as with others in the consulting room. He cracks risqué jokes, teases people, and is quite capable of stating bluntly to an elderly person that he is old and must expect to be weak. Thus the waiting patients and caretakers are frequently drawn into discussions of particular cases. If Jitananda considers that it is a question of bodily weakness, he sells patients bottles of coloured tonic (one for the blood, one for the flesh), and he prescribes certain dietary restrictions. The single biggest category of problems is caused by human malevolence, i.e. by witchcraft or the evil eye. Many who come may suspect this as a cause of their misfortune, and healers such as Jitananda often confirm their suspicions. We heard Jitananda telling patients to bring horoscopes on Monday, Thursday, and Friday, whereas Saturday and Tuesday are for 'Tantric work', i.e. combating witchcraft. Table 9.2 shows that lay people do not heed these instructions and that both types of work seem to be brought on all days more or less equally.

In the vast majority of witchcraft cases the diagnosis is simply 'you have been harmed' (literally 'spoilt': *syākāḥ taḥgu*, Np. *kaiphaṭ* or *bigār*). It is not necessary to name a suspected culprit, and ritual action to reverse the harm done does not require them to be identified or harassed.[4] In a small number of cases diagnoses of the evil eye are made (literally 'the eye has gone', *mikhā wāgu*, or 'the eye has struck', *mikhā dāḥgu*); and in others the magic is described as *tunā* (bewitchment of someone's affections, usually by a member of the opposite sex).

It is relatively rare for someone to state explicitly that they suspect such magical harm. Table 9.2 gives some idea of the range of complaints for which the Nepalese consult healers and mediums in general. A larger number make no specific complaint but simply present their horoscope or pulse for the healer to deduce any problems they may be facing.

Where clients specify a symptom, those one can broadly classify as social or psycho-social slightly outnumber physical complaints. Astrological problems or requests for astrological information generally outnumber both. A considerable number of physical complaints are ascribed to supernatural or social causes. Diagnoses of magical harm may result either from physical, social, or astrological complaints.[5]

Table 9.1: Data on clients consulting Jitananda Joshi on seven different days in 1989 (collected by Uttam Sagar Shrestha)

Day	I Thursday 24/8/89	II Saturday 26/8/89	III Tuesday 29/8/89	IV Saturday 1/9/89	V Monday 4/9/89	VI Tuesday 5/9/89	VII Thursday 7/9/89
TOTAL CONSULTING	71	71	60	55	36	48	73
	(30)*	(67)	(24)	(11)	(10)	(14)	(23)
Number consulted for in their absence	9	1	8	8	2	3	9
Number coming for second time or more	11	14	12	7	9	10	11
Male	31 (11)	34 (25)	27 (11)	26 (6)	19 (4)	21 (7)	39 (10)
Female	40 (19)	37 (42)	33 (13)	29 (5)	17 (6)	27 (7)	34 (13)
ETHNICITY							
Newar	49 (16)	53 (46)	41 (16)	43 (7)	35 (10)	44 (12)	60 (20)
Parbatiya	18 (10)	12 (12)	14 (8)	4 (2)	1 (0)	4 (2)	13 (3)
Tamang	3 (3)	2 (4)	5 (0)	7 (2)			
Other	1 (0)	4 (5)		1 (0)			

(Table 9.1 Contd...)

(Table 9.1 Contd.)

Day	I Thursday 24/8/89	II Saturday 26/8/89	III Tuesday 29/8/89	IV Saturday 1/9/89	V Monday 4/9/89	VI Tuesday 5/9/89	VII Thursday 7/9/89
ORIGIN							
Kirtipur	6	7	9	15	3	6	9
Nearby villages	7	5	11	1	2	5	8
Lalitpur (Patan)	13	14	7	9	4	6	3
Greater Kathmandu	26	28	24	20	14	13	24
	(37%)	(39%)	(40%)	(36%)	(39%)	(27%)	(33%)
Lubhu, Thimi, etc.**	4	5	6		8	6	5
Panauti, Sankhu, Bhaktapur, Banepa	8	10			3	9	14
Beyond	5	2	2	3			5
Not known	2		1	7	2	3	5

Notes: * The figure in parentheses shows the number of accompanying and non-consulting persons
        ** Includes villages south of Lalitpur and north of Kathmandu.

Table 9.2: Symptoms and problems shown to Jitananda Joshi

Day (see Table 9.1)	I	II	III	IV	V	VI	VII
Total cases	71	71	60	55	36	48	73
Physical symptoms	15	19	20	9	7	12	9
Spots		1	1	2			1
Headache		1	1	2		3	1
Pain in chest		1	1		2		
Stomach ache	1		7	1	1		1
Knee, legs, hips		2			1	1	
Other specific pain		4		1			
Generally unwell, weakness, body 'heavy'	9	8	4	1	2	1	2
No desire to eat	2	1					
No desire to work	2						1
No desire to study	1	1		1	1		
Sleeps all the time/inactivity			1			3	
Baby unwell/cries/can't walk			2			2	1
Buffalo/cow doesn't give milk			1				1
Others			2	1		2	1
Pulse shown	28	28	21	23	14	19	15
Social and psycho-social problems	16	15	7	5	4	6	8
Fights at home		3	1	2		1	3
Young man goes out at night	2	2				1	1
Problems caused by alcohol	2		1	2			
Husband attracted to other women/ spoilt by friends	2	1	1			2	1
Husband bringing in second wife	4	4					
Problems with wife	1	1	2	1			1
Work/things not going well	1	2					
Suspected magical harm	2	2	1				
Customers not coming to shop	1		1		2	2	2
Others	1				2		
Astrological/About auspiciousness	25	25	31	24	17	20	44
Showing horoscope/rice	10	12	25	22	11	11	36
Shop earth/incense for shop	6	6	1		2	2	2
House earth shown	5	5	5	1	4	6	3
Others*	4	2		1		1	3

Note: The broad categories are for purposes of exposition only. Neither the broad nor the minor categories are exclusive. It is quite possible to show one's pulse *and* one's horoscope.

* includes asking: whether horoscopes fit for a couple intending to marry; about a child's future; whether an operation should be proceeded with; if a car should be purchased (determined by considering its number plate); if this is a case of a god's doṣ (punishment; literally 'fault').

Treatments are not exclusive. Symptoms of weakness caused by magical harm may be treated both by reversing the magic and with bottled tonic. Magical harm is treated either by brushing and blowing mantras, to remove it from the patient's body, or by the procedure called 'feeding in reverse' (ultā nakegu).[6] In this the afflicted person brings sacramental foods (known collectively as samay: beaten rice, buffalo meat, beans, vegetables). The food is empowered by the healer and then divided in half. One half is kept by the client so that they can repeat the ritual at home in the evening. The other half is then divided in two again. Of this one half is eaten by the patient, and the other, the 'enemy share' (śatrubhāg), is fed to the healer's dog. The dog is an unlovely mongrel with a lame leg, the deformity being ascribed to his diet of hostile magic. Jitananda says that reversing human malevolence is particularly complex when compared to problems caused by gods or ghosts: 'If it's a god's fault, two grains of rice are enough; if a ghost's (bhūt), two grains of broken rice (cwaki); but if it is a human's fault, you have to do so many things'.

The broad categories used in Tables 9.2, 9.3, and 9.4 to classify the symptoms/problems, diagnoses, and treatments are ours. For the purposes of quantification some system of classification has to be used. The assignment of some complaints to one category rather than another is not an unambiguous and simple matter; the distinction between physical symptoms and psycho-social symptoms is obviously not absolute. As Wiemann-Michaels (1989: 45) points out, even swelling can be a psychological symptom in the Nepalese context. The problems 'no desire to work' and 'no desire to study' could equally have been put in the latter category. It is also important to remember that, although some ailments are often seen as purely physical, neither patients nor healers are concerned to impose this kind of classifications on all or even most problems. As far as the broad categories used in Table 9.2 below are concerned, they are purely heuristic, introduced in analysis, and should be discarded where not helpful. In the cases of diagnoses and treatments shown in Tables 9.3 and 9.4, however, we would argue that the broad categories used here do correspond more closely to local conceptions, each category requiring a different type or course of action (though a single complaint may well require more than one such remedial action).

The interpretation

To begin with a methodological observation: the pace at which things occur in the consulting room, the banter and noise which accompany

Table 9.3: Diagnoses made by Jitananda Joshi

Day	I	II	III	IV	V	VI	VII
Total cases	71	71	60	55	36	48	73
Nothing wrong/improving/no doṣ	5	5	4	3	5	4	3
Physical or psycho-physical	16	8	8	10	9	9	7
Types of wind (vāyu)			1	2	3		1
Hot and cold (sardi garam) unbalanced	3	3	1	3	3	3	1
Fever (various types)	3				1		
Weakness	5	5	2	1		3	
Problems with man	1		1	1		1	1
Just ill	1		1	1			
Other specified illness	3		2	2	2	2	4
Magical	28	34	31	15	14	20	22
Harm (syākāḥ, kaiphaṭ)	24	30	28	14	12	10	20
Bewitchment (tunā)	2	2	1			6	1
Evil eye (mikhā)	2	2	2	1	2	1	1
Others						3	
Religious/supernatural causes	6	8	3	4	1	1	2
doṣ (god's 'fault')	1	3		3	1		1
vow (bhākal) or ritual outstanding	4	1	1				
nāg (holy serpent)	1					1	
mulkaṭṭa (headless ghost)		1					
narapiśāc (lit. 'human goblin')		1					
bīr/masān (ghost of murdered man)		2	1				1
sī-mha (ghost, lit. 'dead person')			1	1			
Astrological	22	17	12	15	11	10	34
Bad conjunction (daśā)	10	10	8	12	5	6	18
daśā ok	3	2	3		4		5
Information about house	1	3	1		1	4	2
Others	8	2		3	1		9

Note: A diagnosis is not specified in every case; sometimes two problems are diagnosed for a single case. A few cases where the data were unclear have been omitted.

Table 9.4: Treatments offered by Jitananda Joshi

Day (see Table 9.1)	I	II	III	IV	V	VI	VII
Total cases	71	71	60	55	36	48	73
Physical	16	10	11	6	9	11	5
Gives bottled 'power'	15	7	11	6	9	11	4
Other medicine	1	3					
Magical	28	47	32	22	17	26	27
Brushing, blowing, and/or giving empowered water	6	24	8	11	9	13	13
'Feeding in reverse'	14	18	20	7	6	13	11
Gives empowered powder (*sinhaḥ*) or bewitching powder (*mohanī*)	8	5	4	4	2		3
Religious	22	16	19	15	11	8	20
Worship *nāg*		1	1	1		1	1
Ganesh/Siddhi Vinayak	2	2		3	1		1
Surya	2	1	2	2			2
Eight Mother Goddesses/*pīṭh*	2		1	1	2		2
peepal tree	1	1					
Dharati	2	1	3		1		3
other divinities*			2	3		3	2
Give *dān* (presentation) of fruits or *sagā*	2		2	2			
Bathe/keep purity rules	2		2	2			
Use incense on shop/house	9	10	6	1	7	4	9
Astrological	6	6	1	4	2	4	2
Bad conjuncture will pass after (date specified)	5	3	1	4	2	4	2
Other astrological information	1	3					
*Other***	3	2	3	5	2	3	3

Notes:
    *Includes Bhimsen, Mahakala, Akash, Vishvakarma, placing an offering (*bau*) at the cremation ground at night, determining what the unfulfilled vow is.
    **Includes giving advice, requiring materials for a specific ritual to be brought, requiring the afflicted person to be brought, and declarations that there is nothing to be done.

them, and the fact that two languages, Nepali and Newari, are used side by side, as well as Jitananda's wide-ranging mythological, religious, and idiomatic asides, all mean that no foreigner, however well they may feel they have learnt the local languages, is capable of following every nuance, of grasping what is happening in every detail. Collaboration such as that of the present two co-authors is necessary, as well as desirable for its own sake, in investigations such as these. Moreover, the phenomenon under study is so multifaceted that interdisciplinary cooperation is also advisable. Any truly comprehensive study, as this does not pretend to be, needs to combine biomedical, psychiatric, and anthropological expertise.

Jitananda is used to the attention both of foreign and Nepalese scholars. He is probably the most intensively studied healer in Nepal. To cite only those studies available to us (there may have been others): he figures in Padam Lal Devkota's study (1983: 112–19; 1984) of traditional medical practitioners in Kirtipur; his practice was the basis of a comparison between the psychiatric treatment of a traditional healer and a hospital out-patient clinic by Skultans (1988); and his practice was the source of Wiemann-Michaels' (1989) detailed analysis of forty-six patients diagnosed as suffering from witch-attack (this is undoubtedly the most sophisticated analysis of the problems which arise in trying to compare Jitananda's practice to biomedical diagnosis).

Of these, Skultans's is the most ambitious interpretation of the healer's role. Unfortunately Skultans has not published the figures on which her conclusions are based. What she does say makes it clear that there are some differences in the details of our samples, and these should perhaps be taken to illustrate the dangers of relying on statistical samples which are restricted to a brief period of days in one part of the year. Skultans reports that just over half of her sample of 137 patients came from outside the Kathmandu Valley; Table 9.1 shows that the overwhelming majority of our sample came from inside it.[7] She says that 'the majority are literate and affluent'; we would judge this not to be so. She says that men outnumbered women by 3:2; according to our figures, women generally outnumber men.

This last discrepancy may be due to Skultans's focus on the 67 cases in her sample whom she deems to have complaints 'related to mental illness'. This is a very difficult concept to use; she may have picked out the cases which we have classified as 'psycho-social problems' in Table 9.2. She is certainly right that such patients are 'seen as failing to fulfil their obligations to their families' (Skultans 1988: 973). However, in many such cases, people consult without actually bringing the disturbed person, or the person acting in an anti-social manner, with them, and the conclusion that they are mentally ill should be made with great caution. There is a concept of madness in Nepali and Newari; not a single case of it was brought in the time of our investigation, although Jitananda has a reputation for curing it.

It is the sociological part of Skultans's fluent and stimulating article, however, with which we wish primarily to take issue. Here Skultans's interpretation hinges on a contrast between traditional rural healers and modern 'popular' healers, a designation she uses for both Tantric vaidyas and jhānkris (hill shamans) who operate in an urban environment. Skultans writes:

The present study found that while the majority of patients show a reluctance to consult doctors, they have forsaken village healers in favour of popular healers who have taken over some of the less desirable features of western medical practice such as speed and routinization of treatment. (ibid.: 979)

Earlier she had written that

rural healers are very much like family practitioners. Since the ratio of healers to general population is extremely high, such healers necessarily see few patients and are able to devote considerable time to those they do see. By contrast, there are also healers in the [Kathmandu] valley who offer a new style of treatment ... Their practices are vast. Scores of patients are seen daily and hundreds weekly ... As a consequence the healer has little personal knowledge of the clients' background and problems. The more sought after the healer the shorter the time he is able to spend with any one client. The waiting time, in contrast to the consultation time, is long. (ibid.: 971)

Thus Skultans presumes that whereas traditional rural healers make use of 'detailed theoretical elaboration of witchcraft beliefs [which have] diverse social functions', where the urban healer is concerned (i.e. Jitananda) these 'appear to have been left behind'.

No evidence is presented to substantiate the picture of rural Nepalese healers, other than the estimated (and surely exaggerated) statistic of Shrestha (1980) that there are between 400,000 and 800,000 jhānkris in the Nepalese hills. Thus, while she is certainly right that the diagnoses offered by Jitananda are stereotyped, that he spends little time with each patient compared to their long wait, and that his use of witchcraft terms is 'loose', we find no reason to believe that what he does is distinctively modern or urban. Any impersonality which may creep in to practices such as Jitananda's is due not to its urban context but to his very success and reputation which draw people from considerable distances, a point Skultans herself makes (1988: 978).

Skultans attacks the tendency of medical anthropologists to view the practice of traditional healers as holistic, but she herself seems to think that the traditional, rural healers, with whom she contrasts Jitananda, do practise in a more holistic way, an assumption for which no evidence is advanced. There is one sense in which Jitananda's practice is holistic, however, and that is in not distinguishing types of problem requiring different specialists: physical ailments for the doctor, psychological problems for the psychiatrist or psychoanalyst, social problems for the social worker, spiritual problems for the priest. From a western perspective Jitananda is all of these and an astrologer and exorcist too. Skultans is right, however, that Jitananda makes no attempt to incorporate all such aspects in a rounded diagnosis in the manner of a western holistic healer.

We have no quarrel with Skultans's argument that women generally receive less health care of all types than men. Her description of how witchcraft diagnoses work (the healer providing a vague diagnosis which has to be made to fit by the family) is certainly cogent.[8] But such vagueness is a feature of the diagnoses of ritual healers of all types, whether they are the supposedly traditional jhānkris of the hills or the possessed and usually female mediums (*dyaḥ waipī*) of the towns. These latter, unlike Jitananda, are, by all local accounts, a new, relatively urban and modern phenomenon. A fully sociological theory of ritual healing would have to take them into account as well.[9]

Notes

1. The research for this article was carried out in August 1989. Uttam Sagar Shrestha collected the data given in the tables in physically and intellectually demanding day-long sessions.
2. He told Wiemann-Michaels (1989: 15) that he was born in 1931 and went to India when he was 20. He confirmed to us that he was born in VS 1993, i.e. 1936–7.
3. It concludes with the enigmatic statement: 'Therefore in both truth and untruth' (*tasartha satya tathā asatyamā*).
4. Wiemann-Michaels (1989: 54) writes that only in a single case known to her was Jitananda asked to identify the witch, and he did so only under duress.
5. Wiemann-Michaels (1989: 41, Table 8) lists thirty-five symptoms recounted to her by her sample of 46 victims of witch attack. (She performed two medical examinations of each of them two to three weeks apart.) Symptoms experienced by more than two of them were as follows, in order of decreasing frequency: tiredness (reported by 31 subjects), anxiety (25), aggression (20),

nightmares (19), headaches (18), apathy (15), lack of desire to work (14), sleeplessness (11), abdominal pain (10), lack of appetite (10), avoiding home (9), nausea (8), chest pain (7), irritability (6), back pain (5), fever (3), leg pain (3), cough (3), arm pain (3), weakness (2), weepiness (2), thoughts of suicide (2), swellings (2). It is probable that only those symptoms considered more important will have been reported to Jitananda.

6. *Ulṭā garnu* or *ulṭā khuwāunu* in Nepali (cf. Macdonald 1976: 384).
7. Wiemann-Michaels' (1989: 26, Table 2) figures for her much smaller sample of 46 are roughly similar to ours.
8. On this point much greater detail is to be found in Wiemann-Michaels (1989).
9. See above, Chapters 4 and 8.

10

Lay Perspectives on Health and Misfortune in the Kathmandu Valley

Introduction

Unlike the steep-sided V-shaped valleys of the rest of the foothills in this part of the Himalayan range, the Kathmandu Valley is a roughly circular bowl that was a lake in prehistoric times.[1] It became the capital of the present ruling dynasty in 1769, but it was only in the twentieth century that the country as a whole began to be conceived of as a nation-state and began to be called 'Nepal' (Burghart 1984). Even before the massive social changes of recent decades, there was considerable cultural pluralism. The ethnic group with the best claim to be the indigenous people of the Valley are the Newars: their three cities, Kathmandu, Lalitpur, and Bhaktapur, along with many semi-urban settlements nearby, supported a complex division of labour largely expressed through the caste system (Gellner and Quigley 1995). The Newars practise both Hindu and Buddhist Great Traditions, which coexist in a way that is supposed to be characteristic of north India in the first millennium CE before Buddhism died out there (Lévi 1905). Thus there are healers drawing on both these sacred traditions active in the Valley today. From at least the sixteenth century there have been culturally distinct minorities, such as Muslim traders, north Indian temple priests, and Tibetan Buddhist religious specialists, living in the Valley. Today this cultural complexity has been multiplied many times over. Kathmandu has seen immigration from all parts of the country as well as from India and Tibet. There is a massive foreign aid and diplomatic presence, including the headquarters of SAARC (South Asian Association for Regional Cooperation) and many other South Asian bodies. And there has been a telecommunications revolution that has made South, East, and Southeast Asia, not to mention American soap operas, a permanent presence on the TV sets of the capital within ten years of the first broadcasts by Nepal TV in 1985 (Liechty 1998).

The massive influx of people into the Valley, and the building boom that has accompanied it, has had some very serious environmental consequences, including water shortages, water pollution from chemicals used in carpet manufacture, air pollution from uncontrolled motor vehicles, especially trucks, buses, and the two-stroke engines of Indian-made tempos, and the problem of what to do with urban waste. Kathmandu has long been a popular tourist and pilgrimage destination for Indians; an added attraction was that one could buy East Asian electronics and fashion goods which until recently were wholly unavailable in India. The Kathmandu Valley has also been the main point of entry for westerners seeking trekking, mountaineering, and/or some kind of nature and cultural authenticity (Adams 1996). Economically, there has been a massive influx of foreign money into the Valley. In recent years a modern class system has emerged, in which access to different levels of education and health care have become both signs of social status, and the means of reproducing it.

Health care: what there is in Kathmandu

In attempting to delineate the 'health care system' in the Kathmandu Valley today, it is useful for analytic purposes to distinguish 'systems' of care, on the one hand, from practitioners, on the other. Practitioners may specialize in sub-disciplines within one system or combine two or more systems in various creative ways. These distinctions are outlined in Chart 10.1. The chart is offered as a heuristic device, a means of grasping the complexity of what is on offer to the lay people of the Kathmandu Valley. Other forms of healing could doubtless be added, and some of the types offered could be contested. Reiyukai is primarily a social and religious organization and only very secondarily involved in any sort of healing, but I have included it because of the health benefits claimed to follow from regular practice of its path. Similarly, the Protestant Christian churches that have mushroomed in the freer political climate since 1990 are included since they offer, among other things, healing of some common ailments.

Chart 10.1: Principal types of healing 'system' and practitioner in the Kathmandu Valley today

Systems	Practitioners
1. Biomedicine	government hospitals incl. maternity, eye, teaching; (Christian) mission hospitals; private hospitals ('nursing homes'); government health posts; private clinics; charitable clinics (occasional); 'compounders'/pharmacists
2. Ayurveda (classical South Asian medicine, based on Sanskrit texts)	Ayurvedic hospital, some Ayurvedic health posts, Ayurvedic medical shops
3. Unani (classical Galenic medical system, practised predominantly by Muslims)	one practitioner in Kathmandu (trained in Delhi)
4. Rituals	priests (Hindu or Buddhist), monks, ascetics; offerings by individuals or households to gods such as *wāśyādyah* (the toothache god)
5. Astrology	individual practitioners (Jyotish/Joshi)
6. Imported healing cults	e.g. Seimeikyo/Reiyukai/some Christian churches
7. Mixed divine/Ayurveda/astrology	Tantric healers (*jhārphuke vaidya, jānne mānche, dhāmī*); 3–4 Muslim healers/ exorcists
8. Divine healing (possession)	mediums (*devatā āune*, mostly female) and shamans (*jhānkri*, mostly male
9. Herbal remedies/'herbalism'	family, relatives, midwives

Note: Types 5–9 commonly accept the existence of witchcraft; types 7 and 8 frequently diagnose it. Other, relatively less prominent, systems of healing in Kathmandu are: bonesetting, usually performed by men of the Napit (Barber) caste (Devkota 1983: 63–73); a government-funded homeopathic clinic at Pashupatinath; Tibetan medicine provided by traditional Tibetan doctors and by lamas; Indian fakirs and street magicians; naturopathy (20 clinics in Nepal according to Acharya 1994: 241); and acupuncturists (cf. Durkin-Longley 1982: 93–4).

Chart 10.2: Variations in the naming of different types of non-possessed healer

	Urban Nepal	Rural Nepal
Classical Ayurvedic doctor	*vaidya*	*vaidya*
Tantric healer	*(jhārphuke) vaidya*	*jānne (mānche), dhāmī, jhārphuke,* or *jhānkri*
Herbalist	*jānne* (or *vaidya*)	*vaidya*

Note: See Paneru (1983: 68), Subedi (1982: 31–2), Aryal (1983: Chapter 2), Blustain (1976), and Stone (1988: 15–17) for these usages. Subedi (1982: 21–4, 28) also reports the term *baidang* for a healer who combines the knowledge of a vaidya and a jhankri, and goes into only mild trance.

The term *vaidya* (*baidya*) deserves some comment. It is used for any traditional healer whose knowledge is acquired by training and learning. Thus it includes (i) Ayurvedic doctors, whether trained in modern-style colleges or traditionally; (ii) Tantric healers who combine a variety of methods, both ritual and herbal, and perform exorcisms (known by a variety of different terms in rural areas); and (iii) herbal healers with no formal, scripture-related training who have picked up their knowledge orally and may well be illiterate. Of these three kinds, the first are almost without exception male and urban (see Chapters 8 and 9 above); the second are also overwhelmingly male; the third kind, essentially herbalists, can be either male or female, and seem to be called vaidya mainly in rural areas. What is common to them all is that they do not become possessed and therefore do not speak directly to, or in the voice of, the gods. These different usages are tentatively summarized in Chart 10.2.

Shamans are found among the hill groups of Nepal, and are present particularly among the Tamang population of the Kathmandu Valley. Mediums, mainly women and a few men, heal by becoming possessed by a tutelary deity, usually Hariti, the Buddhist goddess of smallpox, and her offspring. They appear to be a purely urban, and predominantly Newar, phenomenon (see above, Chapter 8).

There is a structural similarity to the 'four indigenous systems of healing' identified by Margaret Trawick (1992) on the basis of fieldwork at the other end of the subcontinent in Tamil Nadu: Ayurveda, siddha medicine, trance healing, and Tamil Shaiva bhakti. The first three of these correspond to types 2, 7, and 8 respectively of Chart 10.1. The fourth, Tamil Shaiva bhakti, is equivalent to type 4 of the chart. The rural study by Carstairs and Kapur (1976: Chapter 5) in Karnataka identified three kinds of healer: the *vaid* (Ayurvedic doctor), *mantarvadi* (Tantric healer), and *patra* (medium or shaman); these too correspond to types 2, 7, and 8 of Chart 10.1. Thus, despite the complexity introduced by new medical practices and new religious movements, the Kathmandu Valley shares, in its broad outlines, a structured hierarchy of healers and practices characteristic of the rest of non-Muslim South Asia: highest status goes to scriptural medicine which is based on Sanskritic learning and the theory of humoral balance (Basham 1976); more widespread, and less elite, are various forms of Tantric ritual healing which combine Ayurvedic concepts with astrology, ritual, and exorcism; finally, the least prestigious, and most popular, form of therapy is legitimated by spirit possession.

Hierarchies of availability

The introduction of western biomedicine as well as foreign therapies of a more religious sort has not done anything to democratize access to health care. The first, most obvious hierarchy is based on the difference between what is available in Kathmandu as compared to what is available elsewhere, and what is available in urban areas as a whole versus the rural areas. Judith Justice's (1986) excellent account of health care bureaucracy in Nepal brings out how invisible the needs and the realities of life in hill villages are to those who live in the capital. Her descriptions of rural health posts where the peon—on paper simply an unskilled dogsbody—was often the only worker present and routinely gave injections, applied dressings, made diagnoses, and distributed medicine, were met with disbelief and denial by officials and planners involved in administering health in the capital (1986: 104–6). As elsewhere in South Asia (Nichter 1992: 243–4), ordinary people find that private practitioners are more polite, more responsive to their needs, and more likely to have medicines than the staff at government clinics. Basundhara Dhungel (1994: 249–50, 253) found exactly the same in two villages in Khabre district, just to the east of the Kathmandu Valley; furthermore, the workers in government health posts were frustrated for exactly the same reasons.

To some extent government health workers are the victims of the same forces affecting teachers and civil servants. They are paid inadequate salaries, they are subject to no checks, and are given no incentives to perform well. They are therefore sorely tempted by opportunities to work outside to supplement their salary, to accept bribes, or to charge for their services. Their chances of promotion or transfer depend on lobbying and networking.[2] Since 1990 and the introduction of political parties, factionalism along party lines has been added to sources of division. In these circumstances, lengthy absenteeism is common.

The background to all this is the increasing monetization of the economy and continual inflation. Biomedical health care has increasingly become available in private clinics and hospitals, and the financial rewards for doctors and nurses are much greater in the private sector. Doctors often manage to combine both. The logical extension of this is that foreign health care is better still. The Nepalese elite like to combine health check-ups and shopping in Bangkok. It seems to be accepted that senior political figures who played a part in the changes of the 1950s, even though they are marginal today, should have the costs of trips to the USA paid by the state, as a thanks-offering from the nation, if they fall seriously ill. Members of the middle class may take serious illnesses to what is considered the best hospital in India, Vellore in south India.

Underlying this are two connected valuations: a service is better if it is foreign in origin (biomedicine is better than indigenous therapies; foreign practitioners are better than local ones); and a service is better if it is more expensive. Exactly the same applies to education. Within the last twenty years there has been a massive expansion of private education in the Kathmandu Valley so that nowadays only the poor send their children to government schools. Many middle-class parents now send their children to boarding schools in India, which are considered better value than private schools in Nepal.

In the same way, anything used by the elite is assumed to be not just more prestigious but more effective. Doctors who have once attended the royal palace will certainly find that this helps their reputation. Ordinary people frequently mention it if the astrologer or doctor they use has this distinction. As Durkin-Longley remarks (1982: 128), 'The Rana period was the heyday for learned vaidyas in Kathmandu whose greatest ambition was to join the palace service ... The chief physician in each of the major palaces was provided with a horse for making his daily rounds.' Biomedical doctors replaced Ayurvedic vaidyas (though without the horses) with the fall of the Rana regime in 1950–1 and the replacement of the Ranas' authoritarian traditionalism with a conscious ideology of modernization.

While Ayurveda today receives some limited government support, there is no comparison between it and biomedicine. The financial rewards and opportunities for promotion in government service, not to mention the rewards of private practice, are many times greater for biomedical doctors than for Ayurvedic practitioners (Durkin-Longley 1982: 157).

There is a single Ayurvedic hospital with 15 beds, attached to the Naradevi Ayurvedic College.[3] Bir Hospital, the biggest, most central government hospital, has more than 300. Foreign donors, who provide the vast majority of Nepal's development budget, are not likely to support anything else. The primacy of biomedicine is an aspect of Nepal's dependency in all other spheres.

Before the introduction of biomedicine Ayurvedic doctors had the highest prestige and certain families still retain high status on this basis, though the sons frequently study biomedicine instead. Like astrology it is acquired though literate study, ultimately based on Sanskrit scriptures. In the hills it is practised predominantly by brahmans, and among the Newars by high castes such as Shresthas and Vajracharyas. Ayurveda, in its 'pure' form, that is to say, practised on its own without ritual therapy, is confined to the cities and a small number of government health posts. It is and has remained an elite form of medicine. Paneru (1983: 77) reports that there is a single Ayurvedic practitioner in Gorkha district: he trained in Benares, worked for the Nepalese government for thirty five years, and only moved to Gorkha on retirement. Significantly he also reports that 'the patients confided that the ayurvedic medicines prescribed by the *vaidya* are expensive and often beyond the means of local people' (ibid.: 81). It is only types 7, 8, and 9 of Chart 10.1—ritual healing, spirit-possession, and herbalism—that reach all the villages.

Thus it is that Tantric healers, mediums, and shamans represent themselves as the 'doctors of the poor' and take pride in the fact that, like brahman priests, they do not charge fixed fees but rather accept whatever the patient can afford to offer. They thereby align themselves with priests as providing an altruistic and religious service, rather than a grasping and irreligious one like biomedical doctors. Biomedical doctors also claim the moral high ground, of course, by occasionally holding free clinics (or in the case of mission hospitals, treating the very poor for free). Free clinics are sometimes run by Hindu and Buddhist organizations, by groups such as the Lions Club, and by some caste associations.[4]

Ayurvedic view of the body but increasingly biomedical practice

There are two common mistakes or oversimplifications in representing the coexistence of biomedical and more traditional forms of therapy. The first is to represent the current situation as a straightforward transition from traditional to modern, and to assume that all the non-biomedical therapies on offer are ancient and traditional. On this view the current situation is simply a mid-point in a changeover which will lead to the eventual triumph of biomedical practice and ways of thinking, and the discarding of the 'backward', 'superstitious' beliefs that support all other forms of therapy. The problems with this view are clear. In the first place, much of what passes as 'traditional' medical practice is in fact relatively new. The numerous female mediums in Kathmandu and other urban areas of the Valley seem to be a new phenomenon, post-dating 1951 (Chapter 8 above). Much of the content of what Ayurvedic doctors do today has in fact been borrowed from biomedicine. Thus Durkin-Longley (1988) has shown how the treatment for jaundice for which Ayurvedic physicians are renowned in Nepal is in fact largely derived from biomedical recommendations now considered out-of-date. Ayurvedic physicians have also accepted much of biomedical anatomy and aetiology, and attempt to compete with biomedicine on its own terms (cf. Zimmerman 1992). A well-known Kathmandu vaidya, Mana Bajra Bajracharya, has published many pamphlets and books in English offering Ayurvedic diagnoses and treatments for ailments such as breast cancer, herpes, migraine, psoriasis, arthritis, asthma, and so on, as well as a compendium of Ayurvedic treatments for cancer (Bajracharya 1987). Thus, in short, far from being a simple transition from one form of medicine to another, all the 'systems' are themselves in transition, and influence each other in various ways. This is not to deny that biomedicine is increasing in importance and will certainly continue to do so.

A second oversimplification, often in reaction to the first, is to posit too much stasis, to see the various systems as equal alternatives, or as having evolved a division of labour with each system specializing in a particular kind of ailment. Enough has been said to indicate that different systems are indeed in competition, as the practitioners are keenly aware, even though lay people do sometimes treat them as complementary. In this there is an analogy with the coexistence of Buddhism and Hinduism within Newar society: Buddhist and Hindu priests are simultaneously in competition with each other, offering alternative forms of the same rituals and/or competing interpretations of common practices, while at the same time often being viewed ecumenically by lay people as different but equivalent (Chapter 14 below). There is another aspect to the analogy between religion and medicine: different generations often have decidedly different preferences in both.

Those who use both Ayurvedic medicine (Nw. *baidya wāsah*) and biomedicines (Nw. *deśī wāsah*) often say that they differ only in the speed of the effect they have. Ayurvedic medicines take longer to have an effect, but the advantage is that they will not cause the illness to 'flip over' and come back. Many like to take Ayurvedic medicine as a preventative 'to keep their stomach clean'.

Treatments of the common cold reveal a broadly Ayurvedic, or at least humoral, view of its underlying causes. It is very widely believed that one should avoid yoghurt during the cold months and keep out of breezes or draughts (even the slightest movement of air). Many drink a glass of hot water a day to warm their body. It is also thought that the impure ghee used to make shop-made sweets and cakes causes colds. Hepatitis is also blamed on impure ghee and on bad water.

There has been, everyone acknowledges, an epidemic of diabetes in the 1990s. Many blame this on the rapid changes in the way of life. A more sedentary way of life is recognized to be part of the cause (even women who never worked outside the home would have had to walk if invited elsewhere, whereas now buses, taxis, and tempos will take them); no doubt the rise of tea-drinking (always with sugar) has something to do with it also.

By some, however, diabetes is connected to a more systematic and ideological representation of social change. According to this discourse, in the past the entire rhythm of life—the local architecture (with its brick-and-wood houses and mud floors), the numerous seasonal foods and feasts, the clean flowing rivers—were all health-giving, appropriate to the time of year, and made people strong. Today, the argument goes, people eat any kind of food, in any place (i.e. ignoring purity taboos and traditional beliefs about appropriateness). They live in modern cement houses that are cold in winter and hot in summer. The rivers have been reduced to open sewers. People have become weak and fat, and susceptible to new diseases like diabetes.

This nostalgic discourse is related to another, which is more explicitly related to the rise of Newar cultural nationalism (Gellner 1986, 1997a). According to this line of argument, Newar culture is highly civilized, and their elaborate feasts are one of its finest achievements to rank beside their fine temples, religious art, and ancient (by Nepali standards) literature. Newar cultural nationalist organizations have organized several 'food festivals' in Kathmandu at the national Exhibition Ground, where tickets are sold partly to tourists, but mainly to Newars themselves, for an extremely elaborate traditional feast, served buffet style, in return for tickets torn out of a special booklet; those serving, whatever their caste, wear traditional agriculturalist-caste dress. It is of course only superficially ironic that this is occurring at a time when private feasts held in Newar houses for weddings or other life-cycle rituals are often *not* in traditional form, but have rather switched to the cheaper option which does not require the mobilization of networks of relatives and caste-fellows, namely hiring the catering service of a large hotel to produce an anodyne, globalized Indian-food buffet.

The switch away from traditional food practices is justified by yet another discourse, much of which, ironically, draws strength from a quasi-Ayurvedic theory of bodily balance. The traditional Newar feast with its sixteen or seventeen dishes is supposed to represent a perfect balance of the six tastes: sweet, bitter, sour, salty, spicy, and astringent. But it achieves this balance by including all six in fairly strong form, and the basis of the feast is always beaten rice (Nw. *baji*, Np. *ciurā*), because this is less susceptible to impurity than boiled rice. Beaten rice, and some of the other dishes, are however notoriously difficult to digest, and many give up traditional feasts, or find they have to refuse parts of them, for the sake of their digestion (as in the case study of KT given below). Some do this with regret, on a purely personal basis, but others dismiss the traditional forms of food as wasteful, old-fashioned, and unsuited to modern times.

The pressures of modern life are seen to require the immediate and easily available cures of western biomedicine (which can be bought at any pharmacist's without prescription). Many feel that they have lost something thereby and that they have to strive to maintain a bodily balance that is threatened by the modernization of Kathmandu and its environs.

Three case studies

Three examples will show how different systems of medicine are used in cases of uncertainty. The first case illustrates well the willingness to consult many different kinds of practitioner as well as the coexistence of a broadly humoral view of the body with the possibility of divine causation and biomedical treatments.

After telling me about when he had typhoid, KT told me: If I eat anything heating (*garmī*) I get spots/pustules (*kaī*) in my mouth: alcohol (*aylā*) or anything with chillis. It's been like that for two years. So [at feasts] I just have the jellied buffalo meat, haricot beans, 'soft' things like that. About six months after my father died I got spots which lasted a whole year and I was very thin. After two months I showed them to my maternal uncle [a Tantric healer] and he diagnosed affliction by (the *doṣ* of) a ghost (*sī*) and a drain spirit (*dhānpwā*). I couldn't do any *pūjā* because I was still wearing white clothes, I wasn't pure yet. He said I should wait till after the year's mourning period was over. So a week after the end of mourning, after everything had been purified, I made the necessary offerings and there was a slight improvement. But after a month it got worse again, so I went to a skin specialist. He told me not to eat anything heating and to rub Bitagel on the spots. It got better in four days. But when I ate 'sour' (*pauñ*) [a fruit used in feasts] and hot things they came back.

Next I took a course of an Indian medicine called '*jaributi* [herbal] grass'. You put water in it at night and drink it next morning ... I got it from an Ayurvedic pharmacist. By the end of the month the colour and taste change ... If your stomach is in a bad way, you get spots; the medicine makes you get better.

Some people said I should try goat's milk. It's very cooling (*sardi*), very good for spots. So I have been drinking it, one quarter measure every morning. There are people who come and sell it door to door. It's very expensive: 32 rupees for a full measure [1 *manā*]. I had tried putting red powder water (*rakta candan laḥ*) [on the spots] while still in mourning. It felt nice and cool but didn't improve things. Now I use Gelora [manufactured in India by Reckitt and Coleman] which stings when you put it on ... The best thing seems to be the goat's milk and watching what I eat ...

One doctor I went to said: 'We should check your blood and that of your wife.' I tried not sleeping with her for a whole month to see if it was from 'sex'... but it got even worse! So I stick to avoiding anything sour, hot, or fried; but that means I tend to be weak. The Gelora makes the spots go away in three days ... But I do wonder if it isn't caused by the *doṣ* of the gods around here; sometimes when chatting with friends I do use bad words inadvertently.

The second case occurred in a household which I would judge is marginally more secularized than KT's and certainly more able to afford biomedicine. It is simpler than the first case, in which the causation was taken to be divine and humoral, and the treatment biomedical. Here there is recognized to be conflict between the two explanations, biomedical and divine, and the two are held concurrently in a frankly experimental manner.

The six-year-old son of PR suddenly had a stiff leg that he could not move. He was taken first to the private clinic of a local doctor who prescribed a course of antibiotics. When there was no improvement, a local midwife (*'ajicā'*, *didi aji*) was invited and she diagnosed the *doṣ* of a well-known ghost, a man who had been hung for murder in the 1930s. He had declared before dying that he would cause people many problems and that offerings to him would need to include a cigarette.

I happened to arrive at PR's house just as the ritual of offering (*bau biyegu*) to the ghost was being performed. PR's mother, the boy's grandmother, was waving small sticks of incense in front of him as he stood in front of a clay bowl filled with broken rice with a cigarette lying on top (the *bau*). She then stuck the incense in the bowl and carried it without speaking or looking back to the spot near the cremation grounds outside the old city walls where the 'ghost' had been hung.

The family were highly amused and slightly embarrassed by my presence, PR's father saying several times, 'You don't believe in this kind of thing in your country, do you? You must think us very backward for doing this.' PR's son recovered almost immediately which the family took as confirmation of the midwife's diagnosis. But, just in case, they continued the course of antibiotics to the end. When I enquired about it later both PR and his elder brother were adamant that the affliction must have been sent by the ghost.

The third case concerns events that happened in Baneshwar, a new suburb of Kathmandu, on 7–8 May 1997, when a woman called Sarasvati Adhikari was beaten so badly under the instructions of Gita K.C.,[5] a female medium, that she died.

A television journalist called Mohan Mainali was awakened at 12.30 a.m. by the noise coming from a house near his apartment. A woman was crying, 'Don't hit me, father of Kumar [i.e. her husband], I'm not possessed by a witch ... Anyway, my chest has stopped hurting now. Aiya ... I am dying. Father of Kumar, please release my legs, I am going to die. Water ... water ... water.' Mainali heard them say that they were trying to make the witch that was possessing Sarasvati talk. He went up to see what was going on but he was told by Gita K.C. that it had nothing to do with him and that if he didn't mind his own business they would kill him by throwing him down the stairs (Maila 1997: 70–1). Following an old procedure, which had been made illegal in 1854 (Macdonald 1976), Gita, Sarasvati's husband, and Gita's landlord, prepared red-hot rice spatulas to brand Sarasvati (the idea being that it is the possessing witch who will be branded); and they also tied her legs, burned them with candles, and poured boiling water over her.

The next day the journalist contacted various women's NGOs and the police. When the police came they found Sarasvati slumped in the corner, unconscious and suffering from burns. She was taken to Bir Hospital but died next day, leaving a daughter of 9 and a son aged 7. She was carried to Pashupatinath, the premier place for Hindu cremations in the Kathmandu Valley, accompanied by a large procession, many of the participants representing women's organizations which were protesting against 'superstition' and the suppression of women.

The accounts of the death of Sarasvati that followed were mostly very hostile to the whole institution of mediums or shamans that diagnose witchcraft, and some clearly saw it as part of the oppression of women that only they are ever accused of witchcraft (Maila 1997: 85). Others, however, were more open to the idea that true mediums did exist: Bhujel's piece (1997: 23) had an interview with a practising medium who claimed to use hot water and ashes in cases of suspected witch-possession and insisted: 'it won't burn those who are ill [i.e. possessed by a witch]'; and the medium condemned Gita K.C. as a false woman merely pretending to be possessed.

There are other crucial differences in the two lengthy journalistic accounts available to me. Virakti Maila's article portrays Gita K.C. almost as much a victim as Sarasvati, indicating that she was forced into her profession as a medium because her husband left for Singapore and never sent her any money, and hinting that she only took up being a medium as a cover for prostitution (Maila 1997: 80). Maila also writes that Sarasvati had visited Gita, who was related by marriage, for healing on several occasions already. He condemns the idea that Sarasvati's husband was having an affair with Gita and that they planned the whole thing, as a bazaar rumour. Bhujel's article, on the other hand, gives a different name for Gita's husband, and claims that she had been a shameless, thieving, sexually voracious hussy from her childhood years, had left her husband, and then later deceived him, taking money for a child that was not his (Bhujel 1997). Bhujel also accepts the relationship by marriage but says that even when, following her brother's advice, Sarasvati stopped visiting Gita, her husband fell completely under her spell (ibid.: 19).

This third case study suggests that the hope often expressed in the early 1980s (e.g. in Shrestha 1980) that traditional medical practitioners might be used to deliver biomedicine more effectively in rural areas was somewhat naïve. The other case studies show that despite the increasing dominance of biomedicine lay people are ready to entertain non-biomedical therapies and interventions, especially (and unsurprisingly) when biomedical therapies are ineffective.

Conclusion

Many studies have drawn attention to the essentially pragmatic and eclectic nature of the ordinary South Asian's approach to illness (Marriott 1955; Amarasingham 1980; Nichter 1978). Beals comments:

The Indian universe is complex, pluralistic, and hierarchical ... The quantity and variety of diseases to be found in any village fully supports the idea of a complicated and pluralistic ecology ... Folk medical knowledge appears to involve the following assumptions: (1) there are many kinds of diseases; (2) different kinds of diseases have different causes and require different treatments and different practitioners; (3) all diseases are curable if the appropriate practitioner can be found; and (4) appropriate practitioners are best identified through personal contacts and particularly through the advice and counsel of friends and relatives. (Beals 1976: 198)

These conclusions would appear to be fundamentally sound even today. However, it seems to me that in attempting to explain lay choice of therapy, one needs also to cite the socio-political context, which includes the competing and incompatible claims of different specialists. In the Kathmandu Valley there is an emerging consensus that biomedicine is the best resort for many kinds of affliction. At the same time, in interpreting the coexistence of biomedicine with other therapies, there is a significant parallel with the way that lay people negotiate and interpret the hierarchically structured religious pluralism with which they live. Thus I would list three main determinants of lay people's choices of practitioner:

1. the social/political context and generally accepted evaluations of different forms of therapy;
2. the pragmatic suck-it-and-see approach which most lay people share when faced with uncertainty and/or chronic complaints;
3. a lively lay appreciation of causal complexity, so that multiple therapies or 'combination' therapy, making use of different 'systems', may often be perceived to be necessary.

Any approach that ignores one or other of these factors lays itself open to the charge of incompleteness.

Notes

1. I thank D. Wujastyk for the invitation which spurred me to write this paper, Alfiani Fadzakir for information on Muslim healers, and Anil Sakya for comments.
2. See Weiner 1989 on this as it affects doctors. Cf. Adams 1998 on the role of doctors in the 1990 People's Movement.
3. Ayurveda enjoyed a brief and marginal revival of status in the eyes of the government in the early 1980s as foreign aid agencies realized that attempts to reach Nepal's villages with biomedicine had largely failed. Consequently, a number of measures to raise the status of Ayurvedic practitioners were undertaken, and the Sixth Five-Year Plan (1980–5) envisaged a 15-bed Ayurvedic hospital and they have been unsuccessful in attracting new candidates into Ayurveda, despite a continuing demand for it from lay people (Durkin-Longley 1982: 135–7). *The Statistical Yearbook of Nepal 1999* reports that Nepal had 495 *kaviraj vaidyas* in 1996–7 (compared to 874 biomedical doctors), and 232 Ayurvedic dispensaries (up from 155 in 1968–9) compared to 736 health posts (down from 816 in 1988–9).
4. For example, the 1995 edition of the annual magazine (*smārikā*) of the Manandhar organization, the Kendriya Manandhar Sangh, reports that on the first of Ashvin 2051 (October 1994) a free clinic was held in the village of Machegaon by paediatrician Dr D.S. Manandhar and physician Dr K. Manandhar between 10 a.m. and 4.30 p.m. The people treated numbered 160, 5,000 rupees worth of medicines were given out free of charge, and the local people were instructed in children's illnesses, hygiene, family planning, and AIDS prevention.
5. 'K.C.' stands for Khatri Chetri: it is often abbreviated and used as a surname in this way.

PART IV

Hinduism and History

11

Hinduism, Tribalism, and the Position of Women: The Problem of Newar Identity

The problem: the Hindu/tribal model[1]

It has often been observed in recent anthropological writing how the politically and culturally dominant group in a given society views those who are peripheral and subordinate to it as inverting its own 'natural' and 'correct' way of doing things. Such views may be applied to people living in remote places, to the subordinate gender, to religiously defined minorities, to 'primitive' man, and even to animals.[2] A good example of this is the way Muslims in India and Nepal are regarded by the majority Hindu population. They are believed to be 'upside down', i.e. to invert the normal order, in everything they do: it is said that they wash their hands and face upwards instead of downwards, that they laugh at funerals, and that Muslim widows wear lipstick and carry leather handbags on the death of their husbands (cf. Gaborieau 1972: 91, 93; 1985: 8–9).

This chapter attempts to show how a similar though more subtle stereotype, originating in the political subordination of the Newars to the Parbatiyas in post-1769 Nepal has impoverished, and occasionally misled, academic studies of the Newars. By identifying some key steps in the reproduction of the stereotype, particularly with reference to the position of women, as well as by reviewing the relevant ethnographic evidence, I hope to throw light both on a scholarly tradition and on the object of its study.

The Newars are the indigenous inhabitants of the Kathmandu Valley. Their language, Newari, is Tibeto–Burman in origin and structure, but has been profoundly influenced by Sanskrit, various Prakrits, Persian, Hindi, Nepali, and (most recently) English. The present state of Nepal came into existence in 1769 when Prithvi Narayan Shah, ancestor of the present king, conquered the three small kingdoms of the Kathmandu Valley and made the Valley his capital. The elite of the new Gorkhali state (so named after Prithvi Narayan's home town and kingdom of origin, Gorkha) was made up of Gurkhali- (Nepali-) speaking Parbatiyas. They consist basically of brahman and kshatriya castes (known locally as 'Bahun' and 'Chetri') and associated untouchable artisans (blacksmiths, tailors, cobblers). These Parbatiyas spread throughout the middle hills of Nepal and absorbed the local ethnic groups or tribes within a wider framework dominated by themselves. Parbatiya migration, often encouraged by land grants, provided the ethnic backbone of the new state, and their Indo-European language, now known as Nepali, provided its lingua franca and official medium of communication.[3]

This historical process has generated an opposition between the 'Hindus', i.e. the Parbatiyas (called *indo-népalais* by French writers), on the one hand, and the 'tribes', most of whom speak Tibeto-Burman languages, on the other. However, it is a commonplace in books on Nepal that the Newars do not fit easily into either category. Thus Höfer (1979a: 43-4) includes the Newars with groups which are linguistically Sino-Tibetan while recognizing that they 'represent a particular case'. Gaborieau (1978: 198), on the other hand, writes that the Newars' 'ethnic profile is paradoxical. They speak a Tibeto-Burman language, but they cannot any longer be classed as a tribe ...' So he places them in his section on caste Hindus, rather than in the chapter on tribes. Finally P.R. Sharma (1978: 1), while arguing that 'the notions of 'Hindu' and 'tribal' here [in Nepal] are perhaps better understood as a continuum than as a dichotomy' and that 'Hindu-tribal synthesis is a fact of Nepal's historicity' (ibid.: 6), refrains from including the Newars in his discussion.

The reason why the Newars are refractory in this way is that, on the one hand, the dominant Parbatiyas consider them inferior and different, as they do the tribes; on the other hand, the Newars are the heirs to an essentially urban South Asian civilization (centred in the three old royal cities, Kathmandu, Lalitpur, and Bhaktapur), and in general do not look at all like a tribe. The Newars are subdivided into numerous castes (many more than the Parbatiyas). They have Brahmans, as well as Buddhist priests called Vajracharyas, who have been dubbed 'Buddhist brahmans'. There are also (to enumerate only those mentioned in the discussion below) high castes, both Hindu (the Shresthas) and Buddhist (Sakya, Tuladhar); a large peasant caste, the Maharjans (Jyapu), with several subcastes; numerous small artisan and ritual specialist castes; an 'unclean' Butcher caste and several untouchable castes.

My purpose is not to argue that the terms 'tribe' and 'Hindu' should be discarded as non-existent categories. They undoubtedly exist. It is also undoubtedly true that today, and for some time past, there has been in Nepal (as elsewhere) a process of Sanskritization. The culture of the dominant Parbatiya group has influenced in various significant ways that of the tribes, so that the tribes have come increasingly to resemble castes. Partly because of this process, a Nepalese scholar, D.R. Dahal (1979), has registered a strong protest against the use of the term 'tribe' in the Nepalese context (he prefers 'ethnic group'). The main point of his critique seems to be that the use of the term by foreign scholars introduces 'biased ideas of social disharmony' and thus undermines the process of nation-building in Nepal. It is not necessary however to use the word 'tribe' in a pejorative sense. In fact, as I have suggested elsewhere (Gellner 1986: 114–18), the terms 'tribe' and 'caste' have come to be understood by scholars of South Asia as the ends of a spectrum, as Sharma says they should be. (It will be noted that where writers on Nepal tend to oppose tribe to Hindu, writers on India oppose tribe to caste; but it is the same contrast which is being made in both cases.)

Some principal aspects of the contrast are presented in Chart 11.1. The groups whom anthropologists of Nepal refer to as tribes do not necessarily have all the characteristics listed under 'tribe', but most possessed them in the recent past. The tendencies listed under the 'caste' heading reach their apogee—maximal elaboration of ritual and other division of labour, maximal proximity to royal centres—in the cities. On this criterion the Newars are the very opposite of a tribe and the very epitome of a Sanskritic, caste-based society. Because outsiders have nearly always approached the study of the Newars via the Parbatiya view of them, scholarly attention has tended to ignore this fact and has concentrated instead on trying to view them as a tribe. What elsewhere in South Asia would simply be labelled folk religion or the Little Tradition, is here immediately seized upon as a historical survival of great significance. The Hindu/tribal model, even when considered as a spectrum and even when dealing with the Nepalese middle hills and leaving the Newars to one side, is, in the words of N.J. Allen (1987: 33), 'exceedingly crude'. Neither category is monolithic or unchanging. The Parbatiyas themselves have changed considerably. The tribes are diverse, have a considerable history of influences from other sources, and are far from being bounded homogeneous units. Toffin (1981b: 39) remarks that 'classifications of the Tibeto-Burman hill tribes into Tamang, Gurung, Magar, Rai, Thakali, etc., correspond only very imperfectly to reality and can only be accepted as working hypotheses. In fact none of these groups forms a homogeneous ethnic group, either culturally or linguistically.'[4] For all these reasons the Hindu/tribal dichotomy should only be used with the greatest care. Where the dichotomy does indeed structure local relationships, this fact should not be taken as natural and self-evident, but explained in comparative and historical terms, as is done for instance in Caplan's (1970) study of brahman/Limbu relations in east Nepal.

Chart 11.1: Aspects of the tribe/caste dichotomy or spectrum as used in South Asian studies

Tribe	Caste
Equality	Hierarchy
Simple division of labour	Elaborate division of labour
Swidden agriculture or pastoralism	Settled agriculture
Position beyond state control	Under state control
Own religious specialists	Brahman and other literate religious specialists

That the Hindu/tribal dichotomy enters deep into the thinking of all those who work on Nepal could be shown by any number of examples. It is worth quoting one, from Acharya and Bennett's statistical analysis of eight studies of women from different cultural groups in Nepal, since it deals with a case (the Newar Maharjan (Jyapu) women of Bulu) which will be discussed again below:

In three of the Tibeto-Burman sample of villages i.e., the Baragaonle, Rai and Magar, only about 15 percent of the women had been married more than once. The Jyapu Newar of Bulu and the Tamang of Katarche seem to have the largest percentage of women who have married more than once [24.4 and 36.2 per cent respectively]. This finding was quite contrary to our expectations since among the Tibeto-Burman speaking groups the Newar and Tamang have been most strongly influenced by Indo-Aryan culture which generally discourages female remarriage even in the case of widowhood. The greater instability of marriages in the more Hinduized Tibeto-Burman speaking communities is possibly due to the greater proportion of arranged marriages in these communities as compared to other Tibeto-Burman groups. (Acharya and Bennett 1981: 82)

The present paper is concerned with the use of the tribal/Hindu dichotomy not for the analysis of the culture of the hill tribes, but for that of the Newars. In view of the much greater density and complexity of Newar society, and its long history of incorporation within the mainstream of South Asian culture, the application of the dichotomy to the Newars, if valid at all, requires even greater care. K.P. Malla (1985), himself a Newar, makes explicit and articulate use of a Hindu/tribal Sanskritization (and cultural imperialism) model to explain the social history of the Licchavi period (fifth to eighth century). Whether or not this is good history, it is mistaken—I hope to show—to use the same terms, without any qualification, to describe the present-day position of the Newars in relation to Parbatiyas.

The problem applied: some views of the position of Newar women

It is often not sufficiently stressed that there is no traditional indigenous way of referring to the distinction between caste and tribe. Both are equally *jāti* or *jāt*.[5] Emic distinctions are indeed made: they are usually in terms of sophistication versus rusticity or humanness versus animality. What western or western-derived discourse calls tribes are for high-caste Hindus the paradigm of uncouth rusticity (*jaṅgalī*), the least 'civilized' (*saṃskṛta*).[6] Much of the discussion of the concept of tribe in South Asia has been an attempt to recapture the fact (which in India missionaries and colonial administrators had various reasons for overlooking), that the caste/tribe or Hindu/tribal dichotomy is really a spectrum without a clear cut-off point. A crucial component of the dichotomy, a criterion of distinction which reappears again and again, at least in Nepal, concerns the treatment of women. With regard to the Newars this is a dominant theme. Chart 11.2 illustrates some of the crude associations which are often made. Different associations are made in different contexts, and only rarely are they all found together. In so far as a similar opposition is made by Newars or other Nepalese themselves, they naturally adjust the terms of the contrast to suit their own circumstances. High-caste Newar Buddhists, for example, would place both Buddhism and the isogamous ideal in the right-hand column. This fact should be sufficient in itself to demonstrate the inadequacy of the Hindu/tribal dichotomy as an analytical tool. The last three contrasts in the chart are too specific to appear in most of the loose image-making which is considered in this section and the next, but they will be seen to be relevant below.

Chart 11.2: Some crude associations of the Hindu/tribal dichotomy as applied to Nepal

Tribe	Hindu
Tibeto-Burman language	Indo-European language
Indigenous origin, or origin to north and east	Origin in India
Clan organization	Caste organization
'Animism' and/or Buddhism	Hinduism
Loose sexual morality	Strict control of women
Remarriage for widows and divorces permitted	Remarriage of widows and divorcées scandalous
Marriage with MBD preferred	Marriage with cousins forbidden
Bride-price or bride service	Dowry
Hypogamous or isogamous ideal	Hypergamous ideal

Since 1769 the Newars have been a subordinate group,[7] and there has been a tendency both on the part of the Parbatiyas, and on that of foreigners who have accepted the dominant or official viewpoint, to assume that what the Parbatiyas do constitutes Hindu orthodoxy, and what other groups do is a deviation from it. In certain circumstances such a view may even be correct; but rather than being accepted as an axiom, it should be treated with suspicion, as a proposition in which many have a strong vested interest; and only when it has been tested against all the evidence, and alternative views also considered, should it be given credence. An example of this view is the proposition that at some unspecified time in the past the Newars practised polyandry.

As far as I know this was first asserted explicitly by Hodgson, although he may well have been developing a remark of Kirkpatrick's (1975 [1811]: 187): 'It is remarkable enough that the Newar women, like those among the Nairs [= Nayars], may, in fact, have as many husbands as they please, being at liberty to divorce them continually on the slightest pretence.' Hodgson wrote:

Upon this I may remark that the traits observed in the Nilgiris are thoroughly Tartar, and as such are widely prevalent in the Himálaya and Tibet. Even the civilised tribe of the Newárs, who, by the way, have a recorded tradition uniting them with the Malabár Náirs—a name identical, they say, with Neyár or Newár (y and w being intercalary letters)—were once polyandrists, and are still regardless of female chastity, whilst the Tibetans were and are notoriously both. (Hodgson 1880 II: 129–30)

The connection with the Nayars of south India was not invented by Kirkpatrick or Hodgson. Certain high-caste Newars, whose clan name was *newā*, claimed descent from them; in doing so, however, one strongly suspects that all memory of the Nayars' polyandry was suppressed, and that only their kshatriya status was remembered. In any case, that a few Newars might be descended from Nayars (which itself is doubtful) does not prove anything about the history of the bulk of the Newar population.

The theory of one-time Newar polyandry was taken up by G.S. Nepali (1965: 238, 277–8), who attempted to give it an etymological foundation. His arguments were based on an inadequate grasp of Newari: he confused the suffix *-bhata*, meaning '-in-law' (from a woman's point of view), with *bhāhta*, meaning 'husband';[8] and he wrongly thought that *bhāhtapī* means 'husbands' (in the plural), whereas in fact it means 'husband's people (i.e. family)'. He also tried to argue deductively that 'the customary freedom of a Newar woman for the successive re-marriages and divorces ... could only be a step forward from the stage of polyandry', and suggested moreover that 'group ownership of women' might be deduced from the custom of distributing to all the bride's relatives betel nuts and special marriage cakes presented by the groom's family (Nepali 1965: 238, 418). Finally he also cited another belief which goes along with these ideas:

... in former days a woman coming to live with her eighth husband, after leaving the previous seven, used to be called Sapta Laxmi and she used to be much welcomed in the house. Though the jealousy of the males would no longer tolerate such laxity on the part of the woman, the traditional belief still exists. (ibid.: 268)

Unfortunately, G.S. Nepali does not record who told him this. All Newars today would reject such a notion with horror. I suspect that he may be recording a Parbatiya saying about the Newars. Deductions like these, which isolate particular customs and label them as pre-Hindu or tribal, are parallel to those with regard to south India which attempt to specify what is Aryan and what is Dravidian. The crass way in which that is often done led Dumont to denounce the distinction altogether: 'The most disastrous of the these imaginary divisions which has been imposed, and still is imposed, on Indian culture is the so-called distinction between Aryan and Dravidian features' (Dumont 1957: 15).

While it surely must be legitimate to ask whether certain contemporary practices predate brahmanical influence, both in south India and among the Newars, obtaining a valid answer is by no means a simple matter.

Historical evidence of the position of women among the Newars

The position of women—their supposed freedom to divorce and remarry at will—is, then, a crucial part of the perception of the Newars as similar to Tibetans and tribals. An important early source for this view was the account of Francis Hamilton, who spent fourteen months in the Kathmandu Valley in 1802 and 1803. It is worth quoting what he wrote in full since it has been relied upon and selectively cited so often:

The Newar women are never confined. At eight years of age, they are carried to a temple, and married, with the ceremony usual among Hindus, to a fruit called Bel (Aegle Marmelos, Roxb.). When a girl arrives at the age of puberty, her parents, with her consent, betroth her to some man of the same cast [sic], and give her a dower, which becomes the property of the husband, or rather paramour. After this, the nuptials are celebrated with feasting, and some religious ceremonies. Among the higher casts, it is required that girls should be chaste till they have been thus betrothed; but in the lower casts, a girl, without scandal, may previously indulge any Hindu with her favours; and this licentiousness is considered a thing of no consequence. Whenever a woman pleases, she may leave her husband; and if, during her absence, she cohabit only with men of her cast, or of a higher one, she may at any time return to her husband's house, and resume the command of his family. The only ceremony or intimation that is necessary, before she goes away, is her placing two betel nuts on her bed. So long as a woman chooses to live with her husband, he cannot take another wife, until she becomes past child-bearing; but a man may take a second wife, when his first chooses to leave him, or when she grows old; and at all times he may keep as many concubines as he pleases. A widow cannot marry again; but she is not expected to burn herself and may cohabit with any Hindu as a concubine. The children, by the betrothed wife, have a preference in succession to those by concubines; the latter, however, are entitled to some share. A man can be betrothed to no woman except one of his own cast; but he may keep a concubine of any cast, whose water he can drink. If the woman's cast is lower than his, the children are called Khas [sic], and are considered to belong to the cast of the mother, but are somewhat elevated on account of their father's birth. (Hamilton 1971 [1819]: 42–3)

There is at least one assertion here which should be dismissed as a mistake: offspring of an intercaste hypergamous union are called *lawa*, *lawat*, or (in some circumstances) *urāy*, never *khas*. But in general what is remarkable about Hamilton's observations is the care with which they are made: he distinguishes different types of Newar, mentions the crucial point that intercaste unions are only acceptable between clean castes, and considers the distinction between primary and secondary marriage (which he calls concubinage).

Details such as these were usually omitted by the reputable authors who repeated Hamilton's observations.[9] Furthermore, the marriage of Newar girls to the *bel* (Nw. *byāḥ*) fruit, and their consequent freedom from widowhood, became one of the quaint customs and historical curiosities of Nepal. Along with the Newar farmer's annual offering to frogs in the rice fields (also first publicized by Hamilton), the 'confusion' of Buddhism and Hinduism, the annual sacrifice of hundreds of buffaloes on the site of the Kot massacre, the story of Prithvi Narayan Shah cutting off the noses of the inhabitants of Kirtipur, and the similarity of Nepalese pagoda temples to those of China and Japan, the bel fruit marriage and the supposed sexual freedom of Newar women, exercised by leaving betel nuts on the husband's bed, are repeated in numerous popular accounts of Nepal.

Further independent evidence of the position of Newar women in the first half of the nineteenth century comes from Hodgson's discussions of Nepalese law. His informants, whom he questioned about numerous aspects of the administration of justice, asserted that a Newar woman remained entitled to her dowry (*strīdhan*) whatever the reason for divorce, whereas a Parbatiya woman who committed adultery lost everything and had her nose cut off (Hodgson 1880 II: 235; Stiller 1984: 180).

Elsewhere Hodgson (1836: 130–1) provides some extra details. If a Newar woman's husband goes to Tibet and she either elopes or her father or brother gives her in marriage to someone else, then she must perform *pārchuke*, divorce. This requires her to go to the head court of the city and give two betel nuts and one mohar (half a rupee) to the judge. Hodgson notes that 'Now, under the Gorkhas, a Newar wife cannot get free without paying two, four, or six, or more up to twenty rupees according to her means.' The judge sends the betel nuts on to the husband, and the wife is free to leave. All this presupposes that her lover is of the same caste and not within the prohibited degrees of kinship, in which case punishments may be in order. If the woman and her lover fail to approach the judge they are subject to a fine of 120 rupees, though only half this amount is normally collected.

The Muluki Ain (law code) of 1854 presents clear evidence of an attempt by the government to regulate Newar marriage and make divorce less easy.[10] It states that, providing her husband continues to support her, a Newar woman has no right of divorce merely because her husband has brought in a second wife and placed her in another house, or because he has gone abroad. She may divorce him at the end of three years if he has gone abroad and left her without means of support; but even this does not apply if he has gone abroad on government business. She may divorce him if he commits theft and is branded, if he becomes a fakir or gets some severe disease or injury (leprosy, loss of a leg, loss of speech, or turns out to be sexless, *napuṃsak*, i.e. incapable of consummating the marriage). A Newar wife is forbidden to return the betel nuts and leave her husband if he is ill; and a Newar husband may not abandon his wife at will (literally: 'saying, "I am leaving this wife whose stars (*graha daśā*) have turned out to be oppressive"'). Providing these conditions were followed, the law code did give divorce among the Newars a recognition not permitted to other groups: however many times a Newar woman had been married, the stipulated divorce payment remained the same, whereas with other groups it diminished with each successive union.

Clearly, the Muluki Ain would not have attempted to prevent something which never occurred. But we have no precise data for the differences between Newar castes. Nor do we know to what extent the law was complied with, and to what extent ignored. The Muluki Ain lists six different payments to be made if a divorce occurred, from 70 down to 10 rupees, according to caste (Höfer 1979a: 137). This corresponds fairly accurately to the different levels of the Newar caste hierarchy. I suspect, however, that those low in the caste hierarchy, and perhaps others as well, simply ignored legal provisions. In many cases they would have been right to do so, since the law specifies in each case 'When they have married and carried through the ritual ...' Since many Newar marriages, even today, occur with little or no ritual (being effected by elopement or by the woman simply joining the man), they thereby fall outside the law. In the past a considerable number of even high-caste marriages were carried out in the same way, or with very simplified rites. On the other hand, that at least some high-caste Newars were deeply committed to brahmanical values is suggested by Hodgson's marginal note: 'The incidence of sati is lower in Nepal than in any part of India. Both Buddhists and Brahmanists alike observe this rite or custom. There may be 30 to 40 satis per annum throughout the Valley' (Hasrat 1970: 66).

Female initiation rites among the Newars

We are now in a position to consider the anthropological debate about Newar marriage and the position of women. Much of this debate has focused on mock marriage (*ihi*), the life-cycle ritual through which Newar girls pass at the age of five, seven, or nine. In Kathmandu it is held whenever a Brahman or Vajracharya priest decides to hold a mass ceremony. In Lalitpur and also in Bhaktapur (if I interpret Vergati 1982: 273, correctly) it can only be performed 'when a god is being established', i.e. either when a new *caitya* or other cult object is being ritually empowered, or (more commonly) when an old person is passing through the old-age initiation ritual of *burā* or *buri jākwa*. All informants agree that the young girl is being married, but opinions differ widely on whom she is marrying. Popularly it is usually said that she is marrying the bel fruit itself. The dominant Hindu theory is that she is marrying Vishnu Narayana, and that the bel fruit represents Shiva, as a witness (Vergati 1982: 278). The dominant Buddhist theory is that she is marrying Suvarna Kumara and the bel fruit is sometimes said to represent the god of wealth Kubera or Jambhala (a Buddhist equivalent of Kubera). Informants of all castes say that the ritual of *ihi* means that a Newar woman will never be a widow, even if her human husband dies. Whether or not one should take this at face value will be considered below. Two important points about the ritual should be noted: first, the central act is the 'gift of a virgin' (*kanyādān*), performed by the father of the girl to the bel fruit or to a symbol of the god; and secondly, there is always an accompanying fire sacrifice. Neither rite is part of the ritual accompanying marriage to a human husband (though optionally, and untraditionally, some wealthy Newars do now perform the fire sacrifice).

The ritual of mock marriage must also be considered alongside that of confinement or 'placing a barrier' (*bārāy* or *bārhāḥ tayegu*). Newar girls pass through this rite at some time after *ihi* but before their first menstruation. They are confined in a room with its windows blocked out for twelve days, during which they cannot look on males or on the sun. In Lalitpur and Kathmandu several girls perform this at once; in Bhaktapur it is always done singly (Vergati 1982: 280). From the fourth or the sixth day, called *bēkegu* (purification), a doll or effigy called a *khyāḥ* shares the room with the girl(s) (either placed in a cupboard or hung on the wall) and it has to be offered some of the food which the girls eat. At the end of twelve days the girls are shown ritually to the sun, Surya (a form of Vishnu). Many Newars state that Surya is in fact the girls' second husband, so that the human husband is only the third; learned informants deny this.

Finally, it is necessary to say something about the types of human marriage practised by the Newars. Among all castes there is a distinction between a ritualized and expensive wedding and an elopement, which avoids the various expenses of ritual, dowry, exchanges between affines, and a feast for numerous guests. High castes must invite a Brahman or Vajracharya priest (and in certain rare cases, both) to conduct the ritual. There is considerable variation in the practice of middle and low castes. They mostly do not use priests: lineage elders perform the ritual. But among them, equally, a ritualized version, with exchanges, feasts, and a marriage procession, can be contrasted with a version in which the bride simply comes to live with the husband without any ceremony.

The exchanges between the bride's and the groom's families are complicated. In essence, there is a long series of prestations and counter-prestations, visits and counter-visits. The central element in the prestations is the betel nut: these are exchanged to and fro; crucially, the groom's family sends betel nuts as a mark of engagement, the bride gives them to all her relatives as a sign that she is leaving them, and she presents them to her husband's relatives (and they accept them) as a sign that she is now a member of their patrilineage (with all the rights and duties this entails). These exchanges are accompanied with appropriate hospitality on both sides. The scale of the celebration is slightly less munificent on the wife-giving side (who are losing someone), but otherwise the rituals balance each other out, and are a clear demonstration of isogamy. Wife-givers are not inferior to wife-takers; the relationship is one of equality.[11] That it is ultimately between two families or lineages, rather than two individuals, is shown by the fact that traditionally the groom did not accompany the procession which sets out to fetch the bride, although nowadays, among many castes, he does so, in imitation of Parbatiya weddings. Only Newar Brahmans, and possibly a few high-caste Chathariya Shresthas, deviate from this isogamic pattern.

Louis Dumont (1964) took up the parallel between the Nayars and the Newars which, as we have seen, was commonly drawn in the old sources. His argument hinged on the distinction between a primary marriage, which has to be celebrated with full rites, including 'the gift of virgin' (*kanyādān*), and is indissoluble, and a secondary marriage, which has much reduced or no ritual legitimation, and is not subject to the same preferential marriage rules. He argued that in both the Nayar and the Newar cases there is a ritualized primary marriage (the *tali*-tying rite in the Nayar case and *ihi* in the Newar one) which then leaves the girl free subsequently to contract less orthodox and unbinding unions. Unfortunately, in describing the Newar case, Dumont had to rely on the work of Fürer-Haimendorf (1956) which, admirable and perceptive though it was, was not based on in-depth fieldwork. Crucially, it exaggerated the ease and the frequency of Newar divorce, as well as the frequency and normality of hypergamous and anagamous intercaste marriages. Furthermore, Dumont believed that the Newars lack castes, and possess only status groups which might on occasion appear like castes. Most of the anthropologists who have done fieldwork on Newars since then have, implicitly or explicitly, cricitized him for saying this.[12]

Dumont's argument was, on the whole, accepted by Vergati, who reasserts that, having gone through ihi, 'Newar women therefore never suffer from the stigma of widowhood in their society' (1982: 283). She does however point out that, in spite of the very considerable differences in social organization between the Nayars and the Newars (matrilineal in the one case, patrilineal and virilocal in the other), both rituals (tali-tying and ihi) act as initiations into adulthood, after which the girl in question is expected to follow the rules and prohibitions appropriate to an adult woman. This suggests that ihi and marriage to a human husband correspond not to Dumont's distinction between primary and secondary marriage, but rather to Fuller's distinction (1976: 105) between 'first marriage', which is a rite of passage by which a girl becomes an adult, and 'second marriage', which legitimates the offspring of her union with one or more men. While most north Indian communities combine first and second marriage in one ritual, among 'traditional' Nayars and among the Newars, as well as in many south Indian cases (Good 1982), they are kept separate.

Perhaps the most interesting contribution to this debate, and the one I want to take issue with, is that of Michael Allen (1982). He provides a full description of both mock marriage and confinement, and uses this for a wider analysis of Newar society. He rightly points out that mock marriage confers full caste membership on girls, just as *upanayana*, *kaytā pūjā*, or *bare chuyegu* does for Newar boys. He has little difficulty in showing that confinement has to do with menstruation and is modelled on the confinement which follows the first menstruation of a girls from orthodox brahman background, after which her husband (if they have been married correctly as children) consummates the marriage. In the Newar case, Allen argues, Surya takes the place of the human husband. He suggests, as a general rule, that

mock-marriages are performed in order to provide some kind of overt commitment to the orthodox Brahmanical purity ideal prior to the establishment of unorthodox sexual relationships. In other words, I would not expect mock-marriages to occur in an isolated tribal community, but rather only where, as in middle India, the tribes are encapsulated in a large caste-structured polity dominated by Brahmans and Ksatriyas. (ibid.: 196)

Towards the end of his paper, Allen remarks that 'after all, most peoples in India and Nepal were, if one could push history back far enough, tribal in origin, and most still retain marriage customs that depart in some way from Brahmanical ideals' (ibid.: 198). Consequently, against Dumont, he argues that the Newars' unorthodoxy lies not in their marriage patterns, nor in their supposed lack of real castes, but in their attitude to women:

the mock-marriages may be said to constitute a formal show of commitment to orthodoxy in Brahman dominated communities within which key values are still strongly unorthodox—especially as regards the status of women and female sexuality and reproductivity. (ibid.: 203)

To this he adds a second explanation, which, as I shall show, is not only unnecessary, but actually undermines the arguments that he so carefully constructs:

Rites seldom exist solely, or even primarily, to provide solutions or solve problems ...There are many features of both *ihi* and *barha* that suggest that it is only after the girl has been, as it were, defused by Suvarna Kumara, by the *khyā* and by Surya Narayana, that a man may safely establish conjugal relations. Put in slightly different terms one might say that the rites seem as much concerned with controlling a potentially dangerous, perhaps even destructive, force as with rendering the girls pure. (ibid.: 203–4)

Until the end of his article, most of what Allen has to say is cogent and forceful. In concluding that confinement is meant to defuse the danger of menstruation he is certainly correct. What he had deduced I was told directly by a Maharjan man:

Where Parbatiyas (*khẽy*) perform *guphā rākhne* six days after the first menstruation, we perform this *bārhā tayegu*, which means that being untouchable [the state of a woman during her period] is abolished (*thiye ma tyaḥ manta*). Women can then cook rice for their families while they are menstruating, although it would be polluting to do so for others. They just refrain from giving money or uncooked rice to anyone, whether family, children, or beggars, and they don't enter the god room.

He added that Maharjan women normally refrain also from sexual intercourse during menstruation, since it is dangerous for the child who might result from it: he or she may be killed by lightning later in life. Among high-caste Hindu Newars, however, the restrictions on a woman during her menstruation remain severe, in spite of having passed through the confinement ritual. She has to refrain from all household work, so that her period is sometimes referred to ironically as *mahārānī juye*, 'being a queen'.

Allen is certainly right that both mock marriage and confinement among the Newars reveal a 'formal commitment' to brahmanical values which are not followed in practice.[13] Newar women have, in reality, relatively high status, a large degree of involvement in economic life, and regular and secure ties to their natal home. Furthermore, one can point to at least two other examples of ritual rather than substantive conformity to brahmanical ideals: the boys' rites which parallel ihi show the same kind of formal and ritualized commitment, in this case to ascetic study in the period before marriage, which in practice is compressed into one day.[14] A second example is the institution of 'living goddesses' (see Allen 1975). Nearly all Newars (except Newar Brahmans) lack the Parbatiyas' hypergamous and filiafocal (i.e. daughter-worshipping) ideology so well described by Lynn Bennett (1983): in this women are considered sacred and worshipped until their marriage, and dangerous, polluting, and inferior once they become sexually active. Newars, by contrast, do not worship their daughters on regular ritual occasions; but in certain ritually defined contexts they do worship certain specifically selected young girls as the goddess Kumari ('the Virgin').

Where I differ from Allen is in his use of a contrast (taken from Dumont) between a caste concern with purity and a tribal concern with protection from danger (Allen 1982: 204). Bennett (1983) shows clearly that the more brahmanical, and caste-like the system of values, the greater the concern with the dangers of uncontrolled female sexuality. Concern for purity and fear of danger (at least the dangers posed by female sexuality) go together and are not opposites. All Allen's arguments about defusing dangers apply *a fortiori* to Parbatiyas and to other Hindus, and therefore fail to explain specifically Newar rituals. Allen argues that the Newars' fear of female sexuality is evidence of a tribal past, when it is evidence of precisely the opposite. In order to make his argument for tribal survivals (to which I shall return below) he should have argued for a *lack* of concern with female sexuality, just as he argued (rightly) that Newar women's status is relatively high (compared to Parbatiyas).

Divorce and widowhood: does *ihi* really prevent 'the stigma of widowhood'?

Due to the practice of ihi, wrote G.S. Nepali (1965: 198), 'marriage is ... not recognised as a sacrament'. R.P. Pradhan (1986: 167), while allowing that in fact high castes do not often divorce, argues that 'the relationship created by the exchange of areca [betel] nuts [in human marriage] is not indissoluble. The relationship almost seems contractual.' If we insist that only kanyādān can be a sacrament, then by definition Newar (human) marriage is not a sacrament and only ihi is. Those Newars who perform the elaborate marriage ritual do however regard it as one of the set of 'ten sacraments' (*daśakarma*).

In connection with the debate surrounding ihi, Quigley (1986: 85, 88) has already stressed that, although the Shresthas of Dhulikhel perform the ritual, widowhood is regarded with 'dread' and there is very little divorce. To this I can add my own experience of high castes (Vajracharya, Sakya, Shrestha) in Lalitpur. Like other Newars, they say that the significance of ihi is that a woman will never be a widow, but in fact a widow does experience considerable loss of status. She may not fill the role of senior woman (*thakālī nakī*) in any ritual, since she is considered to be inauspicious.[15] It is commonly widows who are suspected of being witches (*bwaksī*). Widows living alone or with small children are likely also to be suspected of sexually improper behaviour. Remarriage is very difficult if not impossible. I knew a fifty-year-old Vajracharya priest whose wife had died three years previously. His two sons insisted on living apart, and he lived with the younger son whose wife had a job in a bank. This made it impossible for her to accompany her father-in-law to rituals. His life would have been much easier if he could have married a Vajracharya widow and the family had discussed the possibility. But the sanction of what other people would say (because the inevitable rumours circulated about the woman in question) made it impossible.

Divorce for a woman is very difficult. However unsatisfactory her husband, she will be urged by her parents and her brothers to consider it her own (bad) karma and stick it out. Marriages do sometimes break down and women return to their natal home, usually with their children if they have them; this often leads to conflict between the returning woman and the wives of her brothers, which causes the brothers to separate prematurely from their parents' household. Divorce for a man is somewhat easier, at least early in the marriage. A high-caste woman is not supposed to visit her natal home without being invited, and if she stays the night she should not return to her husband's home without being invited back. Traditionally someone (often a Maharjan tenant farmer) had to be sent to deliver the invitation, though nowadays the telephone is used instead. Wealthy families used to send a sedan chair (*duli*); nowadays they come by car or motorcycle, or send a taxi to fetch her. The young woman must spend main festivals (*nakhaḥ*) at her husband's home or people will begin to wonder about the marriage; but otherwise she often spends long periods in her natal home during the early years of marriage. If, during this time, her husband omits to recall her, there is nothing she can do (although it will of course lead to hostility between the two families). 'Her life is ruined'; her chances of marrying again are small. If she has the chance to elope with someone, he may well be unsuitable and unacceptable to her family, in which case she will have to choose between an uncertain marriage and her family.

The early years of marriage are stressful and insecure for a young woman. At all times she is expected to behave in a demure and submissive manner. She has to please both her husband and (perhaps more important) her mother-in-law, who is certain to tell her that in her day daughters-in-law were more respectful and worked harder. If she fails in either she may be sent back to her natal home (*ma yaḥkāḥ chwayegu*), or simply not recalled from a visit there. If she succeeds only in pleasing her husband, she may be the cause of a bitter and premature separation between her husband and his parents. Her only escape from this period of insecurity and fear is to produce children, especially sons. All this is a far cry from the supposed easy divorce and high status of Newar women. All those whom I asked about the claim that a Newar woman could place betel nuts on her bed and leave her husband denied that this happens. If a wife leaves, she simply goes, and her family may send betel nuts later, to formalize matters, when her husband's family returns her dowry. If the husband sends her away for good she may take her dowry with her and send betel nuts. Betel nuts are returned in a ritually defined place and time only if the husband dies young. In this case, according to a Tuladhar informant from Kathmandu, the young woman places the nuts on his body as a sign that she is going to return home; she then does not have to observe death pollution and may remarry.[16] Informants from Lalitpur say that it is not necessary to place betel nuts on the dead husband's body; the wife simply leaves.

Obviously it is of crucial importance to establish just what the rates of divorce really are. There is unequivocal evidence that some village Maharjans do indeed practise divorce and remarriage with great freedom and without stigma for either party. This is so in Pyangaon (Toffin 1984: 120) and in the nearby village of Bulu (B. Pradhan 1981: 71, 74). At the other extreme, as I have described, high-caste Newar women certainly do suffer considerable stigma, both from widowhood and from divorce, whatever informants may say about ihi; and widow remarriage (unless the woman is young and childless) is even more strongly disapproved of. Associated with the pattern of easy divorce in Pyangaon and Bulu is the practice of a man serving his wife's parents in various capacities throughout his life, culminating in carrying their corpse when they die (Toffin 1984: 166). This is diametrically opposed to the hypergamous pattern, followed clearly and unambiguously by Newar Brahmans (Toffin 1996a: 202) as by Parbatiyas, in which the daughter's husband is identified with Vishnu and served like a god by his affines. In the Pyangaon system the 'prestation surplus' flows in one direction, women in the other. The hypergamous system is asymmetrical in that both women and prestations flow in the same direction.

As Toffin (1981b: 58–9; 1984: 166–7, 418) has made clear, the Pyangaon model is close to that of the hill tribes and to that of the peripheral Newar group, the Pahari. The crucial question is: To what extent do other Newars, and in particular Maharjans both in other villages and in the cities, share the Pyangaon system? Toffin's view is that for the most part they do. High castes, who must once have shared it also, have been Hinduized away from it. The Maharjans represent the 'tribal substratum' of the Newars (Toffin 1984: 19–20, 157, 587, 589).

An alternative hypothesis is that it is Pyangaon which is unusual and that most other Maharjans do not share what I have called the Pyangaon system. If so, the fact that the inhabitants of Pyangaon settled there some two to three hundred years ago and assimilated from Pahari (or Tamang) culture to that of Newar peasants (Toffin 1977: 34–6) would explain why they are different from other Maharjans in these respects. If the latter is the correct assumption, then the similarity of Bulu to Pyangaon has still to be explained. That at least some other Maharjan peasants outside the cities do not share the easy divorce, or the bride-service system, of Bulu and Pyangaon is suggested by a passing report from Sunakothi, another Maharjan village south of Lalitpur. Löwdin (1985: 66) writes that 'the stream of gifts between the two households [wife-givers and wife-takers] should preferably be to the advantage of the husband's household'. He also notes that 'it was difficult to obtain any data on divorces, as they are infrequent and regarded as somewhat stigmatizing' (ibid.). G.S. Nepali (1965: 250) reported from Panga (where the vast majority of the population is Maharjan) that only 3.6 per cent of men and 10.1 per cent of women had experienced divorce or desertion and explained these low figures by saying 'the Newars do not now too frequently avail of the customary privileges of divorce and re-marriage'.

Further evidence that Pyangaon and Bulu are unusual comes from Satungal, a village west of Kathmandu inhabited predominantly by Shresthas and Maharjans, which has been studied since 1970 by the Japanese anthropologist, Hiroshi Ishii (1995). Only 2.3 per cent of the Maharjan men and 3.4 per cent of the Shrestha men inhabiting the village in 1984 had ever experienced divorce, including in this figure both those who carried through a written, legal divorce (equivalent to the procedures described by Hodgson above) and those who were separated from their wives, for whatever reason, and were *de facto* divorced. In Satungal a man (whether Maharjan or Shrestha) has no obligation to serve his wife's parents or to carry their corpse when they die; but he does in fact usually render them considerable help over a long period of time, and he does usually appear at their funeral. In exchanges between wife-givers and wife-takers there is no conscious notion that the exchange should favour either side. At the time of the wedding itself the exchanges seem slightly to favour the wife-takers, especially given that they gain the bride herself; but subsequently, because she often gives gifts to members of her natal family and because her husband often helps them, the balance seems slightly to favour the wife-givers.

This information clearly shows that the Pyangaon pattern is not pervasive throughout the Valley. The Maharjans of Satungal practise ihi, rarely divorce, and do not consider that the son-in-law has to serve his wife's parents. None the less, the fact remains that he does help them and this is a considerable difference from the high-caste pattern, in which the son-in-law's relations with his wife's parents are embarrassed and constrained, and marked by avoidance. My own research suggests that the peasants of Satungal follow practices similar to the peasants of the big cities. Maharjan women in Lalitpur do elope; but divorce carries a stigma for a woman, especially if it happens more than once. A father-in-law who permitted his son-in-law to work in his fields would be criticized for allowing something improper. Lalitpur Maharjans do, however, observe a suggestive custom at marriage. At the next Matsyendra festival (Lalitpur's biggest) after the marriage, the new husband has to stay for four days at the house of his parents-in-law. On the third day his father-in-law takes him to show him his fields. If he is present for the cremation of his parents-in-law he will be asked to carry the bier. But unlike in Pyangaon, there is no obligation to be present.

A three-part model: tribalism, Hinduism, and the Newars

On the basis of the ethnographic evidence presented above, I want to suggest as a hypothesis that Newar society should be interpreted with a trichotomous model in mind, rather than the dichotomous Hindu/tribal one. These three components of the model may be labelled the tribal, the Newar, and the north Indian brahmanic systems. I summarize in Chart 11.3 the main features of each. They are of course ideal types. The Maharjans of Pyangaon may be closest to the tribal system, but they do not marry their (first) cross cousins. To take another example, Newar

Brahmans traditionally did not practise *ihi*; for them kanyādān ('the gift of a virgin') was reserved for the human husband. Now that they marry as adults, many of them have started to have their daughters go through *ihi*. Among the Parbatiyas, Chetris deviate from the north Indian brahmanical system (henceforth NIBS) in that they do sometimes tolerate marriage with the MBD, although they know it is unorthodox and forbidden to brahmans (Doherty 1974: 34; Höfer 1979a: 165–6).

Chart 11.3 depicts the three systems in a row. Many have been tempted to see what I call the Newar system as a mere staging post en route towards the brahmanic one. My purpose in proposing three systems instead of two is to suggest that, although it might be right in some circumstances to see the Newar system in this way, we should not be constrained to do so by the concepts we use. It might perhaps be best to imagine the three ideal-typical systems as the points of a triangle. There

Chart 11.3: Opposed characteristics of three social models used to conceptualize Newar society

Tribal System	Newar System	North Indian Brahmanic System (NIBS)
Cross-cousin marriage preferred or permitted	marriage with cross cousins forbidden	marriage with cross cousins forbidden
Isogamy or hypogamy	isogamy	hypergamy for dominant group
Bride-price or bride service	dowry (primarily woman's property)	dowry and groom-price
DH serves WF	polite avoidance between in-laws	DH worshipped as Vishnu
Divorce and remarriage easy	divorce occurs but difficult	divorce very rare
Widowhood has no stigma	widowhood has stigma	widowhood has severe stigma
Virginal consanguineal girls have no special status	virginal consanguineal girls have no special status; selected girls worshipped as Kumari	virginal consanguineal girls are worshipped
ihi not practised	*ihi* practised	*ihi* not practised
Compatible with Buddhism or Hinduism	compatible with Buddhism or Hinduism	compatible only with Hinduism

might then be a route from the Tribal to the NIBS via the Newar, but alternative routes would be equally possible. In the present cultural and political context the NIBS appears as orthodox and anyone who differs from it (tribes, Newars, low castes) as unorthodox. At an earlier historical period it is likely that the Newar system, at least in this region, was itself the orthodoxy.

The benefits of recognizing the Newar system as autonomous, different from both the tribal and the brahmanic, can be seen if we return to Michael Allen's analysis. In trying to explain why G.S. Nepali's figures for divorce were so low, Allen repeated Nepali's explanation in slightly different words:

Today, despite more than a century and a half of greatly increased pressures towards conformity to orthodox Hindu morality, Newar women still retain their traditional rights to mock-marriage and elopement, ease of divorce and the re-marriage of widows. The move towards greater orthodoxy has, however, led to decline in the actual extent which women exercise these rights, especially those of elopement and divorce. (M. Allen 1982: 200)

One may wonder how it is that women can have traditional rights if they are not free to exercise them. This semantic difficulty results, I think, from imposing a simple Hindu/tribal dichotomy on a heterogeneous group.[17] As we have seen, to talk of 'Newar women' without specifying caste is to simplify beyond what is legitimate. Allen has both compressed the time scale of social change and overlooked crucial differences between different castes. It is hardly surprising that a simple dichotomous model appears insufficient.

There is, further, a paradox which is often overlooked. The peripheral Maharjans of Bulu and Pyangaon who are cited as evidence of high divorce rates among the Newars are precisely those who do not practise ihi (but only confinement). In other words, those Newars who go through the rite which is supposed to prevent future widowhood do in fact consider the remarriage of widows to be shameful, while those who do not consider it shameful, do not practise the rite. This paradox can be explained, however, and exactly in Allen's terms. It is indeed in accord with his main argument (but not his subsidiary one): it is those people who are sufficiently close to brahmanic ideals to share their values, at least in part, who require a ritual 'solution', which however never fully resolves the dilemma of wanting to permit widow remarriage in some cases, while disapproving of it in general.

The historical evidence reviewed above is usually interpreted to mean that all Newars practised divorce freely in the nineteenth century. But as we have seen, Hamilton, on whose report others have mostly relied, specified that high castes required their girls to be chaste before marriage. Whether they divorced frequently is not clear. The Jesuit Desideri who passed through the Valley in January 1722 reported that 'for a widow to remarry is considered disgraceful and almost infamous' (D.R. Regmi 1965 II: 1012). Naturally he was probably recording the ideal, and had no opportunity of observing it in practice. Certainly, the fact (acknowledged in the laws described above) that many high-caste Newar men went to Tibet or elsewhere for trade or to carry on their artisan profession, often only returning many years later if at all, led to the breakdown of many marriages contracted before departure. The lonely wife left behind while her husband is in Tibet is a common theme of Newari folk songs, poems, and short stories. None the less, I suspect that then as now there were important differences of attitude between castes. No doubt there has been Parbatiya influence (mediated *inter alia* by the law code of 1854), but it is mistaken, I would argue, to regard all divergence from the Tribal System as due to it.

Certain aspects and certain levels of Newar society have attracted more research than others. Unfortunately, not only do we lack substantial quantitative data on the Maharjans in the big cities, and on caste differences in the nineteenth century and before, we also lack reliable and detailed ethnographic reports of any kind on Newar low castes. We do know that low Newar castes do not practise ihi. It may be that they, like the peasants of Pyangaon, are close, or at least closer than high castes, to what I have called the Tribal System. If they are, the reason for this is not necessarily that they are of recent tribal origin; it is more likely that their deviation from orthodoxy is required of them by the smallness of their caste and their place in the social structure. Another area in which further information is needed is the history of the NIBS. The term *kanyādān* is old, but whether the hypergamous filiafocal ideology, and the worship of the son-in-law as Vishnu, are equally ancient I do not know. If it can be shown that they are, and that it is plausible to assume that the NIBS—as it is now—has influenced the Newars as long as South Asian culture more generally (i.e. for at least 1500 years), then (and only then) it would be necessary to agree that the Newar System is a compromise, or half-way house, between a tribal origin and Hinduism. If, on the other hand, as I deem more likely, the ideology of brahmanism has itself evolved and developed, then at least three separate interacting systems or patterns of social organization will have been shown to be necessary to explain the complex social history of the Newars.

Conclusion

I have tried to show that in the analysis of Newar social organization and its cultural correlates a trichotomous model is far better able to account for the complexity of present practices, as well as for their probable history, than a simple dichotomous Hindu/tribal one. The persistence of the dichotomous model has been due, at least in part, to the importation of dominant local forms of thought into anthropological analysis. It is worth stressing, however, that much is left open by this argument. In the first place, it may be necessary to identify sub-variants of what I have called the Newar System, when data from different villages are compared with those of the still very little studied urban Maharjans. Second, I have not attempted to discuss the implications of my analysis for the wider interpretation of South Asian society and history. One hypothesis such a line of enquiry might pursue is that both the Newar System and the NIBS are variants of social-structural forms propagated from urban, royal centres at different periods of South Asian history. It is certain that there is wide variation across India in the way in which the NIBS is put into practice and in the degree to which hypergamy is more than just acted out in a ritual context.[18] These variations are very complex and would require lengthy treatment. To mention just two examples: in South India one finds *both* cross-cousin marriage *and* the ideology of *kanyādān;*[19] in west Nepal the local Chetris and Thakuris *both* practise cross-cousin marriage *and* have the ideology of the NIBS, and the Thakuris (the royal caste) are more inclined to both features than the Chetris (Krause 1980). All I have tried to do here is to demonstrate how Newar society should be analysed. While the present argument has lessons which should suggest themselves for the wider cultural field of which the Newars are a part, the demonstration of them would require separate consideration.

Notes

1. For comments on an earlier draft I thank T. Ingold, H. Ishii, R.P. Pradhan, D. Quigley, A. Sanderson, G. Toffin, and P. Webster.
2. On remote places, see Chapman 1978 and Ardener 1987; on women, Moore 1988: Chapter 2; on 'primitives' as viewed by nineteenth-century anthropologists, see Evans-Pritchard 1977: 105 and Kuper 1988: 5; on animals, Tapper n.d. who discusses how patrilineal nomads view their flocks as matrilineal. Two older classic papers which made much the same point are Simmel's short essay on the stranger (in Wolff 1950: 402–8) (today it might have been translated as 'The Other') and Merton's essay 'The Self-fulfilling Prophecy' (Merton 1968: Chapter 13).

3. An excellent introduction to the anthropology of Nepal is Gaborieau 1978, which should now be supplemented by Gellner *et al.* (eds) 1997. On the Newars the standard ethnography is Toffin 1984. On the creation of the modern state of Nepal, see Stiller 1973 and Burghart 1984. I have discussed Newar identity, Parbatiya identity, and the changing reference of the name 'Nepal' in Gellner 1986. On the Parbatiyas, Bennett 1983 is highly recommended.

4. Cf. Fisher 1978: 50, Levine 1987.

5. On the different meanings of *jāt*, see Höfer 1979a: 46, 113, 135.

6. Both these terms may be used both in Newari and in Nepali, although the latter is confined to learned discourse and elsewhere is usually expressed by some phrase such as 'keeping the rules' (*niyam pālan yāye*). The term *jaṅgalī* is also used of rowdy behaviour as such, whoever indulges in it.

7. See Höfer 1979a: 135–41 and Gellner 1995a on the position of the Newars in the national legal code (Muluki Ain) of 1854.

8. Cf. D.R. Regmi 1965 II: 706. Unfortunately Toffin 1975b: 145 followed G.S. Nepali's conflation of *bhata* and *bhāḥta* in his article on Newar kinship.

9. See for instance Wright 1972 (1877): 33; Crooke 1978 (1894): 117; Landon 1976 (1928) II: 240; and Slusser 1982: 257 n. 179.

10. Some of the relevant details are summarized in Höfer 1979a: 137–9, 165. For the Nepali text of the sections dealing with Newars I have relied on J.C. Regmi 1978: 21–8, 46–8. On the position of women under modern Nepalese law, see Bennett 1979 and Gilbert 1992.

11. The two descriptions of Newar weddings which best bring out this equality between wife-givers and takers are Toffin 1984: 408–18 and R.P. Pradhan 1986: Chapter 5, esp. pp. 176–7. More recently, see especially Ishii 1995: 127–33. Other good descriptions can be found in P.H. Bajracharya 1959; G.S. Nepali 1965: Chapter 8; Quigley 1984: 253–61; and Lewis 1984: 281–95. Quigley 1986 is an important general statement about Newar marriage patterns, demonstrating that their basic isogamy has rarely been recognized.

12. See, for example, Greenwold 1975: 49–50; Höfer 1979a: 170; Toffin 1984: 222; Quigley 1986: 93.

13. The idea that a girl is married first to several gods and then only to her human husband occurs in the Rig Veda. (Leslie 1989: 252–4).

14. Or being a Buddhist monk for four days in the case of Sakyas and Vajracharyas (Chapter 5 above).

15. Whereas this is not so in Pyangaon (G. Toffin, personal communication).

16. Löwdin (1985: 65) heard the same. Fürer-Haimendorf (1956: 37) was evidently told about returning betel nuts in exactly this context.

17. Allen's assumption of a tribal/Hindu model is further revealed in two notes (1982: 207 n. 25 and n. 27). He ascribes the strict following of Hindu purity on the part of high-caste Shresthas to Parbatiya influence (when it is likely that those of high status within Newar society were strict in this fashion even before 1769); and he lists three 'tribal features' of Newar society: that *jat* are structured on lineage principles and hold property in

common; that *jat* leadership is based on seniority; and that Newars eat meat and drink alcohol.

18. This is shown in a survey by Milner 1988 which may be consulted for references to much of the relevant literature.

19. It is perhaps no coincidence that Good's (1982) analysis of south Indian female initiation rites, which I read only after completing this essay, also comes up with what may be read as a trichotomous model or spectrum. In this case, however, the end of the spectrum opposed to the NIBS is matrilineal, and the systems which fall in the middle show considerable variation.

12

From Mandalic Sacred Centres to Communist Strongholds? On the Cities of the Kathmandu Valley

Introduction

Since 1970 foreign researchers have been drawn in ever greater numbers to the study of the cities of the Kathmandu Valley. Among these are architects, art historians, Sanskritists, and anthropologists.[1] Perhaps most extraordinary is the number of architects who have descended on the Valley, drawn its buildings, and mapped its cities. They span a spectrum from the highly committed, such as Niels Gutschow, returning year after year to combine scholarly and conservation activities, to undergraduate students in search of a one-month dissertation topic. Why do they come? They come in order to observe a kind of small-scale, cooperative, and religiously sanctioned—in short *gemeinschaftlich*—urban living long since lost in the 'developed', 'societalized' world. Newar individuals are assumed to be encapsulated in collective social and spatial units, and those units organized within the city as a whole, in ways that are both participatory and consensual. The architecture and the spatial organization of Newar cities, towns, and villages encourage such communal organization. In stark contrast to modern, industrial cities, Newar cities, it is thought, do not inhibit or dehumanize the processes of ordinary life.[2] To some extent this romantic picture does indeed correspond to the truth; qualifications to it will be noted below.

When discussing the Kathmandu Valley cities the focus must be primarily on the Newars, the traditional inhabitants of the Kathmandu Valley. However, their relationship to other groups in modern Nepal, in particular to the dominant Parbatiyas, will be an essential factor to consider when discussing the process of modernization.[3] The Newars have their own language, Newari or Nepal Bhasa, which is Tibeto-Burman in origin; it is quite different from Nepali, the Parbatiyas' language which is the national language and *lingua franca*. There are three main Newar cities: Kathmandu itself, Lalitpur (called Patan by Nepali speakers), and Bhaktapur. There are also six or so medium-sized Newar towns in or near the Valley (Kirtipur, Thimi, Sankhu, Banepa, Panauti, Dhulikhel), and perhaps thirty Newar villages of differing sizes and composition. These comprise the Newar heartland, with a total Newar population of around half a million; there are as many Newars again outside this heartland, since the Newars are the shopkeepers, traders, and goldsmiths of hill Nepal, and many have migrated to hill bazaars and trade routes throughout the country over the last two hundred years. In the country as a whole Newars make up 5.6 per cent of the population, but in the cities of the Valley and their hinterlands they are between 47 and 53 per cent of the total.[4]

From the sixteenth century until 1769 the three main cities of the Valley were separate kingdoms, related but frequently at war with each other. In 1768 and 1769 Prithvi Narayan Shah, ancestor of the present king, conquered the Kathmandu Valley and created the modern state of Nepal. Under the Shah dynasty, and particularly under the Rana regime of hereditary prime ministers (1846 to 1951), the social structure of the Newar cities, and much of the urban architecture too, was frozen by a state that supported the caste hierarchy and caste-specific traditions with the full weight of its authority.

In 1951 the Rana regime was overthrown, an event the Nepalese refer to as the coming of 'democracy'. The country was opened to outsiders: tourists, mountaineers, and aid personnel. In 1990 a 'people's movement' (*jan āndolan*) overthrew the Partyless Panchayat Democracy which had been in force since 1959. Nepal now has a multi-party system, and defines itself, in the new 1990 Constitution, as 'a multi-ethnic, multilingual, democratic, independent, indivisible, sovereign, Hindu and Constitutional Monarchical Kingdom.' After national elections in 1991 it had a Congress Party government, while the largest opposition party was the Communist UML (United Marxist-Leninists), which in 1995 was itself to form a minority government for nine months.[5]

Since 1951 there have been manifold and accelerating changes in the Kathmandu Valley: migration to the capital, massive amounts of new building, an influx of foreign aid and diplomatic personnel, rapid growth in tourism, dramatic land price inflation, and a gradual democratization. None the less, much of the pre-1769 social and cultural fabric of these Newar cities can still be discerned, and it is this that the scholars referred to have attempted to describe. It is therefore possible to attempt a kind of 'before and after' picture of modernization, because both the 'traditional' order and the 'modern' exist simultaneously in the minds and actions of different local people, often indeed in the minds and actions of the same person. The terms 'tradition' and 'modernity' are used with all due caution. It is in fact the inverse of my argument to suggest that the traditional situation was stable and unchanging or that processes of modernization are straightforward, unproblematic, unidirectional, and bound to lead either to the values of US American suburbia or to enlightened liberal democracy of the Swedish type.

The traditional order

At the symbolic heart of each of the three cities is the royal palace. Only in one of them, Lalitpur, is the palace at the real centre. In Kathmandu about two-thirds of the old city lies to the north of the old palace, one third to the south. In Bhaktapur, the palace lies even more off centre than this. The model underlying the traditional social and ritual organization of the city is that of the mandala, or sacred diagram. When Newars use the term they mean just this: the powder or carved diagrams used by priests to worship the gods (Gellner 1992a: 45–8, 191–2). The essential features of the mandala may be listed as follows:

 (i) the principal god worshipped is in the centre;
 (ii) the mandala itself has four gates oriented to the cardinal directions;
 (iii) there is a definite boundary marking off the inside from the outside;
 (iv) at the same time there is a series of concentric circles around the central divinity, so that exclusion from or proximity to the sacred can also be a matter of degree;
 (v) the mandala itself can be divided up into sections in a geometric fashion, so that the divine retinue of the central god can be arranged in a regular way around the centre;
 (vi) the members of the retinue of the deity can be seen both as protecting the deity and as lower emanations of the deity.

In accordance with this model, Newar priests performing complex rituals lay out mandalas using powdered rice, flasks of different sizes containing holy water, and offerings of fruit and sweets. (In Tantric rituals meat, beans, and alcohol are also necessary.) However, in the words of Tucci (1969: 23), 'a mandala is much more than just a consecrated area that must be kept pure for ritual and liturgical ends. It is, above all, a map of the cosmos. It is the whole universe in its essential plan ...' Furthermore, since it is used for spiritual exercises, it 'is no longer a cosmogram but a psychocosmogram ...' (ibid.: 25). In short, the mandala is the model which underlies the organization of space, ritually and socially, in Newar cities and former kingdoms. 'The Newar-style temple', Slusser notes (1982: 145), 'is a three-dimensional mandala.' As Tucci emphasizes, in addition to social and political functions to be considered presently, the mandala model includes necessary reference to religious and soteriological ideals.

Shepard (1985: 121) has suggested that the mandala as a means of organization may be reduced to three principles: boundedness, hierarchy, and the importance of the centre. I am happy to accept this formulation, providing it is noted that a mandala involves rather more than simply a centre and peripheries; the latter is a conception which after all underlies urban organization in places which have never heard of mandalas. Just how the various elements of the mandala model apply to the organization of the city will now be considered.

Clearly, in building his palace in the centre of the city, the king wished to demonstrate his closeness to the gods. Each of the three palace squares is filled with temples to the two highest gods of Hinduism, Shiva and Vishnu. The Malla kings themselves claimed to be descended from Rama, one of Vishnu's ten avatars, and appended 'Dev' (god) to their names. They adopted names (forms of 'Narayan') demonstrating their devotion to Vishnu, and Yaksha Malla, who ruled the Valley from 1428 to 1482, called himself an avatar of Lakshmi-Narayan (Narayan is another epithet of Vishnu, and Lakshmi is his consort, the Hindu goddess of wealth and good fortune). At the same time the panegyrics of the kings declared that they were blessed by the dust of the feet of Pashupati, i.e. Shiva. Pashupati's temple is the principal Shiva shrine of the kingdom, then as now, and a major Hindu pilgrimage site. The Malla kings also declared their devotion to their personal goddess Taleju/Maneshvari, whose secret mantra was believed to enable them to hold on to power; they passed it to their son or chosen successor on their death-bed.[6]

The close connection between the king and the gods is evident also if one examines the origin myths of the Newar cities. In the course of a recent analysis, Toffin concludes:

The city is defined in the first place by its ruler. As in the Indian world ... there can be no city worthy of the name without a king, no king without a recognized capital ... [Secondly,] in two cases out of three [in the Valley] ... the king creates the city following the instructions of a god ... The centre of the city is not only the seat of political power. It contains also the temple or the sanctuary of a tutelary deity ... As in many Asian civilizations, the place sacred to the household of the sovereign and/or a particular divinity forms the original focus of the city. Thirdly, the king is required to build other religious monuments inside or outside the walls in order to sacralize the city. (Toffin 1990: 102)

In spite of this closeness to the gods, Toffin (1986) had earlier, to my mind rightly, emphasized that the Malla kings and their present-day successors were not and are not worshipped *as* gods. This contrasts with the *devaraja* cults of the rulers of South-east Asia who were so worshipped, either during their lifetime or after their death. Rather, in a culture which assumed that everyone was related to the gods to some degree, and that everyone could incarnate aspects of some god, the Nepalese king was *closer* to the gods than other people, and he incarnated *higher* gods than other people. But the distinction between the king and the gods remained intact.

The Malla cities had clear boundaries in the shape of the city walls. The site of these is clearly known, and bits of the ruined walls can in some places still be seen. It was one of the duties of the Malla period subjects to maintain the walls. Untouchables were not allowed to live within the walls, but had to cluster in settlements outside the gates. Traditionally they were not permitted to come inside the gates at night, nor during the day unless they had specific business to attend to (e.g. sweeping or removing night soil). The gates formed a vivid symbolic boundary that still today impresses itself on the Newars' imagination. Once a dead body has been carried out of the city gates, it can never return. Stories are told of people who revived on the funeral pyre, or of people whose funeral rites were performed in their absence when the news came (incorrect as it turned out) that they were dead. In either case, the people are socially dead, and may not return or be reincorporated into their family. Indeed it is sometimes said to happen that a person who is taken out as dead and is revived by the heat of the pyre is actually killed there and then (it is assumed that an evil spirit has entered the body of the dead person). In the past people feared to live outside the city walls, where it was thought demons and witches gathered at night.

Just as Lalitpur has its palace most perfectly at the geometric centre of the old city, so Lalitpur, of the three cities, has most clearly four gates in the cardinal directions. It is furthermore the only city where there are four settlements of Untouchables, one outside each of the four gates. The reason for this closeness to the model on the part of Lalitpur may have to do with the fact that it was developed as a royal capital later than the other two cities, only after the mandala model had begun to be considered essential. Thus there were fewer earlier buildings and sacred sites in the way, and Lalitpur was free to be developed in accordance with the now mandatory mandala model. Bhaktapur and Kathmandu, on the other hand, as older royal centres, had to adapt to existing, different frameworks. As Gutschow and Kölver remark,

While we have evidence to believe that ritual delimitation was an essential feature of Patan [Lalitpur] from its very beginning, analogous delimitations have in Bhaktapur been imposed onto a structure that already existed. A system like that of the *Astamātṛkās* [Eight Mother Goddesses] was probably meant to *raise the status* of what had come to be a royal settlement, raise it to the level of other royal cities. (1975: 21; italics in the original)

All three cities have a set of of eight protective Mother Goddesses around them. In fact, compared to the other two cities, the set around Bhaktapur is more complete. In Bhaktapur there are eight temples, each located in one of the eight cardinal directions. Even here, the ideal scheme had to bend before pre-existing facts: one of the temples, that to Mahalakshmi, actually falls just inside the city boundary (Levy 1990: 154–8). In Kathmandu and Lalitpur, by contrast, though the set of eight exists, they are not all eight of equal importance. In Lalitpur, three exist only as isolated stones, never visited except on rare occasions when a local pilgrimage is made around the set of eight. In general, these Mother Goddess temples are associated with cremation grounds; in practice, in all three cities, only three of the eight possible sites actually serve as such. The set of eight temples acts to define the outside, which is dangerous and frightening, and where only low, norm-less, or spiritually very powerful people are at home. The Mother Goddesses are also thought straightforwardly to protect the city from natural disasters and disease.

Thus, in the city as in the mandala, there is a clear inside and outside. At the same time, there are also degrees of closeness to the centre (see criteria iii and iv above). As Gutschow has demonstrated so well with his excellent maps (1982: 49, 119, 162), the lowest of the non-untouchable castes, the Khadgi (Butchers, Milk-sellers) live just inside the city walls, but relegated to their own localities with their own segregated water spouts. Brahmans and the high Hindu Shresthas tend to be found near the centre and near the royal palace (cf. Levy 1990: 172, 177).

Each city had its own hinterland of villages, owing tribute both material and ritual. Thus beyond the city were further concentric circles, more sets of gods and goddesses which incorporated the rural areas also within sacred space. Furthermore, though divided into feuding kingdoms, the Valley as a whole could likewise be seen as a single mandala.[7]

Each of the cities is divided up in several different ways. In Kathmandu there is a well-known division into either two or three parts. Bhaktapur is divided into the upper town and lower town. Lalitpur, being bisected by the main east–west road would have lent itself to a similar binary division rather well, and evidently was thought to be so divided in the early Malla period (Petech 1984: 185). Today, however, such a division is important neither in people's conceptualization of the city, nor in the organization of festivals or rituals. Rather, there are divisions of the city into three parts (according to which cremation ground is used traditionally), a different three parts (according to which day the main [Karunamaya or Matsyendra] festival is celebrated on, or four parts (according to which day the Yenyah/Indra Jatra festival is celebrated). But competition between these parts is not stressed as it is annually between the upper and lower town of Bhaktapur during the Biska festival.

Since the set of eight Mother Goddesses is fully developed in Bhaktapur, each having both a temple outside the city and 'god-house' (*āgāchē*) within it, it gives rise to a division of the city into eight 'mandalic segments' as Levy calls them. During life-cycle rituals each family in Bhaktapur must propitiate its own Mother Goddess. The entire set is worshipped in a prescribed order by the whole city during the main goddess festival, Dasain, which normally falls in the first half of October.

There are still further subdivisions of the cities, into localities called *twāḥ* (Np. *ṭol*). In both Bhaktapur and Lalitpur there are supposedly twenty-four (Gutschow 1982: 39, 168), but even in Bhaktapur, where the structure is clearer than in any other Newar settlement, informants disagree over the exact list (ibid.: 35). They agree, however, that there are twenty-four in all, established by the fourteenth-century king, Ananda Malla (Levy 1990: 183, 490). In the case of Lalitpur, on the other hand, though Gutschow gives a map showing twenty-four twāḥ (1982: 158), it is highly debatable whether today this should be considered anything other than an artificial and rather forced academic exercise. The twenty-four dance platforms where processions of the gods stop on their clockwise processions around the city (ibid.: 168) do not correspond to these twenty-four localities. It is true that some local sources recount how the (mythical) king Bir Dev founded the city with twenty-four localities (e.g. Bhasha Vamshavali II: 1–2), and apparently in 1717 each of twenty-four localities chose a representative to elect the new king, Mahendra Simha (D.V. Vajracharya and T.B. Shrestha 1979: 191). However, the people of Lalitpur today do not talk or think in terms of twenty-four localities.

It remains true that all three cities are divided into named localities with a strong sense of identity, even if the total number of localities is not agreed and the boundaries between localities are not always clear. Each locality must have its essential deities (a Ganesh, a *chwāsā* stone for discarding sacred leftovers, and a Nasadyah, god of music). In addition it is likely to have several particular deities specific to it (e.g. a Buddhist monastery, a Bhimsen, a form of the goddess), usually in or near a central square. Although there are many mixed localities, there are also many with a preponderance of a single numerically large caste, and this gives the locality a definite identity. Attachment to the locality remains strong; each locality considers itself superior to the others. Competition between them sometimes spills over into physical violence, whether occasioned by a competitive festival or not. When such violence occurs it frequently pitches members of the peasant caste against their own affines and sisters living in another part of the city, or sometimes different peasant subcastes against each other.

To continue the parallel between the mandala model and the organization of the traditional Newar city, how did the people who lived in the city relate to its centre, i.e. to the king? In a highly suggestive article, which is unfortunately strewn with factual errors, Jan Pieper has argued that the Malla kingdoms imported oriental despotism, of Wittfogel's hydraulic type, from India and that the mandala model was the ideological means by which the populace was controlled:

The esoteric connotations of the mandala layout, the ritual bonds, the contamination laws, the immobility which the zoning imposed on every member of the community, and all other religious implications described above are part and parcel of the enormous, repressive construction that supported the total power of the Hindu rulers ... It is possible that the most important aspect of Hindu town planning is that it kept the urban masses—in spite of spatial closeness—in small, often rival communities ... Barricades have never been built in any Hindu city ... The great events in the life of the Newar community are the festivals ... Here again, the traditional meaning of the city and its physical structure is most important, since it is the traditional ritual manipulation of the 'great mandala' through mass festivals which requires enormous sums and hence perpetuates the classic situation of unproductive capital consumption. The city was a device to secure the status quo through social atomisation and economic manipulation of the urban masses ... It is, indeed, amazing how well this system of 'sacred lies' [as Nietzsche termed it] worked, and how long it lasted. Urban unrest—so common all through European history—never occurred in India before 1857, and is still an impossibility in the three cities of Nepal. (Pieper 1975: 67–9)

In 1990 there was in fact dramatic urban unrest in all three cities of the Valley; but Pieper could, I suppose, argue that the very fact that it could occur is evidence that the old order had changed radically. In any case, Pieper's formulation has the virtue of asking serious questions about the social, political, and economic consequences of this type of Hindu town planning. However, the suggestion that the Malla kings wielded total and despotic power cannot be accepted in this form. There are well-known problems with Wittfogel's theory even for those parts of Asia which did depend on large-scale irrigation. For the Kathmandu Valley the model is even more inappropriate. The atomization mentioned by Pieper was achieved by the combination of the institutions of caste and attachment to the locality, not directly by the ideology of the mandala, nor by the kings' supposed total power. Thus, Levy (1990: 174), who surprisingly does not refer to Pieper, reports his impression that in Bhaktapur 'antagonism directed toward the relatively distant other city half ... deflects intra-*twa:* [locality] resentments ... to the other city within the city where they can be expressed in comparatively very much less disruptive and dangerous ways.' In other words, overt conflict between castes living side by side does not occur because there are ritualized ways in which conflict happens regularly between symmetrical segments of the city, and this acts as a kind of safety valve.

Conditions for the peasantry in the Malla period were no doubt not easy, but it would probably be a mistake to regard them as oppressed by a system of totalitarian despotism. Geertz's theory of the theatre state, especially as expounded in *Negara* (Geertz 1982) is of some help here. As he describes nineteenth-century Bali, social organization at the village level was so complex and so multi-stranded that the king's controls and sanctions barely penetrated them. The different institutions which administered agriculture, irrigation, and cultural life did not need, and resisted by their very arcane complexity, intrusions from above. Bali,

was a theatre state in which the kings and princes were the impresarios, the priests the directors, and the peasants the supporting cast, stage crew, and audience ... Court ceremonialism was the driving force of court politics; and mass ritual was not a device to short up the state, but rather the state, even in its final gasp, was a device for the enactment of mass ritual. Power served pomp, not pomp power. (Geertz 1982: 13)

As in Bali, local institutions in Malla Nepal were to a large degree self-governing. By and large what a particular local caste segment does internally is its own affair. What was important to the kings and still is to the community is that the caste in question should fulfil its obligations (i.e. ritual duties and festival roles) to the city as a whole, a point Levy has emphasized (1990: 70, 109).

The Malla kings spent part of their time feuding with each other; these were mostly skirmishes which involved rather small numbers of dead. Most of their effort seems to have gone into building temples, practising Hinduism, and writing plays, in which they themselves often starred. The 'theatre state' is therefore a highly appropriate epithet in the literal sense as well. Those castes or caste segments that had to provide the players in these dramas experienced this as a burden, but it was one that could also be held up as a privilege. Many of these ritual obligations continue today, and still receive funding from state-run guthi (religiously endowed) land.[8]

In short, the subjects of the Malla king were indeed seen, and meant to behave, like the retinue of a god surrounding him in his mandala. Like the retinue, they were lower-level functionaries, fulfilling specific purposes. The parallel is often made in reverse by Newars today: when a small divinity is placed in front of a larger one, to receive its offerings, the small image is said to be like a minister, always present before the king.

The modern order

The period between 1789 and 1951, and especially the Rana period from 1846 to 1951, represents a strange transition. The Malla kings were removed, but many of their cults were continued. Newar Brahmans were downgraded, but caste and Hindu orthodoxy were even more rigidly enforced. Consequently Newar practices were by and large frozen in the mould of the Malla period, without the continuing innovations and elaborations which characterized that time. High-caste Newars began to have the facades of their houses plastered with neo-classical stucco pillars, in imitation of the Ranas' palaces, which themselves imitated European originals, but the houses themselves continued to be built to the same plans and in the same places as before.

With the coming of 'democracy' in 1951 many things changed, though not overnight. Caste was no longer upheld by law. Professions were no longer reserved for members of specific castes. Education was, in principle, available to all, and gradually, after some decades, access has, at least within the Valley, and on unequal terms, been made available even to Untouchables. Laws of inheritance changed allowing daughters to inherit in certain circumstances, and allowing the use of wills where there were no children at all. Thus the likelihood of lineage mates inheriting from a man without sons declined virtually to zero. Lineage solidarity has declined markedly, both for this reason, and because there is less need of the security which membership of a cohesive lineage could give. The old cities of Kathmandu and Lalitpur have now merged into one continuous conurbation. The fertile rice land between them and all around is increasingly covered with a proliferation of 'bungalows', that is to say, villas built on separate plots following no coordinated plan, but in accordance with an ideology of private property, individual choice, and a secular environment.

In 1959 after a brief period of parliamentary democracy, King Mahendra, the present king's father, threw the Prime Minister and leader of the Congress Party, B.P. Koirala, into jail, and established the 'Partyless Panchayat Democracy'. This lasted, with certain adjustments (e.g. the concession of direct elections to the National Assembly in 1980), until 1990.

The Panchayat system had its own ideology. This stressed the role of the king as the guarantor of democracy, an equation which was not totally without plausibility because of the role of King Tribhuvan in bringing down the Rana autocracy. Also central to Panchayat ideology was the idea that political parties and class politics were foreign to Nepal's culture, and if introduced would inevitably be divisive and communal in nature. Only a minimal kind of corporatist representation was allowed through what were called 'class organizations' (*sangathan*), which were supposedly harmonious and non-conflictual: there were organizations of women, soldiers, peasants, workers, intellectuals, and students, each with limited representation in the National Asssembly. All other elections were of individuals only; indirect up until 1980, direct between 1980 and 1990. Nepal, it was repeatedly stressed, was the only Hindu kingdom in the world (*ekmātra hindu rājya*). The king was the embodiment of the nation and its unity. He and his family were also the foremost workers for the development of the nation.[9]

Increasingly, however, the Panchayat system came to be seen as corrupt. Since there were no parties, the National Assembly became divided into factions owing allegiance to different personalities, with links to different people within the royal palace. The example of India, a secular republic where political parties and trade unions could operate freely, was continually before people. Finally, and perhaps most crucially, the Panchayat system became associated with economic failures, which ironically the governments in question could probably do little about. This, very briefly, is the background to the unrest of 1990 which led to the downfall of the Panchayat regime.

In spite of the continued use of Hinduism to legitimate the position of the king, and the king's continued sponsorship of Hindu festivals and rituals, Nepal under the Panchayat regime experienced a definite secularization. The state no longer had subjects, treated differently as members of different castes, but citizens, equal before the law. Nepal might be a Hindu kingdom, but purification ceremonies were no longer imposed on those of its citizens who travelled abroad. Political processes were justified primarily in nationalistic, democratic, and developmentalist terms (Gaborieau 1982).

This being so, it is hardly surprising that the religious basis for the social and ritual organization of Newar cities has been eroded. In Kathmandu this has gone furthest of all, since Newars are now in a minority there. The buying and selling of houses, as well as the rental market both for residence and for shops or workshops, all mean that old residence patterns are much changed. To a lesser extent the same process has occurred in Lalitpur; Bhaktapur, being seven miles distant, remains for the moment much as it was. In 1853 both Lalitpur and Bhaktapur had populations of about 30,000. By 1971 Lalitpur had nearly 60,000, and by 1981 over 80,000; the corresponding figures for Bhaktapur are only 40,000 and 50,000. Kathmandu, meanwhile, increased from 150,000 in 1971 to over 235,000 in 1981.[10] Since the 1960s, in short, there has been massive immigration of rural Nepalese, as well as some Indians, to the capital. Increasingly, therefore, Newar cities are inhabited by non-Newars.

Furthermore, the economic boom in greater Kathmandu has changed the economic parameters of Newar life. There are numerous commercial opportunities and a whole new set of demands. The enormous growth of administrative jobs in government, tourism, aid agencies, and foreign missions, means that many Newar towns near Kathmandu, such as Kirtipur, have become dormitory suburbs. In the past, economic opportunities, such as the possibility of trade and artisan work in Tibet, tied Newars in more tightly than ever to their own culture, since the privileges granted to them were conditional on being Nepalese. Today, by contrast, new economic conditions produce very different cultural demands. In the first place, there is education. As everywhere in the world, but possibly more rapidly here than anywhere, there has been a massive inflation of educational qualifications. Hundreds of private schools, calling themselves 'English Boarding' but in fact day schools run by Darjeeling Nepalese and local graduates, have sprung up and successfully persuaded parents that the government schools are not good enough. Near universal education, as it now is in the Valley, creates new bonds and associations which are nothing to do with traditional ties based on caste and locality. It also propagates new languages: Nepali, which used to be confined to men and the worlds of trade and administration, and English, now seen as essential for advancement in almost every field.

Education is in fact one aspect of, and is consciously intended to produce, a new Nepalese culture, shared by all Nepalese. One, perhaps inevitable, response to this situation is a kind of bifurcation. A good example of this is the modern trend in Kathmandu of holding two separate wedding feasts: one, a buffet of pilao rice, which thereby ignores traditional purity rules, is for office mates, colleagues, and foreigners; the other, a traditional, sit-down, beaten-rice and buffalo-meat feast, is for caste fellows and kin. Some Newars have simply abandoned the traditional feast. In other words, the important reference group for many young Newars is now formed by their class mates, office colleagues, and/or business partners. Caste still generally determines one's marriage circle and funeral organization, but not one's aspirations or friends. For all Newars, prestige items now consist of motorcycles, television and video sets, and cement-plastered houses.[11] In the past much of such expenditure went on social religion, thus reinforcing the 'traditional' order. Today those who do sponsor rituals or religious specialists often prefer to switch their allegiances to a non-Newar brahman or to the new Theravada Buddhist movement, which again separates the family in question from local communal ties. The new, highly visible, and totally incongruous Thai-style Theravada Buddhist monastery in the middle of Kirtipur's Naya Bazaar can stand as a symbol of this process.

It would be wrong, however, to exaggerate the extent of the individualization, homogenization, and privatization of the Newars' culture and religion. Maharjan peasants are considerably better off since Land Reform in 1964 and the introduction of higher-yield rice varieties. Some of their new-found wealth has gone into religion and this is often of the locally based type, e.g. the worship of every Vasundhara shrine in Lalitpur, a non-traditional annual event modelled on the festival of Mataya. These processions, of which there are now several a year, reinforce the sense of the city as a sacred space. Although the city walls are no longer in existence, and people live outside them without fear, a great deal of the city's sacred geography remains intact.

What is gradually replacing the old social-structural basis of the Newar city is a strong sense of Newar ethnicity. Traditions and customs are now kept up and defended consciously as an ethnic and national heritage. Ethnicity in some sense surely existed in the past, but was virtually invisible. Now it is stressed. As mentioned above, what Pieper in 1975 confidently declared to be impossible, happened in 1990: the Newar cities of Lalitpur and Bhaktapur put up barricades and effectively excluded the state, thus playing a crucial part in the fall of the Panchayat regime.

One consequence of the creation of the new state of Nepal in 1769 had been the subordination of the Newars to the new elite made up of Parbatiyas, a subordination that was largely supported by the law code of Jang Bahadur Rana, promulgated in 1854. However, it would be an anachronism to see the conflict in the eighteenth century in ethnic terms. There were Parbatiya mercenaries fighting for the Malla kings of the Valley, and there was no solidarity whatsoever among Newars. There is every reason to believe that the Newar populace welcomed the end of the privations which had accompanied the many years in which Prithvi Narayan Shah had blockaded the Valley and that the merchant class, particularly, were happy to be able to continue their lucrative trade with Tibet. Newars accepted the new regime with little difficulty. A strong awareness of Newar identity was only really the *consequence* of the establishment of the present dynasty and did not predate it.

At the same time, there has been in this century a marked process of assimilation to Parbatiya culture on the part of Newars throughout the kingdom. This has passed the point of no return among most of the Newars settled outside the Valley; that is to say, they retain no more distinctiveness than any other group assimilated into the, now informal, Parbatiya caste hierarchy. Within the Kathmandu Valley the high Hindu caste of Shresthas provided civil servants for the Rana regime, and they led the way in adopting Parbatiya customs and in beginning to speak Nepali, rather than Newari, within the home.

Students of ethnic nationalisms elsewhere will hardly be surprised that Newar cultural nationalism grows from precisely this same milieu. It is when a distinctive Newar cultural and linguistic identity is under threat that a movement arises to perpetuate it. The intellectuals who fulminate against Newar mothers who speak Nepali to their children come from the very families where this is happening. Great emphasis is put on the glories of Newar civilization—its architecture, art, scripts, rituals, complex division of labour—precisely at the time when knowledge of these things is rapidly disappearing (Gellner 1986). Appeals to Newar ethnic awareness have considerable force among the burgeoning student population, who are faced with a very uncertain job market, in which Parbatiyas with well-established contacts may seem to have an unfair advantage. What is interesting is that the movement of Newar cultural nationalism seems to have relatively little appeal to what is still the majority of the Newar population, namely the Maharjan or peasant caste, at least to that part of it which has remained attached to the land.

For Newar peasants what has most force is a kind of communist rhetoric, one that is well established in South Asia. The nub of this is that the tiller of soil should receive the benefits of his work; that the idle landlord has no right to the products. (Collectivization is not mentioned.) It should come as no surprise, then, that the city with the highest proportion of agriculturists, Bhaktapur, is the strongest centre of communism. Between 1980 and 1990 known Communist supporters held office there. Both in the 1991 national elections and the 1992 local elections Communists were returned with handsome majorities. All were representatives of the Nepal Workers' and Peasants' Party under its charismatic leader, Comrade 'Rohit' Bijukche. This is essentially a Bhaktapur organization. The rest of the Kathmandu Valley voted Communist in 1991 (8 out of 10 seats), but reversed this in 1992, when Kathmandu and Lalitpur both elected Congress mayors and deputy mayors, as well as a majority of Congress ward representatives (19 out of 35 in Kathmandu, 12 out of 22 in Lalitpur).

Non-Newars who live in Kathmandu experience the Newars as highly communal: excluding outsiders by speaking Newari in their presence, and in many other small ways. It is interesting, then, that in the years immediately following 1990 the Newars lacked explicitly communal or regional parties, such as were attempted in the hills (e.g. among the Gurungs and in east Nepal) and were successfully established in the Tarai (the 'Good Will', Sadbhavana, Party).[12] Rather, Newars' specifically communal demands were expressed through communism. For many intellectuals communism is combined with a 'golden age' view of the past. The Newars' guthis, collective socio-religious organizations, are cited as evidence of primitive communism. (In fact, though egalitarian in operation, they are usually mono-caste and are therefore predicated on the existence of the caste hierarchy, and indeed serve to perpetuate it.) But, as we have seen, many other Newars support the Congress Party too, usually, but not only, the higher castes and better off. In origin a socialist party, it stands today for the middle ground. Dominant or not, the strength of communism in Newar cities bears witness to the fact that the old hierarchical order is moribund. The numerous communist factions, an important part of the explanation of their losing ground in 1992, indicate that Newar fissiparousness, an old feature of their social organization, is still very much alive.

Conclusion

The strongholds of communism among the Newars are two of the most conservative settlements, Kirtipur and Bhaktapur. Opposition to the state is strongest in these cities because they have a large number of peasant cultivators, and because they both have a history of neglect and/or persecution by the centre. Nepalese communists, as noted above, often adopt a romantic view of a supposedly egalitarian Newar past. They stress the need to respect ordinary people's beliefs, and the communist leaders (mostly Parbatiya brahmans) were prominent among those who ensured that Nepal continued to be defined as a Hindu kingdom in the new Constitution, against vociferous Buddhist opposition. Communism, in this context, is by no means as iconoclastic as one might expect. There even seems to be a paradoxical kind of 'elective affinity' between it and those places where the 'old order', though moribund, is clung to most fiercely.

Notes

1. The first manifesto, a cooperative work between the most influential architect and a Sanskritist, was Gutschow and Kölver 1975. Gutschow's book (1982) is the foremost book-length exposition, but there are many others, and numerous articles, e.g. Pieper 1975. Among art historians, Slusser 1982 is the most important source. Among anthropologists, one should see particularly Toffin 1981a, 1984, 1986, 1990; Levy 1990; and Gellner and Quigley 1995. An attractive cooperative work between Toffin and three French architects is Barré *et al.* 1981.

2. Niels Gutschow has pointed out to me that many German architects attracted to Nepal are seeking an alternative to top-down planning, both of the Nazi and post-war eras, which sought and seeks to design community in, but always fails because 'functions' are kept apart in separate zones (personal communication, 21 January 1995).

3. On Newar identity, one should consult Toffin 1975a, 1984: 585–600; Gellner 1986, 1997a, 1999, Chapter 10 above; Quigley 1997; and Grandin 1989: Chapter 6.

4. These figures are based on the advance tables of the 1991 census as analysed by Harka Gurung 1992a, 1992b.

5. Despite its name the UML is essentially a social-democratic party that uses Marxist vocabulary. On the events of 1990 see Raeper and Hoftun 1992 and Brown 1996. On politics since then, see Whelpton 1995, 1999; on the politicization of culture generally, Gellner *et al.* 1997; and on the Newars in particular Gellner 1997a.

6. See Slusser 1982: 310–21; Petech 1984: 174, 205; and Toffin 1986 for these relationships.

7. See Gutschow 1982: 15–27; Gutschow and Bajracharya 1977; Gellner 1992: 191–2.
8. The Newar institution of the guthi, and the tax-free religiously endowed category of guthi land tenure, have been stated by the foremost authority on Nepalese land tenure to be unconnected (M.C. Regmi 1976: 48); but it is evident, on his own data, that it was precisely the land held by these pervasive Newar socio-religious institutions which provided the name for tax-free religious land in the kingdom as a whole after 1769.
9. For more on the Panchayat ideology, see Joshi and Rose 1966; Gaborieau 1982; and Gellner forthcoming.
10. For the 1853 figures, see M.C. Regmi 1974, 1976a; for 1971 figures, see Gellner 1992: 23; and for 1981, Gurung 1981.
11. See Liechty 1998 on the process of class formation engendered by these new consumer goods.
12. For more on this question, see Gellner 1997a, 1999.

13

Does Symbolism 'Construct an Urban Mesocosm'? Robert Levy's *Mesocosm* and the Question of Value Consensus in Bhaktapur

Introduction: structure, consensus, and post-modernism[1]

It has become almost a truism in recent anthropological writing to say that cultures are not coherent, but are made up of conflicting ideas, symbols, and discourses; that concepts are essentially contested; that societies do not just endow people with a way of viewing the world but force problematic choices upon them. In short, cultures are 'constructed', conflict-ridden, and perpetually changing. Some anthropologists have gone so far as to say that we should dispense with the concepts of 'culture' and 'society' altogether, because they imply a degree of systematic integration that never in fact obtains.

This way of thinking rejects in its entirety a theoretical vision, or cluster of theoretical visions, that derive in one way or another from Durkheim. It has been one of the ambitions of social and cultural anthropologists since Durkheim to produce a coherent account of the people they study, an account that reveals their worldview or cosmology as a systematic, interlocking set of concepts. Such an account is produced either as an end in itself or in order to relate the worldview to the underlying social structure.

It is certainly true that Durkheim took the division of the world into national and ethnic units very much for granted; this is somewhat ironic given that he spent much of his life teaching and providing a moral framework for school-teachers, i.e. helping to *create* the very French nation whose existence he never questioned. Unlike Durkheim, and more perhaps than their structural-functionalist and structuralist forebears, most anthropologists today have a lively sense of the way in which units such as nation-states, tribes, and ethnic groups, are not given, but have to be continually policed and created. Does it follow, then, that the cultures which nations are supposed to share are not just imagined, but essentially imaginary? Confronted by numerous third-hand, pseudo-anthropological accounts which essentialize culture and use it as an all-determining explanation for the actions of despised others, many anthropologists understandably despair of the concept and would like to ban it from serious analysis altogether. However, it seems to me that, providing the researcher remains alert to conflict, resistance, debate, polysemy, and so on, the attempt to produce systematic accounts of local cultures is not wrong; providing, that is, they remain aware that they may be systematizing something that is nowhere so systematic among the people they are studying.

On the principle that attack is the best form of defence, let me begin by questioning the arguments used to undermine the attempt to provide coherent accounts of cultures, whether one's own or others'. The argument that it is impossible to do so, that such accounts are inherently partial and that there is nothing to choose between them, is, in the way that it is frequently expounded, caught on a cleft stick. Those post-modern critics who insist on a pervasive lack of order usually wobble between two different arguments: (1) Human social life is inherently chaotic; cultural order and stability are politically motivated myths. (2) The modern world is characterized by a lack of moral consensus, but at other times and places there have been stable and coherent cultural systems.

These two arguments are plainly inconsistent. If all societies are equally chaotic, modern society cannot be more so than others. If, as is surely the case, some societies have been more cohesive than others, it is legitimate to investigate how this has come about and what the conditions of coherence and systematic integration are. To insist that all societies are equally incoherent, equally a cacophony of contesting discourses, is simply the obverse of the old structural-functionalist error, of assuming that the world divides itself up into neatly demarcated, normally stable, and effectively functioning organic wholes. It is exciting, of course, to throw oneself into a bottomless pit where there is nothing but chaos. But the sober truth surely lies with the less exciting alternative, that pluralism and contestation are more characteristic of some periods of history than others and are particularly characteristic of the modern or post-modern world.

I propose to examine an impressive attempt to describe the world and cosmology of what would once have been taken to be a stable and integrated society, that of the Newars of the Kathmandu Valley as seen by Robert Levy in his massive work, *Mesocosm*, and to contrast it with the work of his student, Steven M. Parish, especially in his stimulating book, *Moral Knowing in a Hindu Sacred City*. Both authors are writing about the same place and even with some of the same informants.[2] Levy's title page acknowledges that his book was written 'with the collaboration of Kedar Raj Rajopadhyaya'. Giving such prominence to a local collaborator is certainly laudable. The fact that Rajopadhyaya is a top local Brahman, and the head priest of the Taleju temple at the heart of the city in the royal palace, should be borne in mind when considering the highly ordered (though definitely complex) 'core system' that Levy ascribes to Bhaktapur.

Levy's worldview

Robert Levy is a qualified psychiatrist as well as an anthropologist. He is known particularly for his book *Tahitians: Mind and Experience in the Society Islands* (1973). After that he embarked on fieldwork in Nepal from 1973 to 1976; he chose to look at the city of Bhaktapur in the Kathmandu Valley. When I was carrying out my own fieldwork in Nepal, in Lalitpur, another city in the Kathmandu Valley, from 1982 to 1984, Levy's book was eagerly awaited. It did not in fact appear until 1990.

There is one problem with analysing *Mesocosm: Hinduism and the Organization of a Traditional Newar City in Nepal*. The book is self-confessedly a prolegomenon. Newar society is so complex that Levy felt obliged to write a book of 829 pages, including six detailed ethnographic appendices, in order to lay out the context of the in-depth, psychologically oriented interviews and analyses which are his real interest. So there is always this caveat in describing his work: much of the fascinating detail concerning the ways in which people experience the social order he is describing is yet to come. To some extent one can fill this gap by consulting Parish's books, *Moral Knowing in a Hindu Sacred City: An Exploration of Mind, Emotion, and Self* (1994) and *Hierarchy and its Discontents: Culture and the Politics of Consciousness in Caste Society* (1996).[3] Parish also worked in Bhaktapur, from 1984 to 1986, and had very similar interests to Levy. His book, *Moral Knowing*, takes the social structural and religious analyses of *Mesocosm* as given and, after a brief introduction, focuses on the experiences of six key informants. Four are men, two women. Of the men, one is high-caste, two are middle-caste, and one is an untouchable Sweeper; of the women, one is a Brahman, the other high-caste but poor.

Levy's project, drawn out and incomplete though it is, is impressive for several reasons. It is explicitly comparative; what is especially valuable is that the comparison he makes is not the conventional one between Bongo Bongo Land and American suburbia, but rather between Tahiti and the Newars. Secondly that comparison is placed in an historical framework, so that in fact the comparison is extended to the modern world as well (see Chart 13.1). Thirdly, there is the psychological angle, but this is not an aggressively reductionist programme. Considerable autonomy is granted to social arrangements, so that they do not come out as the epiphenomena of child-rearing practices, as in other, cruder psychological accounts. Finally, there is the great richness of the ethnographic data, organized intelligently with a number of important micro-theories that ethnographers of Nepal should find it good to think with (examples are too numerous to list, but would include his remarks on the meaning of the Swanti festival, on types of priest, on the Nine Durga dancers, on the different identities of key low castes, and many more).

Chart 13.1: Contrasts between Tahiti and Bhaktapur as described by Levy (1990)

Village in Tahiti	Bhaktapur
Small island	capital city of erstwhile kingdom
284 people, 54 households	40,000 people, 6,000+ households
Low division of labour	highly differentiated caste system
Little differentiation of sexual roles	markedly differentiated sexual roles
Fishing and horticulture	farming, crafts, trading
Traditionally non-literate	traditionally highly literate
Face-to-face 'total institution'	complex, opacity
Everything seems 'natural'	people aware how everything is constructed
Seeing is knowing; not seeing merely 'hearing about'	sophistication; awareness of contexts and alternatives
'a resolutely ordinary, daylight, sunny world' (p. 30)	a city of literati; presence of 'symbol hunger', a fascination with symbols (p. 32)

Certain types of criticism of Levy's text I take to be a waste of time. There is no point in attacking him for not doing what he did not set out to do. There is nothing, for example, about politics in the narrow sense (Bhaktapur today is a communist stronghold, and this must be connected, one way or another, to its cultural conservatism,[4] but this would hardly have been obvious in the 1970s when political parties, in so far as they operated at all, had to do so underground). Nor does Levy attempt a class analysis in the Marxist sense. It may well be true that, because of his interest in making Bhaktapur typical of the 'archaic city', he exaggerates its isolation and unchangingness (Miksell 1993), but that alone does not invalidate his project. Nor does Levy investigate the economy or marriage and kinship. All these belong to the background: what he is really interested in is the contribution different caste groups make to the shared symbolic order of the city; their internal organization is of lesser importance. Finally, where an important point of local usage is at issue, I have noted differences of interpretation in the notes. Any ambitious book of this sort is bound to contain errors of detail, as Levy himself recognizes (1990: 5). Whatever the rights and wrongs of these, they do not have any bearing on Levy's larger interpretive project.

Levy lays out his own theoretical presuppositions with admirable clarity in the second chapter of his book. He calls them, with a perhaps ironic coyness, 'conceits'. Three of these 'conceits' relate to history (the notions of the archaic city, axial age, and continent in the great divide) and three to the contemporary workings of Bhaktapur society (ballet, marked symbolism, and climax Hinduism). I shall examine each in turn.

1. *The Archaic City.* Levy's understanding of Bhaktapur's position is summed up in a phrase at the end of the book (ibid.: 619) when says that it 'seems to us to be representative of the kinds of places Islam tried to transform in India, having held out for still a few more centuries against the new kind of world that Islam represented.' There is an echo here of Levy's namesake, the great Sanskritist and historian, Sylvain Lévi, who coined a famous aphorism at the beginning of his three-volume history of Nepal: 'Le Népal, c'est l'Inde qui se fait' (Nepal is India in the making) (Lévi 1905 I: 28). Robert Levy does not, however, quote this, and it is unclear how far he has been influenced by the Frenchman's vision of South Asian history.

A most explicit debt is acknowledged to another and still earlier Frenchman, Fustel de Coulanges and his classic work, *The Ancient City.* Levy leaves to the experts the debate whether Fustel's picture of the ancient city is valid for the early Greek city-states; but he insists that Fustel's characterization of the city as made up of nesting and independent units, each with its own autonomy and its own tutelary divinities, is entirely valid for Bhaktapur (Levy 1990: 22). This, then, is the first crucial notion, that Bhaktapur is an archaic city in the specifically Fustelian sense.

2. *The Axial Age.* Levy moves on to consider the breakdown of the archaic city in the ancient Mediterranean and adopts Jaspers' term, the 'axial age'. Before the axial age, cities were orthogenetic in Redfield's and Singer's sense; that is to say, they represented a sophisticated version of the folk culture of their rural hinterland; they did not purvey a foreign or qualitatively different culture. They were also and very essentially sacred centres. After the axial age, cities became culturally plural and separated from their rural hinterland. In a sense they became modern.

Levy admits that the question whether India passed through the axial age is 'diffusely problematic' (ibid.: 23). His answer is that the revolution, led by 'the heterodoxies', in particular Buddhism, failed. Hinduism represented a kind of Counter-Revolution or Counter-Reformation:

What did prevail was ultimately the static order of Hinduism, which, whatever its peripheral inclusion in their proper place of the socially transcendent gestures of renunciation and mysticism, was hardly any kind of 'breakthrough' into whatever the idea of an axial 'transformation' was meant to honor. All of which is to suggest that traditional India and Bhaktapur, in so far as it may be characteristic of traditional India, are very old-fashioned places, indeed. (ibid.: 23)

3. *The Continent in the Great Divide.* Levy goes on to suggest that Bhaktapur is typical of the 'continent in the great divide' (ibid.). That is to say, in the division of world history between the 'primitive', i.e. pre-literate, and the 'scientific', i.e. industrial, world, Bhaktapur is typical of the agrarian civilizations in between.

There is an immediate problem when we put together these three ideas that Bhaktapur is typical of archaic, pre-axial, and agrarian cities. The archaic and the pre-axial refer to the same thing; but agrarian cities are a much larger category. What Levy necessarily implies is that all post-axial cities are somehow modern. In other words, all cities in the Muslim world and all cities of the Mediterranean world after 800–700 BCE and all Christian cities were not of the same sort as Bhaktapur. Levy does not address the question whether Chinese cities, which knew a post-axial religion, Buddhism, were or were not similar to Bhaktapur.

Levy does not go into great detail about what exactly happened in the axial age, apart from the brief reference to transcendence quoted above. It seems to be taken for granted that transcendence and universality in ideals precludes local cults of the kind found in Bhaktapur. It seems to me that Levy's contrast between pre- and post-axial agrarian cities is much too strongly drawn. Levy underplays *both* the extent to which soteriological and universalist concerns pervade Bhaktapur (he himself does not use this terminology) *and* the extent to which cities in the post-axial but still agrarian West might continue to be organized in the Fustelian kind of way.[5] In short, one may well ask whether the notion of the axial age can really be sustained, particularly when used as a classificatory device for distinguishing types of pre-modern city.

4. *The Civic Ballet.* Turning now to the way in which Levy conceptualizes the workings of contemporary Bhaktapur, the term he begins with is 'civic ballet'. '[T]he civic life of Bhaktapur [is] something like a choreographed ballet. The city space is the carefully marked stage' (ibid.: 16). Roles in the ballet are assigned by descent (usually in the male line) to specific named castes and lineages. In fact the third part of Levy's book, some 200 pages, is taken up with the detailed documentation of the various calendrical festivals which constitute this 'ballet'.

5. *Marked Symbolism.* The next notion that Levy makes use of is that of 'marked symbolism'. The idea here is that some symbolic ideas are 'embedded'; that is, they appear obvious, part of the furniture of the universe, so much so that they barely need to be justified. Other symbols, on the other hand, are 'attention-attracting, emotionally compelling kinds of human communication' (ibid.: 27). The example of embedded symbolism that Levy gives for the Bhaktapurian context is that of ideas relating to purity and impurity. However, Newars, and indeed South Asians generally, are well aware that notions of purity have clear status implications, and that these are publicly marked and can be disputed. To my mind, notions of gender would have made a better example of embedded symbolism: pervasive, important, and far more taken for granted. It cannot be doubted, however, that the pantheon of Hindu gods in Bhaktapur does comprise a system of marked symbolism, as Levy asserts: a set of symbols that are set off from the ordinary world and demand attention and interaction.

6. *Bhaktapur as a Hindu Climax Community.* The final notion that Levy uses is that of the city, Bhaktapur, as a Hindu climax community: that is, in the city, the tendencies of rural Hinduism come to full flowering. This is certainly an important idea. There have been problems in the anthropology of Hinduism which can be traced to the fact that so much of it has been carried out in villages (see Pocock 1960; Gellner and Quigley 1995, esp. Chapter 10). At the same time, Levy pictures

Hinduism as wholly different from the world historical religions: localized, putting its divinity firmly within the world, and ahistorical. I have already criticized the degree of difference this makes between, say, medieval Catholicism and Hinduism. Levy is surely right, however, to assert that the point of constructing Bhaktapur as a sacred space was that it should form a sacred model of the universe, a mesocosm half-way between the microcosm of its inhabitants' daily worlds, and the macrocosm of the universe as a whole.

Levy on caste in Bhaktapur

At the time of Levy's fieldwork Bhaktapur was a city of about 40,000, a compact and elongated settlement on the north bank of the Hanumanti river (actually a small stream except during the monsoon season). About two-thirds of the population were (and are) involved in farming. 'Bhaktapur is an agricultural city surrounded by smaller agricultural towns and villages' (1990: 62). This hinterland used to be part of the kingdom of Bhaktapur before the 'unification' of Nepal by Prithvi Narayan Shah, ancestor of the present king, in 1769. Of the rest of the economically active population, about 15 per cent provided services to others, 8.5 per cent were involved in commerce, and 8.2 per cent in 'manufacturing', i.e. they were artisans of various sorts (ibid.: 67). There are more than 6,000 households in the city. Ninety-two per cent define themselves as Hindu. Nearly all the rest are Buddhists (there are a few Muslims).

As for ethnic affiliation, Bhaktapur is 99 per cent Newar (ibid.: 59, 75). As Levy perceptively notes (ibid.: 76), whether a specific group is considered Newar or not, is the outcome of a long historical process. Some groups, such as the Jha Brahmans and Muslim traders, have lived among the Newars for centuries without being absorbed into what he calls the 'core system'.[6] This 'core system' is a 'caste system', though Levy does his best to avoid the terminology of caste because he wants to 'present Bhaktapur's status system without forcing it into a procrustean bed of generalizing analytic terms' (ibid.: 74).[7] On Levy's analysis, Bhaktapur's Newars are organized into nineteen different castes or clusters of lineage groupings which he calls 'macro-status levels'. These nineteen macro-status levels are of very different sizes: six of them consist of between one and five households; another two levels consist of nineteen and thirty-two households (Tamah/Tamrakar and Brahman, respectively); at the other extreme, level V (Jyapu/high-status peasant farmers) has 1,867 households.[8]

One may well ask whether this 'core system' is not a partial and interested construction by Levy's Brahman informants. Should the Tini

(Tantric Shaivite death specialists who call themselves Shivacharya), placed at level IV with just two households, really be considered a 'macro-status level' on their own? Does this not simply represent a Brahman-inspired attempt at complete and exclusive allocation of all members of the 'core system'—that is, all Bhaktapur inhabitants who are essential to the Brahmans themselves—to precisely the right rank according to Brahman notions of purity? Would this formulation be accepted either by the Tini themselves or by those ranked by Levy and his Brahman collaborator, Kedar Rajopadhyaya, immediately below the Tini? When one considers how Levy treats the Buddhist priests, Vajracharyas and Sakyas, within Bhaktapur, the suspicion that order has been imposed may be confirmed: they are placed outside the 'core system' (1990: 106-7), even though they supply the 'living goddess' Kumari, a key figure in the city's major festival cycle (ibid.: 95), and even though the Vajracharyas' ritual patrons (*jajmān*) are included in the 'core system'.[10] Leaving Buddhist priests out of the 'core system' makes the 'core system' look even more like a Brahman construct. (Whereas other Newars generally put them on a par with, if slightly below, Brahmans, and high-caste Hindus in Bhaktapur treat them like clean-caste 'Jyapus' (ibid.: 106), Brahmans treat Vajracharyas and Sakyas as 'water-unacceptable', i.e. like the low castes from whom water may not be accepted.) Such a Brahman-centred construction can be made to look plausible in Bhaktapur where there are relatively few Vajracharyas and Sakyas (260 households; but this is still nearly eight times the number of Brahman households). It is totally implausible in other Newar cities, where it simply has to be accepted that the dominant order is contested and that there are two competing priestly castes both of which are equally an essential part of Newar society (Gellner and Quigley 1995).

To some extent Levy acknowledges this bias. He admits at the outset of the book that what he has outlined is an 'ideal order' and asserts that 'It is only against this ideal system, that our ultimate enquiry, the dilemmas, conflicts, understandings, and points of view of individuals in Bhaktapur ... can be understood' (1990: 9). He also admits that his elite informants were:

above all Rajopadhyaya Brahmans. The conception of civic order is thus not just that of a sentimental Westerner, it is that of local specialists in symbolic order. The book is, in part, a presentation of *their*, their own, imagery. For Bhaktapur, that conception is not just the wishful ideological thinking and propaganda of precarious elites but a powerful force that in itself helps to create order. Whatever the untouchable, for example, thinks about it all, it is these conceptions which form the matrix of his life. (ibid.: 9; original emphasis)

Of course the question remains whether the brahmanical symbolic order he outlines is as univocal as he sometimes makes it sound.

Levy puts some emphasis on the way in which polluted food is shared within the household as an index of hierarchy (ibid.: 118–20; 386–7; 395). Polluted food is called *cipa* and so Levy refers to this as the cipa system. In general inferiors can and do eat the cipa of superiors, but not vice versa. This applies particularly between husband and wife, it being important that a wife should eat her husband's leftovers, but he does not eat hers. Levy connects this to the wider caste hierarchy in that the untouchable Sweepers eat the leftovers of all castes collected from feasts; the fact that they do this generates strong feelings of disgust on the part of other Newars. Levy's elevation of this into a *system* strikes me as artificial. He claims that 'each "ritually adult" male of the family will accept the cipa of those of either sex older than he is ... [and] women (and girls) generally in the family will eat anyone's *cipa* ...' Does this in fact happen on a regular basis? As far as I know it occurs only between husband and wife, where it is expected that a husband may leave aside a few choice portions as a sign of affection; and it is precisely the fact that they are his *cipa*, which no one else would think of touching, that marks them as intended for her. I think Levy would have been on more solid ground if he had tried to elaborate a systematic set of rules for who should show ritualized obeisance to whom, and on which occasions, similar to those outlined for Parbatiyas by Lynn Bennett (1983: 150–62).

Levy has some very interesting things to say about the interrelations of different castes within Bhaktapur. He points out, quite rightly, that Brahmans are not the only priests. There are also several types of auxiliary priest, as he calls them: lower-status Brahmans who perform the Brahman's functions for lower-status patrons whom regular Brahmans will not serve, and Joshi astrologers who assist Brahman priests in their rituals in the Taleju temple. There are also religious functionaries whom Levy calls 'para-priests': experts in preparing people for their encounters with the sacred. In this category come the Barber caste, as well as others, such as the Mahabrahman death specialists and the Katah, whose women cut the umbilical cords of infants from upper-caste families. He also, I think rightly, posits a basic contrast between these religious functionaries whose public identity is bound up with the preservation of 'the symbolically constructed, hierarchical, civic *dharma*', on the one hand, and, on the other, those castes whose public identity is primarily concerned with material advantage, i.e. craftsmen, farmers, merchants, and so on, including also the king (Levy 1990: 344). Furthermore, this dichotomy appears also within the pantheon, so that there are the 'ordinary deities' who are moral and uphold hierarchy and rules of purity, and there are the dangerous deities who are primarily within the 'realm of force'.

Bhaktapur's priests, including its Brahmans, operate in *both* these realms, both as the exemplary pure (and, in fact, exemplary impure) priests of the ordinary moral realm, the world of the *dharmic*, hierarchical, civic order and also as priests of the realm of power, where purity and impurity and the civic values of interdependency are irrelevant. (ibid.: 344; original emphasis)

This is an important insight, which brings us to the question of the use of 'dangerous' deities.

Levy on the pantheon and Tantrism

Levy's analysis begins with the distinction within the pantheon between the benign and moral divinities, predominantly male but with female consorts, on the one hand, and the 'dangerous' deities, on the other, who accept, and indeed must be offered, alcohol and animal sacrifice. (Such offerings would be unthinkable to high pure gods such as Shiva and Vishnu.) This distinction is, of course, found throughout the subcontinent and has been much discussed in the literature on the Newars.[11] The benign deities sustain the moral order, or *dharma*, which is also, of course, a hierarchical social order. The dangerous deities are used to protect that moral order:

So viewed, the dangerous deities are at a systematically 'higher' level than the benign ones in the sense that they provide the context for the moral religion, respond to the problems that the moral system cannot deal with, and in so doing protect the moral realm. The polytheistic separation and discrimination of deities makes such a two-tiered representation possible, this being one aspect of the complex ordering of the city's pantheon into a fundamentally useful system of signs. (Levy 1990: 602)

This view of the dangerous deities as 'higher' goes against the conventional views of most South Asians, as Levy's use of quotation marks acknowledges.

Be that as it may, Levy devotes far more space to the dangerous deities. He has documented all the festivals of the city exhaustively: 'The dangerous deities are never the focus of primary household events, but they are the centre of more than half of the events in the public city, and of *all* the urban structural focal sequences.' (ibid.: 580; original emphasis).

In other words, the dangerous deities do far more work in producing order within the city. Furthermore, it is *only* when the main locus of the religious event is in public space that the dangerous divinities are dominant in this way (ibid.: 583). Why should this be so? One might suspect that it is their very fierceness that makes them so useful for defining social units; though they worship and honour them, people simply aren't afraid of the benign deities. Levy suggests, tentatively, that the offering of blood sacrifice to the dangerous deities is crucial. People remember how, as children, they identified with the sacrificed animal and feared that adults would sacrifice them as well. Now, as adults, they participate in blood sacrifice, feast on the sacrificed animal, and consume the blood-soaked sacramental foods (*prasād*). Social solidarity is based on shared guilt (ibid.: 574–5).

It is interesting to note, then, that although there are males among the dangerous deities, such as Shiva's fierce form, Bhairava, the dominant figures among them are female. There are four important forms of them within Bhaktapur:

1. the royal tutelary goddess, Taleju, whose temple is within the royal palace, which is symbolically, though not in Bhaktapur at the actual, heart of the old city;[12]

2. Bhagavati, the local name for the form usually known to South Asianists as Durga, the multi-armed goddess who kills the buffalo demon and is the protagonist of the Hindu scripture, the *Devi Mahatmya*;

3. the eight Mother Goddesses, the Astamatrika, whom Levy calls mandalic goddesses;

4. the goddesses of the Nine Durga dance cycle (confusingly, these goddesses, although their troupe is known as the Nine Durgas, actually have the same names as seven of the eight Mother Goddesses; to these seven are added three male figures—Ganesh, Bhairava, Seto Bhairava—and two female guardians, Sima and Duma).

These four forms of the goddess have each a different symbolic place in the life of the city, but are simultaneously viewed as forms of each other. Taleju in a sense pulls them all together. Her cult is on the one hand a closely guarded secret, with access to her shrine strictly controlled. She used to be seen as the guarantor of the Malla king's power in the eighteenth century and before, and the king would pass on her mantra to his son or designated successor on his death-bed. She is also thought to empower all Tantric (esoteric) practice within Bhaktapur so that the 'Brahman Taleju priest is in this context considered the ultimate *guru* of all who have Tantric power' (ibid.: 240). At the same time Taleju is identified with all the other goddesses during the annual festival which focuses on Bhagavati, namely Dasain (Mohani in Newari; Durga Puja in

India). The logic according to which the goddess may be both one and many, supreme and yet impure, is revealed in the stories of the Devi Mahatmya. Levy comments:

The whole includes the part, but may emit it in some way so that the part can be considered as a unit in itself. In this case the part and the whole are in a vertical relationship, share some of the same qualities, and are hierarchically arranged, with the whole superior to the part. Furthermore, the whole tends to be more abstract and less specified, whereas the part is more concrete and more specialized in its function and meaning. (ibid.: 250)

Bhagavati is principally worshipped at the time of Dasain. Levy (ibid.: 425) quotes Bennett's conclusions (1983: 272–4) that Parvati, the gentle wife of Shiva, represents the problems of being a woman from the woman's point of view: 'she must be both sensual and ascetic; flirtatious and faithful; fertile and yet utterly pure.' By contrast, Durga, i.e. Bhagavati, represents the problems of women from the point of view of men: dangerous, needing to be controlled, but fertile and powerful if on your side. It is consistent with this conclusion that the cult of Durga, and knowledge of her scriptures, are almost entirely a male domain, whereas the worship of Parvati occurs primarily in her local form as Swasthani during a fast (*vrata*) that women perform to gain a good husband.

The mandalic goddesses have each a temple around the city. As a set they are believed to protect it from plagues and other dangers. The city is divided into segments each attached to one of the temples, with a ninth central part attached to the shrine of Tripurasundari, who stands at the centre of the mandala formed by the other eight. Inhabitants of each segment visit their goddess during life-cycle rituals; in-marrying daughters-in-law adopt the goddess of their husband's household. The whole city worships all nine in sequence on successive days of the Dasain festival.

Whereas the mandalic goddesses are stationary, and people come to them (the only exception being that the goddesses move between their temple shrine outside the city and their 'god-house' within their city segment), the Nine Durgas move as a troupe through the city and then through the villages which make up Bhaktapur's hinterland in a roughly clockwise sequence. In each location they dance in order to protect the area and receive offerings, especially a young pig, which the man playing Bhairava kills with his bare hands; all the other dancers drink its blood and then shake as a sign of possession (Levy 1990: 564).

Levy's analysis is very detailed and complete and only the barest of summaries can be made here. In essence it focuses on two major cycles, the solar cycle, which begins the solar year with the great festival of Biska (Nepali: Bisket Jatra), and the lunar cycle, the climax of which is Dasain. In analysing both festivals he distinguishes two kinds of integration in the city, which, though Levy does not make the connection, go back to Durkheim's distinction between mechanical and organic solidarity. There is parallel solidarity, which occurs when all households in the city are performing the same rituals on the same days. And there is interactive or syntagmatic solidarity when parts of the city are set off against each other. It should be noted that, although specific castes do have different roles they are expected to fulfil, these public festivals do not focus on hierarchy as such; they do not reaffirm hierarchy by dramatizing conflict: 'Whatever the dilemmas, paradoxes, conflicts, and problems that are explored in the annual festivals, the components of Bhaktapur's social system are privileged and taken for granted' (ibid.: 581). (This is in fact no longer so: even in the 1970s stigmatizing roles in public festivals were beginning to be abandoned by low castes.)

Chart 13.2: Symbolic contrasts of the two major festivals in Bhaktapur (based on Levy (1990))

Biska festival	Dasain (Mohani) festival
Specific to Bhaktapur	observed throughout Nepal
Part of solar cycle	part of lunar cycle (religious calendar)
Marks start of New Year (official calendar)	tied to agricultural year (symbolism of barley shoots)
'King' and brahman tugged passively through the city	'king' and brahman active, but confined to palace (esoteric)
Male dangerous deity dominant	female dangerous deities dominant
Integration through opposition of city halves	integration through opposition of city as a whole to the space beyond
Interactive mode dominant	parallel practices as important as public interactive features
Stories set in ancient legendary past	stories set in timeless mythic realm

The Biska festival consists of many elements, but at its heart are two chariots, the larger carrying an image of Bhairava, the smaller one of the goddess Bhadrakali. At the beginning of the festival there is a tug-of-war between the upper and lower halves of the city to see which can pull the chariot of Bhairava into their half first. Some days later the two chariots are made to clash into each other, which is interpreted both as Bhadrakali being angry with Bhairava and as sexual intercourse between them.

Where Biska is specific to Bhaktapur, Dasain is the most important national festival observed by almost all groups in Nepal. The main events occur over ten days. Households grow barley shoots in their family god-room or corner and offer some form of animal sacrifice on the ninth day (at least an egg). There are important rituals in the Taleju temple, in-cluding buffalo sacrifices. The mandalic goddesses are incorporated by being visited on each of the nine days of Dasain. The Nine Durgas re-ceive a blessing from Taleju who comes out for a short circumambula-tion of the city on the tenth day. The essential meanings of the two festivals and the ways in which the contribute to the city's order can best be summarized as in Chart 13.2. Levy himself, though laying out these contrasts, attempts no such summary. Other hands would have made much of his structuralist or semiological method. At any rate, Levy has clearly demonstrated that the construction of symbolic order at the level of the city depends in Bhaktapur on the contrast between these two central ritual complexes.

Steven M. Parish's view of Bhaktapur

Steven M. Parish's book, *Moral Knowing in a Hindu Sacred City* is a valu-able and path-breaking text: the questions it broaches have hardly been mentioned by previous writers on the Newars, whether Nepali or foreign. He investigates personal experience, emotions, family relatedness, and moral reasoning. The material he presents on honour (*ijjat*) and shame (*lajyā*) is an important addition to Nepalese ethnography as a whole.

What concerns me here, however, is the contrast between Parish's view of the moral order of Bhaktapur and Levy's. Parish sees himself, and I think it would be fair to say, is seen by others, as following in the same line as his teacher. As noted above, he worked in the same place as Levy, used some of the same informants, and above all used very similar methods (detailed taped interviews with selected informants of different castes). On the internal evidence of Parish's first book, it seemed to me that he would have been horrified to be interpreted as having written a critique of Levy. His second book, *Hierarchy and its Discontents*, made me wonder about this conclusion: it is much more overtly an attack on the idea of a 'core order'. Parish is evidently aware that he runs the risk of a bias towards fragmentation:

Just as classical ethnography represented cultures as more unified and static than they actually are, contemporary ethnography runs the risk of representing cultures as more fragmented than they are ... [W]e cannot deny the Newars either their diversity or their unity. I have tried to let this work reflect both in some small way. (Parish 1994: 6)

All the same, there is no doubt that in the debate over the unity of culture Levy's *Mesocosm* and Parish's *Moral Knowing in a Hindu Sacred City* are on opposite sides. In terms of the two propositions about value consensus distinguished above (p. 294), Levy upholds the second and Parish the first: for Levy the modern world has lost an earlier consensus, whereas for Parish it never had it.

Thus, in describing how different informants see the city, Parish writes: 'Different Newars live different lives, often radically different lives ... Thus, Bhaktapur is not one but many cities—a plurality of *imagined* cities within a single urban space' (ibid.: 69; original emphasis).

He concludes the chapter with a passage expressing many of the anti-holistic theoretical impulses I outlined earlier:

This book is just one telling of life in Bhaktapur; many others are possible ... [T]here is a core of shared values, of political and economic structure, of social relations. While this core affects virtually every one in Bhaktapur, shaping and constraining what they know and do, it does not yield one point of view. It would be wrong to privilege one vision ... Newar culture cannot be reduced to a single, dominant conception of reality. Indeed, what is shared—sacred symbols, the religious ethos, the caste system, principles of family organization—far from foreclosing diversity, generates the range of points of view we find, and spurs men and women to create many versions of 'reality' as vehicles for their own socially and culturally embedded lives. Newars may experience even what they share—key symbols and social institutions—in radically different ways. (ibid.: 69–70).

Later on, in discussing the key concept of dharma, he notes that 'Different Newar actors *project different worlds* around the base concept of dharma. In doing so, they generate radically different meanings for this key moral and religious concept' (ibid.: 99; original emphasis). And later:

It seems clear that Newars do not have a single understanding of their moral order ... Rather, Newars 'tell' several different kinds of 'stories' about this moral order ... If the Newars need multiple 'tellings' of the moral order to fit their lives into it then perhaps we need multiple accounts, too, in order to understand what they think and feel, and how they engage social life. (ibid.: 122)

One has to ask whether Parish substantiates his claims. When he claims that his six key informants experience the city in radically different ways, this is ultimately just an assertion. Their very different lifestyles are alluded to in brief pen portraits, but we are given no detailed histories, no long personal accounts, no evidence that they view the structure of the city very differently.[13] However, where the concept of dharma is concerned, there is indeed some evidence that different actors do understand it differently. Brahman priests give Hindu exegetical glosses. The well-off high-caste trader thinks of it in terms of *kuldharma*, the inherited ritual duties of his family. The Untouchable thinks of it in terms of people helping each other out in times of need and setting a good example to one's children. Arguably, this is just where one *would* expect differences of interpretation, in dealing with a highly complex core moral concept. Furthermore, as many studies have shown, in complex societies the polysemy of multivocal symbols can actually serve *to bind people together*.[14]

In another chapter, Parish discusses how Newars view the creation of moral persons, through ritual. The idea here is that children are rendered into full moral persons by going through puberty rituals. It is only after them that they are expected to follow the rules of adulthood (and are entitled to the funeral of an adult should they die). This includes following the strict rules of caste interaction and food avoidance. Here Parish unwittingly provides evidence that in fact all Newars, even Untouchables, do share the same view of these core values. He cites his Untouchable informant giving exactly the same kind of explanation and justification of the puberty ritual (*kaetā/kaytā pūjā*) as his high-caste informants: that only after it does a child have to worry about following the rules concerning who one can eat with. In fact Untouchables often dispense with this ritual, as they do with ihi which Parish's informant also mentions.[15]

The question whether or not Untouchables share in the values of other, higher castes has in fact been fiercely debated in recent years by specialists in the anthropology of South Asia.[16] Parish does not refer to this debate in *Moral Knowing*, though he does engage with part of it in *Hierarchy and its Discontents*. Simplifying somewhat, one can list the positions that have been taken up on the origins and culture of Untouchables as follows.

1. Early evolutionist writers usually assumed that the Untouchables were a 'race' apart, perhaps of tribal origin, perhaps 'pre-Hindu' aborigines.

2. Later materialist, Marxist, or structural-functionalist authors were no longer so inclined to look for racial origins of difference, but tended rather to see the Untouchables as a kind of counter-culture, rejecting in their everyday life and practices the hierarchical worldview of the upper castes.

3. Where previous anthropologists had looked for diversity in South Asia—not hard to find—Dumont's classic, *Homo Hierarchicus*,

argued for a deep structural homogeneity of values throughout the subcontinent. Dumont himself wrote relatively little about Untouchables, but Moffatt wrote a brilliant and authentically Dumontian monograph, *An Untouchable Community in South India*. Moffatt argued, and effectively appeared to demonstrate, that the Untouchables of his village near Madras shared high-caste values. He showed, in context after context, that where they were excluded from high-caste life, they replicated it, including reproducing, as far as they were able, the ritual hierarchies which placed them low in the overall society.

4. In reply to Moffatt's now classic statement there have been a number of reactions: that his village was untypical; that Untouchable myths of origin assert an original equality of all men, a state from which they fell only through others' trickery and their own goodwill; that Untouchables may replicate hierarchy between castes but they are more egalitarian *within* the caste than high castes; that there are different types of low caste, with characteristically different values; and, finally, that poverty and powerlessness are more important to Untouchable identity, both from outside and from their own point of view, than the ritual services that they may or may not provide for high castes.[17]

5. Finally, there is the way which Untouchability is understood by indigenous intellectuals, since this is an increasingly important influence on the way Untouchables are viewed. By one of the ironies of post-colonial development, the view of Untouchables favoured by Untouchable leaders today is the very first, evolutionist one: Untouchables are a race apart, the original, now dispossessed, inhabitants of India. It was this logic which persuaded Ambedkar, the great post-Independence leader of India's Untouchables, to lead his community (initially mostly the Maharashtrian Mahars from which he came, but subsequently many others) into Buddhism. As a mark of communal identity, Buddhism had the great advantage of being simultaneously non-Hindu, indisputably Indian, and yet absent from Indian soil for so long as to have no pre-existing power base.

In *Moral Knowing* Parish does not attempt to place his conclusions in relation to this kind of debate, whether about the place of Untouchables or about the possibility of a holistic view of the total society.[18] We are presented instead with disembodied discourse—discourses with only the sketchiest relation to any kind of structure, whether political, cultural, social, or economic. It really seems as if he has decided *a priori* that Bhaktapur is constituted by different discourses, and so that is what he has found. Some confirmation of this conclusion is provided by *Hierarchy and its Discontents*. In this second book Parish explores the questions left aside in *Moral Knowing*. He writes:

... Dumont and I possess—or perhaps are possessed by—different thematic commitments ... Dumont believes in the unity of culture, while I believe there is an irreducible plurality to cultural life. Dumont looks for unity given by a dominant value or master principle, while I see a plurality of values as characterizing cultural life, a plurality that is the product of human agency engaged with culture. (Parish 1996: 98)

Jan Pieper's view of Bhaktapur

Yet a third view of the city of Bhaktapur is provided by Jan Pieper, a German architect who wrote a paper called 'Three Cities of Nepal' published in 1975. Oddly enough it is referred to neither by Levy nor by Parish. The particular interest of his article in the present context is that he appears to agree with Levy that there is and was a significant degree of value consensus in Bhaktapur and that this was expressed in the great public festivals of the city; but he agrees with Parish that order was maintained by force, or the threat of force, whereas Levy's stress is on the power of symbols and ritual.

As an architect Pieper pays considerable attention to classical Hindu town-planning designs and the ways in which Malla kings attempted to implement these in the Kathmandu Valley. He takes Wittfogel's theory of oriental despotism as his guide, though he recognizes that 'Nepal, with its frequent, moderate rainfalls all the year round, is not a natural home of such a system of total power ...' (Pieper 1975: 66). He is certainly right in his conclusion, despite his misleading reference to year-round rainfall. None the less, he refers to the kingdoms of the Valley as 'oriental, despotic states', lacking a 'wealthy merchant bourgeoisie', where skilled artisans had to be obliged to settle. The 'masses' of the towns were the only threat to the king, and so 'the three cities of the Kathmandu Valley—like any other Hindu township—were designed as devices to control this critical massing of people, as "ruling machines"' (ibid.: 1975: 67). Ritual was used to keep the masses divided into 'small, often rival communities, which were as isolated as the scattered villages in the open country' (ibid.).

The problems with Pieper's use of Wittfogel have been noted above (p. 289). However, Levy agrees with Pieper in seeing the fact that conflict is deflected away from possible friction between castes and on to 'the other city in the city' as an important consequence of the ritualized rivalry between the two halves of Bhaktapur in the Biska festival (Levy 1990: 174). The crucial question is the degree of force that was used in the past to ensure participation in public festivals: I do not know of any clear historical evidence on this question. Levy's focus was on the city as he studied it in the 1970s. By then it was a question of public opinion which ensured that different castes fulfilled their duties, hence his stress on the power of symbols. Already in the 1970s, as noted above, certain castes were abandoning their duties where these were seen as stigmatizing. Presumably none would have risked doing so under the Malla (pre-1769) or Rana (1846–1951) regimes.

Conclusion

How can Levy respond to Parish? How is analysis to accommodate different perspectives on the city while giving sufficient weight to the 'core moral order'? Perhaps the struggle to reconcile these two contradictory imperatives is part of the explanation of the long wait for Levy's second volume on Bhaktapur.

No analysis is likely to be adequate unless it recognizes *both* that there is a shared set of values and symbols in a city like Bhaktapur, which Levy describes and analyses at length, *and* that different actors have different perspectives on them. But this latter assertion needs to be qualified: the degree of difference is strictly limited and there are only a few characteristically different viewpoints. Divergence itself was institutionalized. (Low castes of various kinds constitute a special case.) A city such as Bhaktapur has a great deal more cohesion, and far fewer divergent discourses, than a city such as contemporary London. Part of the explanation for this must lie with political and social organization. It is not enough to say that 'all individuals are unique', 'everyone has their own perspective', and so on. Parish's stress on plural viewpoints can only be made to seem plausible because it is contrasted with an oversocialized conception of people wholly in the grip of a homogeneous culture. Of course, if one has to choose between cultural automata and people as agents, the latter is closer to what one finds in the field—but the point is that one does not have to make that choice. Dumont was quite explicit about the fact that he was attempting to construct a sociology of values (Dumont 1980: 4). Contrary to Parish's claim that he leaves 'no basis in culture for actors who challenge caste hierarchy' (Parish 1996: 68), Dumont's celebrated essay on world renunciation, published as appendix B in the standard edition of *Homo Hierarchicus*, is about precisely that: how Hinduism developed historically through challenges to the status quo by innovative individuals/renouncers.

Ultimately, Levy's and Dumont's frameworks are more satisfying than Parish's because they are explicitly comparative (the interesting question of their grounding in different kinds of ethnography is tangential here). As an analytical strategy the idea that some societies are more cohesive than others, and that some give a greater place to the individual than others, has more explanatory power than the ahistorical, if fashionable, idea that all societies are equally pluralistic.

Notes

1. For comments on an earlier draft I am grateful to participants in the conference on 'The Study of Cultural Semantics in a Time of Discursive Anthropology' organized by Professor G. Aijmer at IASSA, Göteborg University, in June 1996, to participants in discussion at the Royal Nepal Academy, Kathmandu, in January 1997, and to S. Mittal and D. Quigley.

2. There has been some discussion of Levy's work already. See Miksell's Marxist critique (1993), and Chapters 1 and 10 of Gellner and Quigley 1995. For reviews, see Quigley 1991; Gellner 1992b; and Lewis 1992.

3. I found out about and obtained a copy of the second of these books some months after the first draft of this paper was written. As discussed below, certain theoretical assumptions which underline the first book are worked through and stated explicitly in the second.

4. For some speculations on this, see Chapter 12; on Newar ethnicity and politics, see further Gellner 1997a, 1999.

5. For an eloquent attack on the putative contrast between the universalist world religions and particularist local religious in Africa, see Ranger 1993.

6. For more on Newar castes, see Toffin 1984 and Gellner and Quigley 1995.

7. See Quigley's critique of this decision in Gellner and Quigley 1995: 307–7.

8. Levy's level XIX, the Halahulu, does not in fact refer to a group in any sense, but is simply an empty category, referring to whomsoever can be found to accept Dyahla death offerings (Gellner 1995c: 284; cf. Parish 1996: 115–16).

9. There are also problems with Levy's presentation of the local terminology that defines Bhaktapur's caste order (Levy 1990: 102). *ña calae ma ju phu(n)* is translated as 'people from whom water may not be "moved"': *calnu* can mean to move in Nepali, but in Newari *calay juye* or *calae juye* is used only in the more abstract sense of 'to work, to function, to be OK'; thus the expression means 'those from whom [taking] water does not work', i.e. 'people from whom water may not [be taken]'. This refers to what Levy calls levels XIV and below of the caste hierarchy, and also, according to

strict Bhaktapur high-caste Hindus, to level XIII as well. Levy gives the local expression *tiye nae ma tya phu(n)* as an alternative designation of the same group. In more standard orthography this would be *thiyāḥ naye ma tyaḥ pī* which Levy translates as 'people who should not be touched while you or they are eating'. (Similar glosses are given by Parish 1996: 106.) This is wholly implausible both gramatically and culturally: *nobody* should be touched while eating, by anyone of whatever caste. What this means is 'people whose touch renders food forbidden', literally 'having-been-touched, it is forbidden to eat, people'. In other words, cooked food, whether of the sort highly susceptible to impurity, like boiled rice, or of the less impurity-conductive sort, like the beaten rice used in feasts, cannot be accepted from castes who cannot give water (see Ishii 1995: 111–12). Within the low castes there is a still lower category of those who cannot be touched, in particular the Sweepers (known in Nepali as Pode, and in Newari as Pwah, Pohrya, or Dyahla). These categories are laid out and explained for Newars as a whole in Gellner 1995a: 16–19.

10. Levy 1990: 87. Approximately 240 households who were not Vajracharyas or Sakyas identified themselves as Buddhist in the 1971 census (ibid.). They may therefore be assumed to fall into this category of Buddhist laity using Vajracharyas as domestic priests.

11. See the essays collected in Toffin 1993, some of which go back as far as 1979; see also Gellner 1992: 73–80. On Hinduism generally, see Fuller 1992. Levy (1990: 226) reports that the distinction is referred to by Bhaktapurians as that between *gya(n)pugu* (dangerous or frightening) gods and *sadharan* (ordinary) gods, and that in ordinary speech the former are defined by their acceptance of alcohol (*aylā*) rather than their acceptance of meat. I find it surprising that Shiva and Vishnu could ever be referred to as 'ordinary'. In Kathmandu and Lalitpur the dangerous deities are usually defined precisely by their acceptance of animal sacrifice, as *hi phaḥ dyaḥ*, 'gods to whom blood [must be/can be] offered'; to the best of my knowledge, there is no snappy, colloquial term for the high, pure gods.

12. Bhaktapur's palace may once have been more central, next to the now relatively unimportant shrine of Tripurasundari (Levy 1990: 155, 168).

13. Given this basic position, it is surprising that quite a few sentences begin 'Newars feel ...' or 'Newars say ...'

14. See, for example, Humphrey 1984; Gellner 1992: 101–3; and Beatty 1996.

15. Gellner 1995c: 285. Similarly, where Parish argues against Dumont that Newars value individuality equally with 'relatedness', his main example is his informant Bhimsen Lal. From the evidence presented, however, Bhimsen Lal seems to regret deeply that his family split; his values seem to be entirely what Dumont would have expected (Parish 1994: 177–83).

16. See Moffatt 1979; Deliège 1988, 1992, 1993; Mosse 1994; Charsley 1996. I have discussed the position of Newar low castes in relation to this debate in Gellner 1995c.

17. See references in previous note.

18. Parish specifically attacks Moffatt's conclusions in *Hierarchy and its Discontents*, arguing that replication of high-caste structures should be seen as 'a subtle fusion of resistance and collusion ... [which] does start to demystify the system ...' (Parish 1996: 207–8).

PART V

Comparison

14

For Syncretism: The Position of Buddhism in Nepal and Japan Compared

> Héritiers de la logique grècque et du monothéisme juif, nous appliquons d'instinct aux croyances religieuses le principe de contradiction; dieux et dévots se classent à nos yeux en groupes fermés, exclusifs jusqu'à l'antagonisme. Des statisticiens, sérieux à en mourir de rire, calculent le total des Bouddhistes, des Confucéens, des Shintoistes. Un Hindou, un Chinois, un Japonais n'arriveraient pas à les comprendre ...
>
> Sylvain Lévi, *Le Népal* 1: 173

Introduction

In this essay I wish to address the recently revived anthropological discussion of syncretism. By comparing Buddhism in two very different situations, I hope to show *both* how valid the anthropological critique of the concept of syncretism is *and* that it is still possible to apply the term in a non-ethnocentric way.[1]

In their important edited volume, *Syncretism/Anti-Syncretism* (1995), Stewart and Shaw sum up the state of play on the question. It is my impression that most anthropologists would now agree with them that there is no universally valid concept or definition of syncretism and that it is a waste of time to try and decide whether a given tradition is syncretic. On this perspective the only valid questions are: When, where, how, and why do *other people* become concerned about, and fight over, the concept of syncretism? Whether or not something actually is an example of syncretism is a sterile question for which there can never be an objective answer, since all traditions are syncretic. If the specialists of some traditions manage to propagate successfully a claim to authenticity and purity, the only appropriate analytic response is deconstruction and explanation.

Thus Stewart and Shaw (1995: 7) write:

Simply identifying a ritual or tradition as 'syncretic' tells us very little and gets us practically nowhere, since all religions have composite origins and are continually reconstructed through ongoing processes of synthesis and erasure. Thus rather than treating syncretism as a category—an 'ism'—we wish to focus upon *processes* of religious synthesis and upon *discourses* of syncretism. This necessarily involves attending to the workings of power and agency. (original emphases)

While agreeing that it is important to pay attention to discourses of syncretism, I believe it is a mistake to assert that analysts can restrict themselves to the second-order activity of discussing other people's judgements. This would be to erect a barrier between academic discourse, on the one hand, and ideological battles beyond the academy, on the other, which if it ever did exist, ought now to be recognized as an ideal rather than a fact.

Why have anthropologists been uncomfortable with the term 'syncretism'? In the first place, it seems too judgemental to be a legitimate or acceptable part of a social-scientific vocabulary. Are not the observers quickest to slap the label 'syncretic' on phenomena precisely those who are least interested in capturing 'the native's point of view'? Furthermore, does not the use of the term 'syncretism' betray an unanthropological concern with the *origins* of particular practices (e.g. icons, symbols, or rituals) at the expense of a contextualized understanding both of how they work *now* and of what they mean to the people who use them?

These concerns are entirely understandable. All too often external judgements *have* been imposed in exceedingly unhelpful ways. In the description of religious phenomena, this has often been done with great vigour and prejudice. Most anthropologists can cite Victorian condemnations of the religious practices of their area as superstitious, ritualistic, and 'mixed up', i.e. syncretistic. In more restrained language similar descriptions are still being written.

None the less, I shall argue that the term 'syncretism' can still be saved for general social-scientific discourse. However, for reasons to be considered, there will almost certainly never be agreement about just which practices, religions, symbols, myths, etc. are syncretic. The basic definition of syncretism which is tacitly accepted by those who use the concept in academic writings is, I believe, as follows: *the unsystematic (or unsystematized) combination within a single tradition of elements which their originators intended to be kept apart.*[2] Such a definition avoids the extremely pejorative force of some committed usage but does not pass the buck of judgement altogether. As I have indicated, I do not think we should throw up our hands with the post-modernists and say that all traditions are equally syncretic, equally unstable, and equally hybrid.

In his earlier work on supernatural survivals in the modern Greek worldview Stewart advanced a valuable distinction between a *syncretic* situation, for example the Pagan-Christian encounter in the early centuries of the first millennium, and a *synthetic* tradition, for example Greek Orthodoxy in later centuries, when paganism no longer survived as a separate tradition, though elements of it had been absorbed into the now relatively stable Greek Orthodox tradition.[3] From this position Stewart now recants, thinking that he wrongly adopted the viewpoint of his own Greek informants. He asks, 'Once the idea of stable traditions is introduced, how far away can the notion of pure traditions be?' (Stewart 1995: 21). This I think is the counsel of despair. I do not think one is committed to fundamentalism by the simple recognition that some traditions are more stable or more systematic than others, and it is a serious anthropological question to ask why.

All religious traditions take elements from different sources. In different ways most are involved in debates about origins and authenticity. It is surely wrong to argue that anthropologists can never make judgements about the validity of these arguments. Peel (1968) was, I believe, right to say that the Nigerian Aladura churches he had studied were not actually syncretic as the missionary churches charged, since all the elements of their practice were authentically Christian, though not a kind of Christianity the missionaries themselves approved of.

My proposed definition of syncretism is an attempt to capture more or less what lies behind contemporary academic usage. However, even if everyone agreed to this definition (I am under no illusion that they will), they could, with perfect justice, disagree about which phenomena should be labelled syncretic, because of different understandings of the definition's component terms. Even if we take the concepts of 'tradition' and 'system' as unproblematic (and clearly different religions have very different ideas about their relationship to their past and about what constitutes being systematic), different adherents of the same religion frequently have very different attitudes to the 'originators'. Some, the fundamentalists, see the original founder's intentions as paramount; others, the traditionalists, see no way of knowing these outside of the institutions which have passed down the practices and teachings of the religion. For the latter, the succession of priests or cardinals count as originators; for the former, they are no better than distorters of the original message. And these two are by no means the only possible positions. For example, many religions have no single founder; in the case of many 'elements' of religious practice no one knows who the 'originator' was, or, if they do, what his, her, or its intentions were.

Furthermore, even if two parties agreed on what counts as syncretism, they might still evaluate it differently. One side might regard it as a solecism to disregard the founder's intentions; another might believe that the founder's spirit is honoured better in a syncretic synthesis not possible or plausible in the founder's time. There can also be disagreement between adherents of the same tradition over how far a world religion should go in adopting local cultural forms and symbols: one person's inculturation or 'skill in means' is another's syncretic aberration. As Stewart (1995) shows, regional traditions of scholarship have evaluated syncretism very differently: in Africa, thanks to the hostile view missionary churches have taken of African churches, it has been basically a pejorative term; in America, by contrast, it was for long a positive term ascribing some sort of agency to cultural adaptations by those of low status.

Syncretism is an essentially contested concept.[4] The term 'essentially contested concept' was first introduced by Bryce Gallie (1964: Chapter 8), and has since been taken up by several anthropologists, notably by L. Rosen (1984: 185–7). The point is that even if we agree on what syncretism is, it is likely that there will be valid arguments on both sides whenever the question of whether to apply it in a particular case arises. As with concepts like 'democracy' and 'art', contestation is part of its very use. Anthropologists need to exercise caution therefore, but need not excise the term from their vocabulary, as Aidan Southall, for instance, declares that he has done with 'tribe' (Southall 1975: 274), to mention a term once thought relatively innocuous.

What kind of religion is Buddhism?

Buddhism, wherever in Asia it has been practised, in virtually all of its very different forms, has been frequently and vehemently condemned by western observers as syncretic. The basic problem here is that the observers expected Buddhism to be a religion like Christianity: exclusive towards all other religions, and providing for all the possible social and supernatural needs of its adherents. The exclusivity of Christianity as conventionally understood hides from view the fact that religious practices can serve very different social purposes or respond to very different aspects of religion. These may be listed as follows (there may be some I have missed here, but the argument does not depend on this list being exhaustive or definitive):

1. the legitimation and expression of the household or family group.
2. the legitimation and expression of the locality (or village or tribal section or caste, etc.).
3. the legitimation and expression of the nation or ethnic group.
4. the sanctification of the stages of the life-cycle.
5. the socialization of the young and the provision of a moral code.
6. the provision of psychological and practical help in case of misfortune, especially illness.
7. the provision of a path to salvation from all ills, i.e. a soteriology.

Christianity aspired to satisfy all these needs or aspects, and frequently did so. Many religions focus on only one or two of these. Shintoism may be said to lack a soteriology, Hinduism to provide dozens of them. A moral code is frequently lacking from non-scriptural religions.[5]

As far as Theravada Buddhism is concerned, the basic argument was made eloquently by Gombrich in 1971. Early Buddhists set out to provide a soteriology, that is, to provide a path to salvation, and only secondarily, if at all, to help with worldly problems. Early Buddhism, to which the Theravada form remained broadly faithful, also incorporated a moral code, since it was a core part of its teachings that the practice of morality was the indispensable first step on the Buddhist path, but the other five religious aspects it did not aspire to fulfil. This means that Theravada Buddhism is always 'accretive' (Gombrich 1971: 49). It always coexists with some other system or systems which satisfy, for Theravada Buddhists, these other needs. In order to find cohabitation acceptable, Buddhist specialists require that these other systems acknowledge Buddhism as the supreme overarching system, and as the path to salvation, and that their practices do not conflict too blatantly with Buddhism's own teachings. In some contexts this means that Buddhist clerics have accepted animal sacrifices, where these are performed in what are defined as non-Buddhist contexts. At other times and places Buddhists have campaigned successfully for the suppression of such sacrifice.

Mahayana Buddhism, which first emerged some time around the turn of the common era, several hundred years after the death of the

Buddha, maintained much the same position. However, the develop-ment of Tantric Buddhism, several hundred years later again, with its elaborate ritual and its stress on secret teachings defining an initiated elite, encouraged and legitimated the growth of a Buddhist priesthood. As such, Buddhism could aspire to fill all the roles listed above, and could provide rituals and practices for all or most of them. This hap-pened in Nepal (see Chapter 5) and in Tibet (Samuel 1993), where Buddhism became the overwhelmingly dominant political and cultural force. However, in China and Japan, where different literate religious traditions already existed, and responded and reacted to the arrival of Buddhism with new forms and developments, Buddhism remained, as it was in its older form, essentially accretive. In this respect, then, Japa-nese Buddhism is more similar to Theravada Buddhism, the type of Buddhism geographically, historically, liturgically, and scripturally most distant from it, than it is to the Mahayana and Tantric Buddhism of Nepal and Tibet with which it is normally classified.

Let us turn explicitly to the question of syncretism. Just because a given religious system does not provide for all seven aspects, and there-fore coexists with some other tradition(s) and system(s) which pro-vide for the others, this is not sufficient reason to think that we are dealing with syncretism. Even if we take the entire religious field as a single tradition—against the actors' own definitions—there may be a *systematic* relationship between the different subsystems within the field, with one tradition providing the overall framework. Tambiah's *Bud-dhism and the Spirit Cults in North-East Thailand* (1970) is a classic account of the Thai religious field as made up of four different systems, defined in the local context by the differences and oppositions between them: Buddhism; the *sukhwan* rites or brahmanism; the cult of guardi-an spirits; and the cult of malevolent spirits (Tambiah 1970: 338). Good structuralist that he is, Tambiah is not concerned to identify syncre-tism, but simply to show how the different systems are defined in opposition to each other.

Nepal

By 'Buddhism in Nepal' I refer to the Buddhism of the Newar people of the Kathmandu Valley, and exclude the Tibetan Buddhism practised by the Tamangs, the Sherpas, and others of Tibetan culture; this usage may be justified on the grounds that historically, and still for many Nepalese today, the term 'Nepal' refers primarily to the Kathmandu Valley and not to the modern state of Nepal. This Nepalese Buddhism exists in a strongly Hindu context. It is in fact the last surviving remnant of Indian Buddhism and has, for that reason, been of great fascination to Indologists and Sanskritists, from Sylvain Lévi to Bernhard Kölver and Siegfried Lienhard (Lévi 1905; Kölver and Sakya 1985; Lienhard 1984).

The practitioners and followers of Nepalese Buddhism have had continuous contact with Tibetan Buddhism (Lewis 1989), both because Newars have long traded and practised goldsmithing and image-casting in Tibet, and because Tibetans come on pilgrimage to the holy sites of the Kathmandu Valley and have contributed to their renovation. Some Newars have become monks and others lay followers in the Tibetan tradition, and in the late nineteenth or twentieth century most significant Newar Buddhist sites have been adorned with Tibetan-style prayer wheels. These facts notwithstanding, Nepalese Buddhism is not and never has been an offshoot of Tibetan Buddhism. Its natural orientation is to India, and since Indian Buddhism no longer exists, its frame of reference is in fact Hindu.[6]

Whether or not the term 'syncretism' has been used, the cardinal question observers of Nepalese Buddhism have therefore asked them-selves, is this: How much of what Newar Buddhists do is really Bud-dhist? How much is due to the Indian nature of their Buddhism? And how much is a later borrowing from Hinduism, due to the destruction of Buddhism in India, and its encapsulation in Nepal in a thoroughly Hindu environment?[7]

If one adopts a modernist, historical view of Buddhism, as the teach-ing of Sakyamuni Buddha, then all of Mahayana Buddhism is in effect syncretic, since it incorporates forms of worship and scriptures not envisaged by Him. In the same way, Tantric Buddhism, with its still later scriptures, modelled on Shaiva prototypes (Sanderson 1995), and its divinities clearly borrowed likewise from Shaivism, is still more syncretic. Theravada monks do in fact regard Tantric Buddhism as no better than Hinduism, and they seem always to have done so (Gellner 1992: 323).

However, once one accepts Mahayana and Tantric Buddhism as independent traditions with their own originators, the complex rituals and baroque pantheon of Newar Buddhism, similar though they may be to Hindu (Shaiva or Vaishnava) prototypes, are not, in terms of my original definition, syncretic. An example may make this clear. There is a particular form of Avalokiteshvara, the principal bodhisattva of Mahayana Buddhism, known as Srsti-kartr-lokeshvara, or 'Lokeshvara in the process of creation'. The term for creation, *sṛṣṭi*, implies emission from one's own substance, and the icons of this form show Lokeshvara emitting all the Hindu gods from his body. The term, and the icon, are clearly borrowed from the similar Hindu form of Vishnu in the act of creation. But is this syncretism? It is in accord with the Mahayana Buddhist practice of adopting Hindu (or elsewhere, other local cultural) forms and using them to express the ultimate superiority of the Buddhist path. The same logic is also characteristic of relations between the various sectarian traditions *within* Hinduism: Shaivism and Vaishnavism both in different ways try to absorb and include the other as an inferior version of themselves. The copying of the icon of Vishnu in order to express Buddhist ideas is therefore in accord with the intentions of the originators of Mahayana Buddhism (cf. Pye 1978), as far as these can be divined, and it is far from unsystematic.

In cases such as this, one has a mature synthesis of elements of heterogeneous origin. As Stewart remarks (1991: 7) in a passage discussed above, all world religions incorporate elements of diverse origin, and this alone should not be enough to label them syncretic. The *exotika*, the supernatural figures inherited from the Greeks' pagan past and still recognized by the Greeks today, 'form a complementary, although antithetical, part of a whole [namely, Greek Orthodoxy, as popularly practised], not a separate "anti-structure"' (ibid.).

Two further examples may show where the term syncretism can legitimately be applied. Of the three cities of the Kathmandu Valley, Lalitpur is traditionally the most Buddhist. In the royal palace at the city's centre there is a famous gold window. It shows this same figure, Srsti-kartr-lokeshvara. It is said that the as yet unpublished inscription on the window shows that it was given to the king of Lalitpur in the seventeenth century, Siddhi Narasingh, by a Buddhist goldsmith, as was a golden throne. However the window is framed by images which clearly suggest that the figure is not in fact Lokeshvara but Vishnu, in particular Vishnu's mount, Garuda, immediately below it. This combined figure manages to be all things to members of both religions in the city. The Buddhist subject made a donation that was acceptable both to his fellow Buddhists, the majority in the city, and to his Hindu monarch. It was a deliberate piece of syncretism in a particular political situation.

The same interpretation should undoubtedly be made of another striking iconographic form. These are the numerous *caityas* (Buddhist cult objects), dating from the second half of the nineteenth century, all but one of them in the city of Kathmandu, which combine a regular *caitya* form with a water-course which is clearly borrowed from a *śivaliṅga*, the main iconic symbol of Shaivism. This was the Rana period, the most intensely Hindu that the Newar Buddhists have had to live through. It seems very likely that the Buddhists of Kathmandu, the capital, felt this official pressure more than others. This syncretic iconographic form which became so popular among them was, in effect, a way of saying, 'We Buddhists are really no different from Hindus'.

So far I have argued that the Newar Buddhist tradition taken as a whole is synthetic but not syncretic, although certain relatively unimportant parts of it are syncretic. It must be admitted, however, that one important and fundamental feature of Newar Buddhism could well be seen as a syncretic adoption from Hinduism: the fact that its sacerdotal class is made up from two sub-sections of a hereditary caste (see above, Chapter 5). The two sections are the higher Vajracharyas, who are the 'Buddhist brahmans', and the slightly lower Sakyas. The Sakyas, together with the Vajracharyas, constitute the married part-time monks who run the monastic temple complexes that house the important cults of Newar Buddhism. What evidence we have suggests that the originators of both Mahayana and Tantric Buddhism intended their ways of deliverance and/or rituals of initiation to be open to all those of sufficient application and ability, regardless of background. Against this, however, it must be said that the now embattled traditionalist Newar Buddhists hold that the 'originators' of their tradition are precisely their ancestors who *did* intend the positions of Vajracharya and Sakya to be hereditary.

Moving now to consider Newar Buddhists, as opposed to Newar Buddhism, it is necessary to distinguish an inner core, which is largely priestly, from the bulk of the laity. The inner core is formed by the sacerdotal caste, the Vajracharyas and Sakyas, plus the foremost lay Buddhist caste in Kathmandu, known as Uday or Tuladhar. The major practices of the core groups are in general— and with the one important caveat noted—not syncretic by the canons of their own tradition. Ancestor Worship (*śrāddha*) modelled on the Hindu rite is performed, but it is done in a strictly Buddhist idiom. Hindu gods may be worshipped, but they are subordinated to Buddhist bodhisattvas and Buddhas. Just as the Theravada Buddhist may legitimately worship non-Buddhist spirits and Hindu gods, as long as it is not for soteriological purposes, so too may the Newar Buddhist.

It is more complicated as soon as one considers other Newars. These may be divided into three groups: those who have Vajracharyas as their domestic priest, those who have Brahmans as their domestic priest, and those low castes who have neither. In the traditional classification, Newar households who have Vajracharya domestic priests are called *buddhamārgī*, 'those who follow the path of the Buddha'. This includes, of course, all Vajracharyas, all Sakyas, and all Tuladhars. Those families who have Brahmans as their domestic priests are known as *śivamārgī*, 'those who follow the path of Shiva [i.e. Shaivites]'.

For present purposes, it is interesting to consider those Newars other than Vajracharyas, Sakyas, and Tuladhars, who have Vajracharya priests, i.e. the bulk of the Buddhist 'laity'. Among them it is common to find genuinely syncretic attitudes and practices. That is to say, some of them really believe that Buddhist and Hindu paths are equally possible and valuable paths to salvation (an idea other Newars are also liable to express in mixed company); and in their own practice, they often combine the rituals of both religions.

The majority of this group of Buddhist laity is formed by the peasant or Maharjan caste. For them Buddhism provides a framework of life-cycle rituals (aspect 4 above), especially ancestor worship, and ritual assistance in worldly problems (aspect 6). For those few who seek it, it also provides a soteriological idiom (aspect 7). Although Newar Buddhism does provide moral teachings (aspect 5), these reach only the inner core of the religion's adherents, and a few rare individuals from other castes. This indeed is one of the main criticisms made by the Theravada modernists who have so successfully proselytized among Newar Buddhism's traditional followers: that it is a system of ritual, rather than of morality or doctrine. Aspect 2 (expressing solidarity at the level of the neighbourhood or locality) is, again, performed by Buddhism only for Vajracharyas, Sakyas, and Tuladhars. Aspect 3, national solidarity, is not really aspired to by local Buddhism, though it could be said that the divinity/bodhisattva Karunamaya is the national god of the city and one-time kingdom of Lalitpur. It is the Hindu cults promoted by the King which preeminently satisfy this aspect. Maharjan neighbourhood organizations usually focus on Hindu gods such as Bhairava or one of the Mother Goddesses.[8]

To different extents, therefore, and differently according to the caste and individual, Newar Buddhism provides for all seven of the religious aspects listed above. Its specialists have adapted it further in providing life-cycle rituals than any other form of Buddhism: there is a form of wedding ceremony, the central ritual of which (a lustration of the joined heads of the couple) is derived from Tantric initiation. A systematic relationship to Hinduism has emerged which (a) permits the followers of Newar Buddhism to worship Hindu gods, while yet remaining within a Buddhist framework, and, conversely therefore, also provides a bridge whereby any worshipper of a Hindu god can become a Buddhist devotee; and (b) provides alternative rituals, festivals, and divinities, so that Buddhists do not *need* to worship in a Hindu idiom if they do not so wish. The first strategy I have called that of multivalent symbols; worshipping the high Hindu gods Vishnu and Shiva as bodhisattvas is an example of this.[9] The second strategy, following Lienhard (1978), I call parallelism.

One consequence of this complex situation is that individuals and castes have considerable choice in the precise manner in which they articulate and act out their relationship to Buddhism and Hinduism. Just how they present themselves can be seen as the outcome of various pressures, not least among them the attitude of the state. Newar Buddhist clerics, the Vajracharyas and Sakyas, have had to adapt to the Hindu preferences of the local monarchs for a long time, and the development of parallel practices and multivalent symbols is part of their survival strategy. The prominence of Tantric forms of their religion also has much to do with this, since it is apparent to Newars that in the field of Tantric religion Buddhism and Hinduism share a great deal.

Where other (lay) castes are concerned, there is much greater freedom to become Hindu, by degrees. A Nepali proverb says *jasko śakti usko bhakti*: 'whose power, his devotion', or, in other words, 'people tend to adopt the religious style of whoever holds power'. This is particularly apposite for those high-caste Shresthas and middle-ranking Maharjans who have become Shresthas over the last 150 years. In the Malla-period kingdoms of the Kathmandu Valley before 1769 the majority of the Newar population had Buddhist priests. The new Gorkhali rulers, and especially the hereditary prime ministers of the period 1846–51, as already noted, were strong Hindus. Shresthas were increasingly employed as civil servants and it was only natural for them to adopt, increasingly, the religious customs of their masters. Upwardly mobile peasants, who were able to turn themselves into Shresthas, especially in the outlying settlements in the north and east of the Valley, imitated them, by giving up their Vajracharya priests, employing Brahmans, and adopting a Hindu religious style which was very little different from that of the dominant, Nepali-speaking Parbatiya population.[10] For most of these, as for the high-caste Newars who had always been Hindu, it is not usually a question of adopting a syncretic attitude. In fact, it may be rather a question of abandoning a syncretic combination of Hinduism and Buddhism for a predominantly Hindu viewpoint, in which Buddhism is seen as a branch or subsect of Hinduism.

In the large cities of Kathmandu and Lalitpur it may properly be said that the Maharjan or peasant caste has just such a syncretic attitude. They all have Vajracharya priests, but the majority today describe their religion as 'Hindu' when pressed on the question, as in the national census.[11] They accept both religions as equally valid and practise the rituals of both, though they know full well that the priests whom they use are themselves more purist. They are intensely proud of their own traditions, a pride which has probably increased with their improved economic position since 1951. Their syncretic outlook reflects the reality of their position in a double-headed caste system with two Great Traditions: they are the tenants and clients of high castes of both persuasions, and it is in their interest to remain equally attached to both.

To sum up: within traditional Newar Buddhism syncretic attitudes on the part of the laity were not actively combated, but were rather recognized as a lower stage or level of a distinctively Buddhist path. Toleration of syncretism was therefore both a defence against Hinduism and a bridgehead for counterattack. Today, with the introduction of modernist standards of 'purity' and 'authenticity', Newar Buddhism is condemned by western-educated, self-appointed spokesmen for this very strategy, as well as for the similarity of much of its internal organization to those forms of religious relationship identified as typically Hindu.

Japan

Buddhism in Japan presents a very different spectacle to Buddhism in the Kathmandu Valley. It is not just that the population of Japan is 120 million, that of the Kathmandu Valley approximately 1 million; nor is it that Japan is now a rich and successful industrial society, with vibrant Buddhist institutions clearly at home in the modern world. The history of Buddhism there is also very different. There have been many different sects based on different Buddhist scriptures; some were Tantric, practising rituals very similar to those of Nepal and Tibet (the Shingon, and to some extent Tendai, sects), and others were anti-ritualist and anti-elitist (the Pure Land sects). There were, therefore, many different ways of being a Buddhist practitioner, and different ways in which these practitioners related to their main local rival, Shintoism. Such variety was not characteristic of the small world of traditional Newar Buddhism.

In Japan, unlike Nepal, as already noted, Buddhism did not attempt to become an all-encompassing religion. It remained, in Gombrich's term, accretive. There was no strategy of parallelism, whereby whenever a rite was offered by the competing religion, it too evolved its own version for its adherents. Buddhism in the Kathmandu Valley faced a system that provided many rituals and a complete system for life, namely Hinduism. Buddhism in Japan began as the dominant religion of the elite, and it was the native cults which were forced to adapt, to find a name— Shintoism—and textual charters for themselves, and to begin to compete with Buddhism. Until the Meiji Restoration of 1868 Buddhist specialists in Japan could easily tolerate and exist in complementary harmony with Shintoism, since for the most part they were, and saw themselves as, the dominant partner.

Buddhist monks and priests controlled the sphere of death and the afterlife. They therefore provided soteriology (aspect 7); and, through worship of the ancestors, Buddhist ritual symbolized the continuity of the household (aspect 1). The other Durkheimian aspects (2, 3, and 4, death rituals excepted) were happily ceded to Shinto cults. The socialization of the young (aspect 5) came to be conceived of as the task of Confucianism, itself brought from China by Buddhist monks. Dealing with misfortune (aspect 6) was the sphere of a variety of specialists and divinities, some Buddhist, some Shinto, some Taoist, and some a mixture.

The complementarity of Buddhism and Shintoism was not total, however. It was not only that certain Shinto intellectuals rejected its subordination. My own research in a Tokyo neighbourhood focused on the existence of two different types of Buddhist temple, the *danka* temple and the *shinja* temple (see Chapter 15 below). The former are the classic and by far the more common type, specializing in death and open only to the those 'donors' (*danka*) who are attached to them. The latter are open to anyone, to any 'believer' (*shinja*). They include some of the larger and more spectacular temples of Japan. They specialize in worldly matters. In the most paradigmatic case, the temple attempted to avoid any contact with death or worship associated with it as far as possible. This type of temple, its head priest told me, 'is just like a Shinto shrine'. In other words, the possibility of Buddhism providing for all religious aspects was always present. Buddhism existed in pre-Meiji Japan in a complementary synthesis with Shintoism, but in the final analysis it did not actually *need* Shintoism.

As long as Buddhism was recognized as the senior partner, and as the sole guide to salvation, there was nothing in this situation that could be seen as syncretic from a Mahayana Buddhist perspective. The confidence of Buddhist priests in this situation can be seen in the fact that any divinity not strictly Buddhist was defined as Shinto. This is symbolized by the placing of a Shinto holy gate (*torii*) before the altar or shrine. Many Indian or Hindu gods brought to Japan with Buddhism, such as Benten (Sarasvati), were included in this 'Shinto' category, and these gods are, even today, controlled by Buddhist priests.

In the Tokugawa era there were at various places, such as at Ise shrine, Shinto specialists who resisted Buddhist ideological hegemony, and sought to establish a purely Shinto religious perspective, but they were in a minority and do not seem to have been significant in their own time. More characteristic of the pre-Meiji period seems to have been the kind of shrine described by Grapard (1984, 1992), where the practices of the two religions were inextricably melded. Overnight, with the changes introduced by the Meiji reformers, the priests had to decide to become either Shinto or Buddhist; in this case, as in many others, they became Shinto, removed all Buddhist icons, and excluded anything that might be construed as Buddhist. In the pre-Meiji period it was common to find important shrines of, for example, the war god Hachiman, in the precincts of a Buddhist temple and run by Buddhist monks. Now seen as a purely Shinto divinity, he was at that time identified with the Buddhist bodhisattva Maitreya. With the 'reforms' of the early Meiji period, the two institutions were forcibly separated and began to be run by entirely separate functionaries. In the pre-Meiji period what I have dubbed in the Nepalese context multivalent symbolism was evidently common in Japan: Shinto *kami* (gods) were routinely identified with Buddhist bodhisattvas.[12] With the Meiji separation the Japanese had to learn to see Buddhism and Shintoism as two separate religions and not as two complementary religious orientations, aspects of a single way of life.

The new way of viewing religion was inspired by European examples. Where the Tokugawa regime had insisted that all settled Japanese be attached to a local Buddhist temple, and had used the temple's priest as a census taker, the Meiji reformers decided that Shintoism was the truly Japanese religion. They persecuted Buddhism, decided to purify Shintoism, and to use it as the basis of a modern sense of nationhood (Ketelaar 1990). Thus began the process of building what is known as State Shinto with its worship of the Emperor and its view of the nation as a single household under his direction (Hardacre 1989). In short, the old way of practising Buddhism and Shintoism had come to seem syncretic under the impact of Christian-derived views of religion and the power of the West.

And yet even today the ordinary practice of most lay Japanese continues the old complementarity. Most still use Shintoism for rites of birth, youth, and marriage (with considerable syncretism or perhaps rather *bricolage* in the latter), and Buddhism for death (Reader 1991: Chapters 3–4). Among those who stick to traditional forms, and who seek a soteriological practice, most do so as Buddhists. There are, of course, many new religions. Some of these encourage their followers to maintain their traditional attachments; some better known ones, such as Soka Gakkai, are hostile to any other religious attachments; many are frankly syncretic, incorporating Shinto, Buddhist, and Christian elements (Koepping 1995).

Outside the new religions, it is only in the personal rituals of the clergy of the two religions and of the Imperial Palace that there is a determined attempt to break the old complementarity. Buddhist priests now get married in a Buddhist ritual (in the pre-Meiji era it was only in the Pure Land sects that there were married Buddhist priests). Shinto priests have developed Shinto death rituals and Shinto graveyards. The Emperor is now buried in an invented Shinto rite and the new one is consecrated to rule in another. Both of these would have been Buddhist rituals in the pre-Meiji period.[13]

In terms of the earlier analysis, there was an emerging *synthesis* in Tokugawa Japan in which Buddhism was the dominant and accretive partner. This was reversed with the Meiji Restoration so that joint practice of Buddhism and Shintoism has come to seem *syncretic*. It is important to note that both the earlier synthesis and the later separation were the outcome of government action.[14]

Conclusion

This rapid survey of two contrasting situations of Buddhism's coexistence with other religions suggests that we need to distinguish four types of situation.

1. *Bricolage.* The combination of numerous elements of diverse origins with no stable synthesis envisaged. Post-modern perspectives lead to the collapsing of all phenomena into this one kind.

2. *Syncretism.* In this disparate elements are combined, usually of just two traditions; the actors may recognize it and see it as a positive thing, as with the Maharjan peasants or modern ecumenical churchmen, or may be defensive about it and attempt to deny it.

3. *Synthetic traditions*, such as any of the so-called world religions, which are made up of elements of different origin, but combine them in a systematic way, with an internal logic that relates and explains them.

These three should probably be approached as ideal types: in particular situations it is possible that transitions from one form to another may occur.[15] All three of these need to be distinguished from a fourth situation, though they may also be found within it:

4. *Complementary and accretive coexistence of more than one tradition.* This is the situation which I have illustrated with examples from Thailand and Japan. In such cases several traditions coexist, often in a structured hierarchy, but also often in open or tacit competition. The mutual influence of such traditions is highly likely to give rise to some syncretic forms, but the analysis of such situations is extremely complex and all simplistic labelling is to be avoided.

Thus, in applying the term syncretism, I have tried to argue that though one may have good reasons for using it, there are also good reasons for supposing that it will always be controversial. As academic observers we need always to ask whether it is a question of an entire tradition or of a single ritual, or some other aspect of practice. We have to acknowledge that interested participants are very likely to take the part for the whole and make sweeping judgements more detached observers cannot concur in. Questions of power are certainly central to this whole debate. Stewart concludes his latest piece by saying that 'Social anthropologists and sociologists should try to identify where these contests [over syncretism] are taking place and render accounts of them, rather than allow themselves to be trapped into contributing to them' (Stewart 1995: 37). Unlike Stewart, I do not think that academics who make judgements of this sort have necessarily been 'trapped' into contributing to a power struggle. To refuse to do so in the name of ethical and political purity seems to involve abandoning crucial distinctions about the social organization of power, and precisely to weaken the attempt to 'render accounts' which Stewart claims should be the purpose of examining syncretism in the first place.

Notes

1. First written up in this form in 1993, I have benefited from discussion of earlier versions of this argument with members of seminars in Tokyo, Oxford, and Lancaster, and from the comments of Andrew Beatty, Jean-Claude Galey, and Charles Stewart. I should mention also Stefan Palmié's article (1995): I have borrowed and reversed his title.
2. For a useful survey of attempts to define syncretism within religious studies, see Droogers 1989.
3. Stewart 1991: 7. This distinction is an external analytical one; no doubt the protagonists in the early Pagan-Christian encounter had diverse, and more complex, assessments of the relationship.
4. Droogers (1989: 20) also argues that 'the definition of syncretism ought to include the element of contesting ... Syncretism is in the first place *contested religious interpenetration*' (italics in the original). Gallie (1964: 161, 168) lists a number of formal criteria for a concept to be essentially contested, which it seems to me that 'syncretism' satisfies. The only problematic one is that it should be *appraisive*, where 'syncretism' is predominantly pejorative, i.e. negatively appraised. The 'live examples' that Gallie gives are Christianity, democracy, art, and social justice.
5. See Southwold 1978 for a list of twelve criteria, no one of which is found in all religions. Since there is no single ever-present characteristic, Southwold concludes that religion is a polythetic category.

6. On the problems with the category 'Hindu', see Sontheimer and Kulke (eds). 1989. For present purposes Hinduism may be taken as synonymous with Shaivism.

7. I have suggested above (Chapter 2) that the overriding focus on this question is a sign of immaturity in the study of Buddhism.

8. There are occasional exceptions, such as the Maharjans of Gahchen, Lalitpur, for whom the local Buddhist *stūpa* is the main shrine. See Chapter 13, p. 303–4, for a discussion of the predominance of fierce gods and goddesses in the public arena.

9. For an interesting discussion of multivalency in Java, see Beatty 1996.

10. This process has been documented for the town of Sankhu by Rosser 1966.

11. In the changed political atmosphere post-1990 many Maharjans have insisted on being counted as Buddhists instead.

12. See Herbert 1967: 46; Kamstra 1989: 141; Grapard 1992: 74-100; Miyake 1996: 124.

13. See Ketelaar 1990: 44, 92; and, Smith 1995: 31.

14. Kamstra (1989) argues that as far as ordinary Japanese are concerned, Buddhism, Shintoism, etc. are different aspects of a single religious tradition; syncretism is therefore simply not an issue for them.

15. I was pleased to discover that Michael Pye (1994), arguing from within religious studies, has come to a similar conclusion: if carefully done, syncretism can be distinguished from synthesis.

15

Temples for Life and Temples for Death: Observations on Some Shingon Buddhist Temples in Tokyo

Introduction[1]

What sort of comparisons, if any, are appropriate between cultures is a perennial issue in anthropology. More specifically, within regional traditions of scholarship, who has the right to speak authoritatively and which questions it is permissible to ask have also been longstanding problems, if less frequently addressed (Fardon 1985). Among specialists of Japan, both foreign and Japanese, there has been, it seems to me, a tendency to downplay links with Asia and, implicitly or explicitly, to pursue instead comparisons with, and explanations in terms derived from, 'the West'. I am certainly not the first anthropologist whose primary expertise lies outside Japan to suggest that aspects of Japanese culture and society might be helpfully viewed in the light of models derived from elsewhere (Duff-Cooper 1991; Bloch 1992). In the present case I aim to examine similarities in the practice of two traditions of Tantric Buddhism, the Nepalese and the Shingon in Japan, which are distantly related historically.[2] A second aim is to compare the different ways in which these forms of Buddhism relate to their non-Buddhist contexts. The Japanese material is given centre stage here since the Nepalese material has been presented in detail elsewhere.[3]

Shintoism and Buddhism

Are Buddhism and Shintoism separate religions, or two aspects of one Japanese religion?[4] There are arguments on both sides. It depends whether one is talking about priestly families or lay people, and the relationship between Buddhism and Shintoism has changed dramatically since the Meiji Restoration of 1868. It also depends, of course, on what one means by 'religion'.

Opinion polls appear to show that the Japanese are one of the most secular peoples of the world, with 65 per cent regularly claiming to be without religious belief, whereas anything between 60 and 90 per cent claim to have religious belief in such countries as Britain, France, and the USA (Reader 1991: 5). This simply shows how unreliable opinion polls are. If one asks about observance, 75 per cent of Japanese pray to the *kami* (Shinto gods) at New Year, although only 21 per cent affirm that they believe in their existence (ibid.); in other words, 54 per cent of Japanese worship entities whose existence they are at best doubtful about. It would be a mistake to conclude that there is something particularly Japanese about worshipping an entity one does not believe in: according to research in the USA reported in *The Guardian* (11 February 1992, p. 5), 10 per cent of those who do not believe in God pray to Him (or should that be It?) daily. If we look at what Japanese *do*, instead of ethnocentrically confronting them with questions about *belief*, we see that most of them most certainly do participate in Shinto or Buddhist festivals and rituals, and many participate, whether over the long term or for shorter periods, in the many Japanese new religions which amalgamate aspects of both.

The conventional textbook view is that there is a division of labour between Buddhism and Shintoism in Japan such that Shintoism is for life and Buddhism is for death.[5] Thus Japanese perform rituals of birth and the life stages (at the ages of 3, 5, and 7), and later get married, in a Shinto idiom and/or at Shinto shrines. All matters connected with death are carried out by Buddhist priests, and memorials to the dead are to be found in graveyards attached to Buddhist temples.[6] Japanese homes usually have separate offering places within the home, namely the *butsudan*, where offerings in a Buddhist idiom are given to the ancestors, and the *kamidana*, where they are made in Shinto idiom to the Shinto gods.

It is the conflation of Buddhas and ancestors which is the most startling to anyone familiar with Buddhism elsewhere in Asia, since it is combined with a great de-emphasis on the doctrine of karma (rebirth according to one's moral deserts). Robert J. Smith, in his standard work on Japanese ancestor worship, declares it to be a misunderstanding, a Japanese confusion resulting from using the euphemism 'to attain nirvana' (which effectively means to become a Buddha) for 'to die' (Smith 1974: 50). The normal term for ancestor, *hotoke*, is written with the same Chinese characters as *butsu*, meaning Buddha, suggesting that they are the same. Some priests asserted to me that ancestors and Buddhas are indeed the same; others said that they were not. Certainly the widespread and highly expensive ritual of giving a 'death name' to the deceased person can be understood as the Tantric rite of revealing the true 'Buddha nature' of the person. Monks and priests do not need such a new name after death, since they have already received a 'Buddha name' on being initiated.

The separation of responsibilities and complementary associations between Buddhism and Shintoism in Japan has frequently been represented as a series of oppositions, thus:

Buddhism	Shintoism
death rituals	life-cycle rituals
afterlife	worldly aims
temples	shrines
inauspicious/polluted	auspicious/pure
O-bon festival (summer)	New Year (winter)

Buddhist ritual specialists have had to find ways to cope with this association with the inauspicious. Many of the most polluting tasks at death are actually performed by the women of the household. The position of the *burakumin*, Japan's 'outcastes', is connected, among other things, to their performance of death-related tasks (Ohnuki-Tierney 1987: 80, 98).

Several anthropologists have developed this theme of the opposition between Buddhism and Shintoism. Ooms (1976), in a classic structuralist paper, argued that the series of Shinto rituals by which a child is turned into an adult parallel almost exactly the series of Buddhist rituals by which a dead person is turned into an ancestor. Joy Hendry (1981: 229–39) explores and endorses this basic opposition in her detailed ethnography of a Kyushu village, but she ends by suggesting that weddings are such pivotal and protean affairs, with links to divination, funerals, and Buddhist altars, that marriage 'temporarily [overrides] the universal opposition between life and death, just as it brings together male and female' (ibid.: 239). Jane Cobbi (1995) pursues the difference into food preferences: alcohol, salt, and strong-tasting things are associated with men, life, and Shintoism, whereas tea, sweets, and mild-tasting things are associated with women, weakness, and Buddhism. The associations with gender are, as one might expect, rather more complex than such a scheme would at first sight suggest: Martinez's villagers told her that 'Buddhism is for men, and Shintoism for women' (Martinez 1995: 190).

Leaving these symbolic elaborations aside, one might object that a simple opposition between life and death does not capture the full complexity of Japanese religious practice. Even so, the idea that Shintoism and Buddhism are complementary can still be defended. If one lays aside the Judaeo-Christian assumption that all aspects of religion must be provided by the same tradition, it is possible to distinguish at least seven distinct aspects or spheres, as noted above (Chapter 14, p. 328). Buddhism provided for legitimation of the household and for soteriology; Shintoism dealt with the symbolism of the locality and the nation, as well as with the sanctification of the life-cycle; a moral code was provided primarily by Confucianism; and help in misfortune was mainly a Shinto concern (but incorporating many concepts from Taoism). As we shall see, certain types of Buddhist temple also provided and continue to provide considerable competition in this sphere.

Kinds of Buddhist temple

The research on which this paper is based was carried out in the locality of Fukagawa, Tokyo. Fukagawa was part of the 'low town' outside the city walls in the Edo period before 1868 (Waley 1986: 225f). It is one of the few Tokyo localities to have several Shingon temples, including that of the famous Fukagawa Fudo. Fudo, known in Sanskrit as Achala, is a fierce Tantric deity, very popular with the Japanese; his temple here is controlled by the Narita branch of Shingon Buddhism. One of the priests described Fudo to me as 'a rough character with a good heart'. I also visited three other Shingon temples, which I shall call A, B, and C.

The four Buddhist temples considered here present quite a range of types which between them call into question the neat picture of Shintoism for life and Buddhism for death. The neat model can perhaps be accepted as a rough approximation. There are, however, two big problems with it. The first is historical: the separation of the two religions is the outcome of government action in the years following 1868. Viewing the two as distinct and separate traditions does justice neither to the situation before 1868 (which I consider further below), nor to the attitudes of most Japanese lay people today (Grapard 1984).

The second problem is more ethnographic and has to do with the aspirations of the specialists who run many of the larger Buddhist temples.

The neat picture assumes that all Buddhist temples are of the type known as *dankadera*, that is, temples supported by donors or parishioners (*danka*). Indeed, the vast majority of Japanese Buddhist temples are of this sort. But the large and famous ones are not. They are known as *shinjadera*, temples supported by 'believers' (*shinja*).[7] The typical dankadera can be illustrated by Temple C. It is never open to the public. Overshadowed by neighbouring apartment blocks, its recently rebuilt compound encloses a single building which incorporates both the temple and the priest's house. In order to reach the main temple it is necessary to go upstairs. Behind it is the graveyard containing the tombs of households attached to the temple. Except when there is a funeral going on, or during annual festivals for the dead, the place is quiet. Immigration to Tokyo has been so great in recent generations that probably the majority of households there today have no connection to a dankadera in the city. Many have also lost contact with one in their village of origin.

The famous Fukagawa Fudo temple, on the other hand, is a shinjadera and is in complete contrast to the typical dankadera. It is open to the public all day long and there is a steady stream of worshippers, though they tend to be more numerous during the five fire sacrifices held at two-hour intervals throughout day, starting at 9 a.m. The fire sacrifices are impressive rituals involving six or more robed priests and the use of loudspeakers to amplify the prayers. On sale at the shop by the main steps to the temple is a large array of amulets for various purposes as well as *gomaki*, fire sacrifice sticks, and large inscribed boards called *ofuda*. The fire sacrifice sticks may be bought, again for various purposes, e.g. to avoid discord at home, at 300 yen for the smaller ones and 500 yen for the larger ones. They then have the worshipper's name inscribed on them and will be saved by the priests and used in an upcoming sacrifice, so that the petition will ascend directly to Lord Fudo. The ofuda are much more expensive: the cheapest cost 3000 yen. Rather than being placed in the fire, they are waved over it and then taken home by the worshipper to be placed in their *butsudan*. The deity stands at the back of the main hall: he holds a sword and a noose and has a fierce countenance. Most worshippers advance no further than the front of the hall.

At the main entrance to the temple grounds there is a small roof over a water tank; worshippers may purify their hands using small metal cups with long bamboo handles if they wish. Behind this is a series of racks for tying *ema*, small wooden boards on which devotees write what they hope for from Lord Fudo (these too may be bought at the shop). Some record more than one wish. Eighty-one ema were inspected with a total of 90 wishes, which broke down as follows: 40 had to do with success in study (either in examinations, or for entrance to high school or a specific named university, or in particular subjects), 15 wished for health, 9 requested recovery from illness, 6 were for family happiness, 5 for commercial success, 4 for family safety, 3 for traffic safety, 3 for happiness, 2 for romantic love, 2 to grow tall, and 1 for the return of a missing daughter. The preponderance of ema directed at educational ends is apparently standard.[8] To the right of the main entrance to the temple is an altar used for special blessing rituals performed on motor vehicles. The temple has a considerable reputation for this, and the ritual is supposed to ensure that accidents are avoided.

Around the back of the main hall of Fudo are three subsidiary chapels, where many worshippers rarely go. Two of them are dedicated to Dainichi Nyorai (Skt Mahavairocana), the principal Buddha of the Shingon sect, and one to Amida (Skt Amitabha). There are various wall-hangings and statues of other Buddhist figures in these chapels, including Kobo Daishi (Kukai), the founder of the Shingon sect. His birthday and death day are observed as major festivals of the temple. Most of the figures have the appropriate mantra (*goshingon*) written out in phonetic script beneath them: that for Dainichi, for example, is *on bajara datoban* (equivalent to the Sanskrit *om vajradhatu vam*). In the chapel of Amida, there are a few funeral tablets (*ihai*) of selected donors to the temple, the only place anywhere in the temple for the paraphernalia of death rituals.

Also part of the temple complex behind the main hall are a tea-house for performing the tea ceremony, a room for performing *hatsumairi*, the first visit by a child to a Buddhist temple (an equivalent of the more usual first visit to a Shinto shrine), and a room used for calligraphy classes. These are all built around a traditional Japanese garden.

The impression given by this temple is that the priests have made a conscious effort to avoid any connections with death. The two main festivals for the dead, O-bon and Segaki, are not observed. There are not even any statues to Jizo, the popular bodhisattva who is believed to save one from bad rebirths or a bad fate after death. Jizo statues are often found in other well-known shinjadera (cf. Ohnuki-Tierney 1984: 138ff) and often in the form of *mizuko*, the childlike version of Jizo frequently erected for aborted foetuses and decorated with bibs and other childlike paraphernalia.[9]

This impression was confirmed by the head priest, who said that he always refused to perform death rituals for devotees. In five years at the temple he had only acceded to one man, who had requested him so many times that he had finally declared, 'If you ask such a thing you will fall into hell, but OK!' (he laughed as he related this). He added quite spontaneously that, because it rejects anything to do with death, 'this temple is similar to Shinto'.

It can be seen, then, that the life:death opposition repeats itself *within Buddhism*. Here the shinjadera take on the characteristics of the Shinto temple, offering all kinds of help in life, offering Buddhist equivalents to Shinto life-cycle ceremonies, and shunning inauspicious associations with death. Thus, a clear symbolic opposition within Japanese culture reappears within a subculture, in this case Buddhism. This can be represented as follows:

dankadera (e.g. Temple C)	*shinjadera* (e.g. Fukagawa Fudo)
members only	open to all comers
specializes in tombstones and death rituals	no tombstones or death rituals
inauspicious, so avoided for worldly needs	offers help in worldly need including life-cycle rituals

There are, however, two other Shingon temples in the same Tokyo locality—Temple A and Temple B—which fit neither model neatly. Temple B is, in fact, as its priest openly admitted, 'mixed'. One part of it is open to the public on a daily basis: this is the temple to Emma Dai-o (Sanskrit Yamaraj, lord of the dead). This temple has become quite well known because of its incorporation of modern technology. Nineteen offering boxes trigger different tape-recorded messages when coins are dropped into them. When you drop an offering into that labelled 'study', you are told to work hard with a pure mind and that that will ensure success. The other part of the temple is dedicated to Dainichi and has funeral tablets in glass cases down either side. It is open only when the *danka* come to perform death ceremonies. The priest of Temple B was, as his rebuilding of the Emma Dai-o temple would suggest, a dynamic innovator. He was particularly concerned, he said, with the large number of Tokyo residents who nowadays have no effective link with a dankadera and are easily exploited by new cremation companies.

The last temple to be considered, Temple A, is also 'mixed', but in a different way: it is not a regular dankadera with tombs of donors. It has a few tombs, but only of the priests who have served there. It is open to the public every day but it does not reject all connections with death as the Fudo temple priests do. The differences between these four Shingon temples are summarized in Chart 15.1. It will be seen that, in practice, the opposition between the two types of temple produces a spectrum, with some temples conforming to the ideal types of shinjadera and

Chart 15.1: Contrasting characteristics of four Shingon temples in a Tokyo locality

Temple	FF	A	B	C
Ema offered	√			
Facilities for life-cycle rituals and for tea ceremony	√			
Calligraphy classes	√			
Rituals for the safety of new cars	√			
Open daily for worship	√	√	√a	
Observance of Kobo Daishi's birthday	√	√		
Observance of Kobo Daishi's death day		√		
Sale of amulets	√	√	√	
Daily *goma* (fire sacrifice)	√			
Monthly *goma*		√		
Sale of *goma* sticks	√	√	√	
No *goma*			√	√
Tombs		√b	√	√
Ihai (funeral tablets)	√c	√d	√	√
Jizo statue(s)		√		
O-bon, Sekagie observed		√	√	√
Higan observed			√	√

Notes: '√' indicates the presence of the characteristic in question
FF= Fukagawa Fudo
(a) Emma Dai-o hall only; (b) of priests only; (c) selected donors only;
(d) selected donors only.

dankadera but others combining elements of both.

The special position of Temple A can partly be explained by the history of the area. In the pre-Meiji period there was a large Buddhist temple in Fukagawa with grounds far more extensive than any temple or shrine today. At that time the Fudo temple did not exist, though a stat-ue of Fudo was brought on a palanquin from Narita from time to time when invited by *kabuki* actors or other local people. The Buddhist tem-ple of that time incorporated in its grounds the nearby famous Tomioka Hachiman shrine, today a completely separate institution. Hachiman is the god of war and is nowadays seen as an unambiguously Shinto god. In the pre-Meiji period Hachiman was seen as a protector of Buddhism (Herbert 1967: 437) and was therefore identified as a bodhisattva.[10] As his shrine was at that time part of the grounds of a Buddhist temple, his cult was controlled by the Buddhist priests. According to its priest, Temple A, small and inconspicuous though it is, is the successor of the large temple of pre-Meiji times. As all over Japan, large tracts of land were confiscated from Buddhist temples, and the priests of many temples in traditions which combined Shinto and Buddhist practices had to decide overnight to become 'pure Shinto' (Grapard 1984; Ketelaar 1990). In short, in the name of purity and nation-building, the state made a determined attempt to separate the two traditions in an unprecedented way.

Nepal

For a comparison with the Fukagawa Fudo temple, we can consider the large temple-monastery compound called Kwa Bahah (known as 'the Golden Temple' to tourists) in Lalitpur, Nepal (Plate 2).[11] Like Fukagawa Fudo, it receives a regular trickle of devotees throughout the day; locals come *en masse* in the early morning for the high point of the daily liturgy, the washing of the god's face in a ritual mirror and the distribution of the holy water. Like Fukagawa Fudo, Kwa Bahah is on various pilgrimage routes and so is visited as part of a set of holy sites. It has not developed a large range of items for sale as has Fukagawa Fudo, nor does it have a range of instrumental rites it can offer laity or pilgrims as Fukagawa or some Hindu temples in India have. Yet, unlike other local Buddhist temples, it does have a single powerful ritual for instrumental purposes that is sponsored by a wide variety of local people, namely the ritual reading of the text, the 'Perfection of Wisdom in Eight Thousand Lines' (Astasahasrika Prajnaparamita) (see above, Chapter 7).

A big difference from Japan is that Buddhist priests among the Newars of Nepal are part of a caste, with two intermarrying sections, the Vajracharyas and the Sakyas. All Vajracharya and Sakya men are members of a monastery-temple such as Kwa Bahah (though many are much smaller than Kwa Bahah). Only Vajracharyas may be domestic priests for other Newars, but in the context of the monastery Vajracharyas and Sakyas are for almost all purposes of equal status. Kwa Bahah has a very large number of members (over 3000), a majority or near majority of whom live in the vicinity of the temple. The sons of members become members by passing through the ritual of monastic initiation in Kwa Bahah. (Only the sons of members by Sakya or Vajracharya mothers may be so initiated.) They are then added to the membership roll, so that, eventually, in their late forties or early fifties, their turn will come to be responsible for the daily ritual for a month. Thus Kwa Bahah is, in effect, the collective property of a patrilineally defined segment of the Vajracharya-Sakya caste ('the *sā*—i.e. *saṃgha* or Monastic Community—'of Kwa Bahah'). Japanese Buddhist priests of a large temple such as Fukagawa Fudo are functionaries, in effect employees, of the Narita sect, and do not own, even in an extended sense, the temple where they work. On the other hand, priests of dankadera in Japan do own their temples in a way very analogous to the Nepalese situation, though as far as I know the Nepalese pattern of group ownership and rotating duties is not found.

Unlike in Japan, there is in Kwa Bahah no taboo on death rituals or death offerings in the temple, though it is true that there is rarely occasion to perform them there.[12] In Nepal *all* life-cycle rituals are performed in the family's home and the relationship of family to domestic priest, modelled on the Hindu jajman–brahman priest relation, has no necessary relationship to any temple. Unlike in Japan, Nepalese Buddhism expanded to provide a full range of sacraments, so that Buddhist lay people, as well as Sakyas and Vajracharyas (the Buddhist clergy), go through essentially the same set of life-cycle rituals overseen by their Vajracharya domestic priests.[13]

Conclusion

In Japan, as in Nepal, Tantric Buddhism is a ritual system operated by priests for both interested devotees and hereditary parishioners. What is unusual from the Nepalese point of view is the dual separation that has occurred in Japan. In the first place, many Japanese tend to approach Shinto shrines for birth, childhood, and wedding ceremonies, as well as for assistance in worldly matters, reserving Buddhism for death rituals. In the second place, even when Japanese Buddhist institutions offer 'Shinto-type' services, there is a division of labour. The hereditary relationship with a Buddhist temple and its incumbent pertains only to death rituals. For any other service, the devotee is free to approach whatever temple, specialist, or cult they prefer.

When Buddhism coexisted with Hinduism in South Asia (as it still does in the Kathmandu Valley) Buddhist monks and priests were willing to accept gifts, particularly those associated with death, that other religious specialists considered to be tainted with inauspiciousness. But from the monks' point of view, they themselves were beyond such worldly considerations. In very strongly Buddhist societies, such as Burma, Thailand, and Tibet, this monastic view came to be largely accepted by the laity as well: that Theravada monks and nuns accept offerings made on behalf of dead people in no way demeans them in the eyes of those who make them. In Nepal, by contrast, high-caste Hindu Newars are willing to use Buddhist priests as death specialists, but they do not regard them as of equal rank to brahmans. The Nepalese Buddhist priests themselves, for their part, do not accept that their own involvement is particularly problematic. What appears to have happened in Japan, by contrast, is that Buddhist personnel *have* accepted the view of the wider society that the connections with death are inauspicious and have organized themselves accordingly. Both the strategy of the Fukagawa Fudo temple (avoiding connections with death) and the strategies of Temples A and B (combining features of both types of temple) may be seen as creative adaptations to the religiously plural context of modern Tokyo, where mass migration from the villages has meant that many, if not most, of Tokyo's inhabitants no longer have an effective link with a dankadera.

Buddhism began as a soteriology (religious aspect 7, of the spheres distinguished above, p. 323). In spite of the various ways it was adapted to lay life, it has nearly always remained fundamentally a soteriology, and has coexisted with other religious systems which have provided for at least some of the other needs of lay people. Thus there is and was nothing particularly strange about the traditional co-existence of Buddhism and Shintoism in Japan. There is no reason, on this account, to claim that Buddhism was 'Japanized' out of all recognition. Indeed, in specializing overwhelmingly in death rituals, Japanese Buddhist priests remained closer to Theravada Buddhism than the Buddhism of Nepal, whose priests have expanded their ritual repertoire to cover, at least potentially, all seven aspects. The biggest theoretical obstacle to a proper sociological and anthropological understanding of Buddhism, whether in Japan or elsewhere, has been the Eurocentric assumption that there is something illegitimate about such religious specialization and, above all, about its consequence—the coexistence of different religious traditions within a single symbolic field.

Notes

1. For comments, help, and guidance, I am more than usually indebted to my wife, D.P. Martinez. I also thank Roger Goodman and Joy Hendry for useful comments. So many people were helpful in Japan that it would be impossible to thank them all, but I must mention in particular Ishii Hiroshi, Tanaka Kimiaki, Togawa Masahiko, and Hiramatsu Reiko; the last two acted as exemplary assistants and interpreters. The priests of the temples I discuss may prefer not to be named, but I would like to record their unfailing

politeness and their spontaneous and warm hospitality. It will be evident how much I owe to established specialists on Japan, and I hope, though do not expect, that they will excuse an outsider trespassing on their territory.

2. The ritual of fire sacrifice, *homa* in Sanskrit, *goma* in Japanese, is central to both. Many of the same deities are worshipped in both.

3. See above Chapters 5 and 6, and Gellner 1992a.

4. The same question has often been asked about the relation between Theravada Buddhism and the other religious systems with which it coexists (see Chapters 2 and 14, above).

5. Hendry 1995: 146; Reader 1991: Chapters 3 and 14.

6. The English 'shrine' is reserved for Shinto edifices (*miya, omiya,* or *jinja/ jingu* in Japanese), the English 'temple' for Buddhist ones (*dera/otera* or *ji* in Japanese).

7. Alternative names for the the *dankadera* are *ekôdera/ekôin* ('transfer of merit' temple), the term *ekô* referring both to funerals in general and to an essential part of all liturgies; the *shinjadera* are also sometimes called *kitôdera/kigandera,* meaning 'prayer temple'.

8. Reader 1991: 180; Reader and Tanabe 1998: 198.

9. See Lafleur 1992 and Hardacre 1997. I speculate that the refusal of many Buddhist priests to perform such worship of Jizo, reported by Hardacre (1997: 16–17), may in some cases be connected to a general reluctance to have anything to do with death rituals.

10. According to Waley (1984: 238), Hachiman was considered 'an avatar of the Buddha Amida'. Others identified him with Maitreya (see above, p. 332).

11. For further details, see Gellner 1991b, 1992a: 167–79, and on Newar Buddhist monasteries in general, Chapter 6 above.

12. But see above, p. 149ff, for the *bahi* class of monastery in which death purifications are obligatory.

13. The only exception here is that boys from lay castes are not entitled to monastic initiation.

References

Abu-Lughod, L., 1991. 'Writing Against Culture' in R.G. Fox (ed.), *Recapturing Anthropology*, Santa Fe: School of American Research Press.

Acharya, B.K., 1994. 'Nature Cure and Indigenous Healing Practices in Nepal: A Medical Anthropological Perspective' in M. Allen (ed.), *Anthropology of Nepal: People, Problems and Processes*, Kathmandu: Mandala Book Point.

Acharya, M. and L. Bennett, 1981. *Rural Women of Nepal: An Aggregate Analysis and Summary of 8 Village Studies* (The Status of Women in Nepal, 2: Field Studies), Kathmandu: CEDA, Tribhuvan University.

Adams, V., 1996. *Tigers of the Snow and other Virtual Sherpas: An Ethnography of Himalayan Encounters*, Princeton: Princeton University Press..

———, 1998. *Doctors for Democracy: Health Professionals in the Nepal Revolution*, Cambridge: Cambridge University Press.

Allen, M.R., 1973. 'Buddhism without Monks: the Vajrayana Religion of the Newars of the Kathmandu Valley', *South Asia* 2: 1–14.

———, 1975. *The Cult of Kumari: Virgin Worship in Nepal*, Kathmandu: INAS, Tribhuvan University (Reissued 1987 by M.L. Maharjan, Kathmandu).

———, 1982. 'Girls' Pre-Puberty Rites among the Newars of the Kathmandu Valley' in M.R. Allen and S.N. Mukherjee (eds), *Women in India and Nepal*, Canberra: Australian National University. (Included as Chapter 5 of 1987 reprint of Allen 1975.)

Allen, N.J., 1986. 'The Coming of Macchendranath to Nepal: Comments from a Comparative Point of View' in N.J. Allen *et al.* (eds), *Oxford University Papers on India* (Vol. I.1), Delhi: Oxford University Press.

———, 1987. 'Thulung Weddings: The Hinduisation of a Ritual Cycle in East Nepal', *L'Ethnographie* 83: 15–33.

Amarasingham, L., 1980. 'Movement among Healers in Sri Lanka: A Case Study of a Sinhalese Patient', *Culture, Medicine, and Psychiatry* 4: 71–92.

Ames, M.M., 1964a. 'Magical Animism and Buddhism: A Structural Analysis of the Sinhalese Religious System' in E.B. Harper (ed.), *Religion in South Asia*, Seattle: University of Washington Press.

———, 1964b. 'Buddha and the Dancing Goblins: A Theory of Magic and Religion', *American Anthropologist* 66 (1): 75–82.

———, 1966. 'Ritual Prestations and the Structure of the Sinhalese Pantheon' in M. Nash (ed.), *Anthropological Studies in Theravada Buddhism*, New Haven: Yale University Press.

Appadurai, A., 1986. 'Is Homo Hierarchicus?', *American Ethnologist* 13: 745–61.

Ardener, E., 1987. 'Remote Areas: Some Theoretical Considerations' in A. Jackson (ed.), *Anthropology at Home*, London: Tavistock.

Aryal, P.K., 1983. *Use of Traditional Medical Practitioners in the Field of Family Health/Family Planning, Vol. III: Janakpur*, Tribhuvan University, Kirtipur: CNAS.

Asad, T., 1983. 'Anthropological Conceptions of Religion: Reflections on Geertz', *Man* (n.s.) 18: 237–59.

Atkinson, J.M., 1992. 'Shamanisms Today', *Annual Review of Anthropology* 21: 307–30.

Aziz, B.N., 1978. *Tibetan Frontier Families: Reflections on Three Generations from D'ing-ri*, Delhi: Vikas.

Bajracharya, M.B., 1987. *The Ayurvedic Records of Cancer Treatment*, Mahabouddha, Kathmandu: Piyushavarshi Ausadhalaya.

Bajracharya, P.H., 1959. 'Newar Marriage Customs and Festivals', *Southwestern Journal of Anthropology* 15: 418–28.

Banks, M., 1992. *Organizing Jainism in India and England*, Oxford: Clarendon Press.

———, 1996. *Ethnicity: Anthropological Constuctions*, London: Routledge.

Barnes, R.H., D. de Coppet, and R.J. Parkin 1985. *Contexts and Levels: Anthropological Essays on Hierarchy*, Oxford: JASO.

Barré, V., P. Berger, L. Feveile, and G. Toffin, 1981. *Panauti: Une Ville au Népal* (Collection Architectures), Paris: Berger-Levrault.

Basham, A.L., 1967. *The Wonder That was India*, London: Sidgwick & Jackson.

———, 1976. 'The Practice of Medicine in Ancient and Medieval India' in C. Leslie (ed.) *Asian Medical Systems*.

Bayly, C.R., 1983. *Rulers, Townsmen and Bazaars: North Indian Society in the Age of British Expansion, 1770–1870*, Cambridge: Cambridge University Press.

Beals, A.R., 1976. 'Strategies of Resort to Curers in South India' in C. Leslie (ed.).

Beatty, A., 1996. 'Adam and Eve and Vishnu: Syncretism in the Javanese Slametan', *Journal of the Royal Anthropological Institute* (n.s.) 2: 271–88.

Bechert, H., (ed.) 1978. *Buddhism in Ceylon and Studies on Religious Syncretism in Buddhist Countries*, Gottingen: Vandenhoeck & Ruprecht.

Becker-Ritterspach, A., 1982. 'Gestaltungsprinzipien der newarischen Architektur: Beitrag zur Konstruktion und Formgebung', Ph.D. Berlin University.

Bell, C., 1992. *Ritual Theory, Ritual Practice*, New York: Oxford University Press.

Bennett, L., with Sh. Singh 1979. *Tradition and Change in the Legal Status of Nepalese Women* (The Status of Women in Nepal, 1.2), Kathmandu: CEDA, Tribhuvan University.

Bennett, L., 1983. *Dangerous Wives and Sacred Sisters: Social and Symbolic Roles of High-Caste Women in Nepal*, New York: Columbia University Press.

Berg, G.A., 1986. Review of Bloch 1986, *Current Anthropology* 27: 353.

Bharati, A., 1970. 'The Use of "Superstition" as an Anti-Traditional Device in Urban Hinduism', *Contributions to Indian Sociology* (n.s.) 4: 36–49.

Bhujel, B.B., 1997. 'The Plot of Medium Gita under Cover of Exorcising a Witch' (*Boksī jhārne nihūmā dhāminī gītāko cartikalā*), *Satyakathā* 3 (21): 5–24.

Bloch, M., 1971. *Placing the Dead: Tombs, Ancestral Villages and Kinship Organisation in Madagascar*, London: Seminar.

———, 1977. 'The Past and the Present in the Present', *Man* (n.s.) 12: 278–92.

———, 1983. *Marxism and Anthroplogy: The History of a Relationship*, Oxford: Clarendon.

———, 1986. *From Blessing to Violence: History and Ideology in the Circumcision Ritual of the Merina of Madagascar*, Cambridge: Cambridge University Press.

———, 1989. *Ritual, History and Power: Selected Papers in Anthropology*, London: Athlone Press.

———, 1992. *Prey into Hunter: The Politics of Religious Experience*, Cambridge: Cambridge University Press.

Blustain, H., 1976. 'Levels of Medicine in a central Nepali Village', *Contributions to Nepalese Studies* 3: 83–105.

Boholm, A. (ed.), 1996. *Political Ritual*, Göteborg: Institute for Advanced Studies in Social Anthropology.

Boyer, P., 1994. *The Naturalness of Religious Ideas: A Cognitive Theory of Religion*, Berkeley: University of California Press.

Brinkhaus, H., 1987. *Jagatprakāśamallas Mūladevaśāśidevavyākhyāna-nāṭaka: Das älteste bekannte vollstandig überlieferte Newari-Drama*, Stuttgart: Franz Steiner.

Brown, T.L., 1996. *The Challenge to Democracy in Nepal: A Political History*, London: Routledge.

Brubaker, R., 1984. *The Limits of Rationality: An Essay on the Social and Moral Thought of Max Weber*, London: George Allen & Unwin.

Bunnag, J., 1973. *Buddhist Monk, Buddhist Layman: A Study of Urban Monastic Organization in Central Thailand*, Cambridge: Cambridge University Press.

Burghart, R., 1984. 'The Formation of the Concept of Nation-State in Nepal', *Journal of Asian Studies* 44: 101–25 (Reissued as Chapter 8 in Burghart 1996).

———, 1985. 'Introduction: Theoretical Appoaches in the Anthropology of South Asia' in R. Burghart and A. Cantlie (eds), *Indian Religion*, London: Curzon Press.

———, 1996. *The Conditions of Listening: Essays on Religion, History and Politics in South Asia*, C.J. Fuller and J. Spencer (eds), Delhi: Oxford University Press.

Burleigh, P., 1976. 'A Chronology of the later Kings of Patan', *Kailash* 4 (1): 21–71.

Buss, A.E., 1985. *Max Weber and Asia: Contributions to the Sociology of Development*, München: Weltforum Verlag.

Caplan, L., 1970. *Land and Social Change in East Nepal: A Study of Hindu-Tribal Relations*, London: Routledge & Kegan Paul.

Carrier, J. (ed.), 1995. *Occidentalism: Images of the West*, Oxford: Clarendon Press.

Carrithers, M., 1979. 'The Modern Ascetics of Lanka and the Pattern of Change in Buddhism', *Man* (n.s.) 14: 294–310.

———, 1983. *The Forest Monks of Sri Lanka: An Anthropological and Historical Study*, New Delhi: Oxford University Press.

———, 1984. '"They will be Lords upon the Island": Buddhism in Sri Lanka' in H. Bechert and R.F. Gombrich (eds), *The World of Buddhism*, London: Thames & Hudson.

———, 1987. 'Buddhists without History', *Contributions to Indian Sociology* (n.s.) 21(1): 165–8.

———, 1990. 'Jainism and Buddhism as Enduring Historical Streams', *Journal of the Anthropological Society of Oxford* 21(2): 141–63.

———, 1992. *Why Humans have Cultures: Explaining Anthropology and Social Diversity*, Oxford: Oxford University Press.

Carrithers, M. and C. Humphrey (eds), 1991. *The Assembly of Listeners: Jains in Society*, Cambridge: Cambridge University Press.

Carstairs, G.M., 1983. *Death of a Witch: A Village in North India 1950–81*, London: Hutchinson.

Carstairs, G.M., and R.L. Kapur, 1976. *The Great Universe of Kota: Stress, Change and Disorder in an Indian Village*, London: Hogarth Press.

Chapman, M., 1978. *The Gaelic Vision in Scottish Culture*, London: Croom Helm.

Charsley, S., 1996. '"Untouchable": What is in a name?', *Journal of the Royal Anthropological Institute* (n.s.) 2: 1–23.

Christian, W.A., 1989 [1972]. *Person and God in a Spanish Valley*, New Jersey: Princeton University Press.

Clarke, G.E., 1980. 'Lama and Tamang in Yolmo' in M. Aris and Aung San Suu Kyi (eds), *Tibetan Studies in Honour of Hugh Richardson*, Warminster: Aris and Phillips.

———, 1983. 'The Great and Little Traditions in the study of Yolmo, Nepal' in E. Steinkellner and H. Tauscher (eds), *Contributions on Tibetan Language, History and Culture*, Vienna: Arbeitskreis für Tibetische und Buddhistische Studien, Universität Wien.

Cobbi, J., 1995. '*Sonaemono*: Ritual Gifts to the Gods' in J. van Bremen and D.P. Martinez (eds), *Ceremony and Ritual in Japan: Religious Practices in an Industrialized Society*, London: Routledge.

Collins, R., 1986. *Weberian Sociological Theory*, Cambridge: Cambridge University Press.

Collins, S., 1982. *Selfless Persons: Imagery and Thought in Theravada Buddhism*, Cambridge: Cambridge University Press.

———, 1989. 'Louis Dumont and the Study of Religions', *Religious Studies Review* 15(1): 14-20.

Conrad, D., 1986. 'Max Weber's Conception of Hindu Dharma as a Paradigm' in D. Kantowsky (ed.).

Coon, E., 1989. 'Possessing Power: Ajima and her Medium', *Himalayan Research Bulletin* 9(1): 1-9.

Crapanzano, V., 1986. 'Hermes' Dilemma: The Masking of Subversion in Ethnographic Description' in J. Clifford and G.E. Marcus (eds), *Writing Culture: The Poetics and Politics of Ethnography*, Berkeley: University of California Press.

Crooke, W., 1978 [1894]. *The Popular Religion and Folklore of Northern India*, Delhi: Munshiram Manoharlal.

Dahal, D.R., 1979. 'Tribalism as an Incongruous Concept in Modern Nepal' in M. Gaborieau and A. Thorner (eds), *Asie du Sud: Traditions et Changements*. Paris: CNRS.

Das, V., 1982. *Structure and Cognition: Aspects of Hindu Caste and Ritual*, Delhi: Oxford University Press.

Dasgupta, S.B., 1974 [1958]. *An Introduction to Tantric Buddhism*, Berkeley and London: Shambala.

Davis, R., 1984. *Muang Metaphysics: A Study of Northern Thai Myth and Ritual*, Bangkok: Pandora.

De Jong, J.W. 1979. *Buddhist Studies*, G. Schopen (ed.), Berkeley: Asian Humanities Press.

de Sales, A. 1991. *Je Suis Né de Vos Jeux de Tambours: La Religion Chamanique des Magar du Nord*, Nanterre: Société d'Ethnologie.

Deliège, R., 1988. *Les Paraiyars du Tamil Nadu*, Nettetal: Steyler Verlag.

———, 1992. 'Replication and Consensus: Untouchability, Caste and Ideology in India', *Man* (n.s.) 27: 155–73.

———, 1993. 'The Myths of Origin of the Indian Untouchables', *Man* (n.s.) 28: 533–49.

Desjarlais, R.R. 1992. *Body and Emotion: The Aesthetics of Illness and Healing in the Nepal Himalaya*, Philadelphia: University of Pennsylvania Press.

Devkota, P.L., 1983. *Use of Traditional Medical Practitioners in the Field of Family Health/Family Planning, Vol. III: Kirtipur*, Tribhuvan University, Kirtipur: CNAS.

———, 1984. 'Illness Interpretation and Modes of Treatment in Kirtipur', *Contributions to Nepalese Studies* 11(2): 11–20.

Dharmacharyya, Dharma Aditya, 1928. 'Buddhism in Nepal', *Buddhist India* 2(3): 209–16.

Dhungel, B., 1994. 'The Qualitative Community Judgement: The Role of Intermediate Health Practitioners in Nepal's Family Health Services' in M. Allen (ed.), *Anthropology of Nepal: People, Problems and Processes*, Kathmandu: Mandala Book Point.

Dirks, N., 1987. *The Hollow Crown: Ethnohistory of an Indian Kingdom*, Cambridge: Cambridge University Press.

Doherty, V.S., 1974. 'The Organizing Principles of Brahmin-Chetri Kinship', *Contributions to Nepalese Studies* 1: 25–41.

Dougherty, L.M., 1986. 'Sita and the Goddess: A Case Study of a Woman Healer in Nepal', *Contributions to Nepalese Studies* 14: 25–36.

Droogers, A., 1989. 'Syncretism: The Problem of Definition, the Definition of the Problem' in J. Gort, H. Vroom, R. Kernhout, and A. Wessels (eds), *Dialogue and Syncretism: An Interdisciplinary Approach*, Grand Rapids: William B. Erdmans; Amsterdam: Rodopi.

Duff-Cooper, A., 1991. '*Oku* in Aspects of Japanese Ideology' in A. Duff-Cooper, *Three Essays on Japanese Ideology*, Tokyo: Seitoku University, Dept of Humanities.

Dumont, L., 1957. 'For a Sociology of India', *Contributions to Indian Sociology* 1: 7–22.

———, 1960. 'World Renunciation in Indian Religion', *Contributions to Indian Sociology* 4: 33–62. Reprinted in L. Dumont, *Religion, Politics and History in India*, 1970, Paris/The Hague: Mouton, and in Dumont (1980).

———, 1964. 'Marriage in India: The Present State of the Question: Postscript to Part 1: Nayar and Newar', *Contributions to Indian Sociology* 7: 77–98.

———, 1977. *From Mandeville to Marx: The Genesis and Triumph of Economic Ideology*, Chicago: Chicago University Press.

———, 1980. *Homo Hierarchicus: The Caste System and its Implications*, tr. M. Sainsbury, L. Dumont, and B. Gulati, Chicago: Chicago University Press (First published in French 1966, first English translation 1970).

Dumont, L., and D. Pocock 1959a. 'Pure and Impure', *Contributions to Indian Sociology* 3: 9–39.

———, 1959b. 'On the Different Aspects or Levels in Hinduism', *Contributions to Indian Sociology* 3: 40–54.

———, 1959c. 'Possession and Priesthood', *Contributions to Indian Sociology* 3: 55–74.

Durkin-Longley, M.S., 1982. 'Ayurveda in Nepal: A Medical Belief System in Action', Ph.D., Madison University. University Microfilms Int. 8224034.

Durkin [Durkin-Longley], M. 1988. 'Ayurvedic Treatment for Jaundice in Nepal', *Social Science and Medicine* 27(5): 491–5.

Elvin, M., 1973. *The Pattern of the Chinese Past*, London: Eyre Methuen.

———, 1984. 'Why China Failed to Create an Endogenous Industrial Capitalism: A Critique of Max Weber's Explanation', *Theory and Society* 13: 379–92.

Evans-Pritchard, E.E., 1977 [1965]. *Theories of Primitive Religion*, Oxford: Clarendon Press.

Evers, H.-D., 1967. 'Kinship and Property Rights in a Buddhist Monastery in Central Ceylon', *American Anthropologist* 69: 703–10.

———, 1972. *Monks, Priests and Peasants: A Study of Buddhism and Social Structure in Central Ceylon*, Leiden: E.J. Brill.

Fallers, L.A., 1965. *Bantu Bureaucracy: A Study of Conflict and Change in the Political Institutions of an East African People*, Chicago: Chicago University Press.

———, 1973. *Inequality: Social Stratification Reconsidered*, Chicago: Chicago University Press.

Fardon, R., (ed.), 1985. *Localizing Strategies: Regional Traditions of Ethnographic Writing*, Washington: Smithsonian Press.

Fisher, J.F., 1978. 'Homo Hierarchicus Nepalensis: A Cultural Subspecies' in J.F. Fisher (ed.), *Himalayan Anthropology: The Indo-Tibetan Interface*, The Hague: Mouton.

Fitzgerald, T., 1990. 'Hinduism and the "World Religion" Fallacy', *Religion* 20: 101–18.

————, 1996. 'From Structure to Substance: Ambedkar, Dumont and Orientalism', *Contributions to Indian Sociology* (n.s.) 30(2): 273–88.

————, 1997. 'Ambedkar Buddhism in Maharashtra', *Contributions to Indian Sociology* (n.s.) 31(2): 225–51.

Frauwallner, E., 1956. *The Earliest Vinaya and the Beginnings of Buddhist Literature* (Serie Orientale Roma 8), Rome: ISMEO.

Frykenberg, R.E., 1991. 'The Emergence of the modern "Hinduism" as a Concept and as an Institution' in G.D. Sontheimer and H. Kulke (eds), *Hinduism Reconsidered*, Delhi: Manohar.

Fuller, C.J., 1976. *The Nayars Today*, Cambridge: Cambridge University Press.

————, 1977. 'British India or Traditional India? An Anthropological Problem', *Ethnos* 42(3–4): 95–121.

————, 1979. 'Gods, Priests and Purity: On the Relation between Hinduism and the Caste System', *Man* (n.s.) 14: 459–76.

————, 1984. *Servants of the Goddess: The Priests of a South Indian Temple*, Cambridge: Cambridge University Press.

————, 1985. 'Initiation and Consecration: Priestly Rituals in a South Indian Temple' in R. Burghart and A. Cantlie (eds), *Indian Religion*, London: Curzon Press.

————, 1992. *The Camphor Flame: Popular Hinduism and Society in India*, Princeton: Princeton University Press.

Fürer-Haimendorf, C. von., 1956. 'Elements of Newar Social Structure', *Journal of the Royal Anthropological Institute* 86: 15–38.

————, 1964. *The Sherpas of Nepal: Buddhist Highlanders*, London: John Murray.

Gaborieau, M., 1972. 'Muslims in the Hindu Kingdom of Nepal', *Contributions to Indian Sociology* (n.s.) 6: 84–105.

————, 1978. *Le Nepal et ses Populations* (Editions Complexes), Paris: Presses Universitaires de France.

————, 1982. 'Les Rapports de Classe dans l'Idéologie Officielle du Népal', *Puruṣārtha* 6: 251–90.

————, 1985. 'From Al-Beruni to Jinnah: Idiom, Ritual and Ideology of the Hindu-Muslim Confrontation in South Asia', *Anthropology Today* 3: 7–14.

————, 1993. *Ni Brahmanes ni Ancêtres: Colporteurs Musulmans du Népal*, Nanterre: Société d'Ethnolgie.

————, 1996. 'Le Grand Dilemme des Musulmans: Comment Participer au Pouvoir sans le Sacraliser?' in G. Krauskopff and M. Lecomte-Tilouine (eds), *Célébrer le Pouvoir: Dasai, Une Fête Royale au Népal*, Paris: CNRS.

Gallie, W.B., 1964. *Philosophy and the Historical Understanding*, London: Chatto and Windus.

Geertz, C., 1968. *Islam Observed*, New Haven: Yale University Press.

———, 1973. *The Interpretation of Cultures: Selected Essays*, New York: Basic Books.

———, 1982. *Negara: The Theatre State in Nineteenth-Century Bali*, Princeton: Princeton University Press.

Gellner, D.N., 1984. 'Yala Deyā Hiraṇyavarṇa Mahāvihāryā nā danācwāgu Prajñāpāramitā bāre' (in Newari), *Nhasalā* 14: 37–42. (NS 1104.)

———, 1986. 'Language, Caste, Religion and Territory: Newar Identity Ancient and Modern', *European Journal of Sociology* 26: 102–48.

———, 1987. 'The Newar Buddhist Monastery: An Anthropological and Historical Typology' in N. Gutschow and A. Michaels (eds), *Heritage of the Kathmandu Valley* (Nepalica 4), Sankt Augustin: VGH Wissenschaftsverlag (Shortened version reprinted as chapter 6 in this book).

———, 1988. 'Monastic Initiation in Newar Buddhism' in R.F. Gombrich (ed.), *Indian Ritual and its Exegesis*, Delhi: Oxford University Press.

———, 1989. 'Buddhist Monks or Kinsmen of the Buddha? Reflections on the Titles Traditionally Used by Sakyas in the Kathmandu Valley', *Kailash* 15 (1–2): 5–25.

———, 1991a. 'Ritualized Devotion, Altruism, and Meditation: The Offering of the *guru mandala* in Newar Buddhism', *Indo–Iranian Journal* 34: 161–97.

———, 1991b. 'A Newar Buddhist Liturgy: Sravakayanist Ritual in Kwa Bahah, Lalitpur, Nepal', *Journal of the International Association of Buddhist Studies* 14: 236–52.

———, 1992a. *Monk, Householder, and Tantric Priest: Newar Buddhism and its Hierarchy of Ritual*, Cambridge: Cambridge University Press.

———, 1992b. Review of Levy's *Mesocosm*, *Man* (n.s.) 27: 677–8.

———, 1995a. 'Introduction' in D.N. Gellner and D. Quigley (eds). 1995.

———, 1995b. 'From Holy Order to Quasi-Ethnic Group: Sakyas and Vajracaryas' in D.N. Gellner and D. Quigley (eds). 1995.

———, 1995c. 'Low Castes in Lalitpur' in D.N. Gellner and D. Quigley (eds). 1995.

———, 1996. 'A Sketch of the History of Lalitpur (Patan) with Special Reference to Buddhism', *Contributions to Nepalese Studies* 23(1): 125–57.

———, 1997a. 'Caste, Communalism, and Communism: Newars and the Nepalese State' in D.N. Gellner *et al.* (eds). 1997.

———, 1997b. 'The Consecration of a Vajra Master in Newar Buddhism' in S. Karmay and P. Sagant (eds), *Les Habitants du Toît du Monde* (Festschrift for A.W. Macdonald), Nanterre: Société d'Ethnologie.

———, 1999. 'From Cultural Hierarchies to a Hierarchy of Multiculturalisms: The Case of the Newars of Nepal' in SPF (ed.), *Multiculturalism: Modes of Coexistence in South and Southeast Asia*, Washington: Sasakawa Peace Foundation USA.

———, forthcoming. 'From Group Rights to Individual Rights and Back:

Nepalese Struggles over Culture and Equality' in J. Cowan, M.-B. Dembour, and R. Wilson (eds), *Culture and Rights: Anthropological Perspectives*, Cambridge: Cambridge University Press.

Gellner, and D. Quigley (eds), 1995. *Contested Hierarchies: A Collaborative Ethnography of Caste among the Newars of the Kathmandu Valley, Nepal*, Oxford: Clarendon Press (Pbk., Delhi: Oxford University Press, 1999).

Gellner, D.N., J. Pfaff-Czarnecka, and J. Whelpton (eds), 1997. *Nationalism and Ethnicity in a Hindu Kingdom: The Politics of Culture in Contemporary Nepal*, Amsterdam: Harwood.

Ghosh, P., 1994. 'Some Problems with Talcott Parsons' Version of "The Protestant Ethic"', *European Journal of Sociology* 35: 104–23.

Giddens, A., 1976. 'Introduction' in Weber 1976.

Gilbert, K., 1992. 'Women and Family Law in Modern Nepal: Statutory Rights and Social Implications', *New York Journal of International Law and Politics* 24: 729–58.

Giles, L.L., 1987. 'Possession Cults on the Swahili Coast: A Re-examination of Theories of Marginality', *Africa* 57(2): 234–58.

Gold, A. Grodzins 1988. 'Spirit Possession Perceived and Performed in Rural Rajasthan', *Contributions to Indian Sociology* (n.s.) 22(1): 35–63.

Golzio, K., 1984. 'Zur Verwendung indologischer Literatur in Max Webers Studie über Hinduismus und Buddhismus' in W. Schluchter (ed.).

Gombrich, R.F., 1971. *Precept and Practice: Traditional Buddhism in the Rural Highlands of Ceylon*, Oxford: Oxford University Press (1991 reissue as *Buddhist Precept and Practice*, Delhi: Motilal Banarsidass).

———, 1972. 'Buddhism and Society' (Review of Spiro [1970] 1982), *Modern Asian Studies* 6(4): 483–96.

———, 1974. 'The Duty of a Buddhist according to the Pali Scriptures' in W.D. O'Flaherty and J.D.M. Derrett (eds), *The Concept of Duty in South Asia*, Delhi: Vikas/SOAS.

———, 1983. 'From Monastery to Meditation Centre: Lay Meditation in Modern Sri Lanka' in P. Denwood and A. Piatigorsky (eds), *Buddhist Studies: Ancient and Modern* (SOAS Papers on South Asia 4), London: SOAS.

———, 1988. *Theravada Buddhism: A Social History from ancient Benares to Modern Colombo*, London and New York: Routledge & Kegan Paul.

———, 1994. 'A Buddhologist's Impression of Japanese Buddhism' in P. Clarke and U. Somers (eds), *Japanese New Religions in the West*, Folkstone: Japan Library/Curzon Press.

Gombrich, R.F. and G. Obeyesekere 1988. *Buddhism Transformed: Religious Change in Sri Lanka*, Princeton: Princeton University Press.

Good, A., 1982. 'The Female Bridegroom: Rituals of Puberty and Marriage in South India and Sri Lanka', *Social Analysis* 11: 35–55.

Goudriaan, T., 1979. 'Introduction: History and Philosophy' in *Hindu Tantrism* (Handbuch der Orientalistik 4.2), Leiden: E.J. Brill.

Grandin, I., 1989. *Music and Media in Local Life: Music Practice in a Newar Neighbourhood in Nepal*, Linkoping University.

Grapard, A.G., 1984. 'Japan's Ignored Cultural Revolution: The Separation of Shinto and Buddhist Divinities in Meiji (*shimbutsu bunri*) and a Case Study: Tonomine', *History of Religions* 23: 240–65.

———, 1992. *The Protocol of the Gods: A Study of the Kasuga Cult in Japanese History*, Berkeley: University of California Press.

Greenwold, S.M., 1974a. 'Buddhist Brahmans', *European Journal of Sociology* 15: 101–23; reprinted as 'The Role of the Priest in Newar Society' in J.F. Fisher (ed.), *Himalayan Anthropology: The Indo–Tibetan Interface*, The Hague: Mouton, 1978.

———, 1974b. 'Monkhood versus Priesthood in Newar Buddhism' in C. von Fürer-Haimendorf (ed.), *The Anthropology of Nepal*, Warminster: Aris and Phillips.

———, 1975. 'Kingship and Caste', *European Journal of Sociology* 16: 49–75.

Greve, R., 1989. 'The Shaman and the Witch: An Analytic Approach to Shamanic Poetry in the Himalayas' in M. Hoppal and O. von Sadovszky (eds), *Shamanism, Past and Present*, Budapest: Ethnographic Institute, Hungarian Academy of Sciences; Los Angeles/Fullerton: International Society of Trans-Oceanic Research, 2 vols.

Gupta, S., 1979. 'Modes of Worship and Meditation' in *Hindu Tantrism* (Handbuch der Orientalistik 4.2), Leiden: E.J. Brill.

Gupta, S. and R.F. Gombrich, 1986. 'Kings, Power and the Goddess', *South Asia Research* 2(2): 123–38.

Gurung, H., 1981. 'Population Change in Nepal (1971–81)', *The Himalayan Review* 8: 1–22.

———, 1992a. 'Ethnic/Caste Composition of Nepalese Population', *Spotlight* 10(10): 12–13.

———, 1992b. 'Representing an Ethnic Mosaic', *Himal* 5(3): 19–21.

Gutschow, N., 1982. *Stadtraum und Ritual der Newarischen Städte im Kathmandu-Tal: Eine Architektur-anthropologische Untersuchung*, Stuttgart: Kohlhammer.

———, 1997. *The Nepalese Caitya: 1500 Years of Buddhist Votive Architecture in the Kathmandu Valley*, Stuttgart: Axel Menges.

Gutschow, N. and M.V. Bajracharya, 1977. 'Ritual as a Mediator of Space in Kathmandu', *Journal of the Nepal Research Centre* 1: 1–10.

Gutschow, N. and B. Kölver 1975. *Ordered Space, Concepts and Functions in a Town in Nepal*, Wiesbaden: Franz Steiner.

Hall, J., 1985. 'Capstones and Organisms: Political Forms and the Triumph of Capitalism', *Sociology* 19: 173-92.

Hamilton, F., 1971 [1819]. *An Account of the Kingdom of Nepal* (Biblioteca Himalayica 10), Delhi: Manjusri Publishing House

Hardacre, H., 1986. *Kurozumikyô and the New Religions of Japan*, Princeton: Princeton University Press.

———, 1989. *Shinto and the State, 1868–1988*, Princeton: Princeton University Press.

———, 1997. *Marketing the Menacing Fetus in Japan*, Berkeley: University of California Press.

Harper, E.B., 1957. 'Shamanism in South India', *Southwestern Journal of Anthropology* 13: 267–87.

Harrison, S., 1995. 'Four Types of Symbolic Conflict', *Journal of the Royal Anthropological Institute* (n.s.) 1: 255–72.

Hasrat, B.J., 1970. *History of Nepal as told by its own and Contemporary Chroniclers*, Hoshiarpur: V.V. Research Institute.

Heesterman, J.C., 1964. 'Brahmin, Ritual, and Renouncer', *Wiener Zeitschrift für die Kunde Süd- und Ostasiens* 8: 1–31. Reprinted in Heesterman 1985 *The Inner Conflict of Tradition: Essays in Indian Ritual, Kingship, and Society*, Chicago: Chicago University Press; Delhi: Oxford University Press.

———, 1971. 'Priesthood and the Brahmin', *Contributions to Indian Sociology* (n.s.) 5: 43–47.

———, 1974 'Veda and Dharma' in W.D. O'Flaherty and J.D.M. Derrett (eds), *The Concept of Duty in South Asia*, Delhi: Vikas/SOAS.

Hefner, R.W., 1993. 'World Building and the Rationality of Conversion' in R.W. Hefner (ed.), *Conversion to Christianity: Historical and Anthropological Perspectives on a Great Transformation*, Berkeley: University of California Press.

Heinemann, R., 1984. 'This World and the Other Power: Contrasting Paths to Deliverance in Japan' in H. Bechert and R.F. Gombrich (eds), *The World of Buddhism*, London: Thames and Hudson.

Hendry, J., 1981. *Marriage in Changing Japan*, London: Croom Helm.

———, 1995. *Understanding Japanese Society*, London: Routledge (2nd edn).

Henry, E.O., 1981. 'A North Indian Healer and the Sources of his Power' in G.R. Gupta (ed.), *The Social and Cultural Context of Medicine in India*, Delhi: Vikas.

Herbert, J., 1967. *Shinto: The Fountain-Head of Japan*, London: George Allen & Unwin.

Hitchcock, J. and R.L. Jones (eds), 1976. *Spirit Possession in the Nepal Himalayas*, Warminster: Aris and Phillips.

Hocart, A.M., 1950. *Caste: A Comparative Study*, London: Methuen.

Hodgson, B.H., 1834. 'On the Law and Legal Practice of Népal as regards familiar intercourse between a Hindú and an Outcaste', *Journal of the Royal Asiatic Society* 1: 45–56.

———, 1836. 'On the Administration of Justice in Nepal', *Asiatick Researches* 20: 94–134 [see also Stiller 1984].

———, 1880. *Miscellaneous Essays relating to Indian Subjects* (2 vols), London: Trübner & Co.

———, 1972 [1874]. *Essays on the Languages, Literature and Religion of Nepal and Tibet*, Delhi: Manjusri Publishing House.

Höfer, A., 1974. 'A Note on Possession in South Asia' in C. von Fürer-Haimendorf (ed.), *The Anthropology of Nepal*, Warminster: Aris and Phillips.

———, 1979a. *The Caste Hierarchy and the State in Nepal: A Study of the Muluki Ain of 1854* (Khumbu Himal 13(2): 25–240), Innsbruck: Universitätsverlag Wagner.

————, 1979b. 'On Re-reading *Le Népal*: What we Social Scientists owe to Sylvain Lévi', *Kailash* 7 (3–4): 175-90.

Höfer, A., and B.P. Shrestha, 1973. 'Ghost Exorcism among the Brahmans of Central Nepal', *Central Asiatic Journal* 17: 51–77.

Holmberg, D., 1983. 'Shamanic Soundings: Femaleness in Tamang Ritual Structure', *Signs* 9(1): 40–58.

————, 1989. *Order in Paradox: Myth, Ritual, and Exchange among Nepal's Tamang*, Ithaca and London: Cornell University Press.

Holton, R.J. and B.S. Turner, 1989. *Max Weber on Economy and Society*, London: Routledge.

Houtman, G., 1990. 'How a Foreigner Invented "Buddhendom" in Burmese: From *tha-tha-na* to *bok-da' ba-tha*', *Journal of the Anthropological Society of Oxford* 21(2): 113–28.

Humphrey, C., 1984. 'Some Aspects of the Jain *Puja*: The Idea of "God" and the Symbolism of Offerings', *Cambridge Anthropology* 9(3): 1–19.

Humphrey, C. and J. Laidlaw, 1994. *The Archetypal Actions of Ritual: A Theory of Ritual Illustrated by the Jain Rite of Worship*, Oxford: Clarendon Press.

Inden, R., 1986. 'Orientalist Constructions of India' *Modern Asian Studies* 20(3): 401–46.

————, 1990. *Imagining India*, Oxford: Blackwell.

Ingold, T., 1996. *Key Debates in Anthropology*, London: Routledge.

Ishii, H., 1980. 'Recent Economic Changes in a Newar Village', *Contributions to Nepalese Studies* 8: 157–80.

————, 1987. 'Social Change in a Newar Village' in N. Gutschow and A. Michaels (eds), *The Heritage of the Kathmandu Valley* (Nepalica 4), Sankt Augustin: VGH Wissenschaftsverlag.

————, 1995. 'Caste and Kinship in a Newar Village' in N. Gutschow and A. Michaels (eds), *The Heritage of the Kathmandu Valley* (Nepalica 4), Sankt Augustin: VGH Wissenschaftsverlag.

Ishi, Y., 1986. *Sangha, State, and Society: Thai Buddhism in History*, tr. P. Hawkes, Honolulu: University of Hawaii Press.

Jackson, M., 1989. *Paths towards a Clearing: Radical Empiricism and Ethnographic Enquiry*, Bloomington: Indiana University Press.

Jaini, P., 1979. *The Jaina Path of Purification*, Berkeley: University of California Press.

James, W. and D. Johnson (eds), 1988. *Vernacular Christianity: Essays in the Social Anthropology of Religion*, Oxford: JASO.

Jaspers, K., 1989. *Karl Jaspers on Max Weber*, tr. R.J. Whelan, New York: Paragon House.

Jones, R.L., 1976. 'Spirit Possession and Society in Nepal' in Hitchcock and Jones (eds). 1976.

Joseph, M.B., 1971. 'The Viharas of the Kathmandu Valley', *Oriental Art* 17 (1): 121–43.

Joshi, B.L. and L. Rose, 1966. *Democratic Innovations in Nepal: A Case Study of Political Acculturation*, Berkeley: University of California Press.

Joshi, S.M. (ed.), 1987. *Bahcādhāgu Newāḥ Khāgwaḥdhukū (A Concise Dictionary of the Newar Language)*, Kathmandu: Lacoul Publications.

Justice, J., 1986. *Policies, Plans, and People: Foreign Aid and Health Development*, Berkeley: University of California Press.

Kakar, S., 1982. *Shamans, Mystics and Doctors: A Psychological Inquiry into India and its Healing Traditions*, Delhi: Oxford University Press.

Kamstra, J.H., 1989. 'The Religion of Japan: Syncretism or Religious Phenomenalism' in J. Gort *et al.* (eds) [see Droogers].

Kantowsky, D., 1982a. 'Die Rezeption der Hinduismus/Buddhismus-Studie Max Webers in Südasien: ein Missverstandnis?', *European Journal of Sociology* 23: 317–55.

———, 1982b. 'Max Weber on India and Indian Interpretations of Weber', *Contributions to Indian Sociology* (n.s.) 16(2): 141–74 [included in Kantowsky (ed.) 1986].

———, 1984. 'Max Weber's Contributions to Indian Sociology', *Contributions to Indian Sociology* (n.s.) 18(2): 307–14 [included in Kantowsky (ed.) 1986].

———, 1985. 'Die Fehlrezeption von Max Webers Studie über "Hinduismus und Buddhismus" in Indien: Ursachen und Folgen', *Zeitschrift für Sociologie* 6(14) [English version in Kantowsky (ed.) 1986].

———, (ed.), 1986. *Recent Research on Max Weber's Studies of Hinduism*. München: Weltforum Verlag.

Kapferer, B., 1991 [1983]. *A Celebration of Demons: Exorcism and the Aesthetics of Healing in Sri Lanka*, Oxford: Berg.

Katz, N., 1982. *Buddhist Images of Human Perfection: The Arahant of the Sutta Pitaka Compared with the Bodhisattva and the Mahasiddha*, Delhi: Motilal Banarsidass.

Kelly, J.D. and M. Kaplan, 1990. 'History, Structure, and Ritual', *Annual Review of Anthropology* 19: 119–50.

Kendall, L., 1989. 'Old Ghosts and Ungrateful Children: A Korean Shaman's Story' in C.S. McClain (ed.), *Women as Healers: Cross-Cultural Perspectives*, New Brunswick and London: Rutgers University Press.

Kertzer, D., 1988. *Ritual, Politics, and Power*, New Haven: Yale University Press.

Ketelaar, J.E., 1990. *Of Heretics and Martyrs in Japan: Buddhism and its Persecution*, Princeton: Princeton University Press.

Kirkpatrick, Colonel, 1975 [1811]. *An Account of the Kingdom of Nepal*, Delhi: Asian Publication Services.

Kleinman, A., 1980. *Patients and Healers in the Context of Culture*, Berkeley: University of California Press.

Kloppenberg, R., 1977. 'Theravada Buddhism in Nepal', *Kailash* 5 (4): 301–21.

Koepping, K.P., 1995. 'Manipulated Identities: Syncretism and Uniqueness of Tradition in modern Japanese Discourse' in C. Stewart and R. Shaw (eds). 1995.

Kölver, B. and H. Sakya, 1985. *Documents from the Rudravarna-Mahavihara*, Sankt Augustin: VGH Wissenschaftsverlag.

Krause, I.-B., 1980. 'Kinship, Hierarchy and Equality in north-western Nepal', *Contributions to Indian Sociology* (n.s.) 14: 169–94.

Krauskopff, G. and M. Lecomte-Tilouine (eds), 1996. *Célébrer le Pouvoir: Dasai, Une Fête Royale au Népal*, Paris: CNRS.

Kulke, H., 1984. 'Orthodoxe Restauration und hinduistische Sektenreligiositat im Werk Max Webers' in W. Schluchter (ed.), 1984.

———, 1986. 'Max Weber's Contribution to the Study of "Hinduization" in India and "Indianization" in Southeast Asia' in D. Kantowsky (ed.), 1986.

Kunwar, R.R., 1989. *Fire of Himal: An Anthropological Study of the Sherpas of the Nepal Himalayan Region*, Jaipur: Nirala.

Kuper, A., 1988. *The Invention of Primitive Society*, London: Routledge & Kegan Paul.

———, 1994. 'Culture, Identity and the Project of a Cosmopolitan Anthropology', *Man* (n.s.) 29: 537–54.

———, 1999. *Culture: The Anthropologists' Account*, Harvard: Harvard University Press.

Lafleur, W.R., 1992, *Liquid Life: Abortion and Buddhism in Japan*, Princeton: Princeton University Press.

Laidlaw, J., 1995. *Riches and Renunciation: Religion, Economy, and Society among the Jains*, Oxford: Clarendon Press.

Lambert, H., 1988. 'Medical Knowledge in Rajasthan: Popular Constructions of Illness and Therapeutic Practice', D.Phil., University of Oxford.

———, 1992. 'The Cultural Logic of Indian Medicine: Prognosis and Etiology in Rajasthani Popular Therapeutics', *Social Science and Medicine* 34(10): 1069–76.

Lamotte, E., 1958. *Histoire du Bouddhisme Indien, des Origines à l'ère Śaka*, Louvain: Institut Orientaliste (English tr. 1988).

Landon, P., 1976 [1928]. *Nepal* (Bibliotheca Himalayica 16), Kathmandu: Ratna Pustak Bhandar.

Lansing, J.S., 1991. *Priests and Programmers: Technologies of Power in the Engineered Landscape of Bali*, Princeton: Princeton University Press.

Leach, E., 1972. 'Pulleyar and the Lord Buddha: An Aspect of Religious Syncretism in Ceylon' in W.A. Lessa and E.Z. Vogt (eds), *Reader in Comparative Religion: An Anthropological Approach* (third edn), New York: Harper & Row.

Lecomte-Tilouine, M. and B.K. Shrestha, 1996. 'Les Rituels Royaux de Dasai à Katmandou: Notes Preliminaires' in Krauskopff and Lecomte-Tilouine (eds), 1996.

Leslie, C. (ed.), 1976. *Asian Medical Systems: A Comparative Study*, Berkeley: University of California Press.

Leslie, J., 1989. *The Perfect Wife: The Orthodox Hindu Woman according to the Stridharmapaddhati of Tryambakayajvan*, Delhi: Oxford University Press.

Lévi, S., 1905. *Le Népal: Étude historique d'un royaume hindou*, 3 vols. Paris: Leroux; reissued 1986, Kathmandu and Paris: Raj de Condappa, Le Toît du Monde, and Éditions Errance.

Levine, N.E., 1982. 'Belief and Explanation in Nyinba Women's Witchcraft', *Man* (n.s.) 17: 259–74.

————, 1987. 'Caste, State, and Ethnic Boundaries in Nepal', *Journal of Asian Studies* 46: 71–88.

Levy, R., 1973. *Tahitians: Mind and Experience in the Society Islands*, Chicago: University of Chicago Press.

Levy, R. with K. Rajopadhyaya, 1990. *Mesocosm: Hinduism and the Organization of a Traditional Hindu City in Nepal*, Berkeley and Los Angeles: University of California Press.

Lewis, I.M., 1966. 'Spirit Possession and Deprivation Cults', *Man* (n.s.) 1: 307-29.

————, 1970. 'A Structural Approach to Witchcraft and Spirit-Possession' in M. Douglas (ed.), *Witchcraft Confessions and Accusations* (ASA 9), London: Tavistock.

————, 1971. *Ecstatic Religion: An Anthropological Study of Spirit Possession and Shamanism*, Harmondsworth: Penguin.

————, 1986. *Religion in Context: Cults and Charisma*, Cambridge: Cambridge University Press.

————, 1989. *Ecstatic Religion* (second, revised edition), London and New York: Routledge.

Lewis, T.T., 1984. 'The Tuladhars of Kathmandu: A Study of Buddhist Tradition in a Newar Merchant Community', Ph.D., Columbia University.

————, 1989. 'Newars and Tibetans in the Kathmandu Valley: Ethnic Boundaries and Religious History', *Journal of Asian and African Studies* 38: 31–57.

————, 1992. Review of Levy's *Mesocosm*, *American Anthropologist* 94 (4): 968–70.

Liechty, M., 1998. 'Consumer Cultures and Identity in Kathmandu: "Playing with your Brain"' in D. Skinner, A. Pach III, and D. Holland (eds), *Selves in Time and Place: Identities, Experience, and History in Nepal*, Lanham: Rowman & Littlefield.

Lienhard, S., 1978. 'Problèmes du Syncrétisme Religieux au Népal', *Bulletin de l'Ecole Française de l'Extrême Orient* 65: 239–70.

————, 1984. 'Nepal: The Survival of Indian Buddhism in a Himalayan Kingdom' in H. Bechert and R.F. Gombrich (eds), *The World of Buddhism*, London: Thames and Hudson.

————, 1996. 'On Some Key Terms in Newar Buddhism' in S. Lienhard (ed.), *Change and Continuity: Studies in the Nepalese Culture of the Kathmandu Valley*, Alessandrio: Edizioni dell'Orso (CESMEO Orientalia VII).

Lincoln, B., 1987. 'Ritual, Rebellion, Resistance: Once more the Swazi Ncwala', *Man* (n.s.) 22: 132–56.

Ling, T., 1968. *A History of Religion East and West*, London: Macmillan.

————, 1973. *The Buddha: Buddhist Civilization in India and Ceylon*, London: Temple Smith.

Lingat, R., 1989. *Royautés Bouddhiques: Asoka, La Fonction Royale à Ceylan*, G. Fussman and E. Meyer (eds), Paris: Editions de l'EHESS.

Locke, J.K., 1973. *Rato Matsyendranath of Patan and Bungamati*, Kathmandu: INAS, Tribhuvan University.

————, 1975. 'Newar Buddhist Initiation Rites', *Contributions to Nepalese Studies* 2: 1–23.

————, 1980. *Karunamaya: The Cult of Avalokitesvara-Matsyendranath in the Valley of Nepal*, Kathmandu: Sahayogi.

————, 1985. *Buddhist Monasteries of Nepal: A Survey of the Baha and Bahis of the Kathmandu Valley*, Kathmandu: Sahayogi.

Lopez, D. (ed.), 1995. *Curators of the Buddha: The Study of Buddhism under Colonialism*, Chicago: Chicago University Press.

————, 1998. *Prisoners of Shangri-la: Tibetan Buddhism and the West*, Chicago: Chicago University Press.

Löwdin, P., 1985. *Food, Ritual and Society among the Newars*, Uppsala: Dept. of Cultural Anthropology, Uppsala University.

Luethy, H., 1970. 'Once Again: Calvinism and Capitalism' in D. Wrong (ed.), *Max Weber*, New Jersey: Prentice Hall. First published in *Encounter* 22 (Jan 1964): 26–32. Reprinted in S.N. Eisenstadt (ed.) *The Protestant Ethic and Modernization: A comparative view*, 1968, New York: Basic Books.

Lutt, J., 1987. 'Max Weber and the Vallabhacharis', *International Sociology* 2 (3): 277–88.

McClain, C.S., 1989. 'Reinterpreting Women in Healing Roles' in C.S. McClain (ed.), *Women as Healers: Cross-cultural Perspectives*, New Brunswick and London: Rutgers University Press.

McDaniel, J., 1988. *The Madness of the Saints: Ecstatic Religion in Bengal*, Chicago and London: The University of Chicago Press.

Macdonald, A., 1975. 'The Healer in the Nepalese World' in his *Essays in the Ethnology of Nepal and South Asia*, Kathmandu: Ratna Pustak Bhandar.

————, 1976. 'Sorcery in the Nepalese Code of 1853' in J. Hitchcock and R.L. Jones (eds), *Spirit Possession in the Nepal Himalayas*, Warminster: Aris and Phillips.

Mackie, J.L., 1965. 'Causes and Conditions', *American Philosophical Quarterly* 2: 245–64.

Mahapragya, 1983. *Sāhityā Sutā, Karmasthānācārya wa Bauddha Ṛṣi, Mahāprajñāyā Ātmakathā*, D. Newami (ed.), Kathmandu: Sakalopasak.

Mahuzier, L., n.d., (?1974). *Chez les Magiciens et les Sorciers de l'Himalaya*, Belgium: self-published.

Maila, Virakti, 1997. 'Ambushed by Superstition' (*Andhaviśvāsko āḍmā hatyā*), *Tathyakathā* 47: 70–90.

Malla, K.P., 1985. 'Epigraphy and Society in Ancient Nepal: A Critique of Regmi, 1983', *Contributions to Nepalese Studies* 13: 57–94.

Manandhar, T.L., 1986. *Newari-English Dictionary: Modern Language of the Kathmandu Valley*, Delhi: Ecole Française d'Extreme Orient and Agam Kala Prakashan.

Mandelbaum, D.C., 1970. *Society in India*, 2 vols., Berkeley: University of California Press.

Marcus, G.E., 1998. *Ethnography through Thick and Thin*, Princeton: Princeton University Press.

364   *References*

Marriott, M., 1955. 'Western Medicine in a Village in north India' in B. Paul (ed.), *Health, Culture and Community*, New York: Russell Sage.

—, 1976. 'Interpreting Indian Society: A Monistic Alternative to Dumont's Dualism', *Journal of Asian Studies* 36: 189–95.

Marshall, G., 1980. *Presbyteries and Profits: Calvinism and the Development of Capitalism in Scotland, 1560–1707*, Oxford: Clarendon Press.

—, 1982. *In Search of the Spirit of Capitalism*, London: Hutchinson.

Martinez, D.P., 1990. 'The Dead: Shinto Aspects of a Buddhist Ritual', *Journal of the Anthropological Society of Oxford* 21: 199–209.

—, 1995. 'Women and Ritual' in J. van Bremen and D.P. Martinez (eds) *Ceremony and Ritual in Japan: Religious Practices in an Industrialized Society*, London: Routledge.

Mendelson, E.M., 1975. *Sangha and State in Burma: A Study of Monastic Sectarianism and Leadership*, Ithaca and London: Cornell University Press.

Merton, R.K., 1968. *Social Theory and Social Structure*, New York: The Free Press.

Miksell, S.L., 1993. 'A Critique of Levi's [sic] Theory of Urban Mesocosm', *Contributions to Nepalese Studies* 20(2): 231–4.

Miller, C.J., 1979. *Faith-healers in the Himalayas: An Investigation of Traditional Healers and their Festivals in Dolakha District of Nepal*, Kathmandu: Sahayogi (reprint 1987).

Milner Jnr, M., 1988. 'Status Relations in South Asian Marriage Alliances: Toward a General Theory', *Contributions to Indian Sociology* (n.s.) 22: 145–69.

Mitra, R.L., 1982 [1971]. *The Sanskrit Buddhist Literature of Nepal*, Calcutta: Sanskrit Pustak Bhandar.

Miyake, H., 1996. 'Rethinking Japanese Folk Religion: A Study of Kumane Shingen' in P.F. Kornicki and I.J. McMullen (eds), *Religion in Japan: Arrows to Heaven and Earth*, Cambridge: Cambridge University Press.

Moffatt, M., 1979. *An Untouchable Community in South India: Structure and Consensus*, Princeton: Princeton University Press.

Moore, H., 1988. *Feminism and Anthropology*, Cambridge: Polity Press.

Mosse, D., 1994. 'Idioms of Subordination and Styles of Protest among Christian and Hindu Harijan castes in Tamil Nadu', *Contributions to Indian Sociology* (n.s.) 28: 67–106.

Mumford, S.R., 1989. *Himalayan Dialogue: Tibetan Lamas and Gurung Shamans in Nepal*, Madison: The University of Wisconsin Press.

Munshi, S., 1988. 'Max Weber on India: An Introductory Critique', *Contributions to Indian Sociology* (n.s.) 22(1): 1–34.

Munson, H., 1986. 'Geertz on Religion: The Theory and the Practice', *Religion* 16: 19–32.

Nadel, S.F., 1951. *The Foundations of Social Anthropology*, London: Cohen & West.

Nepali, G.S., 1965. *The Newars: An Ethno-Sociological Study of a Himalayan Community*, Bombay: United Asia Publications.

Nichter, M., 1978. 'Patterns of Resort in the Use of Therapy Systems and their Significance for Health Planning', *Medical Anthropology Quarterly* 2: 29–58.

—, 1992. 'Of Ticks, Kings, Spirits, and the Promise of Vaccines' in C. Leslie and A. Young (eds), *Paths to Asian Medical Knowledge*, Berkeley: University of California Press.

Nichter, M. and M. Nichter, 1996. *Anthropology and International Health: Asian Case Studies*, Amsterdam: Gordon and Breach. (First edited by Kluwer Academic, 1989.)

Nietzsche, F., 1967. *On the Genealogy of Morals*, tr. W. Kaufmann and R.J. Hollingdale, New York: Vintage.

Obeyesekere, G., 1963. 'The Great Tradition and the Little in the Perspective of Sinhalese Buddhism', *Journal of Asian Studies* 22: 139–53.

———, 1966. 'The Buddhist Pantheon in Ceylon and its Extensions' in M. Nash (ed.), *Anthropological Studies of Theravada Buddhism*, New Haven: Yale University Press.

O'Hanlon, R., 1985. *Caste, Conflict, and Ideology: Mahatma Jotirao Phule and Low Caste Protest in nineteenth-century western India*, Cambridge: Cambridge University Press.

Ohnuki-Tierney, E., 1984. *Illness and Culture in Contemporary Japan*, Cambridge: Cambridge University Press.

———, 1987. *The Monkey as Mirror: Symbolic Transformations in Japanese History and Ritual*, Princeton: Princeton University Press.

Okada, F.E., 1976. 'Notes on two Shaman-Curers in Kathmandu', *Contributions to Nepalese Studies* 3: 107–12.

Oldfield, H.A., 1981 [1880]. *Sketches from Nepal* (2 vols), Delhi: Cosmo.

Ooms, H., 1976. 'A Structural Analysis of Japanese Ancestral Rites and Beliefs' in W.H. Newell (ed.), *Ancestors*, Paris: Mouton.

Oppitz, M., 1986. 'Die Trommel und das Buch: Eine kleine und die grosse Tradition' in B. Kölver and S. Lienhard (eds), *Formen kulturellen Wandels und andere Beiträge zur Erforschung des Himalaya*, St Augustin: VGH Wissenschaftsverlag.

Ortner, S.B., 1978. *Sherpas through their Rituals*, Cambridge: Cambridge University Press.

———, 1984. 'Theory in Anthropology since the Sixties', *Comparative Studies in Society and History* 26: 126–66.

———, 1989. *High Religion: A Cultural and Political History of Sherpa Buddhism*, Princeton: Princeton University Press.

———, 1998. 'The Case of the Disappearing Shamans, or No Individualism, No Relationalism' in D. Skinner, A. Pach III, and D. Holland (eds), *Selves in Time and Place: Identities, Experience, and History in Nepal*, Lanham: Rowman & Littlewood. (First published in *Ethos* 23/3, 1995.)

Pal, P. and D.C. Bhattacharyya, 1969. *The Astral Divinities of Nepal*, Varanasi: Prithivi Prakashan.

Palmié, S., 1995. 'Against Syncretism: "Africanizing" and "Cubanizing" Discourses in North American *orisa* Worship' in R. Fardon (ed.), *Counterworks: Managing the Diversity of Knowledge*, London and New York: Routledge.

Paneru, S., 1983. *Use of Traditional Medical Practitioners in the Field of Family Health/Family Planning, Vol. IV: Gorkha*, Tribhuvan University, Kirtipur: CNAS.

Parish, S.M., 1994. *Moral Knowing in a Hindu Sacred City: An Exploration of Mind, Emotion, and Self*, New York: Columbia University Press.

———, 1996. *Hierarchy and its Discontents: Culture and the Politics of Consciousness in Caste Society*, Philadelphia: University of Pennsylvania Press.

Parkin, F., 1982. *Max Weber*, London and New York: Tavistock.

Parry, J.P., 1979. *Caste and Kinship in Kangra*, London: Routledge Kegan Paul.

———, 1980. 'Ghosts, Greed and Sin: The Occupational Identity of the Benares Funeral Priests', *Man* (n.s.) 15: 88–111.

———, 1999. 'Preface', *Contributions to Indian Sociology* (n.s.) 33 (1–2): VII-XIV.

Parsons, T., 1965. 'Introduction' in M. Weber, *The Sociology of Religion* [= ES chapter 6], London: Methuen.

Paul, R.A., 1989. *The Sherpas of Nepal in the Tibetan Cultural Context*, Delhi: Motilal Banarsidass. (First published in 1982 as *The Tibetan Symbolic World: A Psychoanalytic Exploration*, Chicago: Chicago University Press.)

Peabody, N., 1997. 'Inchoate in Kota? Contesting Authority through a north Indian Pageant-Play', *American Ethnologist* 24: 559–84.

Peel, J.D.Y., 1968. 'Syncretism and Religious Change', *Comparative Studies in Society and History* 10: 121–41.

———, 1993. 'An Africanist Revisits *Magic and the Millennium*' in D. Barker, J.A. Beckford, and K. Dobbelaere (eds), *Revitalization, Rationalism, and Secularization: Essays in Honour of Bryan R. Wilson*, Oxford: Clarendon.

Petech, L., 1984 [1958]. *Mediaeval History of Nepal* (second edition), Rome: ISMEO.

Peters, L., 1981. *Ecstasy and Healing in Nepal*, Malibu: Undena.

Pfaff-Czarnecka, J., 1993. 'The Nepalese Durga Puja Festival or Displaying Political Supremacy on Ritual Occasions' in C. Ramble and M. Brauen (eds), *Anthropology of Tibet and the Himalaya*, Zürich: Ethnological Museum of the University of Zürich.

———, 1996. 'A Battle of Meanings: Commemorating Goddess Durga's Victory over the Demon Mahisa as a Political Act', *Kailash* 18 (3–4): 57–92.

Phylactou, M., 1989. 'Household Organisation and Marriage in Ladakh', Ph.D. thesis, University of London.

Pieper, J., 1975. 'Three Cities of Nepal' in P. Oliver (ed.), *Shelter, Sign and Symbol*, London: Barrie & Jenkins.

Pocock, D.F., 1960. 'Sociologies, Urban and Rural', *Contributions to Indian Sociology* 4: 63–81.

———, 1973. *Mind, Body and Wealth: A Study of Belief and Practice in an Indian Village*, Oxford: Basil Blackwell.

Potter, K.H., 1963. *Presuppositions of India's Philosophies*, New Jersey: Prentice Hall.

Pradhan, B., 1981. *The Newar Women of Bulu* (Status of Women in Nepal 2: Field Studies Part 6), Kathmandu: CEDA, Tribhuvan University.

Pradhan, R.P., 1986. 'Domestic and Cosmic Rituals among the Newars of Kathmandu, Nepal', Ph.D., University of Delhi.

Puthusseril, A., 1986. 'Charisma and the Interaction between Religious Ideas and Material Interests' in D. Kantowsky (ed.), 1986.

Pye, M., 1978. *Skilful Means: A Concept in Mahayana Buddhism*, London: Duckworth.

———, 1994. 'Syncretism versus Synthesis', *Method and Theory in the Study of Religion* 6 (3): 217–29.

Quigley, D., 1984. 'The Social Structure of a Newar Trading Community, east central Nepal', Ph.D., University of London.

———, 1986. 'Introversion and Isogamy: Marriage Patterns of the Newars of Nepal', *Contributions to Indian Sociology* (n.s.) 20: 75–95.

———, 1987. 'Ethnicity without Nationalism: The Newars of Nepal', *European Journal of Sociology* 27: 152–70.

———, 1988. 'Is Caste a Pure Figment, the Invention of Orientalists for their own Glorification?', *Cambridge Anthropology* 13 (1): 20–36.

———, 1991. Review of Levy's *Mesocosm*, *Cambridge Anthropology* 15 (1): 90–5.

———, 1993. *The Interpretation of Caste*, Oxford: University Press.

Raeper, M. and M. Hoftun, 1992. *Spring Awakening: An Account of the 1990 Revolution in Nepal*, Delhi: Viking.

Raheja, G.G., 1988. 'India: Caste, Kingship, and Dominance Reconsidered', *Annual Review of Anthropology*, 17: 497–522.

Rahula, W., 1956. *History of Buddhism in Ceylon: The Anuradha Period*, Colombo: M.D. Gunasena.

Rajbhandari, S., 1978. 'Hiranya Varna Mahavihar', M.A. thesis, Tribhuvan University.

Rajvamshi, S., 1983. *Bhūmisambandhī Tamsūk Tāḍpattra* (part 1), Kathmandu: National Archives. (VS 2040.)

Ranger, T., 1993. 'The Local and the Global in Southern African Religious History' in R.W. Hefner (ed.), *Conversion to Christianity: Historical and Anthropological Perspectives on a Great Transformation*, Berkeley: University of California Press.

Reader, I., 1991. *Religion in Contemporary Japan*, Basingstoke: Macmillan.

Reader, I. and G.J. Tanabe Jr., 1998. *Practically Religious: Worldly Benefits and the Common Religion of Japan*, Honolulu: University of Hawai'i Press.

Regmi, D.R., 1965. *Medieval Nepal* (4 vols.), Calcutta: Firma KL Mukhopadhyay.

Regmi, J.C., 1978. *Newārī saṃskṛtiko rūprekhā*, Kathmandu: Office of Nepal Antiquary. (vs 2035.)

Regmi, M.C., 1974. 'Population Census Statistics for Bhadgaun, 1853', *Regmi Research Series* 6 (10): 195–6.

———, 1976. *Landownership in Nepal*, Berkeley: University of California Press.

———, 1976a. 'The Population of Patan', *Regmi Research Series* 8 (7): 135.

Riccardi, T., 1980. 'Buddhism in Ancient and early Medieval Nepal' in A.K. Narain (ed.), *Studies in the History of Buddhism*, Delhi: BR Publishing Corporation.

Rosen, L., 1984. *Bargaining for Reality: The Construction of Social Relations in a Muslim Community*, Chicago: Chicago University Press.

Rosser, C., 1966. 'Social Mobility in the Newar Caste System' in C. von Fürer-

Haimendorf (ed.), *Caste and Kin in Nepal, India and Ceylon*, Bombay: Asian Publishing House.

Roth, G. and W. Schluchter, 1979. *Max Weber's Vision of History: Ethics and Methods*, Berkeley: University of California Press.

Said, E., 1978. *Covering Islam*, New York: Pantheon.

———, 1985 (1978). *Orientalism*, Harmondsworth: Penguin.

Sakya, H., 1956. *Nepāl Bauddha Vihār wa Grantha Sūci*, Kathmandu: Dharmodaya Sabha. (BS 2500).

———, 1973. *Mayurvarṇa Mahāvihāryā Saṃkṣipta Itihās* (in Newari), Lalitpur: Bhīchē Bahahyā Sarvasamgha. (BS 2500.)

———, 1979. *Samyak Mahādān Guthi*, Kathmandu: Jagatdhar Tuladhar (NS 1100.)

Sakya, H. and T.R. Vaidya, 1970. *Medieval Nepal (Colophons and Inscriptions)*, Kathmandu: T.R. Vaidya.

Sakya, K. and L. Griffith, 1980. *Tales of Kathmandu: Folktales from the Himalayan Kingdom of Nepal*, Brisbane: House of Kathmandu.

Samuel, G., 1978. 'Religion in Tibetan Society: A New Approach', *Kailash* 6(1, 2): 45–66, 99–114.

———, 1993. *Civilized Shamans: Buddhism in Tibetan Societies*, Washington: Smithsonian Press.

Sanderson, A., 1985. 'Purity and Power among the Brahmans of Kashmir' in M. Carrithers, S. Collins, and S. Lukes (eds), *The Category of the Person*, Cambridge: Cambridge University Press.

———, 1986. 'Mandala and Agamic Identity in the Trika of Kashmir' in A. Padoux (ed.), *Mantras et Diagrammes rituels dans l'Hindouisme*, Paris: CNRS.

———, 1995. 'Vajrayana: Origin and Function' in *Buddhism into the Year 2000*, Bangkok and Los Angeles: Dhammakaya Foundation.

Schluchter, W., 1979. 'The Paradox of Rationalization' in G. Roth and W. Schluchter, *Max Weber's Vision of History: Ethics and Methods*, Berkeley: University of California Press

———, 1981. *The Rise of Western Rationalism: Max Weber's Developmental History*, G. Roth (tr.), Berkeley: University of California Press.

———, 1984. 'Weltfluchtiges Erlosungsstreben und Organische Sozialethik' in W. Schluchter (ed.) (Translated and revised as Chapter 4 in Schluchter 1989).

———, (ed.), 1984. *Max Webers Studie über Hinduismus und Buddhismus*, Frankfurt: Suhrkamp.

———, 1989. *Religion, Rationalism, and Domination: A Weberian Perspective* (tr. N. Solomon), Berkeley: University of California Press.

Schnepel, B., 1987. 'Max Weber's Theory of Charisma and its Applicability to Anthropological Research', *Journal of the Anthropological Society of Oxford* (18)1: 26–48.

———, 1996. 'The Hindu King's Authority Reconsidered: Durga-Puja and Dasara in a South Orissan Jungle Kingdom' in Boholm (ed.), 1996.

Schopen, G., 1997. *Bones, Stones, and Buddhist Monks: Collected Papers on the*

Archaeology, Epigraphy, and Texts of Monastic Buddhism in India, Honolulu: Hawaii University Press.

Schroeder, R., 1992. *Max Weber and the Sociology of Culture,* London: Sage.

Schulte Nordholt, H., 1993. 'Leadership and the Limits of Political Control: A Balinese "Response" to Clifford Geertz', *Social Anthropology* 1: 291–307.

Seneviratne, H.L., 1987. 'Kingship and Polity in Buddhism and Hinduism', *Contributions to Indian Sociology* (n.s.) 21(1): 147–55.

Shankman, P., 1984. 'The Thick and the Thin: On the Interpretive Program of Clifford Geertz', *Current Anthropology* 25: 261–79.

Sharkey, G., 1995. 'Daily Ritual in Newar Buddhist Shrines', D.Phil. thesis, Oxford University.

Sharma, B.P., 1986. *Native Healers of Nepal,* Kathmandu: self-published. (2nd edn).

Sharma, P.R., 1978. 'Nepal: Hindu-Tribal Interface', *Contributions to Nepalese Studies* 6: 1-14.

Shaw, R. and C. Stewart, 1995. 'Introduction: Problematizing Syncretism' in Stewart and Shaw (eds).

Shepard, J.W., 1985. 'Symbolic Space in Newar Culture', Ph.D., University of Michigan, University Microfilms International No. 8520981.

Shrestha, R.M. (with M. Lediard), 1973. *Faith Healers: A Force for Change,* Kathmandu: UNFPA and UNICEF.

Singer, M., 1961. Review of *ROI, American Anthropologist* 63(1): 143–51.

————, 1972. *When a Great Tradition Modernizes: An Anthropological Approach to Indian Civilization,* New York: Praeger.

Sinha, S., 1974. 'The Sociology of Religion' in *A Survey of Research in Sociology and Social Anthropology,* vol.2, Chapter 9, Bombay: Popular Prakashan.

Skultans, V., 1988. 'A Comparative Study of a Tantrik Healer and a Hospital Out-patient Clinic in the Kathmandu Valley', *Psychological Medicine* 18: 969–81.

Slusser, M., 1982. *Nepal Mandala: A Cultural Study of the Kathmandu Valley* (2 vols.), Princeton: Princeton University Press.

Smith, M.G., 1960. *Government in Zazzau 1880-1950,* London: Oxford University Press for IAI.

Smith, R.J., 1974. *Ancestor Worship in Contemporary Japan,* Stanford: Stanford University Press.

————, 1995. 'Wedding and Funeral Ritual: Analyzing a Moving Target' in J. van Bremen and D.P. Martinez (eds), *Ceremony and Ritual in Japan: Religious Practices in an Industrialized Society,* London: Routledge.

Snellgrove, D., 1961. 'Shrines and Temples of Nepal, Part 2', *Arts Asiatiques* 8 (2): 93–120.

————, 1987. *Indo-Tibetan Buddhism: Indian Buddhists and their Tibetan successors,* London: Serindia.

Sontheimer, G.D. and H. Kulke (eds), 1989. *Hinduism Reconsidered,* Delhi: Manohar.

Southall, A., 1970. 'The Illusion of Tribe', *Journal of Asian and African Studies* [Leiden] 5: 28–50.

————, 1975. 'Forms of Ethnic Linkage between Town and Country' in B. Dutoit and H. Safa (eds), *Migration and Urbanization: Models and Adaptive Strategies*, The Hague: Mouton.

Southwold, M., 1978. 'Buddhism and the Definition of Religion', *Man* (n.s.) 13: 362–79.

————, 1982. 'True Buddhism and Village Buddhism in Sri Lanka' in J. Davis (ed.), *Religious Organization and Religious Experience* (ASA Monograph 21), London: Academic Press.

————, 1983. *Buddhism in Life: The Anthropological Study of Religion and the Sinhalese Practice of Buddhism*, Manchester: Manchester University Press.

————, 1985. 'The Concept of Nirvana in Village Buddhism' in R. Burghart and A. Cantlie (eds), *Indian Religion*, London: Curzon Press; New York: St Martin's Press.

Spencer, J., 1990. 'Tradition and Transformation: Recent Writing on the Anthropology of Buddhism in Sri Lanka', *Journal of the Anthropological Society of Oxford* 21(2): 129–40.

Spiro, M.E., 1967. *Burmese Supernaturalism*, New Jersey: Prentice-Hall.

————, 1977. Review of Tambiah 1976, *Journal of Asian Studies* 36: 789–91.

————, 1978. 'Reply to Professor Tambiah', *Journal of Asian Studies* 37: 809–12.

————, 1982 [1970]. *Buddhism and Society: A Great Tradition and its Burmese Vicissitudes*, Berkeley: University of California Press.

Srinivas, M.N., 1976. *The Remembered Village*, Delhi: Oxford University Press.

————, 1987. 'The Indian Village: Myth and Reality' in his *The Dominant Caste and Other Essays*, Delhi: Oxford University Press.

Staal, F., 1979. 'Oriental Ideas on the Origin of Language', *Journal of the American Oriental Society* 99: 1–14.

Stcherbatsky, T., 1977 [1923]. *The Conception of Buddhist Nirvana*, Delhi: Motilal Banarsidass.

Stern, H., 1971. 'Religion et Société en Inde selon Max Weber', *Informations sur les Sciences Sociales* 10(6): 69–112

Stewart, C., 1991. *Demons and the Devil: Moral Imagination in modern Greek Culture*, Princeton: Princeton University Press.

————, 1995. 'Relocating Syncretism in Social Science Discourse' in G. Aijmer (ed.), *Syncretism and the Commerce of Symbols*, Göteborg: IASSA.

Stewart, C. and R. Shaw (eds), 1995. *Syncretism/Anti-Syncretism: The Politics of Religious Synthesis*, London: Routledge.

Stiller, L.S., 1973. *The Rise of the House of Gorkha: A Study in the Unification of Nepal, 1768-1816*, Delhi: Manjusri Publishing House.

————, 1984. 'Hodgson on Justice', *Regmi Research Series* 16 (9–10): 127–60, 16 (11–12): 161–83, 17 (1–2): 1–21, 17 (3): 33–6.

Stone, L., 1976. 'Concepts of Illness and Curing in a central Nepal Village', *Contributions to Nepalese Studies* 3: 55–80.

————, 1983. 'Hierarchy and Food in Nepalese Healing Rituals', *Social Science and Medicine* 17 (14): 971–78.

———, 1988. *Illness Beliefs and Feeding the Dead in Hindu Nepal: An Ethnographic Analysis*, Lewiston, New York.: E. Mellen.

Strenski, I., 1983. 'On Generalized Exchange and the Domestication of the Sangha', *Man* (n.s.), 18: 463–77.

Strong, J.S., 1977. '*Gandhakuṭī*: The Perfumed Chamber of the Buddha', *History of Religions* 16: 390–406.

Subedi, R.P., 1982. *Use of Traditional Medical Practitioners in the Field of Family Health/Family Planning*, Vol. *II: Ilam*, Tribhuvan University, Kirtipur: CNAS.

Tambiah, S.J., 1970. *Buddhism and the Spirit Cults in North-East Thailand*, Cambridge: Cambridge University Press.

———, 1973. 'Buddhism and This-Worldly Activity', *Modern Asian Studies* 7(1): 1–20.

———, 1976. *World Conqueror and World Renouncer*, Cambridge: Cambridge University Press.

———, 1978. 'The Buddhist Conception of Kingship and its Historical Manifestations: A Reply to Spiro', *Journal of Asian Studies* 37: 801–9.

———, 1984a. *The Buddhist Saints of the Forest and the Cult of the Amulets: A Study in Charisma, Hagiography, Sectarianism, and Millenial Buddhism*, Cambridge: Cambridge University Press.

———, 1984b. 'Max Weber's Untersuchung des fruehen Buddhismus: eine Kritik' in W. Schluchter (ed.), 1984.

———, 1985a. 'A Performative Approach to Ritual' in his *Culture, Thought, and Social Action: An Anthropological Perspective*, Cambridge, USA, and London: Harvard University Press.

———, 1985b. 'A Reformulation of Geertz's Conception of the Theater State' in his *Culture, Thought, and Social Action: An Anthropological Perspective*, Cambridge, USA, and London: Harvard University Press.

———, 1987. 'At the Confluence of Anthropology, History, and Indology', *Contributions to Indian Sociology* (n.s.) 21(1): 187–216.

———, 1989. 'King Mahasammata: The First King in the Buddhist Story of Creation, and his Persisting Relevance', *Journal of the Anthropological Society of Oxford* 20: 101–22.

Tapper, R., n.d. 'Pastoralism and Patriarchy: On the Social Structure of Nomads and their Animals'. (Unpublished manuscript).

Tenbruck, F.H., 1980. 'The Problem of Thematic Unity in the Works of Max Weber', *British Journal of Sociology* 31: 313–51.

Terwiel, B.J., 1975. *Monks and Magic: An Analysis of Religious Ceremonies in Central Thailand*, London: Curzon Press.

Thomas, N., 1988. 'Marginal Powers: Shamanism and the Disintegration of Hierarchy', *Critique of Anthropology* 8(3): 53–74.

Toffin, G., 1975a. 'Un Peuple à la Recherche de son Identité: Les Néwar du Népal', *Pluriel* 3: 29-39.

———, 1975b. 'La Terminologie de Parenté Newar: Analyse descriptive et comparative', *L'Homme* 15: 129–53.

————, 1977. *Pyangaon: Une Communauté Néwar de la Vallée de Kathmandou: La Vie matérielle*, Paris: CNRS.

————, 1981a. 'Espace Urbain: A propos des Villes Néwar' in G. Toffin (ed.), *L'Homme et la Maison en Himalaya*, Paris: CNRS. English version in Toffin (ed.), 1991, *Man and his House in the Himalayas*, Delhi: Sterling.

————, 1981b. 'L'Organisation Sociale des Pahari ou Pahi, Population du centre Népal', *L'Homme* 21: 39–68.

————, 1984. *Société et Religion chez les Néwars du Népal*, Paris: CNRS.

————, 1986. 'Dieux Souverains et Rois Dévots dans l'Ancienne Royauté de la Vallée du Népal', *L'Homme* 26(3): 71–95. (Republished as Chapter 1 in Toffin 1993.)

————, 1989. 'La Voie des "Héros": Tantrisme et Heritage Védique chez les Brahmans Rajopadhyaya au Népal' in V. Bouillier and G. Toffin (eds), *Pretrise, Pouvoirs et Autorite en Himalaya* (Purusartha 12), Paris: Editions de l' EHESS.

————, 1990. 'Mythes de Fondation et Symbolique de la Ville', *Diogène* 152: 97–118 (Republished as Chapter 5 in Toffin 1993).

————, 1993. *Le Palais et le Temple: La Fonction Royale dans la Vallée de Népal*, Paris: CNRS.

————, 1996a. 'Tribal Brahmins? The Case of the Rajopadhyaya of Nepal' in S. Lienhard (ed.), *Change and Continuity: Studies in the Nepalese Culture of the Kathmandu Valley* (CESMEO Orientalia 7), Alessandrio: Edizioni dell'Orso.

————, 1996b. 'Histoire et Anthropologie d'un Culte Royal Népalais: Le Mvahni (Durga Puja) dans l'ancien Palais Royal de Patan' in G. Krauskopff and M. Lecomte-Tilouine (eds).

Trautmann, T.R., 1997. *Aryans and British India*, Berkeley: University of California Press.

Trawick, M., 1992. 'Death and Nurturance in Indian Systems of Healing' in C. Leslie and A. Young (eds), *Paths to Asian Medical Knowledge*, Berkeley: University of California Press.

Trevor-Roper H.R., 1967. *Religion, the Reformation and Social Change and other Essays*, London: Macmillan.

Tucci, G., 1969. *The Theory and Practice of the Mandala*, London: Rider & Co.

————, 1980. *The Religions of Tibet*, tr. G. Samuel, London: Routledge & Kegan Paul.

Turner, B.S., 1974. *Weber and Islam: A Critical Study*, London: Routledge & Kegan Paul.

————, 1981. *For Weber: Essays on the Sociology of Fate*, Boston etc.: Routledge & Kegan Paul.

————, 1993. *Max Weber: From History to Modernity*, London: Routledge.

————, 1994. *Orientalism, Postmodernism and Globalism*, London: Routledge.

Vaidya, K., 1986. *Buddhist Traditions and Culture of the Kathmandu Valley (Nepal)*, Kathmandu: Sajha Prakashan.

Vajracharya, B.R. and R.K., 1963. *Nepal Jana-Jivan Kriya Paddhati* (in Newari), self-published (NS 1083.)

Vajracharya, D.V., 1973. *Licchavikālkā Abhilekh* (in Nepali), Kathmandu: INAS, Tribhuvan University.

Vajracharya, D.V. and T.B. Shrestha, 1979. *Pāñcali (Pañcāyat) Śāsan-Paddhatiko Aitihāsik Vivecanā* (in Nepali), Kathmandu: CNAS, Tribhuvan University (vs 2036).

Vajracharya, G.V., 1976. *Hanumān Ḍhokā Rājdārbār* (in Nepali), Kathmandu: CNAS, Tribhuvan University (vs 2033).

Vajracharya, M.R., 1985. *Mañjuśrīpārājikā* (in Newari), Yala [= Lalitpur]: Danbahadur Sakya (NS 1105).

Valeri, V., 1991. 'Afterword' in Lansing 1991.

Vergati, A., 1975. 'M. Greenwold et les Néwars: Doit-on vraiment recourir à deux modèles du système des castes au Népal?', *European Journal of Sociology* 16: 310–16.

———, 1979. 'Une Divinité Lignagère des Néwars: Digu-dyo', *Bulletin de l'Ecole Française d'Extrême-Orient* 66: 115–27.

———, 1982. 'The Social Consequences of Marrying Visnu Narayana: Primary Marriage among the Newars of Kathmandu Valley', *Contributions to Indian Sociology* (n.s.) 16: 271–87.

———, 1985. 'Le roi faiseur de pluie: Une nouvelle version de la légende d'Avalokitesvara Rouge au Népal', *Bulletin de l'Ecole Française d'Extrême Orient* 74: 287–303.

von Rospatt, A., 1999. 'On the Conception of the Stupa in Vajrayana Buddhism: The Example of the Svayambhucaitya of Kathmandu', *Journal of the Nepal Research Centre* 9: 121–47.

von Stietencron, H., 1991. 'Hinduism: On the Proper Use of a Deceptive Term' in G.D. Sontheimer and H. Kulke (eds), *Hinduism Reconsidered*, Delhi: Manohar.

Waley, P., 1986. *Tokyo Now and Then: An Explorer's Guide*, New York and Tokyo: John Weatherhill.

Wallerstein, E., 1974, 1980, 1989. *The Modern World-System* (3 vols.), New York: Academic Press.

Weber, M., 1916–17. 'Die Wirtschaftsethik der Weltreligionen (Dritter Artikel): Hinduismus und Buddhismus', *Archiv fur Sozialwissenschaft und Sozialpolitik* 41(3): 313–744, 42(2): 345–461, 42(3): 687–814. Reprinted in M. Weber 1921, *Gesammelte Aufsätze zur Religionssoziologie Vol II*, Tübingen: JCB Mohr.

———, 1927. *General Economic History*, London: Allen and Unwin.

———, 1949. *The Methodology of the Social Sciences*, trs and eds E.A. Shils and H.A. Finch, Glencoe: The Free Press.

———, 1951. *The Religion of China*, tr. H.H. Gerth, New York: Macmillan.

———, 1958. *The Religion of India: The Sociology of Hinduism and Buddhism*, eds and trs H.H. Gerth and D. Martindale, New York: The Free Press.

———, 1968. *Economy and Society: An Outline of an Interpretative Sociology* (3 vols.), eds G. Roth and C. Wittich, New York: Bedminster Press.

———, 1976. *The Protestant Ethic and the Spirit of Capitalism*, tr. T. Parsons, 2nd edn, London: Allen and Unwin.

———, 1996. *Die Wirtschaftsethik der Weltreligionen: Hinduismus und Buddhismus, 1916–20* (ed. H. Schmidt-Glintzer with K.-H. Golzio; Gesamtsausgabe 1.20), Tübingen: JCB Mohr.

Weiner, S.J., 1989. '"Source Force" and the Nepal Medical Profession', *Social Science and Medicine* 29(5): 669–75.

Whelpton, J., 1983. *Jang Bahadur in Europe: The First Nepalese Mission to the West*, Kathmandu: Sahayogi.

———, 1995. 'Nepalese Political Parties: Developments since the 1991 Elections', *European Bulletin of Himalayan Research* 8: 17–41.

———, 1999. 'Nine Years On: The 1999 Election and Nepalese Politics since the 1990 Janandolan', *European Bulletin of Himalayan Research* 17: 1–39.

Wiemann-Michaels, A., 1989. *Der Verhexte Speise: Ein Beitrag zur transkulturellen Depressionsforschung dargelegt an einem psycho-somatischen Krankheitsbild in Nepal*, Hamburg: Faculty of Medicine.

Wijayaratna, M., 1990. *Buddhist Monastic Life, according to the Texts of the Theravada Tradition*, trs C. Grangier and S. Collins, Cambridge: Cambridge University Press.

Wijeyewardene, G., 1986. *Place and Emotion in Northern Thai Ritual Behaviour*, Bangkok: Pandora.

Wilson, B., 1975. *Magic and the Millennium*, Frogmore, St Alban's: Paladin.

Wolf, E., 1982. *Europe and the People without History*, Berkeley: University of California Press.

Wolff, K.H., (ed. and tr.), 1950. *The Sociology of George Simmel*, New York: The Free Press.

Wright, D., (ed.), 1972 [1877]. *History of Nepal*, Kathmandu: Nepal Antiquated Book Publishers.

Zelliott, E., 1992. *From Untouchable to Dalit: Essays on the Ambedkar Movement*, Delhi: Manohar.

Zimmerman, F., 1992. 'Gentle Purge: The Flower Power of Ayurveda' in C. Leslie and A. Young (eds), *Paths to Asian Medical Knowledge*, Berkeley: University of California Press.

Index

Name Index

Webster, P. 273
Weiner, S.J. 248
Whelpton, J. 82, 291
Wiemann-Michaels, A. 228, 231,
    233–4
Wijayaratna, G. 43
Wijeyewardene, G. 53–5, 59
Wilson, B. 220
Wittfogel, K. 283–4, 311

Wolf, Eric 1, 15
Wolff, K.H. 273
Wright, D. 87, 149, 160–1, 163, 174,
    177, 188, 274
Wujastyk, D. 248

Yaksha Malla (reigned 1428–82) 279

Zelliott, E. 59

Subject Index

ācāḥ luyegu, see Consecration
Achala, see Fudo
Acharya Guthi 120
acupuncture 237
Adibuddha 148
affective, see cognitive
Africa 206–7, 218 n. 4, 322
āgā/āgādyaḥ, see Tantric deities
Agni Matha 193 n. 22
agrarian society 28, 30–1, 298
Akash 230
Amida/Amitabha 133 n. 39, 341
Amoghapasha 148–9
Amoghasiddhi 155
ancestors 54, 200, 327, 338
ancestor worship 14, 54, 223, 327–8,
    331, 337–8
animal sacrifice
    associated with shamanism 56–7
    in Bali 63
    in Bloch's theory 66, 69, 77
    Buddhists against 56, 72, 77; 323
    dancers receive 216, 305
    to dangerous deities 95, 216, 304,
        314 n. 11
    at Dasain 75–7, 307
    Tantrism permits 87–8
animism 52, 53–4, 256
architecture 211, 243, 276–7
Arughat 146
asceticism 23, 27, 31, 36–9, 89, 100–
    101, 117, 119, 161, 200, 265

aṣṭamātṛkā, see Mother Goddesses
astrology 49, 202, 203, 214, 223–4,
    227, 229, 233, 237, 239, 241
Avalokiteshvara 116, 137, 235
Awale 165, 184–5
Ayurveda 97–9, 113–14, 160, 202–4,
    214, 236, 20–1, 245, 248 n. 3
    types of 219 n. 13
axial age 297–9

Bagh Bhairav 222–3
bāhāḥ
    elements of 137, 148
    independent branch 144–7
    lineage 143–5, 164–70
    main 139–42, 147–8
    monastery-by-extension 140, 145–
        6
    opposed to *bahi* 149, 152ff, 159–61,
        171–3
    Three Way structure 120, 149
    types of 139–42, 169
bāhāḥ pūjā 166, 188
bahī 140–3, 193 n. 24
    architecture 152, 169–70
    contrasted with *bahah* 149, 151–61,
        171–3
    elements of 152–8
    groups of 154, 162–3
    history of 151, 160–4, 169–70
    represent monasticism 151–2, 158–
        9, 171–3